Between Preservation and Exploitation

Politics, Science, and the Environment

Peter M. Haas and Sheila Jasanoff, series editors

For a complete list of books published in this series, please see the back of the book.

Between Preservation and Exploitation

Transnational Advocacy Networks and Conservation in
Developing Countries

Kemi Fuentes-George

The MIT Press
Cambridge, Massachusetts
London, England

This book was set in Stone Sans and Stone Serif by Toppan Best-set Premedia Limited. Printed and bound in the United States of America.

Library of Congress Cataloging-in-Publication Data

Names: Fuentes-George, Kemi, author.
Title: Between preservation and exploitation : transnational advocacy networks and conservation in developing countries / Kemi Fuentes-George.
Description: Cambridge, MA : MIT Press, [2015] | Series: Politics, science, and the environment | Includes bibliographical references and index.
Identifiers: LCCN 2015038396 | ISBN 9780262034289 (hardcover : alk. paper) | ISBN 9780262528764 (pbk. : alk. paper)
Subjects: LCSH: Biodiversity conservation—Government policy—Developing countries. | Biodiversity conservation—International cooperation. | Biodiversity conservation—Government policy—Jamaica. | Biodiversity conservation—Government polcy—Mexico. | Biodiversity conservation—Government policy—Egypt. | Non-governmental organizations. | Convention on Biological Diversity (Organization)
Classification: LCC QH75 .F824 2015 | DDC 333.9509172/4—dc23 LC record available at http://lccn.loc.gov/2015038396

10 9 8 7 6 5 4 3 2 1

Contents

Acknowledgments

This book was made possible through the contribution of several people and organizations over the past nine years. While I do not have space to individually thank everyone whose support played a crucial role in this project, I would still like to acknowledge the contribution of the following actors. In no particular order, I would like to thank my parents, Vincent and Verna, for everything. I am additionally grateful for the financial support provided by the National Science Foundation (grant SES-0648473), the Skellig Foundation, and institutional funds from Middlebury College, which made this research possible. I am also thankful for the intellectual support provided by my dissertation committee, Peter Haas, Jane Fountain, James Boyce, and Craig Thomas, as well as the following: David Mednicoff and MJ Peterson at UMass-Amherst, David Rosenberg, Chris Klyza, and my colleagues at Middlebury College, and Amy Kaplan and the participants in the UCD Clinton Institute's "Reading Moby Dick" workshop. I am further indebted to David Pellow, Casey Stevens, Steinar Andresen, Rhiya Trivedi, Carmina Moorosi, Kate McCreary, Marjeela Basij-Rasikh, and Tara Seibold for helping me sort through my ideas.

I would also like to thank the following institutions for providing technical support while I was in field. Their gracious provision of office space, housing arrangements, copying materials, and Internet access proved invaluable in storing and acquiring information. For that, I am grateful to (in Mexico) the Universidad de Quintana Roo, El Colegio de la Frontera Sur, and Simbiosis; (in Jamaica) the Forestry Department, the National Environmental Protection Agency, Windsor Research Centre, and the Southern Trelawny Environmental Association; and (in Egypt), the Nature Conservation Sector of the Egyptian Environmental Affairs Agency. I am thoroughly indebted to all of my named and unnamed interviewees, who took time out of their days to answer my questions and point me in new directions during my research.

Finally, for their patience and unceasing emotional support, I am eternally grateful to Xavier, Aldan, Bennet, and my wife, Lindsey.

Introduction: Transnational Advocacy and Conservation in Developing Countries

The Global Problem of Biodiversity Loss in the Developing World

In the late 2000s, protests, informational campaigns, and lobbying efforts broke out in Jamaica and Mexico, as ordinary citizens demanded that governments put a stop to lucrative, but ultimately environmentally harmful economic development activities. What these campaigns had in common was that they were catalyzed by transnational advocacy networks comprised of researchers, academics, and local activists who had spent the better part of two decades gathering information about increasingly alarming threats to biodiversity in these regions. Despite the fact that powerful business interests in Jamaican bauxite mining and Mexican tourism strongly opposed any change in the status quo, the mass public in these countries mobilized around the networks' information. With the support of sympathetic governmental agents, they successfully pushed for new regulations to conserve globally important biodiversity.

Although these networks based their claims in part on the scientific implications of biodiversity decline, their influence on policy and practice in these cases is not attributable solely to their ability to speak as scientific experts in a complex issue area. Rather, scientific claims about biodiversity were married to local demands for resource access and environmental justice by marginalized populations who were threatened with displacement by large-scale mining and tourism. Countering both preservationist claims and economic exploitation, networks and mass publics successfully argued that local populations should retain traditional access to land. Only by doing so, they argued, would it be possible to use natural resources in a sustainable manner. So it was that scientific data produced by transnational networks comingled with historic narratives about slavery, colonial resistance, regional identity, intergenerational tradition, and in some cases threats of bloodshed, to influence new environmental regulation to conserve biodiversity. More significantly, this was done in the face of opposition by industrial developers in mining and tourism who, along with the government, argued that new regulation would hamper the economic growth sorely needed in developing countries.

At the same time that transnational networks were influencing the passage and implementation of environmental legislation in Jamaica and Mexico, two other networks were attempting to influence conservation in the interior of southern Mexico and along the Red Sea in Egypt. As in the aforementioned cases, transnational networks produced scientific information arguing for new regulations that would conserve biodiversity in the face of significant threats from nationally prominent industries. Industrial practices from large-scale agriculture and tourism were similarly threatening to displace local and marginalized populations in Mexico and Egypt who depended on natural resources for small-scale commerce and subsistence. However, whereas transnational advocacy networks of scientists were able to influence environmental action along the coast of Mexico and in Jamaica, they were unable to do so in southern Mexico's interior or on the Egyptian Red Sea coast. Not only did governmental agents and industrial actors challenge the policy implications of the scientists' information, so too did members of the mass public who were unconvinced by the stated reasons for conserving biodiversity in times of poverty. And so, efforts at building effective regulatory instruments to conserve biodiversity failed in these two cases.

While these contestations over environmental policy played out at a very local level, they nevertheless had important implications for global environmental governance. As scholars like Rosendal and Schei and Swanson have noted, international conservation treaties like the Convention on Biological Diversity depend for their implementation on the ability of developing countries to change domestic behavior among communities and subnational units.[1] Without commitment at the local level, multilateral environmental agreements (MEAs) and other institutions will be ineffective at addressing the problems of ecosystem decline.[2]

In this book I discuss four cases of transnational advocacy networks that participated in the design and implementation of biodiversity conservation projects in the developing world. I use these cases to ask the following questions: why were transnational advocacy networks able to persuade policymakers and private sector actors to change environmental behavior in the mountains of Jamaica and the coast of Mexico, but not in Egypt or inland in southern Mexico? How important is scientific information in explaining when networks can influence policymaking? Can networks reconcile scientific arguments for behavior with appeals to culture? Should transnational networks even promote conservation in developing countries, if conservation impedes economic productivity? Or can the environment be conserved in a way that serves the most needy and vulnerable populations in developing countries?

I am particularly interested in exploring how people and institutions approach the problem of biodiversity conservation in developing countries. Biodiversity or biological diversity is defined by the international community as follows: "The variability among living organisms from all sources including, inter alia, terrestrial, marine and other aquatic ecosystems and the ecological complexes of which they are part; this includes diversity within species, between species and of ecosystems."[3] For a variety of reasons, including different rates of industrialization, colonization, and accidents of evolution, most of the world's remaining biodiversity is found in the developing world.[4]

Global biodiversity loss is one of the major environmental problems of the modern era, a fact illustrated by increasingly alarming data gathered by the international community. For example, the 2005 Millennium Ecosystem Assessment tells us that biodiversity is being lost at a rate that is currently "up to one thousand times higher than the fossil record," primarily due to human activity.[5] The 2010 *Global Biodiversity Outlook*, published by the Secretariat of the Convention on Biological Diversity, tells us that the human activity causing biodiversity loss, including anthropogenic habitat change, overexploitation, and pollution, is either remaining constant or increasing in intensity.[6] Moreover, the *Global Biodiversity Outlook* and the 2012 report on the Millennium Development Goals illustrate that at best, we have slowed the rate of biodiversity loss in only a few areas.[7] As humans drive various species of mammals, birds, aquatic life, and plants to the brink of extinction, we are faced with as-yet unknown, but potentially severe environmental problems. At a minimum, we are faced with the loss of forms of life that took millions of years to evolve and are irreplaceable. More alarmingly, biodiversity loss can have ripple effects. As each species in an ecosystem is lost, there is a risk that complex and poorly understood relationships may be irrevocably disrupted, leading to sudden declines and ecosystem collapse. In addition, poor and rural people are more vulnerable to ecosystem decline. They depend more directly on biodiversity and ecosystem services than urban dwellers, and poverty makes it more difficult for vulnerable populations to purchase substitutes of natural resources, or relocate in order to escape problems caused by environmental decline.[8]

Because biodiversity is generally contained within a state's borders, there is less need to coordinate environmental regulations across different political systems, which makes managing biodiversity less problematic in some ways than regional or internationally managed problems such as acid rain, ozone depletion, and transnational waste movement. However, the international society still has to find ways to convince governments of developing nations to implement meaningful and potentially costly environmental reforms if global biodiversity is to be saved.

The cases studied here center on the domestic implementation of the UN Convention on Biological Diversity (CBD) but involve other biodiversity-oriented MEAs, such as the Ramsar Convention on Wetlands and the Convention on Migratory Species (CMS). As a framework convention, the CBD leaves substantial room for states to interpret treaty obligations. Article 8 of the CBD recommends that parties create and manage protected areas for in situ conservation, while the World Conservation Union (IUCN) has also recommended that parties to the CBD adopt an internationally standardized approach to defining and managing protected areas. However, in a system of international sovereignty, states complying with the CBD are free to manage protected areas to the extent that policymakers see fit.[9] In practice, this means that protected areas can range from zones restricted only to scientific researchers for the purpose of knowledge and data gathering, to "cultural landscapes" with human populations daily utilizing the natural resources within, to regularly accessed sites of tourism, to "paper parks," legally created areas that have no effective management practices in place.[10]

Technically, states may be in compliance with biodiversity treaties if they create additional protected areas, regardless of whether the creation of these areas leads to a real change in behavior at the local level or not. This points to one of the challenges of using regime compliance as a measure of good environmental governance. If a regime's obligations are substantively vague or otherwise poorly designed, it may be difficult to determine if the parties are meeting them. In fact, as Victor and others have illustrated, regimes may have requirements that are so thin, that they do little more than codify existing behavior such that states comply with them by default.[11] In other words, regime compliance does not always mean good environmental behavior. As Mitchell has noted in a recent volume edited by Young, King, and Schroeder, a regime can only be effective if it leads to a meaningful change in behavior among key actors.[12]

This is a problem that has been picked up on by the international society. The report on the Millennium Development Goals demonstrates that even as the total coverage of protected areas has increased globally, biodiversity has steadily declined. Galaz and others in the Young, King, and Schroeder volume attribute some of this discrepancy between the growth in institutional norms and local regulations and the steady decline in biodiversity to the problem of "fit." Problems with institutional fit emerge when the instruments designed to address an environmental problem do not meet the needs of the biophysical and social systems in which they are deployed.[13] The authors point out that if institutions have jurisdiction over too small an area, then even positive regulatory changes may cover too little an ecosystem to arrest an environmental decline.

In addition, one of the challenges of environmental governance is that human society creates regulatory instruments with imperfect and incomplete knowledge about the precise effects of current and future anthropogenic stress on natural resources. For example, ecosystems may reach tipping points earlier than anticipated, due to the introduction of new stresses, or because some causal relationships were overlooked. If institutions do not respond dynamically to observed changes, then regulations that may have been initially well designed could quickly become obsolete. Fortunately, as their volume indicates, institutional "fit" may be improved if decision makers have access to the right information at the right time. To that end, transnational advocacy networks can play a crucial role in helping existing and future regimes become more effective tools in conserving biodiversity. Transnational networks can do this if they use information to influence which geographic areas are considered relevant to biodiversity management, how to evaluate appropriate management policies in protected areas, and how to identify and measure improvements in biodiversity indicators.

Transnational Scientific Networks, Activism, and Environmental Governance

Although the barriers to entry are great and the successes are hard won, the history of global activism shows that advocacy networks of ordinary people, motivated by strongly held ideas, can influence how governments and institutions treat the environment. Scholars such as Khagram,[14] McCormick,[15] Wapner,[16] Keck and Sikkink,[17] and Haas[18] have described how advocacy networks, using only the power of persuasion, have influenced the content of international treaties such as the Montreal Protocol on Ozone, and the environmental practice of institutions like the World Bank in funding dam development projects in less developed countries (LDCs). Moreover, institutions in the UN constellation have recognized that nonstate actors matter to global environmental governance. Responding to the global problem of biodiversity loss, international organizations like UNESCO and the Global Environment Facility have asserted that local communities, environmental nongovernmental organizations (ENGOs), and civil society researchers should be involved in designing and managing governance mechanisms, such as protected areas and sustainable use practices.

However, even though civil society advocates can, and arguably should, make a difference does not mean that they always will. As advocates have realized, at the international level the proliferation of networks and advocacy organizations has not always led to influence. Participation in treaty drafting or at international summits is ultimately circumscribed by the will and interests of states who function as arbiters of civil society legitimacy.[19] Moreover, at the local level, governments have ways of jealously guarding their authority. Although international institutions like the Global Environment Facility (GEF) and the World Bank encourage governments to include nonstate actors in decision-making processes, they are unable to legally require local governments to listen to the recommendations of the civil society. As these cases show, governments may establish institutions with impressive titles like State Advisory Council, create formal seats for representatives of the civil society, and then either circumscribe the agenda to which civil society advocates have access, or ignore all policy recommendations that do not already fit with vested interests.

In addition, network advocacy may fail to gain influence if networks do not act appropriately in choosing, framing, and deploying arguments.

The literature is rife with examples of conservation networks in developing countries that managed to alienate potential supporters in the civil society and government by adopting an environmental agenda that was insufficiently attentive to the needs of local populations. Therefore, network advocacy may succeed or fail based on characteristics of the networks themselves, such as their ability to build cooperative relationships with target audiences, as well as characteristics of the political system in which they are engaged.

So for those interested in learning about the possibilities of environmental activism, the question remains: if nonstate actors matter to global environmental governance, under what conditions and when are they most likely to do so? By comparing the case studies examined here, I contend that transnational advocacy networks will have to meet at least three conditions to improve the likelihood that they will influence environmental policymaking. First, they will have to generate an internal and intersubjective scientific consensus on the causal dimensions of the area in which they are interested. Second, they will have to link conservation to environmental justice concerns among local communities. Third, they will have to establish social links with target audiences in critical regulatory and civil society institutions.

By asserting that transnational advocacy networks can persuade other powerful actors, such as governments and institutions, to change their behavior, I am asserting that ideas matter in international relations. This claim places my research firmly in the interpretivist school of international relations theory. Interpretivism is not, strictly speaking, one approach, but contains many schools that focus on the role of ideas, including constructivism, feminism, and critical race theory.[20] In contrast, rationalist approaches like neorealism and neoliberalism downplay the normative role of ideas, and claim to explain important global phenomena by focusing on the quantifiable material capabilities of key actors (usually states), such as the distribution of military capabilities, differences in the gross domestic product (GDP) of powerful countries, and economic incentives.[21]

These two approaches differ significantly in the causal power and import they attribute to transnational advocacy networks. Transnational advocacy networks (TANs) are loosely organized coalitions of "actors working internationally on an issue, who are bound together by shared values, a common discourse, and dense exchange of information and services."[22] Unlike corporations and governments, transnational networks cannot use political force, military coercion, or massive economic resources to influence outcomes. Rather, they have to appeal to norms, or widely held ideas about appropriate behavior in a particular issue area, in order to persuade other important actors to change behavior.

From a rationalist perspective, this means that TANs have limited ability to shape outcomes. Governments may rely on TANs for information at critical junctures, but only to clarify preexisting interests. In other words, TANs function primarily as informational resources for governments trying to maximize fixed, hierarchically ordered preferences.

For constructivism, one of the interpretivist approaches, interests are not fixed, but are constituted by norms, and hence subject to change in ways not entirely dependent on material realities. In other words, while there are undoubtedly aspects of our world that exist independent of our thinking about them (such as nuclear weapons, colonialist policies, international differences in military power, and racial inequality), our understanding of, and approach to, these problems can be altered if we think about them in different ways. Since ideas affect the conduct of international relations, actors who can shape them—like transnational networks—have power. In fact, *influence* is a kind of power that networks exercise when they convince policymakers and other actors to take action that they ordinarily would not have. This knowledge-based view of power is not materialistic, nor is it manipulative, in that it does not depend on networks convincing policymakers to act against their objectively determined interests.[23] By exercising knowledge-based power, networks do more than bring problems to light. They attempt to negotiate meanings and shape the discourse around an emerging issue area.[24] This is particularly relevant to nature conservation. Although the lay public thinks of environmental places like ecosystems, watersheds, and ecoregions as being objectively "out there," our understanding of the natural environment and what environmental management "means" is shaped by social understandings.

Constructivist scholars have written extensively about how norms have shaped the conduct of international relations. For instance, Risse-Kappen argues that the Soviet Empire was brought down in part by internal conflicts between supporters of political and economic liberalism and supporters of Soviet statism, and not entirely by changes in the distribution of military power between the two international poles.[25] Klotz posits that the international society, including the United States and the United Kingdom (both of which had economic ties to South Africa), imposed crippling sanctions against the apartheid regime to protest its institutionalized racial hierarchy because of new ideas about racism's moral failings.[26] Dimitrov contends that states have adopted a norm of environmental multilateralism, and thus create treaties and institutions to address problems such as global deforestation, even when there is no additional problem-solving capacity gained by doing so.[27] Finally, Price and Tannenwald assert that although contemporary conventional weapons may exceed the destructive power of nuclear weapons, the fact that the international society has not used them in almost seventy years despite ample opportunity can be attributed to a sentiment of international revulsion against the idea of nuclear weaponry.[28] In all of these examples, norms affected how governments acted internationally and domestically.

Further, several contemporary studies have also clarified how civil society advocates have used ideas and persuasion to affect global environmental governance in important ways. Rodrigues describes a case wherein TANs persuaded Brazilian policymakers and the World Bank to endorse public participation in environmental impact assessments of Amazonian development on indigenous communities.[29] Skodvin and Andresen give evidence that TANs lobbied states to push for the adoption of a moratorium on commercial whaling in the International Whaling Convention (IWC) because of deeply held ideas about the intrinsic value of cetacean life.[30] Khagram's work argues that networks convinced the World Bank to allow independent review of the environmental and social impact of dams in India, while Levering and Keck and Sikkink point out that networks also assisted states in negotiating the UN Convention on the Law of the Seas.[31] TANs and advocacy groups thus matter at all levels of global environmental policymaking. They use ideas to shape international outcomes by constraining the language and negotiation of international treaties, or by using domestic, grassroots activism to change the behavior of other members within a state or subnational political system.[32]

However, the literature is also clear that, for good or ill, transnational advocacy networks are not always successful in promoting new ideas. If this were so, the relationship between global environmental activism and state policymaking would look very different. While the number and activity of ENGOs has grown exponentially in the past four decades, they certainly have not had untrammeled influence over global environmental governance, to the dismay of climate activists, conservationists, and environmental justice advocates.

As I have argued, networks that have a scientific consensus are more likely to influence policymaking. This argument is based on the study of *epistemic communities*, which comprise one subset of TANs. Epistemic communities are knowledge-based networks of individuals who are recognized as experts in a given issue area, and who agree about the causal relationships, scientific validity claims, reasons for action, and appropriate policy recommendations in this area.[33] Like all TANs, epistemic communities are motivated in part by principled beliefs. Unlike most TANs, they exercise a particular kind of authority in making knowledge claims by virtue of the fact that they can rest their arguments on an internally held consensus that is generated by a shared epistemology about the way the world works in their field of expertise.

The use of consensually validated knowledge claims distinguishes epistemic communities from other kinds of networks, as moral claims do not rely on hypothesis testing and the validation of causal relationships pertinent to an emerging problem.[34] To be clear, the fields of expertise of epistemic communities include natural science, but these networks may also be comprised of social scientists, including economists and legal scholars.[35] While scientific research forms one category of knowledge in which actors, recognized as experts, can claim authority, epistemic communities can emerge in any field where individuals "1) share professional judgment on a policy issue; 2) weigh the validity of their policy goals in their area of expertise; 3) engage in a common set of practices with respect to the problem area ... 4) share principled beliefs."[36] As Cross points out, these individuals could just as well be military experts making claims on nuclear arms control, as faith leaders in the priesthood.[37] Nevertheless, since this manuscript focuses on environmental policymaking, I draw from the literature that examines epistemic communities as networks of scientists.

Epistemic communities are generally seen as more likely to exercise policymaking influence in cognitively complex issue areas like environmental management. Scientific reasoning and shared causal beliefs not only distinguish epistemic communities in environmental advocacy from other kinds of advocacy networks, but also are the causal mechanisms by which epistemic communities shape governance. Scientific knowledge claims are commonly seen as "objective," "competent," and "valid," and science portrayed as derived from a "permanent, ahistorical" truth.[38] When science-based communities generate a consensus on causal relationships in a problem area, they have a powerful cognitive tool to convince target audiences, including state policymakers, corporations, and secretariats of international institutions to adopt a certain understanding of the world and act appropriately. Epistemic communities and their scientific authority have been influential in shaping: the development of the UN Economic Commission for Europe's convention on Long Range Transboundary Air Pollution (LRTAP),[39] the creation of a Mediterranean Action Plan to manage oil pollution,[40] and the negotiation of the regulatory Montreal Protocol of the Vienna Convention on the Protection of the Ozone Layer.[41]

While these studies have focused primarily on the influence of epistemic communities on governments and state leaders, Cross also points out that, particularly in an era of multilevel governance, we should examine what effect epistemic communities have on nonstate actors.[42] In other words, environmental epistemic communities are trying to change not only policy, but also the actions of people in the private sector, like corporate leaders and community groups, that influence how we use natural resources. McCormick, for instance, studies how epistemic communities mobilized the mass public to campaign against breast cancer.[43] The argument that network influence can be strengthened when networks agree about the science underlying an issue is a well-established one, but influence operates at multiple levels. In order to measure it, scholars need to pay attention to the effect, if any, of knowledge on the behavior of actors other than policymakers.

At the same time, epistemic communities depend on more than getting the science right. While scientific authority is an important cognitive tool available to epistemic communities, civil society networks nevertheless have to persuade target audiences, whether policymakers or CEOs, that their claims are salient and congruent with preexisting interests.[44] This requires that epistemic communities and TANs negotiate the social and political norms in which they operate, as causal arguments that violate institutionalized norms will be dismissed by target audiences, even if the underlying science is valid.[45] It is this need to appeal to domestic norms that suggests that epistemic communities will have to frame their arguments in language that is likely to appeal to the worldview of target audiences. The ability to choose appropriate *frames* (or the set of metaphors, symbolic representations, and cognitive cues used to interpret an issue, provide a rationale for action, and mobilize support)[46] is an additional important cognitive tool through which epistemic communities and other kinds of advocacy networks may exercise influence. When emerging problem areas are framed in such a way as to resonate with the predetermined interests and institutionalized norms of target audiences, managers are more likely to self-identify as potential stakeholders, and internalize the arguments presented.[47] With this in mind, my second broad argument is that transnational advocacy networks will have to frame conservation in a way that supports local environmental justice claims. In doing so, networks will be more likely to ground their claims in a way that attracts public support and legitimacy for conservation.

This argument is perhaps the most contentious, as it seems to contradict one of the major contemporary approaches about the best way to promote environmental management in developing countries. Over the past twenty years, neoliberalism has emerged as the dominant framework in creating environmental governance mechanisms. Bernstein describes the rise of "neoliberalism" as a dominant approach in environmental governance as *liberal environmentalism*,[48] while Bakker and others more recently describe this as the rise of *neoliberal environmentalism.*[49]

Although scholars like Bakker and Castree are very critical of the overuse of the term "neoliberalism" as an excessively vague rhetorical tool lambasting the attitudes and practices of multinational corporations, the literature is clear that there are certain practices and norms that fit within the typology of neoliberalism. Moreover, these practices distinguish neoliberalism from other approaches to environmental management. For instance, liberal environmentalism (or environmental neoliberalism) is characterized by the use of mechanisms such as privatization of water and natural resources; commodification and marketization of biodiversity; deregulation of public lands and goods; monetization of ecosystem services; and the delegitimization of nonmarket (i.e., cultural, emotional) perspectives of valuing nature.[50] Neoliberalism also acts in the service of global capital, by disseminating norms and attitudes that privilege a capitalist mode of conceptualizing appropriate policies to manage nature.

In practice, this has meant that conservationists have focused on drawing a parallel between the goal of conservation—healthy ecosystems—and the economic benefit of these ecosystems to major economic sectors in the developing world. In doing so, this approach advocates a straightforward economic approach to framing, understanding, and rationalizing the value of nature conservation: conservation is important because of its contribution to functional national and global markets, and therefore conservation mechanisms should be designed to provide continued economic growth opportunities to major economic sectors. Currently, academics,[51] international organizations,[52] and treaty secretariats alike[53] have all spent considerable effort trying to "translate" the worth of the environment into the mutually intelligible language of neoliberal[54] economics to convince policymakers and economic actors of the validity of action.[55] Proponents of neoliberal environmentalism frame stable ecosystems and healthy biodiversity as economically profitable by pointing out that environmental services such as soil stability, forest health and water quality provide unrecognized, but nevertheless quantifiable economic benefits to industry, and hence to GDP. The impetus behind this argument is that governments in developing countries will be more likely to conserve biodiversity once they are convinced that doing so is economically profitable.

To be sure, the argument that economic language should shape environmental behavior in developing countries seems intuitive, and has been encouraged by policymakers and researchers alike. Since the 1972 Founex Report, published in preparation for the first UN conference on the environment at Stockholm, academics and policymakers have argued, sometimes convincingly, that to solve the environmental and economic problems of developing countries, the most important thing to do is promote national economic growth and development. This argument is based on a variety of claims and observations.

First, rather than being primarily affected by global "green" environmental issues such as biodiversity loss and ozone depletion, the pressing environmental issues facing LDCs are predominantly those associated with local, "brown" developmental problems. These problems, which embody challenges to human welfare such as low access to sanitary drinking water, exposure to communicable diseases, and a chronic lack of adequate housing[56] are all exacerbated or caused by poverty, technological disadvantages, and low capital development. Second, global environmental problems such as climate change and ozone depletion are predominantly the result of action taken by highly industrialized countries (HICs) during the era of industrialization.[57] LDCs that do experience negative externalities of these global problems (for example the low-lying Maldives and poverty-stricken coastal Bangladesh are both experiencing climatic disruptions and rising oceanic levels), are suffering from the poor environmental behavior of other, richer states. Third, LDCs are highly indebted. The pressure of debt servicing in the global South, as well as the dependence of these countries on the export of agricultural commodities means that LDCs are stuck in a perpetual game of catch-up to the model of development exemplified by the developed world. In order to close this developmental gap, LDCs place a great deal of stress on their natural resources by attempting to increase production of primary goods and agriculture.[58] As a result, not only is economic development and industrialization seen as a possible solution to the problem of environmental vulnerability, it also is seen as a corrective to the injustice inherent in shifting the costs of climate change and other environmental problems from rich to poor countries.[59]

Further, from an economic perspective, curbing deforestation or addressing biodiversity loss might be environmentally friendly at the global level, but comes at a domestic cost for developing countries, which have to limit, among other things, road construction, agricultural expansion, and the construction of living areas for a growing population.[60] Therefore, unless it can be conclusively demonstrated that conservation contributes to productivity in major economic sectors, LDCs would under this logic be better served by focusing on domestic economic development to address local problems of "poverty, malnutrition, illiteracy, and sheer misery."[61] As this book demonstrates, antiregulatory policymakers in Jamaica, Mexico, and Egypt have used elements of these claims to argue that the best way to conserve biodiversity is to use biodiversity to protect major economic activities, like tourism, agriculture, and mining, even when these processes were the primary threats to biodiversity in the first place.

Finding Environmental Justice between Preservation and Exploitation

However, while economic arguments seem seductive, environmental justice frames are more likely to appeal to local populations who would otherwise be marginalized by a neoliberal paradigm. Biodiversity loss has important global socioeconomic dimensions that make environmental justice concerns an inescapable part of management. Environmental injustice arises when the distribution of environmental goods and bads are such that marginalized populations pay a disproportionately high share of the costs, and receive a disproportionately low share of the benefits of (mis)management.[62] In the literature on environmental justice, the delineation of the marginalized is almost always informed by economics, as they are overwhelmingly relatively poor, but the difference between marginalized and privileged populations may also be informed by race and gender.[63]

These costs may be manifested in various forms. Pellow and Newell build on 1980s studies of patterns of toxic waste sitings in minority communities in the United States to show that the racism of waste movement is global: nonwhite communities in Asia, the Caribbean, Latin America, and Africa have now become the depositories of toxic waste and e-waste, even though they do not equally share in the benefits of industrialization and the rewards of the technological revolution.[64] In a volume on environmental inequality edited by Carmin and Agyeman, Ali and Ackley describe how residents of Fiji suffer from growing water, soil, and air pollution while the FIJI corporation exports their "pristine" water to be sold as a luxury good in the developed world.[65] A 2005 study on women by the UN Division for the Advancement of Women illustrates how gender relations in Zimbabwe, Kazakhstan, Gambia, Tanzania, among other countries, leave women more vulnerable to water-borne diseases and increasing water scarcity.[66] While the specifics vary from case to case, the literature shows that sociopolitical marginalization exacerbates environmental vulnerability.

The vast literature on environmental justice is also clear: the benefits from which marginalized communities are generally excluded are often economic, but may be procedural as well. Too often, marginalized communities are excluded from participating in political decision making over natural resources by a range of sociopolitical and economic power structures. This disenfranchisement may occur both internationally, as marginalized communities have low rates of participation in treaty negotiation, and locally, as domestic political systems make it more difficult for marginalized groups to participate. Although political disenfranchisement is a global phenomenon, it may be particularly severe in post-transitional and autocratic countries. This is evident, for instance, in Carruthers's volume on environmental justice in Latin America, wherein indigenous communities and *campesinos* have a difficult time setting the terms of how natural resources and pollution are to be managed, due to linguistic, geographic, and political barriers to participation.[67] As Hiskes and others have pointed out, environmental justice is not just a matter of substantive changes in environmental harms.[68] Rather, environmental justice depends on people having some control over their own destiny in the use of natural resources.

Further, marginalized communities may be excluded from other kinds of benefits, such as cultural and symbolic uses of natural resources, if the environment is degraded beyond a certain point. As critical literature in ecological economics points out, the neoliberal economic model is only "one of the many metaphors necessary to comprehend the complexities of environmental changes and their impacts on humans."[69] What is described as "effective management" under the neoliberal economics paradigm may be incompatible with different paradigms. For example, in 2005, representatives of the Hopi, Navajo, and Havasupai Nations sued the Snowbowl Ski Resort in Arizona for planning an expansion that would use recycled sewage in artificial snow on peaks deemed "sacred to at least thirteen formally recognized Indian tribes." In 2007, the Nations won an appeal in the Ninth Circuit Court of Appeals, effectively blocking the use of recycled sewage. However, in 2008, the Ninth Circuit Court revisited the case, and found that although "the presence of recycled wastewater on the Peaks is offensive to the Plaintiffs' religious sensibilities [and] will spiritually desecrate a sacred mountain," this did not count as a "substantial burden" to the Nations. In short, the Court found that "the sole effect of the artificial snow is on the Plaintiffs' subjective spiritual experience." From an economic perspective, since this is impossible to quantify and since there was no material impact caused by the use of recycled sewage, the Court dismissed the Nations' case.

In the cases studied here, local communities were critical of narrow economic arguments as reasons for managing natural resources. In the mountains of Jamaica, local residents pointed to the cultural history of the land as a refuge for runaway slaves and guerilla resistance during the colonial era. Along the coast of Mexico, fishermen spoke of the practice of subsistence fishing being passed down through generations. Further inland, peasants and agricultural communities invoked a familiarity with the land dating, in some cases, through the history of the Mayans. In all these cases, local communities were clear that economic market valorization did not capture the depth of value that natural resources and biodiversity had.

Moreover, linking conservation to the interests of major economic sectors does not always address the needs of the mass public or the environment in developing countries. First, under the neoliberal economic paradigm, the timeframe of payoffs is of paramount importance. While degraded natural environments may impose costs in the long run, economic firms tend to heavily discount future costs and benefits, particularly if avoiding future (and ultimately unknowable) costs means sacrificing immediate gains. Second, although the advocates of neoliberalizing nature recognize that commodification is only one part of valuing nature,[70] if natural resources are evaluated based on their economic value, it may be economically rational to engage in short-term, ecologically unsustainable exploitation. Moral concerns arise when the interests of dominant economic forces marginalize alternative perspectives. Practical concerns arise when different groups of actors have different ideas about what biodiversity "is," and what nature "is," and therefore what "appropriate policy" is. After all, managing a protected area to conserve intergenerational history and legends may require significantly different policies than would maintaining an area for the quarterly profits of economic sectors. Because of these concerns, using neoliberal economics as an exclusive model to approach environmental management is likely to exacerbate the socioeconomic inequity that characterizes the developing world. Thus for issues of practicality and justice, networks seeking to ground their claims in political systems should make their arguments resonate with the mass public, rather than with vested elites who have different frameworks for evaluating biodiversity conservation.

As indicated earlier, transnational networks should also try to generate usable and consensually held scientific arguments in order to improve their chances of influencing policy. But using science as a basis for policy can also promote injustice, if doing so discriminates against marginalized populations. That science is seen as authoritative does not mean that those people interested in justice should accept scientific findings uncritically in environmental policymaking. While scientific inquiry aspires to a positivist epistemology, it is still only capable of presenting a partial view of the world.[71] If science is used, it should be framed to reinforce environmental justice claims of local populations to avoid further disenfranchising them.

The argument that science should be critiqued in the interest of justice certainly seems problematic. However, recent research on epistemic communities and transnational science networks by authors like McCormick[72] and Karvonen and Brand[73] have built on earlier work in critical theory and feminism by Forsyth,[74] Haraway,[75] and others to raise questions about the ability of science to make universal claims—what Haraway describes as "the

God trick." In short, a scientific explanation of a problem is necessarily limited in scope. Scientific validity tests do poorly in explaining, for example, how and why people derive cultural or religious meaning from the natural world. Moreover, scientists, like any other group of people seeking to explain social phenomena, impart their own biases or worldviews on what they study. Scientists have to engage with issues like which features of an emerging problem are most important, and which are less so. Their arguments address questions like: why is action important in the first place? How do we understand the costs of inaction—are they emotional, physical, or economic? And, since environmental governance is ultimately a political issue, who pays what cost of action? Scientific cause-and-effect claims can (if done properly) adjudicate some questions and show us parts of an objective truth.[76] But because humans have a finite capacity to process information, scientists make decisions about which relationships to highlight in making policy-relevant arguments, and which to elide. As Longino points out, these decisions are informed by the social context from which scientists emerge—their cultural experiences, prior beliefs, and so on.[77]

Problematically, as Forsyth tells us, the narrative of scientist-as-expert does not address the fact that scientific explanations offer a partial and contestable look at the world.[78] Moreover, the designation of "expert" is an act of power and, since all power is relational, it is one that privileges some actors while marginalizing others. In other words, the language of "expertise" asserts that there are some kinds of knowledge claims (and hence, claimants) that are "better" than others.

In practice, expert knowledge is only possessed by those who have "a certain kind of training that provides them with the legitimacy of that expertise."[79] It is contrasted with lay or "embodied" knowledge, which is "often gained simply through living in a locale, is not codified in any set way, and is generally not considered in the evaluation of cost-benefit analysis."[80] Ultimately, the designation of "expert" is a social one, since it depends on the recognition by others about the experts' authority, as well as the drawing of a boundary between experts and lay people (or nonexperts).[81] Moreover, the borders that are drawn between expert and nonexpert are often determined by social markers, rather than the content of knowledge itself.

Forsyth asks us to understand who recognizes epistemic communities as experts, and "how they may reflect other forms of political power."[82] What feminists like Cohn and other scholars have shown is that this power is bound in one's ability to speak the "right" language, to attend the "right" schools, get access to funds from the "right" institutions, and present oneself in the "right" way. Those who are unable or unwilling to do so (arguing from emotion, rather than logic; using indigenous or vernacular forms of language, rather than the dominant form) are thus excluded from the conversation, and made to feel like an outsider.[83] For a host of structural reasons, in global environmental governance these are disproportionately women, non-Westerners, and low-income people of color. Indeed, as Mohai and others point out, one of the lasting criticisms of modern environmentalism is its "history of excluding people of color from leadership of the ecology movements."[84] Even when marginalized groups get access to the halls of power, there is no guarantee that they will act in a way to advance the interests of the disenfranchised. By describing how women in science tend to adopt an antifeminist discourse of expertise, Phipps illustrates that marginalized populations are just as likely to reinforce the social discourse establishing boundaries between Expert and Other.[85] It is possible and certainly desirable to make more accurate claims about the world within a scientific epistemology. However, since the use of scientific arguments can create power imbalances, it is not clear that we should always privilege scientific epistemologies over others. Rather, we should recognize and value other epistemologies as part of our multiple bodies of knowledge.

The designation of "expert" would not necessarily be problematic, if not for the tendency of scientific claims to marginalize the voices and preferences of local populations in developing countries. For example, scholars like Dowie and Chapin have described how conservationist networks and NGOs have pushed for highly restrictive policies in Uganda, Brazil, and elsewhere in the developing world, justifying them in the name of "sound science."[86] In response, those governments created reserves in areas like the Mgahinga that expelled local tribes from their land in the name of biodiversity conservation, creating "conservation refugees."[87] As Dowie and Chapin note, this fortress style of conservation only made sense if you accepted a worldview, propounded by the NGOs, that nature is something separate from humans, and must therefore be protected from them.

More recently, Vermeylen and Walker discuss the role of science in managing genetic resources among the San tribal people in southern Africa.[88] They illustrate how the corporations Unilever and Pfizer, as well as the state agency Council for Scientific and Industrial Research (CSIR) created a management protocol with the San people to conserve the Hoodia plant, recently discovered to hold appetite suppressive qualities. This protocol was based on scientific calculations about the range of the plant and what conservationists deemed best practices for conservation. One of the problems with this agreement was that it required all stakeholders, including the San, to commodify the plant and calculate its commercial value to the global pharmaceutical industry. Vermeylen and Walker are clear that this had costs for the San, who had this elite-driven process of marketization and governance imposed upon them from outside. In one interview, they quote a San member who described the effects of commodifying Hoodia: "When you eat the Hoodia you can feel the supernatural powers coming from above ... You can not experience these powers and energies of the Hoodia in pills; we gave the power away for money. Everything we had here is gone because we traded the supernatural powers for money, for simple things."[89]

Fortunately, while Dowie, Chapin, and Vermeylen and Walker illustrate how science-based conservation can alienate rural dwellers, scientific networks and science-based arguments do not necessarily contribute to sociopolitical marginalization. In fact, McCormick and Karvonen and Brand describe how scientific movements can and have advocated for environmental policies in ways that empower lay people and lay knowledge. For instance, anti-dam movements in Brazil managed to delay (but not stop) the construction of a controversial large dam in Belo Monte when transnational networks of scientists mobilized with indigenous groups and social activists to resist the state's policies.[90] Far from being simple recipients of expert wisdom, the nonexperts in Brazil used their agency to shape the production of environmental knowledge. For example, nonexperts and scientists together framed the impact of large dams by linking them to the emotional costs that indigenous rural people bore when displaced by dams—emotional costs that were not part of the official calculations of the government's resettlement and rehabilitation matrix.[91] These emotional appeals helped sustain the anti-dam movement in its campaign against a government that was willing to use violence to get its way.

In that case, the presence of scientific experts certainly helped undermine the pro-dam forces' arguments about the negative impact of dams on riparian ecosystems and water sedimentation, and the production and use of anti-dam knowledge was shaped by participation between experts and lay activists, rather than transmitted by experts to the lay public in a top-down manner. Examples like these show the possibility of real cooperation between scientific experts and nonscientists in the mass public. Compare this, for instance, to the cases Chapin describes, where a biologist from Conservation International said about working with indigenous people in the Lower Xingu region of Brazil: "Quite frankly, I don't care what the Indians want. We have to work to conserve the biodiversity."[92]

For those interested in strengthening democracy in developing countries, this argument that conservation depends on local justice and equity claims suggests that environmental management and democracy are linked. This suggests that transnational scientific networks may play a role in strengthening democracy if they use their position as keepers of privileged scientific information to empower local disenfranchised populations in making claims about the proper use of natural resources.[93] Certainly, McCormick makes this clear when she describes networks of scientists who empower the mass public as "Democratizing Science Movements."[94]

However, as set forth in this chapter, this will only occur if scientific knowledge is generated in a participatory, rather than an exclusionary way. Of course, a truly participatory model of knowledge generation is not going to be easy to establish. It will depend on scientific experts being willing to let lay people influence the environmental policy agenda, including deciding what natural resources should be used for, and with what worldview to evaluate proper policy. As a result, scientists will also have to cede some of the terrain of knowledge-as-power to other kinds of actors.

But as Karvonen and Brand ask: "Why should experts sacrifice their relatively privileged social position?"[95] In other words, why should scientists encourage nonexperts to participate in generating and shaping knowledge about environmental processes, when doing so may weaken the ability of scientists to shape the policy agenda? The fact is, participatory and democratic knowledge generation strengthen the ability of networks to exercise influence. As McCormick describes in Brazil, or as Pellow discusses in anti-waste movements in Zimbabwe and Haiti, participatory knowledge generation can lead to environmental solutions that are more socially acceptable and hence more likely to endure and effect change.[96]

In addition, there is an ethical reason to promote participatory knowledge. Environmental justice scholars recognize that justice has a crucial procedural element. That is, no matter what the substantive outcome is of a policy, it is unlikely to be rooted in justice if the people primarily affected by it are alienated from the process of designing the policy. The lack of participation is why, while the fortress conservation policies described by Chapin and Dowie or in Zebich-Knos's study of ecotourism in Mexico[97] may be environmentally good (depending on your worldview), they are also criticized as unjust.

Participatory knowledge generation and environmental justice depend on scientists promoting socialization between themselves and target audiences in the mass public and political arena. *Socialization* describes the process of regular communication, including face-to-face meetings, where actors exchange information and ideas, and learn about one another. Socialization may be manifested by such processes as jointly conducted reports between "norm entrepreneurs" and their target audiences, mutual participation in workshops, and exchange of staff. Norm entrepreneurs are particularly crucial in building support for new ideas. They are actors who call attention to new issues by using language or frames to increase the visibility and importance of an emerging problem.[98] In other words, they act as proselytizers of a particular issue, and may play an important role during the process of socialization by attempting to shape the policy agenda. Since socialization depends on the exchange of ideas, it can contribute to the development of shared perceptions among connected actors, and improve the chance that knowledge produced among interacting agents will be mutually accepted and legitimated. Socialization is therefore more intimate than simply producing knowledge and communicating it to target audiences.

In describing how global environmental assessments become influential, Clark, Mitchell, and Cash argue: "the process by which information is generated and delivered affects the potential of that information process to influence outcomes."[99] Actors who are socialized in the generation of information and knowledge associated with an emerging problem are more likely to adopt the normative implications associated with that knowledge and consider the conclusions relevant to their own interests. Socialization can also promote *framing alignment*,[100] or the development of shared interests, values, and beliefs among various groups.[101] When these social relationships are absent, it is unlikely that policymakers will respond favorably to new demands for action, even if made by networks of scientific experts. Knowledge matters not solely because of its content, but also through how it is produced.

This presents certain unavoidable obstacles for successful advocacy networks. If socialization matters, then undemocratic political systems will make it difficult for networks to gain influence, since the institutions that contribute to socialization, such as free movement and open access to policymakers, are likely to be curtailed. Even in countries that have recently transitioned to democracy, civil society environmental networks are likely to find obstacles to participation. Axelrod, in a volume edited by Axelrod and VanDeveer, illustrates how decades of authoritarianism in socialist Czechoslovakia have limited the development of a mass public that can effectively participate in state policymaking in some highly contested areas, including nuclear energy.[102] In addition, Perrault describes how the transition to institutional democracy in Bolivia brought with it worsening economic inequality, and a model of natural resource use that was based on "rapacious resource exploitation, social exclusion, and impoverishment."[103] Clearly, post-transitional regimes are not necessarily free of problems in promoting democratic participation.

This is not to say that democratic transitions are meaningless. As states create more political opportunity structures like popular elections and autonomous and accountable regulatory institutions, the civil society will generally have more chance to socialize with policymakers on their own terms. Hochstetler, in a volume edited by Steinberg and VanDeveer demonstrates that the transition to democracy (aided in that case by membership in the EU) has strengthened civil society participation in post-Soviet states, although this improvement was uneven.[104] Certainly, Hochstetler's research, along with studies by Botcheva among others, shows that civil society participation and environmental performance were markedly better in countries like Romania and Brazil after their governments liberalized.[105] This suggests that the mechanisms for civil society participation in, and hence influence over environmental policymaking may be stronger in democratic systems, even if Bolivia and former Czechoslovakia show that democratization is not a guarantee of stronger participation.

On the other hand, it is also possible that socialization between expert networks and policymakers may be stronger in closed or autocratic political systems. In autocratic systems, the production of policy-relevant knowledge is more likely to be controlled by policymakers concerned about the implications of allocating scarce benefits to political constituencies.[106] Political elites are therefore more likely to be invested in the design of high-profile research programs, and thus more connected to channels of communication with scientific experts.[107] Scientific community members may also be drawn from government bureaucrats or state agencies, as states may wish to be more involved in producing, and therefore controlling, policy-relevant knowledge. If ties between scientific networks and policymakers become strengthened by the state's involvement in producing information, scientists may end up socializing very systematically with policymakers. As an interesting paradox, autocracy may thus occasionally foster socialization.

For example, Teets describes how China uses a model she calls "consultative authoritarianism" to foster civil society engagement in policymaking.[108] Under consultative authoritarianism, closed political systems cede some authority and autonomy to nonstate actors in areas in which the state finds it difficult or ineffective to exert direct control. In addition, Sowers points out that in autocratic systems like Egypt (also covered in this book), policymakers may allow scientists and other experts control over knowledge generation in complex areas. This is similar to Teets's discussion, although Sowers describes this model as "embedded autonomy."[109] Further, as policymakers in autocratic systems are by definition more insulated from potentially messy and possibly distributionist popular demands, they may be in a better position to limit rampant consumption, and mitigate pork-barrel policies.[110] Authoritarian systems can respond very quickly to new information, even if their response is not necessarily just or fair. However, as Sowers and Teets point out, embedded autonomy is likely to be ephemeral. If policymakers in autocratic systems decide they would rather not have freely flowing information available, advocates may find themselves abruptly excluded from policymaking authority.

Whether a country is democratic or autocratic also matters for scientific advocacy, insofar as political regime type can affect scientific credibility. For science to be considered credible, the conclusions drawn should not be derived from an already-established political agenda, but rather based on a neutral (as far as possible) assessment of the facts at hand, as knowledge that is produced with a visible political bias is easier to de-legitimate.[111] Scientific credibility is more likely to emerge in politically open states, where ENGOs and academic research institutions are free to formulate ideas and research programs, communicate with policymakers, and establish relationships with transnational researchers.[112] This is not a given, however. Contemporary discussions about climate change in the United States show

how, even in democracies, political actors and lobbyists can muddy the scientific debate by aggressively funding science that fulfills a political, antiregulatory agenda. Since domestic politics affect how transnationally held knowledge is used to affect environmental governance, this book pays attention to variation in political systems and whether this affects transnational scientific advocacy.

Biodiversity Management in Developing Countries: A Research Methodology

In summary, I point to three main factors in the production of ideas that affect the success or failure of transnational network advocacy: the presence of a knowledge consensus, environmental justice issue framing, and socialization with target audiences. When all three are present, transnational advocacy networks are more likely to influence how policymakers respond to emerging environmental problems.

In this book, I conduct a comparative study of transnational advocacy in developing countries to understand which of these factors are sufficient or necessary or both to generate influence, and how they affect one another. For example, if knowledge consensus is the only variable that corresponds with network influence in LDCs, then a narrowly focused epistemic-communities approach would suffice. This would undermine the argument that environmental advocacy depends on justice framing, or factors other than the content of scientific knowledge. However, if knowledge consensus does not correspond with influence, and the primary predictor of influence is justice-based issue framing, then the most important element in generating influence over environmental conservation in LDCs would not be scientific consensus, but carefully chosen symbols and metaphors. Further as indicated previously, the relationship between socialization and political openness and influence is ambiguous. Whether democracy is more likely than autocracy to lead to social ties between scientists, policymakers, and the civil society is not predetermined. Of course, there are other ways in which transnational networks may use these cognitive resources to influence policy. It is possible that the three independent variables—framing, consensus, and socialization—all interact together to lead to network influence. In this section, I explain the methodology I used to parse the interrelationship of consensus, justice, socialization, and network influence.

Given the practical limits of conducting this kind of qualitative research, I nevertheless tried to study countries that could be meaningfully compared, and that were as representative of the developing world as possible. First, since I wanted to investigate how local contestations affect regime implementation, I chose countries that were actively implementing the Convention on Biological Diversity (CBD) by carrying out projects funded by the Global Environment Facility to conserve biodiversity. Since these projects were explicitly linked to the CBD, I could avoid studying cases in which conservation projects were created independent of global governance institutions. I also did not want to study countries with low institutional capacity according to measures like the World Bank Governance Research Indicators Database (GRID), as these were more likely to have projects fail due to a lack of capacity, rather than a lack of will. As a result, this book does not speak as directly about research on environment and conservation in the least-developing countries.

The challenges to governance in these countries can be seen in Stephenson and Schweitzer's study of activism and environmental justice in the Niger Delta.[113] There, decades of military rule, kleptocracy, and corruption have so enervated the nation-state, that it has become a "fragile" actor in the politics of oil regulation, and is now unable or unwilling to curb environmental abuses in the Niger Delta. In other words, the state's failure to regulate corporate-caused environmental pollution is overdetermined: Stephenson and Schweitzer note that it could be attributed to "powerful state disinterest, Nigerian governmental fear, federal officials' willingness to discriminate against the minorities in the region, or corruption."[114] Thus environmental advocacy in the least-developed world may fail not because advocates use improper framing strategies, but simply because the state is unable to implement policy and shape behavior, which makes them poor tests of the effects of framing. Nevertheless, there are studies on environmental governance in the least-developed nations by Vermeylen and Walker, Stephenson and Schweitzer, and Rosendal.

Second, I used measures of political democratization, such as Freedom House ratings, the Reporters sans Frontiers Press Freedom Index, and Polity IV studies to find countries with different levels of political openness and democracy. By doing so, I could speak to the existing comparative literature exploring how environmental movements negotiate different political contexts to advocate for changes in governmental policy, including

O'Neill's chapter in Steinberg and VanDeveer's volume.[115] Among the cases I have chosen, Jamaica is the most democratic, Mexico is still transitioning away from seven decades of authoritarianism, and despite recent political upheaval, Egypt has an entrenched and politicized military that has sharply curtailed civil and political liberties.

I then used qualitative research methods to recount network advocacy from project design to implementation in these three countries. These methods included over a hundred in-field, open-ended interviews with identified network members, policymakers, community residents, and academics over the following periods: three months in Jamaica in 2006; six months in Mexico in 2008; three months in Egypt in 2008; and one month each in Jamaica and Mexico in 2011 and 2012 respectively. I supplemented these interviews with participant observation, by assisting research organizations in the field gather data on biodiversity. I also conducted analyses of media releases and archival materials, such as project documents, workshop reports, meeting minutes, and joint produced studies. By analyzing these data, I could identify the members of advocacy networks and key actors involved in environmental policymaking. I could also measure the extent to which network members developed an internal consensus by examining whether members of a network agreed on the causal relationships relevant to an emerging issue area, whether they were aware that agreement within the network was shared, and whether they were accurate in their assessment of the causal relationships under study.

One of the more difficult things to measure is the extent to which changes in policy and practice are due to network influence, as influence is not a necessary outcome of advocacy, nor are policy changes necessarily a sign of influence.[116] Moreover, as scholars of the developing world are aware, changes in policy do not necessarily mean changes in practice. Recent research on China, for example, shows that one of the most enduring challenges to environmental regulation, especially in rural areas, is not the lack of new regulation, but a lack of implementation of existing state policies.[117] As Mostafa Tolba, former UNEP executive director from Egypt said: "The parliaments in our part of the world—the Third World—we produce the most outstanding laws. But they are never implemented. ... It's a puzzle that we can't find the solution to.[118]

Rather, *influence* exists when policymakers and managers look to epistemic communities for information and theories, accept the conclusions drawn by scientists, and change policy to reflect the conclusions of the advocacy groups. Policymakers and managers then have to change behavior to conform to these policy changes, as legislative changes alone are not a sufficient sign of improved environmental management.

Therefore, when networks have influence, target audiences will change their behavior, policies, and practices to converge on the preferences of the advocacy networks. Ideally, this will lead to measurable improvements in indicators of biodiversity health over time, but this is not certain, as natural disasters, time-lag problems, external threats, and a lack of clear information may all undermine the efficacy of new environmental policy and practice.

Measuring influence was also made more complex by the fact that biodiversity management is an issue that crosses multiple sectors. Network influence over conservation in Jamaica, Mexico, and Egypt was determined by their aggregate influence over various regulatory agencies, including national and local institutions in environment, agriculture, tourism, mining, energy, and forestry. Networks also tried to convince actors in the private sector, from subsistence farmers and small-scale fishermen to entrepreneurs in the hotel industry, to change their operating practices. Finally, networks attempted to design the GEF projects such that they reflected the networks' understanding of globally important biodiversity before the projects were even started.

Therefore, I considered that networks successfully influenced policy by looking at a range of possible outcomes. First, networks may have shaped project design in dimensions such as the choice of indicators, or the specification of management tools. Second, project design has to be followed by governmental implementation. For example, if the responses of policymakers and managers are limited to general exhortative statements extolling the virtues of conservation, but without real efforts to regulate environmentally harmful activity, or if policymakers create empty policy, such as "paper parks," no influence over policy can be said to have occurred. Third, influence occurs if the network's recommendations lead to changes in the practices of private sector actors, such as corporations, fishing associations, community organizations, or other nonstate entities. Given these observations, it is clear that influence is not dichotomous. Advocacy networks may have more effect shaping private sector behavior than over policy (or vice versa), which means failure to influence one area does not mean that a network has been unable to generate any influence.

I admit that there are still some remaining questions about the generaliz-ability and representativeness of my case selection. Although I have selected cases that give some geographic representation of the developing and tran-sitioning world by selecting a country in the Caribbean, a Latin American case, and a case in MENA, there are clearly areas that are not addressed in my book. I do not discuss post-Soviet countries in Eastern Europe, nor do I discuss post-communist countries in Asia, even though natural resource management and environmental challenges are no less serious there. Since I do not address these cases, my book is not perfectly representative of the developing world experience. However, there are existing studies on these cases, cited throughout this chapter, and future research could certainly fur-ther engage with the effect of scientific consensus, socialization, and local justice framing on transnational scientific advocacy in different political contexts.

Outline of the Book

In chapter 1, I describe the case study of the *Project for Sustainable Conserva-tion of Globally Important Caribbean Bird Habitats* carried out in the Cockpit Country of Jamaica. Jamaica, as a parliamentary democracy, represents the most liberal case in the states discussed in this book. In that case, a transna-tional epistemic community emerged during the 1990s and early 2000s to advocate for the protection of sensitive ecosystems in an area threatened by bauxite mining. The epistemic community, concerned about the ecological integrity of the Cockpit Country, had to contend not only with various nat-ural resource policymaker agencies in the environmental and agricultural ministries, but also managers in the powerful bauxite industry, and peas-ant and agricultural residents, all of whom had sometimes incompatible preferences. By linking a scientific consensus to local demands for justice and autonomy over natural resources, the epistemic community was able to promote changes in behavior in national policymakers, who agreed to adopt a moratorium on bauxite mining in Cockpit Country. Despite oppo-sition from bauxite industry leaders and their allies in the government, popular support for conservation was powerful enough to override the neo-liberal argument for exploitation. However, their influence was limited to those agencies with which network members were able to socialize.

Chapter 2 presents the *Proyecto para la Conservación y Uso Sostenible del Sistema Arrecifal Mesoamericano* (MBRS Project) carried out in Mexico. This covers a coastal and marine ecosystem off the eastern coast of the Yucatán Peninsula that was threatened by large-scale coastal tourism and overfishing from the 1970s onward. Again, this case involved an epistemic community engaging with competing interests of various actors. Here, these consisted of policymakers in the environmental and agricultural ministries, managers in the transnational hotel sector, and peasant and subsistence populations. Although Mexico is comparatively more autocratic than Jamaica, the mass public was able to link scientific arguments for conservation to local environmental justice demands to promote changes in behavior in federal regulatory environmental and agricultural agencies. However, state agencies that were not socialized with the epistemic community remained critical of regulation, and resisted environmental protection, going as far as to campaign for the overturn of new federal legislation.

Chapter 3 investigates a case that also takes place in Mexico, under the *Proyecto para la Consolidación del Corredor Biológico Mesoamericano—México* (CBMMx Project). This case study did not involve an epistemic community, as the transnational network that emerged to advocate for improved biodiversity management did not hold an intersubjective consensus on relevant causal relationships. The advocacy efforts of the TAN in this case focused on natural resource policymakers and marginalized agricultural populations throughout the Yucatán. In this case, the lack of a consensus on biodiversity allowed policymakers to impose their own preferences on project management despite socialization between network members and governmental agencies. Most importantly, policymakers determined how biodiversity was imagined under the project with little local input. The final result was a feeling of mutual alienation and dissatisfaction from scientists and local communities about project management, and a lack of cooperation on implementation and biodiversity conservation on all sides.

Chapter 4 presents the final empirical case study, the *Project for Sustainable Conservation of Migratory Soaring Birds* carried out in Egypt. As with the CBMMx Project case study, this project involved a transnational network that did not generate an intersubjective consensus. This chapter also suggests that autocracy limits the possibility of network socialization, as policymakers in key regulatory agencies created systematic barriers to communication between state institutions and the civil society. I conclude by describing how a lack of consensus and low socialization allowed the state to capture the GEF project funds, exclude the civil society, and undermine the environmental and social goals of conservation.

In chapter 5, I link these descriptions of local contestations over biodiversity governance to the study of international relations. As mentioned earlier, all of these countries were carrying out the projects in order to implement their obligations under the Convention on Biological Diversity (CBD) and other regional agreements. Besides these, the debates over appropriate policy invoked state obligations to other, non-biodiversity institutions, including the World Heritage Convention and the UN Framework Convention on Climate Change (UNFCCC). In each case, a constellation of different treaties and institutions had rules that overlapped with the CBD and each other governing the management of protected areas. These overlapping rules and institutions gives rise to a condition Young and others describe as "regime complexity."[119]

I argued that the growing regime complexity that these scholars describe in this and other areas gives transnational actors more space to shape the conduct of global environmental governance. As states try to govern issue areas that are affected by more, occasionally conflicting, and non-hierarchically ordered institutions, their obligations will become more ambiguous. Nonstate actors can help shape the ambiguity emerging from regime complexity by addressing the following questions: when do institutional rules overlap in a given issue area? When do rules conflict, and when are they synergistic? And how do governments, communities, and subnational actors adjudicate possibly conflicting rules?

I find that transnational networks are particularly crucial in this regard because of their ability to shape ideas. Transnational networks affect how states and other actors respond to regime complexity by making normative—not just technical—pronouncements about how to interpret rule ambiguity. For instance, whether a protected area should be managed as a site of cultural heritage under rules set by the World Heritage Convention, or a site of biodiversity preservation under the CBD (or some mix of the two, or even other institutional rules) is an issue that can be settled only by appeals to norms. As such, I link my comparative study of activism and environmental justice to constructivist schools of thought that claim that ideas about appropriate behavior matter.

In the conclusion, I use my comparative study of transnational activism with constructivist arguments about the role of ideas to underline the importance of justice claims to global environmental governance. In exploring these links, I link debates on international environmental justice with literature on environmental regime effectiveness and neoliberal ecological economics.[120] When networks generated a consensus, socialized with policymakers, and invoked norms consonant with local justice, they were more likely to persuade policymakers. Absent one or more of the variables, conservation projects were implemented poorly, or simply rejected by states.

Therefore, even though Young and others[121] are skeptical about whether it is possible to include "fairness or justice, stewardship [and] participation"[122] in implementing environmental regimes, these aspects go to the heart of effective management. They reflect the important normative questions behind biodiversity management, including what biodiversity consists of, what it is being managed for, and for whom it is being conserved. If conservation and biodiversity management is to be subsumed under state-sponsored development policies,[123] this begs the question of "development for and by whom?" The literature on environmental justice is very clear: if growth and development are driven by dominant economic actors, their preferences may be mutually incompatible with those of other actors, primarily marginalized or politically disenfranchised communities at the local level.[124] Instead, if networks can link conservation to local justice, they will be more likely to foster political support from the mass public and promote long-lasting environmental policy change.

1   Jamaica and the Conservation of Globally Important Bird Habitats

Introduction

"It will not happen," said Colonel Sydney Peddie. "Or else there will be war." Peddie, the leader of the Accompong Maroons, a fiercely independent community of descendants of escaped slaves and anticolonial rebels, was addressing the Caribbean branch of the BBC in 2007. That year, Accompong Maroons living in Cockpit Country joined forces with a transnational network of environmental advocates and the Jamaican diaspora to publicly oppose the extension of bauxite mining in the area. While this opposition was based in part on scientific appeals about the proper way to conserve biodiversity, the Maroons, descendants of runaway slaves and indigenes then led by Colonel Peddie, used the language of war and cultural survival to oppose mining.

For the Maroons, opposing bauxite mining was not just about preventing biodiversity loss. Rather, bauxite mining also threatened to irreparably damage the land that was bound to their identity, livelihoods, and history. Further, the agencies responsible for promoting bauxite mining have historically excluded rural communities like the Maroons from participating in making decisions that affected their local land use, and excluded them from the lion's share of revenue generated by mining. Thus, the bauxite industry itself was seen as antipathetic to the interests of the Maroons. In this, Jamaica bears out a pattern seen in studies of other developing countries, like Brazil[1] and Mexico.[2] In short, those poised to bear the burden of environmental degradation were excluded not only from the decision making shaping industrialization, but also from its benefits. Thus, in ways familiar to scholars like Carruthers,[3] Pellow,[4] and Carmin and Agyeman among others,[5] contestations over environmental management in Cockpit Country became struggles over environmental justice.

For the opponents of mining, these struggles have been successful so far. Under political pressure from the advocacy network and the mass public, and with support from sympathetic policymakers in the Forestry Department and the Ministry of Environment, the government of Jamaica (GoJ) and the Ministry of Agriculture agreed to place a moratorium on mining in Cockpit Country in 2007, "saving" biodiversity, at least temporarily.

However, if justice claims were all that were needed to get policymakers to listen to the concerns of the marginalized, the history of land conservation in the developing world and in other parts of Jamaica would look very different. In this case, a transnational advocacy network of scientific experts holding a consensus on causal explanations and policy recommendations played a catalytic role in influencing political and public support for the campaign to save Cockpit Country. Scholars of global environmental governance generally describe a network that holds all of these characteristics as an *epistemic community*. As described in the introduction, epistemic communities increase the likelihood that policymakers will listen to certain claims about appropriate policy, due to the perception that they are authoritative experts with privileged knowledge in specific issue areas. Here, the epistemic community was helping the GoJ carry out the Project for Sustainable Conservation of Globally Important Caribbean Bird Habitats, an effort funded by the Global Environment Facility (GEF) to conserve nesting areas for Black- and Yellow-billed Parrots endemic to Cockpit Country. I describe the development of the project later in this chapter to show how the epistemic community became engaged in global governance efforts in Jamaica.

At first glance, this seems like a highly local issue. Cockpit Country is rural and isolated. Many of the inhabitants rarely, if ever, travel to Jamaica's capital, Kingston, much less to the foreign countries from which several epistemic community members arrived. Moreover, it is likely that the endemic species in Cockpit Country could go extinct without materially changing the lives of people in Kingston, much less those outside the country.

However, it is precisely this kind of local action that we need to study to understand how well international environmental regimes on protected areas are being implemented. In Jamaica, like the rest of the cases discussed here, the GEF cited the project being carried out as relevant to the Convention on Biological Diversity (CBD). Moreover, as I described in the introduction, and as addressed by scholars like Rosendal,[6] Rosendal and Schei,[7] and

Swanson,[8] the effectiveness of the CBD and global governance mechanisms can only be seen in the steps that states take (or fail to take) to manage local ecosystems.

Successful biodiversity governance requires the coordination of activity across multiple levels, and the case in Jamaica was no different. The epistemic community engaged in advocacy work at all stages of the project. At the international level, the epistemic community lobbied institutions like the GEF and World Bank to commit funds to conserve Cockpit Country. Nationally, members tried to get the government of Jamaica to adopt the CBD's recommendations on managing protected areas. Finally, members mobilized a variety of supporters within Jamaica and transnationally to defend Cockpit Country against the onset of mining. Thus, as with other cases of transnational activism "from Santiago to Seattle,"[9] the networks studied throughout this book were actively engaged in advocacy efforts in domestic and international political opportunity structures simultaneously. This chapter explores how these efforts, buttressed by a scientific consensus, socialization between the network and policymakers, and appeals to local environmental justice claims shaped the GoJ's willingness to take new steps to conserve and manage biodiversity.

When people refer to Cockpit Country, they are describing an isolated, rural region of karst limestone located in the parishes of Trelawny, St. Elizabeth, and St. James in the northwestern section of Jamaica (see figure 1.1), and characterized by rainforest laid over a closely packed series of conical hills and plunging valleys. From the air, it resembles an egg carton turned upside down and covered with trees, or perhaps the cockfighting pits that gave the area its name. These isolated hills and depressions have, in combination with poor species dispersal capability, led to the creation of numerous microhabitats and specialized evolution,[10] giving the area a wealth of biodiversity recognized by the World Bank, the UN, and Jamaican policymakers and civil society.[11]

However, despite a general shared understanding among policymakers, local residents, and academics about where Cockpit Country is situated, it is not a legally defined place with officially recognized borders. Most residents of Cockpit Country belong to agricultural and peasant communities. Some are descended from populations of Maroons, the escaped slaves and indigenous peoples who fled to the hilly terrain during guerrilla wars against the British. For these communities, Cockpit Country provides

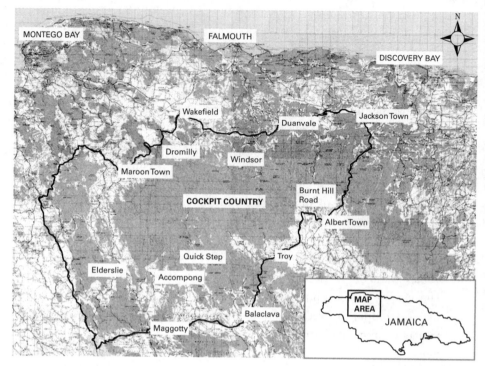

Figure 1.1
Cockpit Country region with Ring Road boundary. *Source:* Used with permission from The Nature Conservancy, Jamaica.

subsistence, fuel, and commerce through forest products, timber, and yams, one of the primary agricultural products of Trelawny, a parish in the northwestern section of the island.[12] As far as the Maroons and other residents are concerned, Cockpit Country is delimited by a peace treaty signed by the British on January 6, 1738, which ceded an area of still-debated size to the sovereign control of the Maroons.[13]

These local perspectives are contested, however, by the imaginaries of other actors who have radically different ideas about the size and content of what is to be defined as Cockpit Country. The Forestry Department of Jamaica has declared 300 square kilometers of Cockpit Country as a forest reserve. Epistemic community scientists have mapped 450 square kilometers of what they consider Cockpit Country, based on subterranean water cycles and internationally important genetic endemism.[14] The Maroon community, based on their understanding of the colonial peace treaty and their knowledge of past battles fought against the British, has asserted that Cockpit Country is defined by a map declaring the area to comprise 1,142 square kilometers.[15] In contrast, Jamaican government regulatory agencies for mining and transnational bauxite companies have mapped Cockpit Country as a site of untapped mineral deposits. A recent government-commissioned study by the Jamaica Bauxite Institute declared Cockpit Country to be only 288 square kilometers.[16]

These contestations about how to define and name an area, an issue shared by all the cases studied here, is a common theme in the conservation politics of developing countries. West's study of Papua New Guinea[17] and both Cervone's[18] and Sawyer's[19] accounts of Ecuador are just some of the recent literature showing that the struggles of land management are cartographic, as much as they are physical. Maps embody several political and power claims about land, which are too often not recognized. They are not subjective. Maps are constructed by making choices about what a land is: from what perspective it is to be assessed, what are the characteristics that define one area, and what distinguishes it from other areas. These choices involve a range of assessments about the importance of observed ecological relationships, geographic characteristics, and the migration and activities of residents. Once these choices are inscribed on a map and legitimated by a government, alternate views become marginalized, and possibly erased. As in Papua New Guinea, Ecuador, and countless other places, a government's definition of a community or region may differ from how local people understand it—the borders might not fit. Groups who locals saw as outsiders might be lumped into one district or other kind of land-based unit for the ease of central administration. Nomads and hunters may have radically different ideas about the location of appropriate travel routes and pastoral lands. But maps present a static, single picture of what a place is that, once accepted, is then reified by state agencies and the exercise of state authority. As Henderson and Waterstone note, maps are an expression of power.[20]

Agriculture, Mining, and Environmental Injustice in the Cockpit Country

Biodiversity conservation in Cockpit Country has also been shaped by the socioeconomic inequity that characterizes patterns of resource use in the region. The fertile soil in the myriad valleys provides excellent arable land to the primarily agrarian population in and around the area. The residents of Cockpit Country carry out a variety of activities that affect biodiversity conservation such as subsistence agriculture, logging, charcoal production, hunting, and very occasionally acting as ad hoc tour guides for tourists.[21]

Nationally, the parish of Trelawny is the primary yam and yam stick producing parish.[22] Yam production, one of the main agricultural practices, requires the harvesting of "yam sticks," or cut saplings, stripped and used to provide a support for the biomass of the plant.[23] The removal of saplings prevents the regeneration of the forest, contributing to overall deforestation. In turn, this exacerbates forest degradation caused by the conversion of forest cover to monoculture in agricultural production.[24]

Besides yams, another agricultural threat that has been specifically identified as problematic is marijuana cultivation. Due to its official status as an illegal crop in Jamaica, farmers have to create inroads into virgin territory to find hidden lands for cultivation.[25] Indeed, one of the potential challenges to physically studying biodiversity in rainforest regions in Jamaica is the ever-present risk of literally stumbling into a marijuana plantation during field research. At such times, the standard practice is to carefully pick one's way through the plants, cognizant that the crops' owner, probably armed, may be watching for damage to their lucrative trade. Ironically, marijuana cultivation could in some cases promote de facto conservationism, as farmers prefer to keep old-growth, broad-leaved trees intact, to act as camouflage from the air.

The practice of legal agriculture creates additional stresses as well. Clearing the forest for agriculture or logging creates ecological vulnerabilities and gaps that may allow invasive species to gain access to sensitive areas. Agricultural crops may act as alien invasive species.[26] Industrialized agriculture is particularly problematic, in that it depends on the introduction of chemicals from pesticides and fertilizer, which may leach into soils and enter the hydrological regime as biological toxins.[27]

Like many developing countries in Latin America and the Caribbean,[28] agriculture and land use practices in Cockpit Country are highly inequitable, with low-income agricultural communities extremely vulnerable to economic and environmental marginalization. In the Cockpit Country, 3 percent of landowners control 62 percent of the available farmland in the area, and as such, small farmers have to rent or lease land from larger property owners or otherwise conduct incursions into virgin forested areas. In turn, this contributes to migratory farming and fragmented and dispersed agricultural plots.[29] As agricultural productivity decreases, farmers turn to logging for fuelwood and timber production to generate income.[30]

The other main threat to biodiversity—bauxite mining—is also shaped by socioeconomic inequity in rural areas. Besides containing highly productive arable land, the depressions of Cockpit Country are believed to contain substantial deposits of bauxite, a mineral ore used to produce aluminum (see figure 1.2).[31]

Mining and production have since the 1950s been promoted in Jamaica by different actors for differently constructed interests. While Jamaican agencies in the mining sector now treat bauxite as a symbol of national development and autonomy, the industry came to Jamaica to serve the interests of powerful countries in the world's economic core. In the 1950s, while Jamaica was still under British administration, the United States developed a powerful need for readily available bauxite. The Korean War broke out at the start of the decade and, with the Cold War arms race heating up,

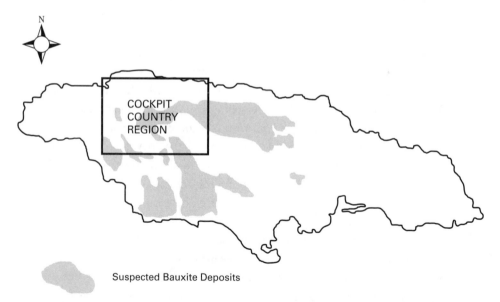

Figure 1.2
Suspected bauxite deposits in Jamaica. *Source:* Author's reproduction of map provided by The Nature Conservancy, Jamaica. Used with permission from The Nature Conservancy, Jamaica.

created a strategic demand for aluminum to service and supply military machinery. Given Jamaica's proximity and the sizable amounts of easily accessible bauxite, the U.S. government gave financial aid to multinationals to help them extract the increasingly valuable ore. In this, the American government covered 85 percent and 16 percent of Reynolds's and Alcan's initial capital investment in the island respectively.[32] While direct investment by the U.S. government and Department of Defense in stimulating production of Jamaican bauxite ended with the 1950s, civilian demand for bauxite and aluminum products continued apace.

Consequently, the contemporary use of aluminum in civilian commodities like planes, ground transportation, and household items, combined with Jamaica's proximity to the United States and the fact that Jamaica's ore is close to the surface (and hence comparatively easy to mine) have made the small island state into a major global player in bauxite production. While Jamaica's share of total production has since fallen, it is still considerable. In the 1970s, Jamaica was the second largest exporter of bauxite in the world, peaking at 18.1 percent of global supply. In 1999 production stood at thirteen million tonnes per annum, or 7 percent of the total world supply.[33] Between 2002 and 2006, Jamaica produced the fourth-highest quantity of bauxite globally, exporting 4.5 million tons to the United States alone.[34]

Thus, the extraction of this natural resource has become the primary mechanism through which Jamaica became integrated into the global production of capital. As in other developing countries that export primary products, most of the value added to this resource is done so outside of the country. To be sure, the kinds of resources that developing countries produce vary significantly. In Ecuador, the primary product is oil; in Fiji, water.[35] But the pattern where foreign interests extract natural resources at low costs, and then turn them into goods that developing nations have to purchase at much higher costs holds here as well. While Jamaica eventually developed smelters to convert ore into alumina, the later stages wherein alumina is turned into aluminum (and eventually machinery and consumable goods) are carried out in refineries in industrialized countries, like the Gramercy refinery in Louisiana. Certainly, scholars writing in the 1970s, like Walter Rodney,[36] Norman Girvan,[37] and Eduardo Galeano[38] would not be surprised at this relationship between natural resources and global capital and developing countries even if, as Galeano himself later admitted, their descriptions were somewhat crude.

This is not to negate the benefits that bauxite production has brought to Jamaica. Since its launch in earnest in the 1950s, production and export have been major contributors to Jamaica's foreign revenue stream. Notably, former Prime Minister Michael Manley took a deliberate role in strengthening bauxite's role in Jamaica's economic growth in the 1970s. In 1974, Manley passed a Bauxite Levy on the production of ore, nationalized 51 percent of both Kaiser and Reynolds and 6 percent of Alcoa and Alcan, and fostered the creation of the International Bauxite Association (IBA), a cartel of bauxite producers modeled on OPEC. In 1975, the GoJ created the Jamaica Bauxite Institute (JBI) to protect the government's interest in the production and global commercialization of bauxite.

As with Nigeria's nationalization of oil production, the goal of the Manley government was ostensibly to strengthen the position of the state with respect to the transnational bauxite corporations, and gain a more equitable distribution of resources. Indeed, the 1970s oil crisis underlined how vulnerable Jamaica was in the global economy, and illustrated the power that developing countries could exercise with greater sovereign control of their own natural resources.[39] In involving the government in bauxite production, Manley enhanced the importance of the industry to national development. In the context of other cases of successful and attempted nationalization in the Third World in the 1970s, Manley's policies and rhetoric about national control fit the narrative of growing Third World independence and reasserted sovereignty.[40]

It is also clear that national support for the bauxite industry led to impressive growth in revenue for the GoJ in the post-Levy era.[41] By the end of the 1970s, taxes paid by the industry climbed to J$200 million, nearly ten times what they were in the 1960s. Domestically, production has contributed from 5.4 percent to over 10 percent of GDP between 1999 and the present.[42] Between 2004 and 2006, the JBI received J$5 million in interest from bauxite deposits and J$11.5 million from commercial projects. The GoJ has 50 percent ownership in Clarendon Alumina Production, one of the bauxite companies possessing prospecting leases in the Cockpit Country.[43] Bauxite interests have also been highly placed in other agencies. In the mid-2000s, the director of the JBI, Parris Lyew-Ayee, was appointed to the directorship of the National Environment Planning Agency (NEPA).[44] Given its role in Jamaica's political economy, it is understandable that, at a 2013 announcement of a partnership between the JBI and Nippon Light

Metal Company to extract rare earth metals from Jamaican ore, Lyew-Ayee commented enthusiastically: "our bauxite is really God blessed."[45]

However, Manley's policies may have softened the inequities in the relationship between global capital and Jamaica in bauxite production, but his policies did not eliminate them. The GoJ's share of revenue certainly increased, and the government supported Jamaica's technological growth, by creating refineries in the parishes of St. Elizabeth, Clarendon, and St. Catherine to turn raw ore into alumina. However, since Jamaica was so reliant on imported energy, the country never developed the technical capacity to progress to the final stages of aluminum production. Moreover, while most of the value of bauxite and aluminum production is generated outside of the country, and certainly outside of the parishes in which bauxite is found, many of the ecological costs are borne locally by the low-income rural communities who live in and near subterranean mineral deposits. Ore is extracted through the *standard open-cast* method, which entails removing the entire layer of topsoil and vegetation covering a deposit. Immediate impacts of this process include deforestation, forest degradation,[46] and the emission of potentially toxic fumes and dust.[47] In addition, the use of heavy machinery in mining areas requires the construction of access roads, which segment ecosystems, allow further access into formerly pristine areas, and contribute to deforestation.[48] The interaction of these processes can cause widespread soil erosion, downstream run-off and sedimentation, exacerbating the loss of forest cover, in turn causing eutrophication in aquatic ecosystems.[49]

But perhaps the most symbolic example of bauxite-related ecological devastation is the presence of red mud lakes throughout rural Jamaica. When bauxite ore is refined, it is mixed with caustic materials to dissolve the alumina and then extract it. The leftover residue, called "red mud," is then stored in tailings ponds, which are either abandoned bauxite mines, or natural valleys. To date, Jamaica has produced an estimate of 60 billion tons of red mud in such lakes.[50] These lakes contain caustic materials and metals in sufficient quantities to be toxic to plant and animal life.

Unfortunately for the communities surrounding these lakes, the harms they pose are not limited to the lakes themselves. Red mud lakes in Ewarton and Kirkvine have leached alkaline minerals and sodium into groundwater, damaging crops of nearby communities and ruining household water supplies.[51] As the lakes dry, the dust and fine particulates on the surface become airborne, sometimes visibly coating the neighboring landscape. In the district of New Building, near the Alpart refinery in Nain, St. Elizabeth, residents have complained bitterly about the effect of mining on their daily lives. Lenford Bailey, a New Building farmer, described the effects of mining thus: "The pollution a kill we. The dust is a real problem for us who live near to the plant. When you get up in the morning and see the white stuff you step [on], you wouldn't believe [it]. The acid carry a stinking stench."[52]

For the rural communities near bauxite production plants, these environmental hazards make it increasingly difficult to conduct basic subsistence activities, as well as creating untold health problems. Adding insult to injury, residents who lose their agricultural livelihood, either because their crops wither and die, or because they are removed from the land, do not find reemployment in the bauxite sector. Due to increasing automation, bauxite mining is no longer a major employer of Jamaica's surplus labor, and those who do find jobs tend to be the younger population, leaving older farmers vulnerable.

If this were not enough, the industry has developed a reputation for predatory practices in rural communities. Consider the stories shared by agricultural districts in St. Ann, by the names of Prickly Pole, Glasgow Lodge, Eight Miles, Nine Miles, Stepney, Hessen Castle, and Murray Mount. There, the company Noranda has repeatedly bulldozed agricultural lands months before the deadline given to farmers to clear out. When the company did pay compensation to farmers displaced from intergenerationally held lands, the settlement given was several times lower than what was claimed to be fair valuation for the destroyed agricultural crops. In 2011, Gerald Lawrence, the president of an association representing these districts spoke to the *Jamaica Observer*, describing these and other practices experienced by the agrarian communities. "We want the whole Jamaica to know what we are going through," said Lawrence. "Our lives have become hell."

So it is that bauxite mining in Jamaica has hampered the goal of sustainable development. The global nature of bauxite production means that, despite greater governmental control over local operations, the control over capital and the lion's share of wealth from bauxite remains in the hands of multinational corporations and elites in Jamaica's political economy. In ways similar to Ali and Ackley's description of Fiji's water-exporting sector, the process of globalization and global production means "the potential for environmental harm from external agents that are only remotely connected to the culture and have little to lose in this context becomes magnified."[53]

Thus, the vulnerability of rural populations in these local communities to global ecological inequity is heightened. First, as citizens of Jamaica, rural residents are subordinate to differences in productive capacity and capital development between their own country and the industrialized countries in which aluminum companies are located. Second, as rural residents within Jamaica, these communities are vulnerable to exploitation from the local activities of bauxite corporations and political elites in the bauxite sector who, despite being located in Jamaica, are comparatively able to distance themselves from the ecological costs of extraction. To borrow a phrase from Newell, this exploitation in Jamaica simply underlines the fact that, even in countries located in the global South, there are "Norths-in-the-South," wherein citizens of developing countries are made economically and eco-logically vulnerable by their own political elites.[54] Mike Schwartz, a Brit-ish-born researcher who lives and works in Cockpit Country, described the relationship between the political center and the rural periphery around bauxite as one of modern colonialism: "[The] Mining Act of 1947 is colo-nial in nature. It was hurriedly brought in by the British when they realised how much value was in bauxite (discovered in Jamaica around 1942). The purpose was to extract value from the colony and send it back to UK. Inde-pendence has not changed the Act: it is still colonial, but now it's not white man in England but black man in Town [Kingston] who is colonial!"[55]

These stories have certainly informed the attitudes of Cockpit Country residents to the prospect of bauxite mining. When asked about the possibil-ity of mining in Cockpit Country, Viris Pingue, a yam farmer and owner of a rustic bed and breakfast told a story about what happened in the neigh-boring parish of St. Ann: "They were talking about bauxite mining and jobs, persons would be getting jobs, and all of that. But after we learned about it, you know, what happened in St. Ann—because you know about what happened in St. Ann? They took away the best part of the land for bauxite mining, and the persons were pushed further away. And it turned out that most of the persons who were told they would get jobs, didn't get any jobs."[56]

Management of this complex of environmental and social issues is spread across several governmental agencies. First are the agencies in the environmental branch of the GoJ. The National Resources Conservation

Agency (NRCA) was created in 1991 as the executive agency of the Ministry of Environment.[57] In 2001, the NRCA was merged with two urban planning agencies, the Town Planning Department and the Land Development and Utilization Commission, to form the National Environmental Planning Agency (NEPA). The Ministry of Environment, lead agency of the NRCA/NEPA, can propose certain areas to be managed as National Parks with the approval of the Cabinet.

Second are agencies in the agricultural branch. The Ministry of Agriculture contains three relevant agencies in the Forestry Department, the Mines and Geology Division, and the Jamaica Bauxite Institute (JBI).[58] The Ministry of Agriculture itself regulates the issuance of mining licenses over the Cockpit Country to bauxite companies. The Forestry Department, executive agency of the Ministry of Agriculture, gains jurisdiction over resource management when the ministry declares areas as Forest Reserves. In these reserves, the department can regulate activities such as tree clearance, road construction, and the killing of wildlife, in particular avifauna.[59] Since the 1950s, most of the area known as the Cockpit Country has been declared a Forest Reserve (see figure 1.3).

The Department of Mining in the Division of Mines and Geology grants mining licenses and evaluates the environmental soundness of post-mining activity.[60] Its research division in the JBI acts as the GoJ's technical adviser in mining and regulates and monitors the activities of industrial bauxite companies.[61] The JBI also conducts environmental impact assessments (EIAs) on mining activities and, where necessary, develops planning strategies for population relocation and post-mining land use and restoration.[62] These agencies were the main political actors within Jamaica that the epistemic community network targeted with their advocacy efforts.

Scientific Authority and Racial Identity

The Cockpit Country network exemplified the transnational nature of epistemic community advocacy. The academics, environmentalists, and policymakers who comprised the network came from several countries and backgrounds, even though they all shared a common interest in conserving biodiversity and a shared background in scientific training (see table 1.1). In the 1980s and early 1990s, L. Alan Eyre, a British-born Jamaican and founder of the Department of Geography at the University of the West

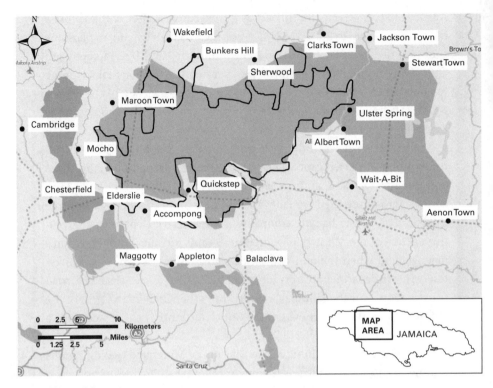

Figure 1.3
Cockpit Country forestry reserve. *Source:* Author's reproduction of map provided by the Centre for Environmental Management, *Public Consultations on Defining the Boundaries of the Cockpit Country* Kingston: Centre for Environmental Management, 2013), 172. Base map copyright held by OpenStreetMap. Used with permission from OpenStreetMap and the Centre for Environmental Management.

Indies (UWI) began writing passionately about what he saw as unconscionable lack of national attention to the environmental qualities and threats in Cockpit Country. Disturbed by what he described as "dangerous ignorance" among policymakers about its ecological importance, Eyre called for the GoJ to protect the region in accordance with what he saw as its potential status as a World Heritage Site.[63]

Through the 1990s, other civil society actors emerged to support Eyre's arguments about conserving Cockpit Country. In 1995, the Gosse Bird Club, a Jamaica bird-watching organization under the leadership of Catherine

Table 1.1

Partial list of epistemic community members

Organization	Individuals	Functions	Science training
Windsor Research Centre	Mike Schwartz	Population monitoring (fauna). Conducts training of Forestry Department personnel. Habitat health evaluation.	Biology
	Susan Koenig	Population monitoring (fauna). Conducts training of Forestry Department personnel. Habitat health evaluation.	Ornithology
Southern Trelawny Environmental Agency	Hugh Dixon	Population monitoring (fauna). Socioeconomic surveys.	Ecology
The Nature Conservancy	Kimberly John	Population monitoring (fauna). Underwater ecology.	Freshwater ecology
	Ann Haynes-Sutton	Population monitoring (fauna)	Conservation ecology
The Forestry Department	Owen Evelyn	Population monitoring. Flora taxonomy. Habitat health evaluation.	Botany
	Kevin Porter	Population monitoring (fauna). Flora taxonomy.	Botany
	Respondent	Population monitoring (fauna). Flora taxonomy. Habitat health evaluation.	Botany
University of Manitoba/ University of the West Indies	Balfour Spence	Habitat health evaluation	Geology/ geography
Clearing House Mechanism	Dayne Buddo	Population monitoring (fauna)	Marine ecology
University of Wisconsin	Mick Day	Karst limestone ecology. Habitat health evaluation.	Geomorphology
University of the West Indies	Peter Vogel (deceased)	Population monitoring (flora, fauna)	Conservation ecology
	George Proctor (retired)	Habitat health evaluation	Botany
Jamaica Environment Trust	Diana McCaulay	Environmental advocacy	Environmental policy
Birdlife Jamaica	Catherine Levy	Population monitoring (fauna)	Ornithology

Levy, changed its name to Birdlife Jamaica to receive some funds and scientific support from Birdlife International for conservation projects.[64] Birdlife Jamaica and Peter Vogel, a herpetologist from the Department of Life Sciences at the University of the West Indies (UWI), began gathering data showing a global decline in populations of migratory Yellow- and Black-billed Parrots in the region. This information strengthened Eyre's arguments for conservation, as 95 percent of the world's population resides in the Cockpit Country.[65]

In 1996, Birdlife Jamaica hired Susan Koenig, an ornithologist from Arizona completing her dissertation, to assist in a study of parrot populations and bird habitat management in Cockpit Country.[66] Koenig moved to Windsor, a colonial military garrison used by the British stationed in Cockpit Country during the guerilla wars against the Maroons. Windsor then was still inhabited by a British citizen, Mike Schwartz, who was an immigrant amateur birdwatcher and self-described "freelance researcher." When Koenig's dissertation research began winding down, she and Schwartz began planning to create a research center at Windsor in the heart of Cockpit Country. This would allow them to receive financial and technical support from larger transnational conservation NGOs like The Nature Conservancy (TNC) and institutions like the Ford Foundation while continuing to work on local conservation.[67] As Koenig explained in an interview on the screened-in veranda at what became the Windsor Research Centre (WRC), this seemed like a natural progression. She could stay involved in conservation, in an issue she clearly cared about, and in a region with which she was already familiar: "I was finishing in 1999, when Mike said 'what are you going to do with the rest of your life?' and I said, 'I don't know, probably be a biologist for hire, and amble the world, saving the world.' I really had no desire to go into academia, so what was I gonna do with my life? So Mike said 'Hey, let's start a research center.'"

So it is that two white foreigners came to Cockpit Country and created what became one of the key agencies in the emergent epistemic community. At the time of creating the WRC, Koenig and Schwartz were assisted by the Southern Trelawny Environmental Association (STEA), a local environmental and rural development NGO started by Hugh Dixon. Dixon, a black Jamaican who grew up in one of the small towns in Cockpit Country, returned to Albert Town and created STEA in order to, as he described, bring "conservation and economic opportunity projects" to Cockpit Country in a way that would "bring benefits on both sides to the community and to conservation for generations to come."

In 1999, Birdlife Jamaica, WRC, and The Nature Conservancy, a transnational organization with a branch in Jamaica, successfully applied for funds from the Global Environment Facility for what was called the Cockpit Country Conservation Project. That project was to be implemented by the NRCA to conserve Cockpit Country as an area of bird habitats and sensitive biodiversity. The GEF agreed that this project was relevant to the Convention on Biological Diversity because it would support conservation in a way that would help the government of Jamaica comply with Articles 7 and 8 of the CBD.[68] However, that project was aborted in 1999 when the government of Jamaica refused to use World Conservation Union (IUCN) classification to create a protected area in Cockpit Country, precipitating a withdrawal of World Bank financing.[69]

Although the project was aborted, the organizations and researchers who produced the studies that informed it became the nucleus of an emerging transnational advocacy network. By the end of the project in 1999, this network held a core pool of knowledge on Cockpit Country biodiversity. This knowledge included several studies, such as a biodiversity assessment of Cockpit Country conducted by Koenig, George Proctor (a botanist from UWI), and Ann Haynes-Sutton from TNC. Another UWI academic, geologist Balfour Spence, produced a Land Management Assessment illustrating some of the potential and actual threats to biodiversity in the region, including agriculture and bauxite mining. These studies were then circulated among research organizations that had developed ties with one another in the advocacy process, namely Birdlife Jamaica, TNC, the WRC, and STEA.[70]

These data also clarified the policy implications of network knowledge. First, they identified the major threats to biodiversity, in particular unregulated agriculture, mining, and the introduction of invasive species.[71] Second, they began clarifying what the network understood Cockpit Country to be. At the time, Koenig, Proctor, and Haynes-Sutton used the commonly understood boundary, and one advanced by Eyre in his earlier work on Cockpit Country. This boundary was circumscribed by the Ring Road, a military perimeter established by the British in the eighteenth century, around approximately 450 square kilometers of karst limestone forest (see figure 1.1).[72] The scientists in this group described this boundary as "anthropologically rather than geologically defined."[73] This distinction between "anthropological" methods of defining an area and "geological" methods reemerged in later debates among scientists, local communities, governmental agencies, and environmental advocates about whether to use culture or science to define the borders of the region. At the time, however, the Ring Road boundary used by Eyre served as the basis from which the epistemic community began its advocacy efforts in Cockpit Country.

In 2001, Birdlife Jamaica spearheaded a proposal from Jamaica for international funds to conserve Cockpit Country as a site of biodiversity and as a habitat of migratory birds. Birdlife joined a regional effort with environmental NGOs in the Dominican Republic and the Bahamas. These organizations lobbied for GEF funds to create the Project for Sustainable Conservation of Globally Important Caribbean Bird Habitats, introduced earlier. As stated in GEF project documents, this would help the member states comply with their obligations under several Articles of the CBD, including Articles 7 and 8.[74] With a total budget of almost US$2 million, the Project for Sustainable Conservation in Jamaica was slated to begin in October 2003 and was scheduled to run for forty-two months under the implementation of the United Nations Environment Programme (UNEP) and Birdlife Jamaica.[75] Due to early involvement by network members in project design, the GEF adopted the 450 square kilometer area given in the 1999 biodiversity assessment study as the spatial definition of Cockpit Country.[76]

After 2001, the network continued to grow, as researchers from international academic institutions and domestic organizations began contributing information and support relevant to Cockpit Country conservation. These included non-Jamaicans, such as Mick Day, a University of Wisconsin specialist in karst geography, and Jamaicans like Dayne Buddo, a researcher and the former Focal Point of the Jamaica Clearing House Mechanism (CHM), a biodiversity database established pursuant to Article 7 of the CBD.[77] The core network of the epistemic community consisted of a group of approximately twenty to thirty researchers, fourteen of whom are listed by name, training, and organizational affiliation in table 1.1.

This network maintained cohesion through a variety of linkages, including frequently if irregularly held informal or semiformal face-to-face meetings and electronic communication. The physical meetings took place either in the Cockpit Country itself, or in Kingston. The WRC in Windsor and STEA offices in Albert Town, with their provision of room and board to visitors, electricity, and (admittedly spotty) Internet access were natural gathering spaces for researchers studying Cockpit Country. WRC also offered training in bird monitoring methodologies that, in addition to Koenig and Schwartz's habit of sharing an evening bottle of rum with visitors on the veranda of the main building, provided substantial face-to-face contact among visiting researchers from UWI and foreign academic institutions.

Because of the logistical difficulties in traveling from the mountains of Trelawny to the nation's capital, Dixon, Koenig, and Schwartz were less frequent attendees at the meetings held in Kingston, which were primarily attended by researchers from UWI and The Nature Conservancy. Buddo spoke of a series of ad hoc committee meetings between network members, ranging in frequency up to three times a week. Besides these meetings, researchers in the network were able to share information at virtual conferences held by TNC and WRC, and through online databases managed by WRC and the CHM.

Despite differences in background, training, and national origin, network members all shared a concern about the possibility of biodiversity loss in Cockpit Country. The primary environmental worry for all members was the risk that losing vital species in flora or fauna would trigger a domino effect, or push ecosystems past the threshold of sustainability. As network members were well aware, the limestone rainforest of Cockpit Country provides a habitat for local and migratory fauna. Arthropods, invertebrates, and crustaceans, as well as charismatic species of Giant Swallowtail butterflies and Black- and Yellow-billed Parrots, all contribute to ecosystem stability by maintaining intricate trophic relationships.[78] In Koenig's 1999 biodiversity assessment, she laid out an early description of the possibility that this interconnectivity between different parts of the ecosystem could come under threat from activities like logging: "Selective removal of large timber species could cause unpredictable losses of biodiversity, far greater than predicted by the proportion of forest removed, because of the associated losses of host-specific parasites, epiphytes or other symbiotic and commensal organisms."[79]

Later, network members used the same language of interconnectivity to describe the potential risks to biodiversity management of species loss, albeit in more poetic language. For example, Buddo in an interview conducted at the Clearing House Mechanism emphasized the potential irreparable loss caused by the extinction of endemic species in Cockpit Country.

If you lose elements of biodiversity ... whether it's trophic levels, relationships, you're going to impact the entire [system]. And sometimes, you know, you don't lose something because of a direct impact; you lose it because of an indirect impact, because you moved its food source ... and you end up wiping out these endemic species, these rare species. There's one section in Cockpit Country where there's this particular road, right? There's this part, these plants are only found in that section, in that place, and *nowhere else* in the world. I mean, that is remarkable! Only in that section, that *one* small section.[80]

These ideas would be repeated again in reports and interviews with members of STEA, WRC, TNC, and UWI who participated in networked meetings and various forms of information sharing. Throughout, there was a shared sense that something would be irrevocably lost with the destruction of Cockpit Country biodiversity.

What was happening by the early 2000s is that network members were increasingly describing Cockpit Country biodiversity loss with language that transcended their initial specialization. Moreover, network members consciously organized around a shared scientific epistemology, as well as a belief in appropriate policy. This process is described in the literature on social movements as *framing alignment*, where actors in a network converge on a set of norms, by exchanging information and ideas and building horizontal links.[81] In particular, the effort toward creating mutually intelligible information required that researchers conduct investigations and create relationships with specialists outside their area of expertise. This process led to a shared understanding of the integrated ecological relationships in the Cockpit Country, as described in the following quote by Susan Koenig: "[When] you start doing one little bit of research, then the system has its story to tell you, and you start seeing the interactions with the other animals and the system. ... Also, I was kind of the resident biologist. ... So everyone kind of directs the questions to me and so I started doing bat monitoring for Windsor Great Caves, because 'birds fly, bats fly, so therefore Susan must know something about bats.'"[82]

As the advocacy network became constituted around the ecological importance of Cockpit Country biodiversity, other nonstate actors emerged to support the conservation studies and the GEF-funded project. These actors consisted of a range of organizations including: community based organizations (CBOs) of Accompong Maroons, descendants of escaped slaves and indigenous Indians, the Jamaica Caving Organization (JCO), and the Jamaica Conservation and Development Trust (JCDT).[83]

This mobilization was not motivated by strictly scientific reasoning, nor did these groups share an ecologically generated concern about Cockpit Country. For example, organizations like the Accompong Maroons valued Cockpit Country not only for its role in providing economic opportunities, but also for its cultural importance as a historic site in which rebel slave garrisons resisted British colonialism.[84] Nevertheless, they assisted the advocacy efforts of the network by, among other things, contributing funding to the Project for Sustainable Conservation and carrying out research through organizations like The Nature Conservancy, thus aiding in the generation of scientific knowledge.[85]

Besides the use of a scientific epistemology, demography is what distinguished the epistemic community from the community-based organizations and networks that emerged in Jamaica to lobby for Cockpit Country conservation. Cockpit Country residents are largely agricultural workers, have comparatively low incomes, and few if any have a formal education beyond the secondary level. They are also almost exclusively black. In contrast, with the exception of Hugh Dixon of STEA and the WRC, none of the organizations or people identified as scientific experts were from the area. Further, although they live in Cockpit Country, Koenig and Schwartz of the WRC, like most of the researchers they host, are white foreigners who chose to care about biodiversity in the area, rather than having it be a natural part of their lived experience. Even among the Jamaican organizations, there are significant social differences between those publicly recognized as experts on the environment of the region, and those who live within it. Several members of the Jamaican NGOs were either white Jamaicans, like Diana McCaulay of the Jamaica Environment Trust (JET); white immigrants, like Ann Haynes-Sutton of TNC; faculty at UWI, the Caribbean's top university (several of whom, like Alan Eyre, were also white); or from state agencies. Almost all of these organizations, including the state agencies and UWI, were based in Kingston, rather than in Cockpit Country.

Far from being a liability, the preponderance of white and/or foreign scientists in the epistemic community was seen as a mark of authoritativeness. As McCaulay herself noted, "foreign-ness" can give knowledge claims heft in Jamaica, independent of the actual content therein: "We have a respect for outsiders and what they say. Jamaican scientists could be saying the same thing, but if it comes from a foreigner, somehow you think that's better."[86]

Within the epistemic community, some of the members also uncritically acknowledged the social authority of foreign-ness and whiteness. One researcher who was based in the WRC during field research in 2011 categorically described black Jamaicans as "lazy" (intended "as a compliment" since it meant they were shrewd enough to find the easiest way to accomplish tasks) and intimated that the role of the primarily white scientific elite in the campaign was to provide the expert knowledge upon which to make rational decisions. It is not surprising that whiteness and foreign-ness should play this role. In Jamaica, the lasting effects of the economic, gendered, and racial project of colonialism have given whiteness a great deal of social cachet in making authoritative claims. Fully parsing the history of whiteness and social authority in Jamaica is beyond the scope of this book, but there are several publications in the fields of history, anthropology, and poetry that do so effectively.[87] Of course, Jamaica is not unique in this among postcolonial states, and authors like Hall have conducted comparative work on this relationship in other political systems.[88]

In any case, these discussions illustrate that socially constructed markers, such as skin color and place of origin, constitute some of the bases from which scientific claims can derive their authority. As I noted in the introduction, this underlines some of the core arguments of critical theory scholars such as Litfin, Forsyth, Haraway, and McCormick about the role of science in policymaking: determining who is an expert, who gets to speak with authority about an issue area (and therefore, what kinds of knowledge claims constitute "expertise"), is not a value-neutral undertaking. Instead, the category of "expert" (which entails the exclusion of those who are not seen as experts) is determined in part by a range of social, economic, and political power relationships, and not just "objective" technical merit, were such a thing possible. So, in the case of Jamaica, when Forsyth says that there is a "need to understand who these experts are, and how they may reflect other forms of political power,"[89] we can see that the power structure that defines "expertise" in Jamaica is informed by race as well as the usual markers of technocratic discourse.

To be clear, whiteness was not the only social marker that mattered. The staffers in Jamaica's Forestry Department, and several UWI researchers, like Kurt McLaren, were black Jamaicans. All the same, they were members of socially and politically elite institutions, and all spoke the language of science. To be sure, during the initial period of mobilization against bauxite mining, this socially constructed distinction between expert and nonexpert on Cockpit Country did not have a perceptible effect on epistemic community advocacy. Scientists in the epistemic community and sympathetic policymaker institutions agreed with Maroons that mining should be prevented in Cockpit Country, and, as long as mining was on the table, debates about drawing the borders of Cockpit Country were postponed. Eventually however, this difference led to cleavages in the conservationist movement over the proper way to manage natural resources in the area. I will address this in more detail in chapter 5, but for now, I return to the early stages of epistemic community mobilization.

As described, by the end of the 1990s, a transnational network came into being, constituted around a concern for the ecological integrity of Cockpit Country and a shared scientific epistemology. Based on their understanding of the issues facing Cockpit Country, this epistemic community identified bauxite mining as the primary threat to environmental sustainability. Their opposition to mining solidified as it became clearer that the government of Jamaica and the bauxite industry were seriously contemplating extending mining operations in the mountainous region. As early as 1999, Spence's report for the aborted Cockpit Country Conservation Project noted that none of the available management strategies that the GoJ identified to restore mined lands could cope with bauxite mining, stating: "It should not be allowed in the Cockpit core because land reclamation will not restore the original ecosystem to acceptable levels."[90] Dayne Buddo later supported this observation: "[Forest management] would be obsolete if bauxite mining takes place in Cockpit Country. There will be no trees to take anyway. That's a *huge* threat. Really above what an NGO can do, really above what scientists at the University [of the West Indies] or Institute [of Jamaica] can do. ... You can't have bauxite mining in the Cockpit Country. It's the last place that you want to have that."[91]

After 2000, national policy developments and industrial practices in the bauxite sector indicated mounting national interest in developing access infrastructure in Cockpit Country. At that time, the government of Jamaica began planning the construction of a major thoroughfare traversing the southern coast of the island, with a link between the north and south coast passing through Cockpit Country.[92] Although this plan was postponed due to the foreseen difficulties of constructing the highway within Cockpit Country, the initial proposal indicated that the government was considering the possibility of major and unprecedented infrastructure development.[93] Further, as bauxite deposits were being depleted nationwide, it increasingly seemed as if Cockpit Country with its projected reserves would be an imminent target for mineral extraction.[94] Consequently, by 2001, the network agreed internally that mining was an imminent concern. As Schwartz noted: "[Now, the TNC's] analysis *or* our analysis gives bauxite mining as the biggest threat. And we certainly agree with *that.*"[95]

By the time the project started in 2003, the network members all shared Spence's 1999 policy goal of banning mining by declaring Cockpit Country as a protected area. This idea that mining should be forbidden was also strongly supported by local agricultural residents, who feared the destruction to natural resources posed by the practice. In the press conference described earlier, Colonel Peddie was very clear that mining should be abandoned as "we [Maroons] cannot afford to let them destroy us like that."

At the same time, there was some dissent within the network about the role of agricultural practices among rural communities in Cockpit Country. The method of yam harvesting, namely the use of yam sticks, still widespread in the late 1990s and early 2000s was universally seen as problematic because cutting yam sticks has a high potential to clear vast tracts of land and contribute to deforestation by preventing the regeneration of the forest.[96] Some Jamaican-born scientists agreed with local residents that sustainable agriculture in the Cockpit Country buffer zone was acceptable. Sustainable agriculture, if managed correctly, could incorporate local communities into governance efforts, promoting biodiversity conservation while simultaneously maintaining economic well-being for marginalized and rural populations. In explaining their views of conservation in Cockpit Country, Hugh Dixon of STEA and Ann Haynes-Sutton of The Nature Conservancy respectively emphasized the possibility of sustained use for human benefit:

[When] you get the little bits of research ... you start to say, "Hey, I can use the resource, because I know it's renewable. And I can know what levels I can use it, to make it renewable to sustain it over time," as against indiscriminate use of it.[97]

I do not agree that there are species that should never be used for economic purposes, nor do I agree that there are some uses (such as hunting) that should never be considered, provided such use can be shown to be consistent with the conservation of the species. ... I believe that conservation of biodiversity is not just important but fundamental to the maintenance of humanity.[98]

However, a small fraction of the network, four of the approximately two dozen identified members, quietly opposed the idea of continued agricultural incursions into Cockpit Country, even those meeting the subsistence needs of marginalized populations in the region. In off-the-cuff conversations and interviews, these respondents took a very preservationist approach to management, going so far as to suggest that permitting infrastructure development, such as access to electricity and improved roads, for communities in Cockpit Country, would have a detrimental effect on the greater good of biodiversity management. In one instance, white foreigners within the network unfavorably described the poor black inhabitants of the region as "cockroaches" who failed to understand the richness and importance of Cockpit Country's endemism. Less virulently, Schwartz and Koenig, in one of their veranda chats, seemed to argue that humanity itself was a threat to the goal of biodiversity conservation:

I'm part of the human plague that has descended upon this planet ... I would be very happy if everyone on this planet voluntarily decided to go extinct and leave it to the rest of the animals to have a chance to exist [*laughing*].[99]

So, we need to set a good example to this future species that takes over the world. ... [We] should voluntarily go extinct to protect the rest of biodiversity.[100]

The idea that network members may have radically different ideas about the merit of including local needs in biodiversity conservation raises important questions about the normative principles of transnational networks. Since conservationists may prefer policies that marginalize low-income populations, knowledge-based transnational advocacy networks like epistemic communities cannot—as Forsyth, Haraway, and McCormick note—uncritically be called "progressive" or normatively "good."[101] In addition, as indicated earlier, this network derived its authority as a voice of expertise through social systems (racial, discursive, and class based) that institutionally discriminated against the average Cockpit Country resident. Thus, reiterating studies of conservation in developing countries by Dowie,[102] and Karvonen and Brand,[103] among others, science-based conservation may be highly problematic for local communities if scientific discourse, which already excludes some populations, leads to policies that further disenfranchise the socially vulnerable.

However, this internal tension did not undermine the ability of the network to support community-based calls to prevent bauxite mining. While epistemic community members were recognized as knowledge claimants through sociopolitical power structures that subordinated the "lay" Cockpit Country resident, both residents and scientists were confronting the political power of the state and its bauxite interests. As a result, these comments did not become a visible part of the internal policy debate, since maintaining cohesion against the overarching threat of bauxite mining remained the primary goal of the advocacy network and its allies.

The network strengthened its scientific basis for opposing bauxite mining by the ability of members to generate a clear consensus on the dangers of mining to Cockpit Country's environment. The very short causal links between human action and ecological damage facilitated this process. First, it was easy to identify the likely causes of mining in Cockpit Country, as the only companies with Ministry of Agriculture–issued mining licenses for bauxite were Alcoa and Clarendon Aluminum Production. Second, agreement about the consequences of mining was also easily attained, as the bauxite industry has standardized its extractive processes, giving clear signals to network members about the possible impact on local biodiversity. In reports produced in the early 2000s like The Nature Conservancy's *Cockpit Country Conservation Action Plan*,[104] and STEA's *Biodiversity Manual*,[105] members emphasized the irreparable damage posed to local ecosystems. One outspoken UWI faculty member who will be identified as John Doe, was clear that the consequences of mining would be dire: "[Any] kind of intrusive land cutting that the bauxite company would do would just basically kill the area. There would be nothing left."[106]

While mining has not taken place yet, the network has developed projections about the likely scope and expected extent of damage based on shared maps illustrating the presence, size, and location of bauxite reserves in Cockpit Country (see figure 1.2). These maps and figures were cited in reports such as the 1999 biodiversity assessment conducted by Koenig of the WRC, Vogel of Birdlife/UWI, Haynes-Sutton of TNC, and Proctor of UWI,[107] and the Land Management Assessment conducted by Spence,[108] and contributed to a growing alarm about the likely scope of bauxite extraction activities in the area:

[Mining] is the biggest threat. It's an inevitable threat, and it's going to be a significant impact on the Cockpit Country.[109]

[The] whole issue that they will face in the near future, as you probably would have heard, is that [the Cockpit Country is] supposed to be a huge bauxite reserve. And so if we do run out of areas of bauxite outside the Cockpit Country, they're going to actually head in there.[110]

In contrast, consensus on the contribution of agriculture to environmental degradation was less robust. This was due to a lack of clear information in some sectors, differences in methodology within the network, and a qualitative difference between the network's approach to understanding the ecological impact of bauxite in comparison to agriculture. First, in discussing the causes of agricultural degradation, there was some uncertainty about which farmers and practices were the primary threats. Marijuana cultivation is illegal in Jamaica, though regularly carried out as part of the informal economy. Similarly, unauthorized logging and unauthorized farming of licit crops takes place in Cockpit Country. In these cases, activities that are hidden from the view of policymakers do not follow any formal reporting systems. Thus, for some agricultural activities, it is difficult to isolate specific actors and practices and to conduct accurate models of the environmental impact of agricultural activity.[111]

Second, a lack of clear information also inhibits the collection of scientific information about the consequences of subsistence agriculture and logging on biodiversity. For example, a 1995 study of subsistence agriculture in Cockpit Country revealed samples of small farmers who completely bulldozed forested areas for cattle, but also indicated that other farmers painstakingly conserved the natural forest during crop cultivation.[112] As a result, precisely accounting for the impact of agricultural activity on biodiversity in Cockpit Country would require an extensive qualitative survey of decentralized, under-reported activity. Failing this, the current models have some inescapable element of uncertainty.

Finally, the fact that agricultural activity was considered to be a less severe threat than bauxite mining contributed to another element of uncertainty. With bauxite mining, the epistemic community described the likely outcome as equivalent to complete destruction of the local biodiversity. Since agricultural activity was less clearly devastating, the network relied on more finely gradated assessments of environmental degradation, which led to some differences when network members could not agree on a shared methodology for measuring the extent of biodiversity loss. The differences in projections about the extent of contemporary environmental degradation were visible in the data the epistemic community used to describe the state of Cockpit Country. The Forestry Department used its LANDSAT study to fix the rate at 0.1 percent loss of forest cover per annum, a figure that is also recognized currently by The Nature Conservancy.[113] At the same time, UWI scientists have produced reports positing a range from a low of 0.03 percent to a high of 11.3 percent loss per annum.[114] Spence's 1999 Land Management Assessment claimed the rate of deforestation in Cockpit Country between 1961 and 1991 at 0.97 percent, and the 1999 biodiversity assessment cited studies by L. Alan Eyre fixing the rate of loss at 2.8 percent.

Thus, on one hand, there was universal agreement on the dimensions of bauxite mining and its causal impact on biodiversity loss. On the other, there was some disagreement between TNC and the rest of the network about the precise *causes* of agricultural degradation, some diffuse uncertainty about the *consequences* of agricultural degradation, and despite an official acceptance of the Forestry Department's figure, acknowledgment by all members of disagreement on the *extent* of agricultural degradation in Cockpit Country. Nevertheless, these disagreements did not surface in the network's policy discussions, and although consensus was certainly higher in the case of bauxite mining, network members universally agreed that Cockpit Country should be protected.

The network was able to generate a consensus, but the members' ability to communicate it to policymakers was affected by how well they were able to socialize with target audiences. In this, the epistemic community took advantage of the political opportunity structure to build strong social ties to the Forestry Department. These political opportunities to socialize with the Forestry Department emerged due to the desire of the conservator, or the leader of the Forestry Department, in the late 1990s and early 2000s to modernize their approach to forest conservation. For example, in 2002, the Forestry Department as well as the Environmental Foundation of Jamaica and TNC provided funds to WRC to create a program to train people in bird banding, one of the techniques used to monitor bird populations. The Forestry Department was motivated in its part by a grant it received from the Canadian International Development Agency (CIDA) to launch the Trees-for-Tomorrow project, a capacity building exercise intended to help states conserve natural resources. After the bird-banding program was launched, WRC continued working with and training Forestry Department staffers throughout the conduct of the project, despite the fact that staffers and field agents received no extra pay for participating.[115]

Additionally, the Forestry Department took the initiative in strengthening the relationship between itself and local NGOs. In 2001, the department launched a program of local forestry management committees (LFMCs) to share information on subsistence agriculture and promote environmentally friendly practices among residents of local communities.[116] In doing so, the Forestry Department made official arrangements with WRC and STEA to help manage the LFMCs and promote sustainability among local populations.[117]

The Forestry Department further adopted epistemic community information wholesale into its management approach. The department used the 1999 biodiversity assessment to determine areas of critical importance.[118] In 2001, TNC began a Parks in Peril (PiP) project to set priorities for biodiversity management and recommend appropriate management strategies,[119] and the Forestry Department used this research to design internal strategies for the conservation and management of forest resources and biodiversity.[120] In some cases, the borders between the Forestry Department and the civil society were even more porous, as individuals like John Doe moved between the department and an academic position at UWI. In fact, the Forestry Department functioned as part of the epistemic community. This is not uncommon in relationships between regulatory agencies and scientific networks. Craig Thomas has written about the participation of the Bureau of Land Management in an epistemic community involved in promoting biodiversity management in California,[121] and the literature on the epistemic communities involved in ozone regulation also clarifies that policymakers may also serve as environmental advocates and as parts of epistemic communities.[122]

In short, researchers from the civil society and the governmental agency shared information and knowledge about causal relationships and the importance of biodiversity in the region through joint reports, training sessions, and information exchanges.

Not surprisingly, the Forestry Department staff shared the perspective of the network that bauxite mining was the single greatest threat to biodiversity conservation in Cockpit Country. The Ministry of Agriculture, which is the parent agency of the Forestry Department, did not share this view, and was only too happy to endorse bauxite mining in the region. But back in Kingston, Owen Evelyn, then senior director of the science department within the Forestry Department, voiced concerns held by the Forestry Department about carrying out forest conservation, given the impending possibility of bauxite mining. As Evelyn stated: "The primary threats, or potential threats, is bauxite mining. Okay? We regard it as probably the most significant threat, because most of the Cockpit is bauxite. ... Other threats are not *that* extensive. But the bauxite is extensive, because if they go inside, it will affect all the biodiversity planning that we have identified.[123]

While the epistemic community was able to socialize with the Forestry Department, other regulatory agencies in the government of Jamaica were less willing to create such close relationships with the civil society. In fact, the relationship between the network of scientists and the environmental agency NEPA was almost antagonistic. This was not always the case. Prior to 2001, when the agency was still referred to as the NRCA, members of the emerging epistemic community did establish strong relationships and created a pattern of information sharing with the environmental agency. For example, the NRCA commissioned a series of Sector Assessment Reports in 1999 to prepare for the construction of a National Biodiversity Strategy and Action Plan (NBSAP), one of the requirements of the CBD.[124] In order to draft the NBSAP, the then NRCA recruited a number of researchers associated with the epistemic community, including Peter Vogel and Ann Haynes-Sutton.

However, after the government of Jamaica restructured the agency in 2001, the relationship between the scientists and what was now known as NEPA began to deteriorate.[125] First, network members like Schwartz criticized the process of creating NEPA through the merger of the NRCA with the Town Planning Department, since the NRCA and the Town Planning Department had conflicting mandates in the past: "[The Town Planning Department] wanted to do [a housing scheme], and suddenly they found to their surprise and amazement that they couldn't do it, because NEPA— NRCA—had refused permission, because of the environmental impact. And the government took the shortcut route and said, 'Well, we'll fix you. We're going to amalgamate Planning and NRCA into one, NEPA, so this doesn't happen again.'"[126]

Second, after this restructuring, NEPA's staff was almost entirely new, with little institutional continuity from the NRCA. In interviews not for attribution, former high-ranking NRCA staffers admitted that this change in staffing and organization weakened the regulatory authority of the agency. In short, they blamed this restructuring for a loss of expertise, institutional continuity, and morale, which in turn severely hampered the credibility and capacity of the organization to assess and evaluate environmental processes.[127] Civil society members were similarly critical of this change, with a UWI researcher identified here as John Doe describing the contemporary version of NEPA as an agency facing underlying and systematic staffing problems: "The problem with NEPA from what I understand, is how the appointments are made. The high echelon people are people who are appointed by the government, and they might not have any interest in anything per se, other than just doing their jobs. And they aren't necessarily the best people for this position."[128]

Added to these challenges was the fact that NEPA, like all natural resource agencies in Jamaica and other developing countries in general, has persistent funding issues, given its low priority in the national budget. The perceived decline of the NRCA/NEPA as a regulatory power later contributed further to the rupture of communication between the civil society and the agency. In 2005, tensions between the civil society and NEPA came to a head when members of the network and NGOs such as the Jamaica Caves Organization (JCO), JET, and community-based organizations in St. Ann sued the agency. At the time, a consortium of Spanish developers, Grupo Piñero, planned to build a tourist resort in Pear Tree Bottom in St. Ann's Parish. After NEPA approved the project through an environmental impact assessment (EIA), the NGOs and community groups objected, arguing that the EIA did not consult local communities, failed to address a range of environmental problems, and was thus fundamentally flawed. At first, Jamaica's Supreme Court Justice Brian Sykes agreed, finding in 2006 that the EIA was highly problematic. Noting that NEPA, in planning its EIA, had failed to consult the Jamaican public, and failed to consider how the project would affect local wildlife and important elements of oceanography, Justice Sykes concluded: "The empirical work on the EIA was really poor. This requires serious fieldwork. There is no evidence that this was done."[129]

However, any success here was short-lived. Two months later, Sykes allowed construction on the hotel to continue, despite finding that the developers were not adequately prepared to respond to the NGOs' lawsuit. The environmental advocacy network was able to manage only a temporary delay of construction, rather than a halt. Further, since the NGOs blamed NEPA for conducting a poor EIA, this lawsuit created suspicion and animosity between the NGO community and NEPA. Perhaps understandably, NEPA became very reluctant to work with NGOs afterward. Anecdotally, during my field research, I was only allowed access to NEPA's archives once it was clear that I was not an NGO member.

While less confrontational, other relationships between civil society epistemic community members and natural resource management agencies were characterized by far less socialization than was the case with the Forestry Department. Channels of communication between the various populations of social actors were not institutionalized, but rather ad hoc and irregular. Most of the communication to policymakers took place through letter-writing drives and media efforts by a few elite actors—in particular, Mike Schwartz of the WRC, Ann Haynes-Sutton of The Nature Conservancy, and Diana McCaulay of JET—who wrote letters to the Ministry of Agriculture and issued press releases during 2005 and 2006. Occasionally, epistemic community organizations would attempt to create more formal communication between the populations of policymakers and civil society researchers. For example, in planning for the Conservation Action Plan, TNC held a series of workshops with epistemic community organizations from 2004 to 2006, and invited policymakers from the JBI, the Ministry of Agriculture, the Ministry of Environment, NEPA, and the Forestry Department to attend.[130] However, only the Forestry Department participated while the JBI, NEPA, and people in the Ministry of Agriculture outside the Forestry Department abstained, a pattern of minimal agency participation characterized as typical by network respondents.

So why was the epistemic community able to create such strong ties to the Forestry Department? Some of this was due to the ability of network members to use the bird-banding program to demonstrate their knowledge about conservation and hence their value to the Forestry Department's mandate. But much of this would not have been possible were it not for changes within the Forestry Department, independent of epistemic community activity. In 1996, the Forestry Department hired Owen Evelyn, a Jamaican graduate of the British Columbia Institute of Technology, and Marilyn Headley, a UWI graduate and the first (and so far only) woman to serve as head conservator. After they arrived, Evelyn and Headley became crucial access points for epistemic community advocacy. Epistemic community members were clear that Evelyn and Headley's willingness to work with NGOs and listen to new information was unparalleled, with the aforementioned John Doe noting that after Headley became conservator in 1996, "she seemed to have actually pushed them in a [new] direction."

Koenig noted that this approach and openness were a stark contrast with previous relationships between the civil society and regulatory agencies. Reflecting on the bad relationship between NGOs and NEPA after its restructuring, Koenig observed: "When I first came here in 1995, the reverse was the case. Forestry Department was absolutely languishing under the former conservator, and NEPA was the shining star at the time. They were supportive of the parrot project, and just completely different organizations."[131]

Koenig also noted the potential downside of charismatic individuals shaping organizations, saying "it really is exciting and also [*sighs*] worrisome that essentially one personality in an organization can completely turn the organization around."

To be clear, any changes in the Forestry Department's management approach after the 1990s cannot be attributed solely to the arrival of Evelyn and Headley. While their presence was critical in establishing a relationship between the department and the civil society, the epistemic community provided new information that shaped how the department engaged in conservation in Cockpit Country, as will be discussed. However, the dependence of the epistemic community on the timely arrival of Evelyn and Headley, especially in contrast with NEPA's later antipathy, illustrates the capricious nature of political opportunity structures.

The First Advocacy Period and the Neoliberal Approach: 2001–2006

For the purpose of this chapter, network advocacy can be divided into two periods. In the first, which took place roughly between 2001 and 2006, the network of scientists deliberately adopted the language of economic cost–benefit analysis in the belief that this would make its claims "intelligible" to policymakers. During this period, network members focused on communicating neoliberal arguments to policymakers in the Ministry of Agriculture, mining agencies, and the Ministry of Environment. In the second advocacy period, after it was clear that policymakers preferred the economic gains from continued exploitation, the focus changed. From 2006 onward, the network's arguments about conservation became integrated in a mass public effort that held local environmental justice claims for Cockpit Country residents to be central to advocacy.

As already noted, the primary goal of the network was an official moratorium on bauxite mining in Cockpit Country.[132] Existing environmental regulations were simply ineffective, and the threat of bauxite mining was too great to environmental, cultural, and social concerns in Cockpit Country. Under Jamaican law, environmental regulations require that companies restore mined land, governed by certification processes from the Department of Mining.[133] However, mined lands do not have to be restored to their previous ecological relationships, but can be converted to commercial agriculture, or simply to grasslands. In fact, between 1995 and 2000, the bauxite companies Kaiser and Alcan planted a total of three million trees (the vast majority of them commercial fruit trees), grass, and other fast-growing plant species,[134] in a process that epistemic community members derided, despite its certification by the Department of Mining.[135] As STEA argues: "[Mining restoration] is complicated, because once the soil is removed, the hydrology of the area is altered, and we don't really understand the relationship among soil dwelling microbes, fungi and all other plant and animal species, such as pollinating roles, seed dispersal and chemical relationships."[136]

As a result, network members rejected the idea that mining restoration would be an adequate environmental management strategy in an area as ecologically rich as Cockpit Country, pointing out in a 2005 workshop on Cockpit Country that "you cannot restore forest which has been completely cleared."[137] Local residents like Viris Pingue were similarly skeptical of restoration based on their awareness of mining activities in other parishes:

On your way to Mandeville, there is this big massive piece of land, where the bauxite water used to flow. That is Alcan [the bauxite company]. ... You're going up to Mandeville, and there is this big, huge hole down there. It was a part of mining. Yes. I saw it. So, how are they going to restore it in three years? Yes. How are they? How is it going to be restored? Because the land is damaged. And nothing can plant there again. Yes. Nothing at all. ... So, can it be restored? No, you can't restore farmland. Not easily. It has been damaged. You can't fool us. They can't fool us.[138]

To be sure, there was some disunity in the community's campaign with the Ministry of Agriculture in this regard. Instead of supporting the network's hardline stance against mining, the Forestry Department recommended new regulations on post-mining activity, advocating that companies reforest mined areas, or an equivalent area elsewhere, with comparable species. This proposal, referred to as the "no net-loss"[139] strategy, contrasted with the preferences of the civil society members of the epistemic community who did not think restoration was adequate.

However, in interviews, Forestry Department personnel admitted that the removal of forest cover would permanently change the biodiversity composition of the area, and that restoration was far from an optimal response. Marilyn Headley noted that the compromise position was a second-best preference, chosen only in light of the fact that in 2006, bauxite mining in Cockpit Country seemed inevitable:

Well, what we are trying to get across to the bauxite companies is that ... if you're taking out forest land, you should really start thinking that you need to replace some forest somewhere. ... Purists don't agree because they say that you've lost the forest. Well, we've lost the forest. So our next step now is to get them to put a forest somewhere else.

But you know, you can't really replace the Cockpit Country. You can put a forest somewhere else, you can pay for a forest to be planted somewhere else, but you can't replant the Cockpit Country.[140]

At the time, the epistemic community members based their arguments for a moratorium on an approach that claimed that mining and the projected ecological damages would negatively affect the economic revenue potential of the tourist industry, Jamaica's other flagship economic sector. When placed beside bauxite mining, tourism is a comparable contributor to national development, bringing a similar amount of foreign revenue. In 2003, tourism contributed 10 percent of GDP and 50 percent of national foreign currency earnings. Including auxiliary employment, tourism is credited with contributing to the creation of one in every four jobs in Jamaica.[141]

The idea was to persuade the government of Jamaica that Cockpit Country was important for tourism and hence for the Jamaican GDP, by virtue of its watersheds, which provide municipal and drinking water to tourist centers in the northwestern section of the island.[142] Diana McCaulay of the Jamaican Environmental Trust indicated that transnational and Jamaican ENGOs undertook at least three such studies between 2003 and 2010, and a fourth began under the Windsor Research Center in 2011. In 2006, Dayne Buddo rationalized the use of economic arguments as a self-evident means of effectively communicating to policymakers in the government: "We're trying to communicate to [policymakers] in dollars and cents. Which is a language that they more understand than to say, 'This is a particular species that is only found in Jamaica.' They probably don't relate to it as much, as then saying, 'If you lose this, you stand to lose millions of dollars in tourism.'"[143]

Similarly, Kimberly John, a Trinidadian researcher at The Nature Conservancy who participated in drafting one of these valuations in 2003, pointed to the strategic choice of neoliberal economic arguments as a necessity in environmental advocacy.

Since our decision makers, I don't think they are really well educated about ecology and so on. ... I think it's best we, to frame the message of biodiversity management in something that in a sense seems [economically] conservative, what we were going to do is attach a cost, that there's a price associated with the clean water that's supplied by the Cockpit Country. ... If you compare water with bauxite mining ... [compare] the benefits to the society and the economy of maintaining the resources.[144]

In 2005, The Nature Conservancy, led by John and Ann Haynes-Sutton, completed their valuation and distributed their findings to the Forestry Department, the JBI, NEPA, the Ministry of Environment, and the Water Resources Authority.[145] Their report emphasized the use of water services to the "very significant municipal, agricultural and tourism interests downstream," in order to "provide a compelling cost-benefit analysis" to mitigate the economic arguments of bauxite mining.[146] It is also somewhat ironic that the initial arguments for conservation rested so much on appeals to tourism, given the fight between NEPA and Jamaican NGOs about the EIA of Pear Tree Bottom in the mid to late 2000s. In any case, these efforts were supported initially by members of the network who were closely associated with local communities. Hugh Dixon, for instance, argued that the neoliberal economic arguments showing the benefits of Cockpit Country's water supply to the tourism sector would be most likely to persuade regulators to halt bauxite mining: "[Bauxite] brings revenue into a weak economy, so, you let the land, and mine the bauxite, and get out as much as possible, and let's rake in the money. ... [The] only thing that is going to stem that exploit, indiscriminate exploit, is the ability of the communities to put forward a case on the value of the water."[147]

While these valuations were being conducted, network members noted that the neoliberal approach, focusing on the contribution of services to the tourist industry, was limited in its ability to understand the value of Cockpit Country's biodiversity. Speaking on behalf of one of the most maligned and pestilential inhabitants of the Cockpit Country rainforest, Mike Schwartz ruminated on the economic approach: "So, to some extent, we have to find, we have to—to make a rational decision, you should know what's the value of the biodiversity, of the geo-diversity, and compare it with the value of the bauxite. That's one approach, the economic approach. ... [But] we have sixty-seven or something different species of mosquito in Jamaica, and they're all valuable, and some are endemic, and we love them too. I mean, how do you value them? So it is, there is a problem."[148]

Owen Evelyn of the Forestry Department echoed Schwartz's concern in 2006 about the ability of the economic approach to pick up other kinds of values "How do you put a value on some of these things? ... We're talking about plant material, you know? I mean, apart from actually *timber*, you know? How do you value these other, other targets that we have identified? We're talking about the yellow Boa, and the butterfly. How do you put a value to these?"[149]

Besides banning mining, epistemic community members called on the Ministry of Environment to create an internationally recognized National Park to define the borders and management strategy of Cockpit Country. In 2004, Ann Haynes-Sutton of The Nature Conservancy, citing the Programme of Work on protected areas adopted at the 7th Conference of Parties (COP-7) of the CBD, called for the adoption by the Forestry Department and NEPA of IUCN classification to create an internationally standardized, protected area.[150] If adopted, this policy would require the government of Jamaica to legally establish the buffer zone and core areas of Cockpit Country, and increase the size of the area currently protected under Forest Reserve status (see figure 1.3).[151] Like the proposed moratorium, this suggestion rested on the network's attempt to use economic arguments to highlight the benefits of environmental management, by stating that IUCN classification would raise the international profile of Cockpit Country, encouraging international donors to contribute funds for domestic biodiversity management.[152]

IUCN status was also expected to generate tourist revenue by improving Cockpit Country's marketability as a zone for ecotourism. Funds would be generated by charging user access fees for low-impact recreational activities in protected areas of the Cockpit.[153] An ancillary benefit gained by promoting ecotourism in Cockpit Country would be the alleviation of pressure caused by the concentration of the tourist market on large-scale development in high-traffic coastal areas, which have been showing signs of degradation, beach erosion, and shallow water pollution.[154]

While the arguments presented to the Ministry of Environment and Agriculture and mining agencies emphasized the market value of biodiversity in Cockpit Country to the tourist industry, network members focused on getting the Forestry Department to promote conservationist activities that benefited marginalized, agrarian populations. Jamaican researchers from UWI and STEA in particular were very concerned about the possibility that conservation would prohibit agricultural and subsistence activities,[155] creating additional environmental stress for lower-income populations. There were ecological concerns embedded in this as well, as farmers who were prohibited from developing agricultural plots openly would very likely take agricultural activity into secluded and virgin territory in order to escape governmental scrutiny.

For these reasons, network members like Dixon have been working since 1999 with the Forestry Department to foster sustainable agriculture among marginalized populations, particularly in yam farming.[156] STEA had developed in 1999 a program to promote hedgerows in Cockpit Country, where fast-growth trees used for yam sticks are planted in rows with cash crops cultivated in the "alleys" between the rows. Besides functioning as renewable sources of yam sticks, hedgerows can minimize surface runoff and erosion.[157]

At the end of the first advocacy period, the network had attained very limited influence over Cockpit Country conservation policies. The network did have some influence over agenda setting at the international level, as the GEF accepted the spatial definition of Cockpit Country as proposed in 1999. In addition, the network had some influence over local policy and management approaches of the Forestry Department. The department's 2001 Management Plan incorporated recommendations by the epistemic community to produce and distribute seedlings for quick-growth trees. These seedlings, provided for free to subsistence and agricultural communities, were intended to be used as yam sticks, replacing the unsustainable practice of cutting saplings.[158] The Forestry Department also worked with the epistemic community in the LFMCs to promote sustainable agriculture in local communities. However, there was no new protected areas designation, and bauxite mining was still on the table for the region.

All the same, the Forestry Department's changes to management after 1999 were very encouraging for environmental advocates. John Doe for instance, had been highly critical of the department's earlier activities, which focused on promoting commercial pine plantations in sensitive ecosystems. Although the department was intended to sustainably manage forest resources, its emphasis on planting commercial pine exacerbated biodiversity loss in National Parks like the John Crow Mountain Park in the eastern part of the island. As Doe described: "I mean, most of the, especially like in the John Crow Mountains, most of the deforestation that was created in John Crow was by the Forestry Department. You have this little stupid man basically going in and clearing an area of forest, of natural forest, to plant up pine and all kinds of crap."[159]

By the time the project concluded in 2007, the Forestry Department had changed its environmental approach. Of the Jamaican natural resource management agencies, the Forestry Department's regulatory articles and the Forest Act of 2001 are the only specific references to biodiversity management.[160] In discussing the department's approach, Headley described its ecological perspective of the connection between trees and forests to wildlife habitat as a new development: "[Biodiversity] is a new discussion, and I suppose what has changed [are] the views of managing forest for different, different reasons. ... So everybody is talking about the ecosystem, and the habitat, and we even talk about birds and bats, which we didn't do, in the Forestry Department before. When we started as the Forestry Department, it was just the trees, we just never overlapped."[161]

Further, Headley was clear that this shift was most pronounced among those agents who participated in the training exercises carried out by WRC.

We've stopped using the phrase "paradigm shift," that was the phrase we all used in the late 90s. But it *did* shift, it really did shift, the paradigm did shift in that direction. And it took a little dragging and kicking of feet you know. But, surprisingly, all the field staff are on it. The managers are actually the last ones to come on board. But the field staff are all community foresters [who] overlap with the bird information, so they go to bird banding courses. And there's another one who does the bat identification, so they overlap that way.[162]

Thus, the strong social ties seemed to have an effect on the Forestry Department's willingness to listen to new information from the civil society. However, the success of the epistemic community in promoting ecological practices in the Forestry Department marked the only instance of the network's direct influence on natural resource management in the first advocacy period. While the environmental ministry seemed either unwilling or unable to incorporate the claims of the epistemic community, the Ministry of Agriculture and the mining regulatory agencies were clearly antipathetic to the preferences of the transnational civil society network.

In 2004, the Ministry of Agriculture granted Alcoa and the Clarendon Alumina Production exclusive licenses to prospect for bauxite deposits.[163] In 2006, it dismissed the first study on the link between tourism and Cockpit Country's water supply as unsubstantiated.[164] Claims of projected revenues through conservationist activities like ecotourism, or the value of water's ecosystem services for the tourist sector, were described as too long term, too vague, and too small to offer a convincing counterbalance to mining's role in GDP. In 2011, Diana McCaulay of the Jamaican Environment Trust was explicitly skeptical about the ability of past and future economic valuations to actually convince policymakers that conservation was profitable: "Good luck with [economic valuation] is what I think. I was actually in the room when decisions were taken about things, about natural resources that *had* had economic valuations. It didn't even come up."[165]

The Second Advocacy Period: 2006–2012 and Government Retrenchment

In 2006, the prospecting licenses issued to mining companies expired.[166] Although the Ministry of Agriculture asserted that mining was not planned and that the licenses would not be renewed,[167] local communities reported in September that bauxite companies had in fact begun prospecting, and were relocating residents from lands with identified deposits.[168] After the network requested information about these reports, the JBI and the Ministry of Agriculture insisted that extractive mining was not planned for Cockpit Country, that the licenses would not be renewed, and claimed confidentiality to avoid discussing mining plans.[169] Unconvinced by these claims, the network began pressing for a firm commitment by the Jamaican government to protect Cockpit Country from mining.

In October and November 2006, epistemic community members used the press, radio, and private meetings with mining regulators to argue for a mining moratorium. Concerned about what seemed like stonewalling, the epistemic community and organizations created the Cockpit Country Stakeholders' Group (CCSG). The CCSG began a public campaign to mobilize local and transnational grassroots political pressure through petitions, letter writing and by threatening public demonstrations in order to pressure the government.[170] In December, the government seemed to relent and invited members of the epistemic community to participate in a private consultation with the Minister of Agriculture and the Jamaica Bauxite Institute. However, the minister revealed at the consultation that the licenses had already been issued, whereupon the epistemic community members "storm[ed] out"[171] of the meeting and issued a public repudiation of the process two hours later.[172]

As described earlier, the network by this time had formed links with local agricultural and Maroon communities by living with and producing knowledge alongside these residents. This knowledge then formed the nucleus of a budding coalition of local agricultural and Maroon communities, the Jamaican diaspora, and environmental activists in Kingston. Moreover, this coalition converged around a mix of cultural, historic, socioeconomic, and ecological arguments about the value of the natural environment.

First, local communities critiqued the government's claim that bauxite mining in Cockpit Country would bring "development" to the rural poor of the area. For example, they referred in interviews to the example of bauxite mining in the parish of St. Ann, where bauxite companies displaced low-income and agricultural residents of mineral rich lands, "took away the best part of the land for bauxite mining," and failed to fulfill their promises of employment after exploiting the parish's natural resources.[173]

Second, even where there was potential gain to be made by accepting payment for relocation, respondents resisted the destruction of Cockpit Country, as doing so would mean losing a core component of the identity of yam farmers and Maroons. As Pingue put it, "We have to defend what's ours. We can't let the foreigners come in and take it all away. Because then we'll have nothing left."[174] As she later added: "People love farming, because that is your livelihood. So, you're going to throw that away [for mining]. And then, when you throw that away, you're going to enslave yourself to a man. And remember, when first you were working for *your-self*. And it's not for sure now that you're even going to get a job. Especially an older person. Because most of the persons that are farming now are older persons. So can you tell me that my husband now can get a job with bauxite mining? No."

In response, members of the epistemic community and the diaspora signed petitions and sent letters to the Cabinet and Ministry of Agriculture. Epistemic community organizations such as the Jamaica Environment

Trust and the Windsor Research Center held public denunciations. Maroon communities and local farmers also threatened that "blood will be shed" if mining and its attendant problems, such as water pollution and coerced displacement, were to take place.

Both those who supported and those who opposed the extension of bauxite mining in Cockpit Country noted that this resistance was driven by "nonscientific" arguments. One senior mining official who did not want to be identified dismissed the resistance as entirely "irrational" and "emotional." Agreeing that the resistance against mining was not entirely scientific, but far less dismissive about this, Diana McCaulay observed in 2011: "Not everybody is swayed by the science. ... There was this, sort of factual based approach that said 'It's an important source of water,' all of that kind of thing, and then there was this more, 'this is part of our history, our culture, our most significant remaining natural resource,' and that appealed to another set of people."[175]

McCaulay had good reason to believe that history and culture mattered to the antimining movement. In 2007, in the start of the second advocacy period, Melville Currie, a member of the Maroon Council of Trelawny stated this explicitly to the Jamaican press. "We do not want any bauxite mining up there at all and we will have to fight it until the last Maroon is dead," said Currie, adding: "It is a sacred area where our ancestors fought and died, so we think it should be preserved."

In the end, this public mobilization mattered, as the campaign shifted away from a scientific neoliberal core argument to one that included these claims of local culture and justice. In 2007, under political pressure, Minister of Agriculture Clarke issued a hold on mining and prospecting leases, pending a definition of Cockpit Country's legal borders. After parliamentary elections, the Ministry of Agriculture asserted that Cockpit Country would be permanently off limits to mining. This was an outcome attributed by policymakers and epistemic community members to the concerted activism of the local community, described in the final report of the GEF as "most successful advocacy work."[176]

However, tensions between the mining regulatory agencies and the civil society continued, as both sides failed to agree on what, exactly, Cockpit Country entailed. The network reiterated its call for the borders to comprise the area defined in the 1999 studies, but now, along with Maroon communities, claimed an additional portion of the Cockpit Country region. New maps disseminated after 2007 proposed increasing the size of what would be Cockpit Country from 450 to 1,142 square kilometers, while UWI geologist Parris Lyew-Ayee Jr., the son of JBI Director Lyew-Ayee, indicated in a study commissioned by the JBI that the Cockpit Country ecosystem should only comprise 288 square kilometers (see figures 1.4–1.5).[177]

The conflict seemed to abate after the 2007 parliamentary elections, when Bruce Golding's government appointed Christopher Tufton as the new Minister of Agriculture, who then asserted that Cockpit Country would be permanently off limits to mining. This development, while positive, emerged less from the persuasive knowledge claims of the network

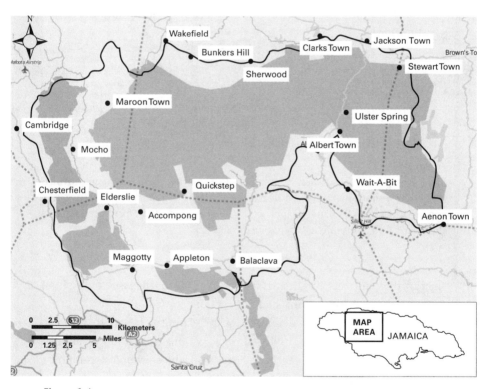

Figure 1.4

Revised epistemic community Cockpit Country map. *Source:* Author's original drawing, based on map provided by the Windsor Research Center, "Map of Cockpit Country and Principal Communities," http://www.cockpitcountry.org/CCimgmap.html, accessed August 2015. Base map copyright held by OpenStreetMap. Used with permission from OpenStreetMap and Windsor Research Center.

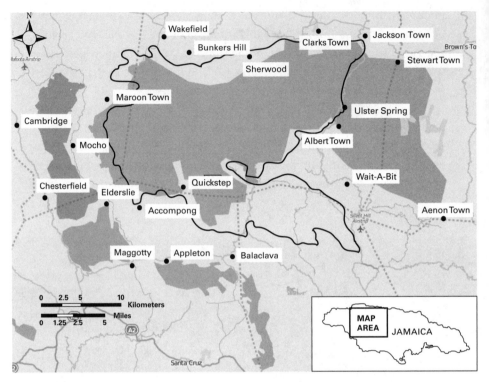

Figure 1.5
Parris Lyew-Ayee map. *Source:* Author's original drawing, based on map provided by the Center for Environmental Management, *Public Consultations*, 175. Base map copyright held by OpenStreetMap. Used with permission from OpenStreetMap and the Centre for Environmental Management.

than from public mobilization. However, as of 2015, the issue of the legal definition of Cockpit Country had not yet been settled.

Ironically, the issue of defining Cockpit Country began to generate cleavages between community-based organizations in the conservationist movement and some of the technical experts in the epistemic community, especially in the Forestry Department. With the temporary success in halting mining, underlying differences between members about the role of science and culture and the appropriate framework for understanding Cockpit Country came to the fore. As these differences also involved debates over which international institutions applied to Cockpit Country management, I will return to them in chapter 5.

Conclusion

This chapter supports the argument that socialization, consensus, and justice framing improve the likelihood that networks will influence policymaking. As I have described, the epistemic community network socialized extensively with the Forestry Department, which by the late 1990s had become highly integrated into the production of knowledge with the epistemic community. As a result, the Forestry Department demonstrated a singular interest in learning from the transnational network, promoted sustainable practices by issuing seedlings for hedgerows and fast-growth trees to minimize yam stick harvesting and adopted an ecological approach to biodiversity management emphasizing the forest's function as a habitat and food source for local and migratory fauna. This contrasted with the department's previous management approach, which emphasized the production and rapid turnover of commercial timber. In contrast, other agencies that did not socialize with the epistemic community, namely the rest of the Ministry of Agriculture, its mining agencies, and NEPA were either environmental laggards or actively opposed to implementing policy recommendations.

This chapter also supports the argument that local justice framing strengthens conservationist arguments. In this case, the economic valorization of ecosystem services made the promotion of biodiversity conservation more politically problematic. Although the neoliberal models used in the first advocacy period attempted to link biodiversity protection to "national development," low-income communities in rural Trelawny were far more supportive of stronger regulation and restrictions on natural resource use than mining regulators.

Local communities were also less inclined to believe that biodiversity should be managed as an engine of national economic growth. In large part, this was because they and their allies in the network were not convinced that marginalized agrarian populations would be included in bauxite-driven development. When asked in 2011 about the contribution of mining to national economic growth and poverty alleviation, Diana McCaulay noted that "mining has maybe enriched the mining companies, and perhaps the Jamaican government, and perhaps the Jamaican government has squandered that money. You know?" McCaulay went on, speaking about the attempt to commodify water sources in Cockpit Country in the water valuation efforts: "Is that not going to create more poverty, where those who have money can pay, and those who are taking their water from resources like clean rivers, don't get water? I think our ideas about how poverty is alleviated, and how development is 'real development,' are completely wrong."

Furthermore, these low-income local communities, and their allies in government agencies and the advocacy network, adopted a far broader conception of what biodiversity was, and what it was for, than that promoted by policymakers and managers in state-led models of development. By linking natural resources to autonomy, subsistence, and the cultural and aesthetic needs of local populations, communities in Jamaica lobbied the state to protect a Cockpit Country area five times larger than that preferred by mining policymakers in the government. Members of the advocacy network were skeptical that economic arguments, divorced from consideration of intangibles like culture and history, could be used to encourage biodiversity conservation. As McCaulay argued: "The thing with the economic argument is that if you say that water brings in x amount of money for tourism, then the natural thing is that if you get y amount of money from bauxite mining, it makes sense to go ahead and mine."[178]

This chapter alone is agnostic about the effect of a scientific consensus on advocacy efforts. A consensus was present throughout the advocacy campaign, in both the failed and successful attempts of the community to influence policy. This indicates that consensus is insufficient to lead to influence and deployed in a concerted effort by publicly recognized experts. Further understanding the effect of economic and political factors on epistemic community advocacy requires additional analyses of case studies, which are addressed in the chapters that follow.

2 Tourism, Development, and the Mesoamerican Barrier Reef

Introduction

"The people of the state aren't going to live by eating mangroves." So said Miguel Ángel Lemus, then president of the Association of Owners and Investors in the Riviera Maya (APIR), in 2007. Ángel Lemus and APIR were arguing against a recently adopted environmental law extending federal protection over natural resources on the nation's coast.[1] This law, Article 60 Ter, legally barred hoteliers and other developers from cutting and stripping coastal mangrove swamps, or otherwise negatively affecting the hydrological flow of mangrove zones.[2] Ángel Lemus and APIR were joined by other business and tourist associations in the state of Quintana Roo, as well as representatives of the *quintanarroense* government, who asserted that this law would impede economic development by making it difficult, if not impossible, to construct the beachfront hotels representative of the Cancún tourist model. Despite the efforts of Ángel Lemus and others, the federal government has kept this law on the books as a tool of environmental protection of coastal biodiversity.

The federal government, in extending protection to the coast, was influenced by a transnational epistemic community of experts, concerned about biodiversity loss in marine ecosystems. The impetus for this epistemic community advocacy was the federal government's interest in implementing a GEF-funded project relevant to Mexico's obligations under the Convention on Biological Diversity (CBD). This project, the Proyecto para la Conservación y Uso Sostenible del Sistema Arrecifal Mesoamericano (MBRS Project), was a regional effort by Mexico, Belize, Guatemala, and Honduras that invoked several articles of the CBD, including Article 8 for in situ conservation and Article 10 promoting sustainable use of biodiversity.[3]

As occurred in Jamaica, this community influenced biodiversity conservation and regime implementation at multiple levels. The community
shaped how local, national, and international actors "imagined" the Mesoamerican Barrier Reef System (MBRS), by changing ideas about the interconnectivity of the zone, and clarifying the cause-and-effect relationships
between human activity and environmental health. When the epistemic
community linked biodiversity conservation arguments to local claims for
autonomy and environmental security, they generated enough political
support to counter the demands of antiregulatory business interests. This
chapter supports my findings from chapter 1, that a transnational network,
equipped with a scientific consensus and socialization with key actors can
use local environmental justice claims to strengthen improved environmental governance.

The MBRS has since the mid-1990s been imagined as a transnational
ecoregion comprising the territorial waters of four countries: Mexico, Honduras, Guatemala, and Belize. At present, Mexican jurisdiction in the MBRS
extends across approximately four hundred kilometers of coastline, from
Yum Balám in the northern part of the Yucatán Peninsula to Banco Chinchorro, in the southern coast of the state of Quintana Roo (see figure 2.1).

Like the Cockpit Country, it is a site of internationally recognized high
biodiversity. The coral reef, formed by the deposits of calcium by polyps
presents one of the most visibly striking components of the system. The
genetic diversity is literally visible within healthy sections of the reef, as
the many-hued different species of fish and crustaceans share space with
fantastically colored corals and other forms of marine life.[4] A sample of
biodiversity at Mexican sites at Sian Ka'an, Xcalak, Banco Chinchorro, and
Majahual (see figure 2.1) yields over ninety species of coral and a thousand species of flora and fauna, including endemic and IUCN Red List-
registered species.[5] In all, reefs may house up to three thousand species of
marine life.

But important biodiversity is also found in less aesthetically pleasing,
if no less important coastal mangrove zones and seagrass pastures. With
densely laid, finger-like roots, mangrove zones provide shelter to reef-
dwelling populations of scaled fish and crustaceans in juvenile and larval
stages.[6] They also act as filters, removing sediment and organic matter
from river outlets and coastal runoff, and preventing sedimentation in
the reef.[7]

Figure 2.1
WWF-defined ecoregion. *Source:* Author's reproduction of map available at http:// www.wwfca.org/nuestro_trabajo/mares_costas/mesoamericano_reef/, accessed August 2015.

Tourism, Fishing, and Development: Environmental Justice in the MBRS

The GEF project documents and various conservation projects launched in Quintana Roo and the MBRS recognize that overfishing and improper capture practices among coastal populations can drive resource overexploitation. Although fishing in Quintana Roo is not a massive sector of employment, with only approximately one thousand registered fishermen out of a population of 1.5 million,[8] it is a source of environmental stress on the basin. Coastal communities and fishermen extract resources for subsistence and commerce, catching 3,800 tons of seafood with a total value of almost MX$150 million in 2006.[9] Certain species of scaled fish and shellfish that are targeted for commercial use have, since the late 1980s, experienced precipitous declines in population due to overexploitation.[10] As fishermen systematically target the largest animals, the average size of adult fish in commercial populations continually diminishes.[11] Worse, declining commercial stocks cause fishermen to target species lower on the food chain, increasing the chance of population and ecosystem collapse.[12]

Species loss can also have ripple effects. For example, herbivorous Parrotfish and other species find shelter in coral reefs and feed on the algae that compete with coral for nutrients and living space.[13] Without these fish, algae will lose one important check on their growth, putting additional stress on the viability of reefs and broader marine ecosystems. Albert Franquesa of the Mexican environmental NGO Los Amigos de Sian Ka'an used the metaphor of a living body to describe this series of relationships, underlining the importance and integration of each part of biodiversity in the ecoregion: "[It's] like the different organisms that we have in our bodies. Everything has a function, and we can live without a piece, or without one organ. ... The same thing happens with an ecosystem. ... If you remove one of the species, you would probably think that the ecosystem is not going to collapse. But each time you remove one, and another, and another, you're closer to the point where the ecosystem stops functioning."[14]

However, the environmental impact of low-income users does not occur in a vacuum, but is linked through Mexico's political economy to the large-scale coastal tourist development that characterizes the northern third of the state. Since the 1970s, the federal and state governments have promoted northern Quintana Roo for tourism by offering very attractive tax incentives and financial support to developers. The federal agency El Fondo Nacional de Fomento al Turismo (FONATUR) contributed critical support for this development between 1974 and 1998 by providing federal credit and investments for infrastructure, and granting the political backing necessary to build and advertise Cancún and the Riviera Maya as a major tourist destination.[15] Through this investment, the number of hotel rooms in the Riviera Maya increased between 1997 and 2003 from 4,000 to 28,000. By 2008, Cancún and the Riviera Maya combined had 73,709 rooms.[16]

This development (and the subsequent transformation of the land-scape of Quintana Roo) thus bears a remarkable similarity to the neoco-lonial model of development that environmental scholars see in modern Latin America. In Brazil, for instance, Wolford describes how the cerrado was remade into an agroindustrial center by the settlement policies of the Brazilian government, as the state began expanding its control over the countryside.[17]

This settlement was discursive, as much as it was physical. As part of the process of creating roads and infrastructure and subsidizing agroindustry (particularly in large-scale soy production), the government had to reimag-ine the cerrado—including its natural resources and its native population—as a "wasteland ... cluttered with scrub bush and a few small trees."[18] The Amazon was likewise reimagined as a blank landscape during its partial settlement by the modern Brazilian state. In Brazil, this settlement was explicitly neocolonial, as the government carried it out as a military-backed project for the political and economic capture of natural resources. In much the same way that the Europeans did in their colonization of the New World, this project was framed as intended to control and capture land and natural resources for the good of the state and security. As Hochstetler and Keck put it: "It was an imaginary landscape of wealth there for the taking—a 'land without people for people without land,' as the Brazilian military said, whose indigenous people and other local populations were quite sim-ply painted out of the picture."[19]

Similarly, Cancún was brought into modernity by a government with a particular vision of the nation-state and its developmental needs. Like the neocolonial model of Brazil, this also was informed by the authority of a state backed by the power of violence. Although Mexico was not technically a military dictatorship in the way that Brazil was in the 1960s through the 1980s, the ability of the hegemonic Partido Revolucionario Institucional (PRI) to use the military to defend its power was evident in the Tlatelolco massacre of 1968, when the military fired on students who were protesting state repression. Similar to the Brazilian Amazon, Cancún and Quintana Roo state had been a zone of refuge for indigenous people, first from Span-ish control and then from Mexican rule post-independence. As Reed noted in his history of the Yucatán Peninsula, the Quintana Roo Maya region functioned as a de facto independent nation until its official incorporation into the modern state of Mexico in the 1930s.[20] As a result, the narrative of the state was that it was a "backward area associated with the questionable activities of smugglers, *chicle* gatherers, and forest-dwelling Indians."[21] Like the cerrado and the Amazon, it would have to be made modern by transforming the land through massive infrastructure projects in a "highly visual and material form," as Pi-Sunyer and Thomas put it,[22] and then brought into the political economy of the center. In doing so, the state transformed not only the geography of the land, but also its demographic makeup at a "tempo of change [that] is unparalleled."[23] The population of Cancún, for instance, grew from six hundred in the 1960s to over thirty thousand by the 1990s, to more than six hundred thousand at present. The vast majority of these new inhabitants was nonindigenous, and came from outside the state of Quintana Roo, brought there by the prospect of jobs, largely in the newly modernizing tourist sector. As Albert Franquesa summarized, the settlement treated pre-incorporated Cancún and Quintana Roo as just as blank as other indigenous spaces in Latin America. In describing the process of settlement by the influx of people over the past thirty years, Franquesa explained: "They were all saying the same thing. 'Before it was horrible, because there was nothing here. There was nowhere to go shopping, nowhere to, I don't know—go have fun. You'd take four hours to get here from the airport because they hadn't even built up the highways.'"[24]

This colonization, however, paid off in a windfall of foreign revenue to federal and state coffers. From 1999 to 2006, between 28 percent and 38 percent of the total tourism revenue in Mexico and between 75 percent and 80 percent of the total state revenue of Quintana Roo came solely from earnings based on Cancún and the Riviera Maya.[25] The growth of this industry has also visibly transformed the physical geography of the region. In 2012, a tourist standing on the beach of the hotel zone (or *zona hotelera*) would see the landscape commanded by a continuous wall of all-inclusive resorts from transnational companies like Sandals and Hyatt. All along Highway 307, from Cancún through Tulúm and all parts south, billboards promise further expansion in the future. As Enloe described in discussing the role of tourism in international relations, all of these processes have become the major means through which Mexico has been integrated into the global economy.[26]

Fishing, though less economically significant than tourism, is still an important source of income for coastal communities, and the political economy of this practice similarly contributes to the impact of this activity on the reef ecosystem. Although fishing contributes around 0.8 percent toward internal state revenue, the three thousand registered and nonregistered fishermen in the state earned an average of MX$60,939 per year, or approximately US$6,000, an attractive sum to marginalized populations.[27]

Given its prominence in the Mexican political economy, it is not surprising that tourism is the most significant systematic threat to environmental health in the MBRS. Despite their ecological importance, mangrove zones are not generally marketed as part of the tourist package of Cancún and the zona hotelera. They are an excellent habitat and breeding ground for mosquitoes, onerous to navigate, and difficult to advertise to visitors to all-inclusive resorts. As a result, hoteliers developing beachfront property drain, cut, and fill mangrove zones with concrete in order to provide brochure-ready recreational opportunities to tourists. To create the beachfront aesthetic, hoteliers place multi-story buildings as close to possible to the shoreline.

Unfortunately, the removal of beachfront vegetation combined with the construction of massive hotels and associated infrastructure interrupts the rate of replenishment of beach sand, and contributes to a loss of coastline and increased beach erosion. This in turn contributes to sedimentation, run-off, and nitrification in the basin, depressing the regeneration and growth of corals.[28] Further, the destruction of mangrove zones inhibits the ability of fishermen to make a living—as havens for fish are destroyed, this puts additional pressure on vulnerable species, and therefore on the fishermen who depend on them. Even cruise tourism causes stress, as improperly docked ships collide with reefs, and poorly regulated waste disposal practices can contaminate marine environments.[29] Once constructed, docks and ports for cruise ships interrupt the flow of marine currents, often causing shorelines to recede, worsening coastal erosion.[30]

Ironically, the tourist industry in Cancún then sustains itself by advertising the "natural beauty" of Mexico to the visitors, mostly foreign, who arrive. Since this same industry is increasingly responsible for the destruction of the natural environment, this advertising strategy relies on a simulacra, a fantasy representation of the Yucatán's environment that chooses to be unaware of the degradation that the industry is causing. For instance, in order to sustain the white sand beaches that are eroding due to poor coastal construction, the governments of Mexico and Quintana Roo are spending multiple millions of U.S. dollars dredging sand from the ocean floor and trucking it in to prop up the beaches for tourists.

According to the common narrative of hoteliers and state development agencies like the Secretariat of Tourism (Secretaría de Turismo del Estado de Quintana Roo, or SEDETUR), this modern, large-scale tourism is necessary for the socioeconomic development of the state and the country, to low-income populations and policymakers alike. High tourist traffic contributes to demand for seafood, driving up the final sale price of these fish, and putting extra revenue in the hands of low-income communities.[31] Hotel construction and operation provides previously unavailable job opportunities to residents, who work as tour operators and guides, as well as creating a wider market for artisanal goods. All of this is promoted by the state under what Enloe described as "the tourism formula for development."[32] In asking why a state would be complicit in an economic project that has such high environmental costs, Pi-Sunyer and Thomas note: "At least part of the answer must be sought in the influence of a general myth of development (shared by Mexican and international technocrats alike) that holds that the poverty of poor countries arises from an inadequate spread of market forces. It follows that the recommended solution to poverty is increased capitalist penetration."[33]

For supporters of this model, the ability of tourism to attract benefits like an increase in foreign revenue and international prestige are clear arguments in its favor. But while these benefits are real, this kind of tourism carries particular costs for some of the more marginalized residents of the region. First, tourism and tourist development compete with the subsistence and commercial needs of local residents. The same tourist demand that leads to an increase in the price of fish also drives scarcity among overharvested species, especially lobster. In addition, recreational tourism undermines the sustainability of marine natural resources. Tourists interested in enjoying coral reefs arrive in motorized access boats that agitate the ocean floor, scattering sand on the reef polyps. Improperly supervised snorkelers or divers may intentionally or accidentally touch the highly sensitive polyps. Even highly conscientious tourists introduce the chemicals present in most kinds of sunscreen that are highly toxic to the local biota.[34]

The principal threat is tourism ... not just because of the people who are maybe directly diving, or fishing, or stepping on the reef. ... [If] you have 10 million tourists a year in one place, these tourists generate solid residues ... waste water from human activity, from bathrooms, from whatever. ... When there's fishing in certain places, the fish will probably be overexploited. ... If there weren't tourism, fishermen wouldn't need to fish these enormous quantities to support the demand.[35]

Second, tourism in the Yucatán can physically and economically displace low-income and rural residents. Attracted by the promise of employment, inland residents of Quintana Roo and neighboring states have flocked to the Riviera Maya and the coast. This migration has led to a massive increase in the population of coastal towns and cities. In the municipality of Felipe Carrillo Puerto alone, in-land migration of low-skilled workers seeking employment in the tourism center of Cancún and the Riviera Maya has contributed to a tenfold population increase between 1970 and 2000.[36] Unfortunately, this migration has led to sprawling shantytowns springing up around hotel sites; these "support communities" provide cheap labor for hoteliers, generally in the form of custodial services or construction. Because these shantytowns develop spontaneously, they are not covered by municipal planning and services, nor are they incorporated into the water and sewage treatment plans of the hotels. Poor oversight in combination with absent treatment facilities means residents have little recourse other than to dump refuse directly into the ocean or in hastily dug pits that in turn leach polluting materials into the water table.[37]

To members of the civil society, the fact that hotel investors in large-scale tourism were primarily either foreigners or from outside of Quintana Roo (an observation borne out by the data on hotel ownership) meant they could avoid the long-term environmental impacts of coastal degradation in ways that the average *quintanarroense* could not. Further, despite promises that tourist development would lead to increased employment opportunities for the marginalized populations, studies of the human and political geography of large-scale hotels in the Riviera Maya indicate that tourist zones function more as exclusive enclaves, with minimal links to peripheral areas.[38]

For instance, low-income residents of Cancún have been effectively barred from accessing a growing number of the beaches for which Cancún is known. In 2014, residents of four neighborhoods in the Solidaridad municipality formed a human chain in front of the beach Playa Punta Esmerelda, to protest the closure of one of its public access points.[39] This point was closed by the construction of a large wall, which also functioned to seclude a tourist hotel from its surroundings. To add insult to injury, the government then spent public funds to restore these restricted beaches, in places like Playa Car, to mitigate the environmental impact of tourism. Indeed, throughout Cancún, formerly public beaches were being restricted, by regulation or by practice, such that low-income *quintanarroenses* came to tourist zones primarily as workers, and not as people similarly engaged in recreation. In Puerto Aventuras, residents were allowed access to beaches only if they purchased something from the hotels installed on the beach-front. In response to this social exclusion, community members like Orlando Cox Tun created local movements that demanded the restoration of free access to beaches in their own districts. As Cox Tun said: "We don't want to have to press the issue with the Puerto Aventuras Trust, where they give us provisional passes, and make us leave our credentials to get access to the beaches. We want an access that is free and dignified and available right now. Puerto Aventuras does not have it, so we're protesting."[40]

Despite its promises of bringing development to all, large-scale tourism attracts migrants seeking employment, but without the attendant sharing of benefits promised by the model.[41] What made this more problematic is the observation that hotel investors, as Gonzalo Merediz Alonso described it in 2012, "made their earnings, and are enjoying their profits, while we here are suffering the environmental costs of destroying the beaches, the economic cost of fixing the beaches, and the bad image that eroded beaches are giving the destination."[42] In other words, the costs of environmental degradation are borne primarily by those already marginalized, while polit-ical economic elites are able to avoid its long-term consequences. Further, elites are able to accrue the benefits of environmental overexploitation through the processes described earlier. As the literature on environmental justice indicates, the aggregation of social, economic, and environmental costs in the hands of the marginalized is one of the defining features of injustice.[43]

Occasionally, conflicts among different interest groups in Mexico over natural resources can turn violent, and even lethal. As this chapter makes clear, one of the focal points of biodiversity conservation campaigns in the MBRS is the maintenance of mangrove zones along the coast. In 2011, enough environmental activists were targeted and killed in Guerrero state, among them Fabiola Osorio Bernáldez of the environmental NGO Guerreros Verdes, that the Inter-American Commission on Human Rights described activists as "a group in a special situation of risk, in view of the grave and multiple aggressions that they suffer in relation to their activi-ties."[44] Osorio's former companions in Guerreros Verdes have explained her death, though unsolved to date, as a result of her vocal campaigns against the cutting of mangrove zones and subsequent construction of a tourist pier at Pie de la Cuesta on the Guerrero coast. As a federal employee in the environmental secretariat (SEMARNAT) recounted with some relief, in Quintana Roo "normally this [conservation advocacy] does not generate violence." Nevertheless, it is clear that environmental policy and conservation are not simply esoteric concerns, but of direct relevance to the lives of ordinary Mexicans.

Managing all of these competing environmental claims falls under the jurisdiction of a mix of federal and state agencies. Although the MBRS lies entirely within the coastal waters of Quintana Roo state, the Mexican constitution and laws like the General Law of Wildlife (La Ley General de Vida Silvestre, or LGVS) and the General Law of Ecological Equilibrium and the Environment (La Ley General del Equilibrio Ecológico y la Proteción al Ambiente, or LGEEPA) mean the federal branch has primary responsibility in biodiversity and coastal management.[45]

The most relevant federal agencies are located in the environmental secretariat, SEMARNAT, and the agricultural secretariat, SAGARPA. In 1996, the executive branch created the environmental and fisheries secretariat, La Secretaría de Manejo Ambiental, Recursos Naturales y Pesquería (SEMARNAP). In 2002, Vicente Fox's newly elected Partido Acción Nacional (PAN) transferred control over fisheries to the agricultural secretariat, La Secretaría de Agricultura, Ganadería, Alimentación y Desarrollo Rural (SAGAR), and turned SEMARNAP into SEMARNAT and the agricultural secretariat into SAGARPA.[46] Currently, SEMARNAT can propose the creation of federal Natural Protected Areas (ANPs) and Marine Protected Areas (AMPs) to the executive branch, and establish appropriate land-use policies and management plans for these areas. Further, SEMARNAT can pass regulatory declarations called Normas Oficiales Mexicanas (NOMs) that restrict or authorize appropriate environmental activity within all protected areas. For example, SEMARNAT uses the NOM-059 series to protect species identified as nationally important or under threat or both.[47] In 2000, the Zedillo administration created the National Commission for Natural Protected Areas (La Comisión Nacional de Áreas Naturales Protegidas or CONANP) as an autonomous agency of SEMARNAT to help in the creation and management of federal protected areas.[48] CONANP at present can conduct EIAs, and monitoring of activities.[49]

In the next tier of importance are the federal agencies within the agricultural secretariat, SAGARPA. By taking on fisheries, SAGARPA and the national fisheries commission (La Comisión Nacional de la Pesca, CONAPESCA) are now responsible for designating appropriate areas for commercial and sustainable fishing and evaluating appropriate fishing techniques.[50] CONAPESCA has a mandate to record catch sizes and set harvest quotas with assistance in determining officially sanctioned rates of capture from the National Fisheries Institute.[51] CONAPESCA also authorizes the creation of fishing cooperatives, or associations of fishermen that share investment capital, resources, and profits, and requires permits for access in sensitive areas.[52]

Since Quintana Roo state is the geographic seat of Mexico's authority in the basin, state governmental agencies matter. The state Secretaría de Desarrollo Urbano y Medio Ambiente (SEDUMA) can create zoning ordinances through the Programa de Ordenamiento Ecológico Territorial (POET), a regulatory framework allowing SEDUMA to assess environmental loading capacities and determine appropriate land use policies for biologically sensitive sites. Zoning can function to endorse or proscribe adoption of certain activities in a geographically described area.[53] The state tourist secretariat of Quintana Roo (Secretaría de Turismo del Estado de Quintana Roo or SEDETUR) is responsible for promoting the development of tourism. In practice, this means acting as a liaison for tourist interests to state and federal environmental agencies, clarifying regulatory policies applicable to prospective construction and hotel development, and developing recommendations for best practices, for example, in hygiene and hospitality.[54] In addition, the government of Quintana Roo can propose protected areas to be administered at the state level. Similar to the federal government, the state can determine appropriate borders wherein restrictive policy applies and file areas as protected under law. As a result, the state has certain legal competencies.

However, epistemic community members suggested that, in practice, federal agencies are far more likely to have the capacity and will to implement meaningful environmental regulations. POETs are almost exclusively restricted to the northern third of the state, while in the southern two thirds, only the Laguna Bacalar, a small town north of the capital city Chetumal, was assigned a POET at the time of writing. SEDUMA was planning to design a POET for the Othón P. Blanco municipality, which contains sites crucial to the MBRS Project, like Xcalak, Majahual, and Banco Chinchorro.[55] But even so, the civil society remained skeptical of the putative impact of POETs on the environmental effects of untrammeled development: "[POETs] have not been sufficient to apply the brakes on uncontrolled economic development. Instead of allowing a fixed quantity of construction per unit area, whenever there is a certain interest, the quantity is changed and increased, which permits greater degradation than what was originally intended."[56]

But management of natural resources is not solely under the authority of public officials. Private sector actors in fishing, tourism, and narcotrafficking also shape daily management of the coastal environment through their ordinary practices. Since state and federal governments cannot feasibly monitor all formal and informal activities along the coast and in marine environments, advocacy networks have to consider how to engage with these actors if they hope to influence conservation.

Fishing communities along the coast of Quintana Roo are organized into profit- and equipment-sharing cooperatives. Membership size varies, ranging from the nine-member Private Civil Society Organization for Fishermen (SCPP) Horizontes Marino, to the ninety-member SCPP Laguna Macax.[57] In addition to serving as a source of income to marginalized and low-income populations, fishing has some cultural importance, as the occupation is transferred intergenerationally. Cooperatives can help determine who has access to fishing rights, and can create internal norms governing the kinds of equipment and techniques employed.

Hoteliers also strongly affect local governance. Whereas the fishing community consists of decentralized actors, hotel capital and ownership is concentrated in the hands of a few actors, who in turn have formed statewide neocorporatist business associations for the protection of tourist interests. The primary associations in Quintana Roo are: the Asociación de Propietarios e Inversionistas de la Riviera Maya (APIR), Grupo Quintana Roo, la Asociación de Clubs Vacacionales (ACLUVAC), and the Centro Coordinador Empresarial y del Caribe (CCEyC).[58] Hoteliers have considerable leeway in determining the point of construction of hotels, as well as the size of hotel infrastructure, the number of rooms, and the presence and extent of treatment facilities. In addition, because hotel chains may provide reef access to tourists as part of vacation packages, policy and regulations on recreational diving influence how people interact with the reef.

On occasion, narcotraffickers may also play a part in coastal resource management. Due to their proximity to international borders, on the one hand, the isolated mangrove zones of Quintana Roo make excellent hiding and transition points for traffickers coming from points south, who therefore have an interest in maintaining the coverage of these tree species.[59] On the other hand, other traffickers in coastal states, like Sinaloa, use mangrove swamps as impromptu laboratories and waste storage sites for manufacturing methamphetamine, dumping toxic residue in the sensitive ecosystems.[60] While some traffickers would therefore have an interest in conserving mangrove zones, it is nevertheless unlikely that they can be counted on to be good environmental stewards for these and other reasons.

Transnational Mobilization around the Mesoamerican Barrier Reef

As development in Quintana Roo continued after the 1970s tourist boom, a network of self-identified stakeholders in Mexico, other countries implicated in the basin, the United States, and international governmental and nongovernmental organizations mobilized to address mounting problems facing reef governance. By 2001, a core group of actors had emerged, sharing specific policy proposals, an intersubjective consensus on the relevant causal relationships, a shared understanding of processes, and shared policy preferences and tactics for engagement. In other words, they became an epistemic community, as described by the literature and outlined in chapter 1 and the introduction (see table 2.1).

One of the civil society actors first involved in reef advocacy is the Mexican branch of the World Wildlife Fund (WWF-México), which had been conducting research in discrete sections of the Mesoamerican reef system since 1982. That year, the state government of Quintana Roo established the Sian Ka'an Biosphere Reserve after the *Centro de Investigaciones de Quintana Roo* (CIQRO) published research indicating the importance of its biodiversity to the UNESCO Man and Biosphere Programme.[61] In 1986, WWF-México lobbied the federal government to create a federal protected area at the Sian Ka'an Biosphere Reserve. After the federal government declared it in 1986, Cancún-based Los Amigos de Sian Ka'an emerged to monitor human activity and environmental processes in the newly created area, and promote compliance with environmental regulations. By promoting local and transnational governance efforts for reef and coastal management in

Table 2.1

Partial list of epistemic community members

Organization	Individuals	Functions	Science training
Los Amigos de Sian Ka'an	Gonzalo Merediz Alonso	Protected areas monitoring. Habitat health evaluation.	Marine biology
	Albert Franquesa	Protected areas monitoring. Habitat health evaluation.	Marine biology
UNU-INWEH	Peter Sale	Designing monitoring methodology	Ecology
The Nature Conservancy	Juan Bezaury Creel (formerly of Los Amigos)	Protected areas monitoring	Land use planning
	Will Heyman	AMP monitoring	Marine sciences
CONANP	Alfredo Arellano Guillermo	Population monitoring. Habitat health evaluation. National Reef Committee coordinator.	Marine biology
	Rosa Loreto Viruel (formerly of Los Amigos)	Protected areas monitoring. Puerto Morelos AMP management.	Marine ecology
	Juan Domínguez Calderón	Protected areas monitoring	Marine biology
	Patricia Santos	Population monitoring (fauna). Flora taxonomy. Habitat health evaluation.	
URI-CRC	Pamela Rubinoff	Monitoring methodology	Coastal management
ECOSUR	Eloy Sosa	Reef ecology monitoring	Marine ecology
	Felipe Serrano	Reef ecology monitoring	Marine ecology
	Laura Carrillo	Reef ecology monitoring	Marine ecology
WWF-México	Melanie McField	Threat analysis, monitoring methodology	Conservation ecology
	Álvaro Hernández Gil	Habitat and marine fauna monitoring	Ecology
CINVESTAV	G. Acosta-González	Reef coverage / pollution	Oceanography
UQROO	Héctor Carlos Gamboa Pérez	Reef ecology and monitoring	Marine ecology

Quintana Roo, WWF-México therefore acted as a catalyst in a process of network building among other organizations and agencies.

By the 1990s, concern about reef management in Mexico became transnational, as Mexican stakeholders created cost- and information-sharing links with a growing network of domestic, regional, and international actors. For example, in the Mexican town of Xcalak, local fishermen became concerned that tourist development would, by harming coral reefs, lead to losses in fish stocks important for subsistence and commercial production.[62] In 1994, these fishermen and local activists formed the Xcalak Community Committee (XCC) to articulate and aggregate interests and lobby for the protection of Xcalak's reefs. An older fisherman and longtime resident of Xcalak who will be identified as El Papá remembered the initial drive for conservation in an interview in 2012: "The people asked for the national park, to conserve the reefs, birds, and so on. They were planning to develop a tourist complex, which would have affected the ecology of the whole place."[63]

In 1995, the XCC contacted Los Amigos and WWF-México, requesting assistance in their plans to lobby the federal government to create an AMP in the reefs, which would grant local fishermen exclusive access to fish resources.[64] In the process of assisting the XCC, Los Amigos and WWF-México partnered with the Coastal Resources Center of the University of Rhode Island (URI-CRC) to conduct studies on populations and migratory patterns of reef fish.[65]

At the same time, Los Amigos and The Nature Conservancy (TNC) were conducting studies in the Sian Ka'an Biosphere Reserve, and determined that the protected area would need a carefully monitored buffer zone to maintain ecosystem integrity.[66] In 1998, the federal government responded to their advocacy by establishing an additional 100,000 hectares in 1998 at what is now known as the Área de Protección de Flora y Fauna Uaymil in the south, and at the reefs off the coast of Sian Ka'an. Currently, the Sian Ka'an Biosphere Reserve constitutes the single largest contiguous national protected area in Quintana Roo, with a surface area of 528,147 hectares.[67]

Quantitatively, the mid- and late 1990s looked like a time of unprecedented success in biodiversity conservation in Mexico. Between 1994 and 2000, over 700,000 additional hectares of federal and state areas were declared in Quintana Roo.[68] Mexico therefore seemed well on the way to implementing its obligations to the CBD, which it ratified in 1993, particularly Article 8 on in situ conservation.

However, it was not clear to the emerging network that simply expanding coverage of protected areas would lead to effective conservation without commitment by policymakers and the public to carefully designed regulations. For example, although the addition of the Sian Ka'an Reef and the Área de Uaymil increased the total coverage at Sian Ka'an, the three sites had management plans that were developed in isolation from each other.[69] Other protected areas, including at Puerto Morelos and Xcalak, completely lacked management plans when they were first created.[70] In fisheries, management at the time focused on conserving individual species, with little attention to important interspecies dependence.[71] While well intentioned, this piecemeal regulatory approach did not arrest the alarming declines in ecosystem health visible in the late 1990s. Coral reef coverage was being lost at a rate of 3 percent per annum, beaches were eroding, and fish stocks continued falling.[72]

Throughout the late 1990s to 2001, the emerging network began responding to this information and adopted a new approach emphasizing the interconnectivity of the MBRS. Recognizing this interconnectivity would be essential in the network's perspective to proper management. Thus, whereas the MBRS was once considered a collection of separate reefs, epistemic community members described it as a unitary reef system, second in size only to the Great Australian Barrier Reef, by the mid-1990s.[73]

As members began gathering information on the challenges and stresses on the reef, Mexican NGOs like WWF-México and Los Amigos began reaching out to researchers worldwide through a variety of transnational forums and workshops. Some of these were managed by the International Coral Reef Initiative (ICRI), an umbrella NGO consisting of marine ecologists and researchers that contributed to the development of shared ideas and knowledge. In 1995, ICRI held a series of workshops in Cancún on Caribbean reef management and its interdependence with marine currents, benthic habitats, and trophic webs along the coast.[74]

In 1996, the Central American governments and Mexico created a critical political opportunity for the network to do something meaningful with this new knowledge. That year, the Central American Commission for Development (CCAD) called on the Central American countries to take a regional approach to improving environmental management.[75] In response, the governments of Mexico, Belize, Guatemala, and Honduras drafted the Tulúm Declaration, pledging to coordinate activities, and invited WWF-México and the World Conservation Union to design what was to become the GEF-funded Proyecto de la Conservación y Uso Sostenible del Sistema Arrecifal Mesoamericano.[76] To the emerging transnational network, the Tulúm Declaration and the planned CCAD project offered "a framework for perhaps the most viable and transcendental opportunity on the planet for carrying out a multinational conservation effort."[77]

From 1998 onward, the network formulated the core organizing principles of what was to become its members' preferred approach to reef management, dubbed Integrated Coastal Zone Management (ICZM). ICZM was explicitly ecological in focus. It emphasized interconnectivity of coastal regions, and delegitimated the earlier, piecemeal methods of conservation. Network members developed the methodologies and investigative techniques of ICZM through a variety of transnational meetings. These included a symposium in Australia to evaluate ICZM application at existing and proposed Mexican AMPs at Xcalak, Yum Balám, and Sian Ka'an,[78] and at meetings held for the Atlantic and Gulf Reef Rapid Assessment (AGRRA) project, under the UN Institute of Water, Environment and Health (UNU-INWEH) in 1998 and 1999.[79]

In 1999 Juan Bezaury of TNC, formerly of Los Amigos, and Bessy Aspra de Lupiac of Honduras conducted a study, the *Threat and Root Cause Analysis*, which invoked ICZM to evaluate the primary anthropogenic threats to biodiversity in the Mesoamerican basin.[80] This became one of the primary sources of scientific information on the reef for the GEF project. At this time, the network had grown to include: Mexican academic institutions el Centro de Investigaciones y Estudios Avanzados (CINVESTAV) and el Colegio de la Frontera Sur (ECOSUR, formerly CIQRO); the Belizean agency CZMA/I, and staffers at the Hol Chan reserve; governmental staffers at the Cayos Cochinos Research station in Honduras; and federal employees from marine parks at Punta Cancún and Punta Nizuc in Mexico.[81]

While the GEF project was developing, WWF-México staff were planning their own project on reef management, using information produced by some of the same actors involved in the CCAD efforts. In 1999, WWF-México held workshops in Cancún and Belize to study the ecological features of the basin, including its habitats, marine and downriver current flows, and physical characteristics.[82] In 2000, WWF-México launched the

WWF Mesoamerican Reef Alliance Project (WWF MAR Project), which used ICZM and an ecological focus to advocate for reforms to fisheries management.[83] The WWF MAR Project also provided a crucial way through which nonexperts could participate in knowledge generation. As I will discuss, this project institutionalized the exchange of information between lay people in the fishing community and formally recognized experts in the conservationist NGO network and state agencies.

In 2001, the CCAD launched the Proyecto de la Conservación y Uso Sostenible del Sistema Arrecifal Mesoamericano (MBRS Project) on November 30.[84] The Unidad Coordinadora del Proyecto (UCP) coordinated the project's regional goals, which included, among other things, recommending areas of focus (such as monitoring techniques, modernizing and standardizing protected areas management, and identifying legislative gaps) by creating yearly Plans of Action.[85] The Mexican government created a National Reef Committee, headed by CONANP and staffed by civil society actors from Los Amigos and WWF-México, to manage the project. Under CONANP regional director and marine biologist Alfredo Arellano Guillermo, the National Reef Committee was responsible for studying biodiversity and recommending new management approaches, like creating federal protection under more robust conservation protocols.[86]

In carrying out the project, CONANP reached out to the available pool of civil society experts. CONANP established Memoranda of Understanding with agencies such as ECOSUR and CINVESTAV for assistance in monitoring and analysis in specific aspects of the MBRS Project, in matters such as chemical, physical, and pollution analyses at selected sites.[87] In 2002, Global Visions International (GVI), a British environmental NGO interested in coastal ecosystem integrity, created a formal relationship with CONANP and Los Amigos to conduct research and recreational expeditions in Sian Ka'an.[88] Like the Forestry Department in Jamaica, CONANP functioned both as a policymaker organization and as an epistemic community organization, gathering data as part of the National Reef Committee, contributing members to research gathering workshops, and recruiting from civil society agencies in the epistemic community network.

In addition to the MBRS-focused epistemic community, a network focused on the national management of mangroves emerged in Mexico in the 1990s. Like the epistemic community, the mangrove network argued that mangrove swamps were important as repositories of biodiversity and as buffer zones against coastal erosion and hurricanes.[89] Further, since mangrove zones are critical to the activities of local fishermen, this network campaigned for increased protection alongside residents who were worried that overdevelopment would destroy local livelihoods.

For example, in 1995, a fishing community in San Blas, Nayarit, became alarmed about proposals by the municipal and state government to create an industrial shrimp farm for the aquaculture company *Granjas Aquanova* in their traditionally used mangrove zones.[90] That year as well, the state planned to convert 3,500 hectares into tourist facilities, like golf courses and luxury hotels.[91] In response, a local NGO called Grupo Ecológico Manglar-San Blas mobilized to protest both plans, through street protests, marches, and official complaint letters.[92] In 1996, inspired by shared stories of resistance against the loss of mangroves in Honduras, Ecuador, El Salvador, and Guatemala, a network of environmental NGOs in these countries and worldwide launched RedManglar. This was a transnational network to save mangroves from tourism and industrial shrimp farming for local use. In Mexico, RedManglar began campaigning for protection in sites throughout the country, including in the states of Sinaloa and Nayarit, but also for key coastal sites in Quintana Roo that were part of the MBRS. These included mangrove zones in the Cancún-Tulúm corridor, Sian Ka'an, Xcalak, Chetumal, Cozumel, and Banco Chinchorro.[93]

This mangrove network consisted of stakeholders from transnational NGOs like Greenpeace, research organizations such as the National Autonomous University of Mexico (UNAM), national advocacy groups like the Mexican Center for Environmental Rights (CEMDA), and groups local to states such as Grupo Ecológico Mayab (GEMA) of Quintana Roo and Pronatura Noroeste of Baja California. One of the primary goals of this network was the integration of environmental conservation with civil and political rights for vulnerable populations. As CEMDA has consistently argued, a healthy environment requires the "free, prior and informed consent" of local, marginalized, and indigenous peoples.[94] This participatory based argument echoes the environmental justice literature in seeing participation in environmental policymaking as at least as important as policy outcomes in establishing sustainable environmentalism.[95]

Consequently, to this network the overexploitation of natural resources in areas by activities like tourism was inextricably linked to the disempowerment and political rights of already marginalized peoples. The mangrove network was concerned not only about the effects of ecological degradation on local populations, but also their ability to participate in the decisions that led to changes in land use. As a national movement, this group also had visible political support in the early 1990s from then–environmental minister Lichtinger and party members in the Green Ecological Party of Mexico (PVEM) and the Institutional Revolutionary Party (PRI), particularly from assumed PRI presidential successor Luis Donaldo Colosio.[96]

Although the mangrove network was not an official part of the MBRS Project, some of the member organizations like CEMDA worked with Los Amigos and TNC in gathering information on the contribution of mangrove zones to coastal integrity. In 2008, for instance, Los Amigos and CEMDA launched a project in Quintana Roo with SEMARNAT, CONANP, and PROFEPA to study the socioeconomic impacts of environmental degradation along the coast of Quintana Roo. As I indicate later in this chapter, the mangrove network was crucial in supporting one of the most significant policy developments on mangrove protection relevant to the epistemic community's campaign.

Like the epistemic community, this mangrove network relied on scientific knowledge produced by experts to strengthen conservationist claims. Unlike the epistemic community, the network had a more diverse epistemological base, and included human rights groups like CEMDA and fishing cooperatives. The cooperatives in particular had members who were not formally educated in the way that a graduate of UNAM or ECOSUR would be, although they had a wealth of the kind of "embodied knowledge" that McCormick, Haraway, Karvonen and Brand, and others describe as "gained simply through living in a locale."[97]

By 2001, the core actors of the reef-based epistemic community had established a comprehensive series of network links, and a broad network comprising various actors from a range of organizations in the public and private sector. As table 2.1 indicates, this community was defined by access to formal training. Its members were drawn from highly visible research organizations, like transnational NGOs, international institutions, and academic organizations in Mexico and elsewhere.

This network was substantially larger than the seventeen members listed in table 2.1. Comprised entirely of epistemic community actors, Los Amigos alone has fourteen members. ECOSUR, based in Chetumal, counts another eight more members, while URI-CRC has an additional eleven.

A very conservative estimate of this epistemic community suggests that there are more than sixty, and perhaps as many as one hundred, members involved in advocacy over reef management in the basin.

Epistemic community members built social ties with one another in formal meetings, and by recruiting staffers from each other's agencies, as both CONANP and TNC did, hiring staffers away from Los Amigos between 1997 and 2000. Between 1998 and 2004, URI-CRC conducted six meetings in Chetumal with UQROO and local actors, five in Xcalak with Los Amigos and the XCC, and additional meetings in Belize and Cancún with ENGOs involved in Mesoamerican reef management. After the MBRS Project was launched, epistemic community members met several times a year in technical workshops held in rotating countries, and in periodic "Meetings of the Experts" held by the UCP, one held in 2001–2002, three in 2002–2003, and two in 2004–2005. Further, epistemic community members shared knowledge and causal arguments through jointly authored reports, like the *Threat and Root Cause Analysis*, an electronic database on reef research operated by UQROO, and through financial support, particularly from TNC, which gave research grants to Los Amigos and Global Visions International (GVI).

The Epistemic Community and Advocacy in the MBRS

By 2001, Mexico had an active epistemic community, concerned about the ecological integrity of the Mesoamerican basin, and worried that rapid declines in one area would irreparably harm the region. This was a problem not only for the aesthetic and intrinsic value of healthy coastal environments, but also for the employment and subsistence opportunities for marginalized communities that depended on access to and the exploitation of natural resources.[98] In other words, maintaining "biodiversity and ecosystem equilibrium" was crucial for economic resource generation and sustained consumption among low-income populations, in addition to providing ecological goods.[99]

The Normas Practicás studies produced by Los Amigos, WWF-México, and URI-CRC linked mangrove loss to declines in the health of fish nurseries and populations.[100] They illustrated the importance of mangroves in buffering against marine surges during storms and hurricanes.[101] Further, the WWF-MAR studies noted that biodiversity in fish populations has a symbiotic relationship to coral reefs. They described how fish "[provide] corals the capacity to maintain their vital functions in healthy conditions for their growth, reproduction and development, while the presence of numerous coral structures gives the fish places where they can be protected, where they can find food, reproduce and maintain other vital functions."[102]

In his Cancún offices in 2008, Álvaro Hernández Gil of WWF-México explained why conservation mattered, using the same language of interconnectivity invoked by the Cockpit Country epistemic community described in chapter 1: "There is a very close relationship between the mangrove and the health of the reef. Because for many species of fish and other species that keep the reef healthy, part of their life cycle is developed in the mangrove zone. Then, when someone destroys this part of the ecosystem, the mangrove, people generally think, 'The reef is over there, and what I'm destroying are these trees here.' But all these species have a very important interaction."[103]

José Juan Domínguez Calderón, also of CONANP, made similar points, noting as did Hernández Gil that the mass public was generally unaware of the complex of relationships affecting environmental management on the coast: "If you remove coastal material, in the mangrove and the forest, it's a chain that affects everything. In other words, the forest that is over here, contributes energy to the mangrove, and the mangrove contributes energy to the lagoon, to the reef lagoon, and the reef lagoon—but then people don't understand this trophic or ecological chain."[104]

To be fair, the epistemic community had to arrive at the idea that effective management required an approach that integrated formerly isolated areas. Even core epistemic community organizations like Los Amigos had to learn that, as Gonzalo Merediz Alonso put it in 2008, "it wasn't making sense to have a Reserve being conserved like an island, right? Sian Ka'an exchanges water with its surroundings, the reefs are linked, the forests are connected."[105] But this idea was only possible once the epistemic community began the process of exchanging information through transnational links about the challenges of reef management.

Having adopted this ecological approach, the epistemic community universally opposed the continuation of the tourist model that Cancún and the Riviera Maya are built upon. According to their research, this model of development not only degrades the reef ecosystem, but also competes with the land ownership claims of indigenous and lower-income populations,[106] threatening the economic sustainability of these communities by preventing sustainable use of natural resources.[107] Halting or reversing the environmental impacts of tourist development in the northern third of the state, near Cancún and the Riviera Maya is, according to some epistemic community members like Rosa Loreto of CONANP in 2008, "a little difficult" since (as she put it) "the place is already pretty well developed."[108] Four years later, this view that Cancún and the Riviera Maya were done deals had not changed within the epistemic community. In a 2012 interview in the Cancún offices of Los Amigos, Gonzalo Merediz Alonso observed dryly that "in the Riviera Maya and in Cancún, the situation is already a little behind—we're already a little too late to do some of the things we want."[109]

Nevertheless, there is still space to ensure that the development planned for the southern third of the state, including in rural and undeveloped areas such as Majahual, is carried out sustainably.[110] Eloy Sosa of ECOSUR was very clear that the model of development would have to be changed to keep the ecological integrity of the south intact: "So, if they repeat the northern style development [in the south], it's going to have a *very* big impact. That's what I'm telling you, yeah? Because we're talking about the southern part, where the most important biodiversity in Quintana Roo is, right? And that's why so much of us are lobbying for a kind of development that's more measured than what they learned to do in the north."[111]

For this is what the advocacy network wants. Placing a moratorium on tourism in the way that the Cockpit Country epistemic community network demanded on mining would be virtually impossible, as well as politically undesirable. Instead, recognizing that people should make a living from using natural resources, network members wanted to make sure that the abundant resources of the coast were used in a sustainable manner, whether by small-scale fishermen, or large-scale developers. To quote Álvaro Hernández Gil: "In Cancun, where anyone can come and fish, and they don't need a permit, we don't imagine that this is sustainable. ... At the same time, if we want sustainability in fishing, we want tourism to become sustainable as well."[112]

In order to carry this out, the network campaigned throughout the project to change the behavior of different groups of actors. They wanted the federal government to create additional protected areas, but were clear that these would have to use management approaches that incorporated ICZM and recognized the importance of ecological interdependence, rather than simply expanding the size of area covered. As Eloy Sosa of ECOSUR described, piecemeal management could leave problematic gaps in regulatory coverage that would not satisfactorily arrest ecosystem decline, even if those areas that were protected were carefully managed: "When we get into this topic, when we get into biodiversity, the government acts like everything is OK. Because they argue: 'In Quintana Roo, we have a high percentage of coastal areas as protected areas. We *are* carrying out management.' ... For me, the concern is where there aren't any protected areas, right? There, there has been a very strong impact."[113]

Recognizing that state and federal regulatory capacity could only go so far, they also wanted hotel developers to change their standard operating procedures, for example by limiting the size and location of hotels, and for fishing cooperatives to adopt sustainable practices.

In addition to sharing a rationale for action based on an ecological understanding of the reef, this network shared a causal consensus on the relationship between human activity and environmental degradation. Perhaps even more important, network members agreed that they agreed about the causal arguments. Patricia Santos of CONANP explained that this emerged for three specific reasons: "First, because the data is generated by experts. Experts that almost all of us know, because we are friends, or colleagues, or teachers, or students. Or, we know they're experts because we read each other's publications. Second, because the methodology that is used is standardized, which makes it trustworthy. Third, there is no reason for anyone to dress up the information being collected."

This consensus was facilitated by short chains between cause and effect, a shared methodology for studying the problem, and at least in the case of tourism, a limited group of suspects in anthropocentric environmental degradation. First, since large-scale hotels are easily identified it was clear to the network which actors were causally responsible for coastal overexploitation. Second, having studied coastal construction in documents like the *Threat and Root Cause Analysis* produced for the MBRS Project, the network was clear about the consequences of tourism-based development for the ecological health in the reef. Members universally acknowledged that large-scale tourism-based development depleted mangroves, which in turn caused a chain reaction of coastal erosion and loss in reef cover, and exposed shorelines to tidal energy.[114]

Third, the epistemic community had a widely shared measure of the projected and current aggregate extent of environmental degradation in the

Mesoamerican reef. In 2005, the epistemic community concluded a baseline study of reef conditions in the four countries in the basin. In Mexico,
the sites studied were Cozumel in the north and Banco Chinchorro and
Xcalak in the south, all sharing parts of the MBRS. In this study, researchers
gathered comprehensive information on indicators of reef and ecosystem
health including: the size, density, species, and average cover of coral species; the diet, nesting patterns, and biomass of twenty-three indicator species of fish; the quantity of seagrass; and the density of mangrove cover as
measured by number of trees per hectare.[115] In addition, studies of pollution in the Bay of Chetumal generated figures on the presence of chemical
and organic compounds from agricultural pesticides and plaguicides, such
as polychlorinated biphenyls (PCBs) and DDT, as well as generating information on the chemical and physical composition of water.[116]

Some studies were more narrowly tailored toward specific threats. For
example, CONAPESCA and the Food and Agricultural Organization (FAO)
had conducted longitudinal studies on declines in catch size and populations of important commercial species, such as spiny lobster, snapper,
and conch, dating back to the 1970s.[117] The CONAPESCA and the baseline
studies were shared among epistemic community members through member participation in the various threat assessment workshops and research
methodologies workshops conducted among network participants for the
MBRS Project. This shared consensus strengthened the epistemic community's belief about the threats posed by tourism such that, even among
network members from the federal agency CONANP, there was a widely
shared belief that "the primary threat is tourism."[118] As Álvaro Hernández
Gil said, "We believe that coastal development, particularly in the case of
Mexico, is the principal threat to the integrity of the ecosystem. Coastal
development, which, in the majority of the cases, is associated with tourist
development."[119]

There was some uncertainty about the *causes* and *consequences* of fishing-
related declines in the MBRS, however. As occurred within farming and
marijuana agriculture in Jamaica, a sizable portion of this activity is carried out clandestinely, as outsider fishermen frequently emerge to poach
from resources claimed by registered cooperatives, to their dismay. Since
it is impossible to determine which fishermen are responsible for overharvesting, by how much they are overfishing, and other reliable indicators of
human impact on fish stocks, attaining precise measures of fishing's impact

on coastal resources is impossible. Nevertheless, the epistemic community was clear in interviews and project documents that overfishing can collapse fish populations and spawning sites, or areas in which fish gathered to reproduce.[120] As a result, the epistemic community had a very robust scientific consensus on the relationship between coastal development and fishing on environmental health.

In this case, the epistemic community established strong socialization ties with federal agencies, particularly SEMARNAT and CONANP in the environmental secretariat, and comparatively weaker ties to state policymakers. As described earlier, the National Reef Committee that managed the MBRS Project was staffed by CONANP and by epistemic community organizations Los Amigos and WWF-México. The technical working groups that provided recommendations to the coordinating agencies of the project were also comprised of members of CONANP and NGOs from the epistemic community. During the MBRS Project, CONANP held meetings with researchers from epistemic community organizations such as ECOSUR and CINVESTAV to help manage protected areas.[121] These ties were strengthened by the exchange of personnel and training between CONANP and the civil society. CONANP employed former staffers of Los Amigos for reef monitoring during the period of field research, and participated in regional workshops with civil society actors on protected areas management.[122]

During the 2000s, WWF-México also strengthened this relationship and exchange of knowledge through its WWF-MAR Project. During this period, the NGO met with the federal agencies CONANP and SAGARPA, as well as academic organizations CINVESTAV and ECOSUR to share new knowledge on fisheries management and conservation.[123] The epistemic community did create additional ties to agencies in the state government of Quintana Roo, but these were comparatively weakly established, largely because the management of marine and coastal resources falls primarily under the federal authorities.

The WWF-MAR Project was also crucial in establishing strong social ties to local community groups, particularly among fishermen in Quintana Roo. Moreover, these ties were oriented around the idea that local fishermen, despite their lack of formal training, had access to knowledge that was crucial to environmental management. For example, the federal government and WWF-México invited cooperatives to planning workshops on conservation precisely because of the recognition that fishermen were skilled at: identifying common sites of capture, measuring diversity within and among fish species, and identifying the capture techniques that were commonly employed in the region.[124] Further, WWF-México was able to identify important fishing zones near Holbox by having the most experienced fishermen meet in March 2006, vote on the importance of zones to managing fish stocks, and come to a consensus with other fishermen on how to identify threats and solutions in the area. An instruction manual produced by WWF-México was clear that the decisions by fishermen about which zones to conserve should determine the organization's monitoring strategy. Clearly, this participatory approach had benefits to both local actors and the conservationist NGO. As the WWF-México noted:

> Undertaking this type of workshop, with the input of fishermen, is very important for the selection of [critical habitats]. It also helps build trust with the fishermen with respect to [ecosystem based fisheries management], and provides legitimacy with the fishing communities ... they know the fishing sites, they know which areas are dangerous for sampling, they have a good idea of the species present and they reduce monitoring costs as they can receive comparatively lower compensation than a team of divers specialized in ecological monitoring.[125]

As a result, the outcomes of these workshops, including manuals and recommendations for safety precautions, appropriate fishing techniques, and population monitoring,[126] were grounded in the lay knowledge of non-experts. In this, the WWF MAR, like the Cockpit Country Stakeholder's Group in Jamaica, served as a way in which recognized experts generated knowledge through a model based on civic engagement. Returning to Karvonen and Brand's question: "Why should experts sacrifice their relatively privileged social position?,"[127] we can see here the positive outcomes of participatory knowledge generation. Importantly, this approach was not new to the epistemic community. As indicated earlier, epistemic community organizations like Los Amigos took their cues about conservation at Xcalak from the community-led mobilization against tourism in the mid-1990s.

At the same time, while the epistemic community was socializing with lay actors in the fishing community, they were carefully cultivating ties with the hotel sector. In tourism, Los Amigos and URI-CRC conducted periodic studies on the relationship between coastal construction and environmental degradation, issuing recommendations in the Normas Prácticas studies to hotel operators in the Riviera Maya.[128] In addition, transnational epistemic community organizations such as Conservation International and

Los Amigos established the Mesoamerican Reef Tourism Initiative (MARTI), an informal association of hoteliers and civil society researchers. Like the Normas Prácticas studies, the MARTI initiative was created to promote voluntary good environmental practices in the tourism sector, including in the operation of cruise ships, reef visitation practices, and hotel operation and construction.[129]

As I have described, the community generated a robust intersubjective consensus on two of the primary anthropogenic threats assessed here: fishing and coastal hotel development. Second, the community created strong social links to policymakers in the environmental and fishing governmental agencies, particularly in the federal level, as well as with private sector managers in the hotel and fishing sectors.

As in Jamaica, the environmental advocacy networks used a variety of framing strategies to argue for improved management in their respective ecosystem. However, unlike Jamaica, the framing choices were not divided into two distinct advocacy periods, but used to target different audiences. In particular, epistemic community members seemed initially convinced that hoteliers and the state government of Quintana Roo would respond primarily to neoliberal arguments about the economic benefit of conservation. This formed a strategic choice, as interview respondents indicated that the network continued to be internally motivated by broader concerns about biodiversity and ecosystem integrity. The following section assesses the success of the community in influencing biodiversity policies and practices in the Mesoamerican basin.

Epistemic community advocacy took place in the MBRS at different levels. At the international level, the epistemic community used its position as public experts involved in project design to advocate to the GEF to adopt its imaginary of what the ecoregion "was." The area described as the MBRS in the 1999 *Threat and Root Cause Analysis* was chosen to "approximate the limits defined by World Wildlife Fund (WWF) for the Meso-American Caribbean Reef Ecoregion" (see figure 2.2).[130] This also allowed the epistemic community to include references to ecological management in the project, such as the necessity of including coastal with marine management. When the central coordinating agency of the project, the Unidad Coordinadora del Proyecto (UCP), adopted this map, it included as areas relevant to biodiversity management in the reef coastal and marine environments, like mangroves and seagrasses.[131] As a result, initial project design reflected

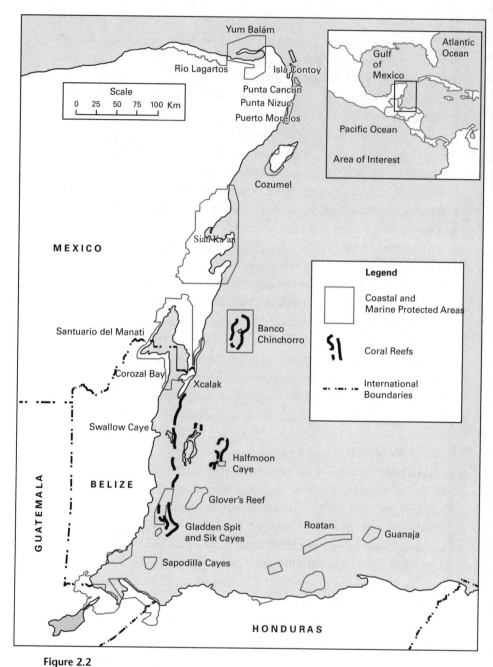

Figure 2.2
Mesoamerican Barrier Reef System political map. *Source:* Author's reproduction of
map provided by the Centroamerican Commission of Environment and Development (CCAD) and the National Commission of Protected Areas (CONANP) (2006),
http://www.reefresilience.org/images/mesoamerbarreefmap.gif, accessed June 9, 2015.

some of the core principles of ICZM developed by the emerging scientific network during the late 1990s. The outcome of this process was that the community exercised influence on the eventual management approach taken by federal environmental policymakers in Mexico by shaping the agenda of the project.

The epistemic community also wanted to ensure that ICZM informed the standard monitoring methodology used to evaluate reef health. Although there was no standard approach to measuring reef health at the start of the project, the epistemic community got an opportunity to change this in 2002, when the CCAD and the UCP requested a standardized, scientifically valid monitoring program for the MBRS.[132] In May of that year, a transnational consortium of researchers headed by Peter Sale of UNU-INWEH held a workshop in Cancún to this end. Over thirty-five scientists from the four countries and the international community participated in this workshop, including members of Mexican epistemic community organizations, Los Amigos, WWF-México, and CINVESTAV, and organizations such as CZMA/I from the broader regional reef advocacy network.[133] The methodology developed by the consortium was called the Programa de Monitoreo Sinóptico (PMS), and was synthesized from earlier studies, including the 1999 AGRRA workshops and the ICZM symposia.[134] The PMS specified monitoring methods, environmental modeling, biodiversity indicators, and relevant sites of investigation in the region, and by using the ecosystem framework developed in ICZM, incorporated coastal mangrove zones and seagrasses in the monitoring approach. Much as occurred with the geographic area defined in the 1999 *Threat and Root Cause Analysis*, the transnationally generated PMS was incorporated as part of the regional management approach in the MBRS Project, legitimized by the multilateral institutions of the CCAD and the GEF.

At the federal level, a minor campaign in the epistemic community advocacy attempt was the goal of reforming a coastal zone referred to as the Zona Federal Marítimo-Terrestre (ZFMT). The ZFMT consists of the coastal area measured twenty meters from the average tide level, in which large development projects such as hotel construction are subject to an environmental impact assessment, and have to be approved by SEMARNAT and PROFEPA.[135]

However, at present the epistemic community considers the ZFMT as an inadequate management tool. Studies of beach erosion cited in the Normas

Prácticas studies have demonstrated that large structures between the first sand dune and the coastline are severely disruptive of sand replenishment and contribute to beach erosion. As the location of the first sand dune on a beach may be substantially more than twenty meters away, hotels constructed out of the ZFMT and hence free from this federal oversight may nevertheless contribute strongly to coastal erosion and reef sedimentation.[136] Nevertheless, this became a site of policy advocacy for a small subsection of the epistemic community, as the Normas Prácticas studies of Los Amigos and URI-CRC recommended that the federal government expand the ZFMT from twenty meters to a construction-free zone extending up to five meters behind the first sand dune.

In addition, the epistemic community sought the reform of SEMARNAT's and CONANP's practices in managing federal protected areas in the MBRS. Los Amigos recommended the addition of federal status in then noncovered areas, primarily at Majahual and Xaban Ha, an area near Cozumel.[137] Los Amigos and other epistemic community organizations, including ECOSUR and WWF-México, sought the use of ICZM principles in existing protected areas, both in those without plans, and in those with insufficiently designed plans. This was explicitly advanced to CONANP and SEMARNAT: in 2003 civil society organizations and CONANP participated in a series of workshops in Belize to discuss incorporating ICZM-based principles, like ecosystem loading capacity in protected-areas management.[138] Throughout the conduct of the MBRS Project, epistemic community members in WWF-México and ECOSUR sought to persuade CONANP to redraft existing plans at Xcalak and at the "buffer zones" at Sian Ka'an, Área de Uaymil, and the Reefs of Sian Ka'an to better comport with the ideas of ICZM.

The network was clear that advocacy at the federal and international levels should be informed by scientific causal arguments, such that protected areas management would conform to, as Álvaro Hernández Gil put it, a "scientific or ecological point of view of biodiversity."[139] This is not to say that epistemic community members were unconcerned with the economic potential of natural resources. In a state where so much of the local economy depends on tourism, ignoring the economic value of biodiversity would be tremendously misguided. However, epistemic community members were clear that this economic value was only one part of the worth of biodiversity, and that policy should recognize all potential values, including scientific, environmental, and economic. Patricia Santos of the federal agency CONANP, and an epistemic community member explained: "But I believe that what should be recognized is that the [natural] resources have a value per se. ... They're valued not just because they might be valuable to mankind. Or, they're not just valuable because we can get some money from them. They're valuable per se, by the fact of their existence, from all that they represent for evolution, all the complexity and their place in the biosphere."[140]

In fisheries management, the epistemic community tried to get both federal agencies and fishing cooperatives to promote sustainable harvesting in a way that would lead to long-term resource use. The epistemic community did this through the MBRS Project, and through the WWF MAR Project, by working with CONANP and WWF-México to promote sustainable fishing practices, such as the voluntary adoption of size restrictions on lobster, compliance with fishing regulations, and protection of spawning sites among cooperatives.[141]

At the policy level, epistemic community members recommended that CONAPESCA establish regulations identifying and protecting fish spawning sites. In 2002, TNC and other organizations conducted a study under the MBRS Project to identify spawning sites throughout the Mesoamerican basin.[142] The epistemic community urged CONAPESCA to ban or restrict fishing in these sensitive zones crucial to fish biodiversity.[143] Moreover, community members recommended that CONAPESCA, CONANP, and SEMARNAT make new protection compatible with the interests of local fishermen. For example, federal agencies could create protected areas over fish spawning sites and grant conditional permits to fishermen, giving registered cooperatives sole legal access to such zones. In exchange for this exclusive access, the cooperatives could then contribute to reef governance by monitoring for illicit activity and pledging to adopt sustainable practices.[144]

Epistemic community members combined this approach with encouraging fishermen to curtail the quantity of fish extracted for commerce or subsistence by shifting toward other forms of income generation including, as Eloy Sosa described, "sport fishing, so that they move toward tourism, ecotourism."[145] The epistemic community sought to persuade cooperatives to take this action by arguing through the WWF MAR Project that these restrictions would improve the long-term viability of fish resources necessary to continued economic exploitation.[146]

Moreover, the sustainability of commercially harvested fish populations was linked not only to overharvesting per se, but also to the maintenance of health of other populations and the degradation of terrestrial and marine ecosystems external to the reef.[147] Throughout, epistemic community members, through reports and interviews, were clear that the danger of overharvesting would have economic impacts on the interests of local fishermen. Advance reports for the GEF project during its run warned that "overfishing and a lack of regulations in reproductive and nursery sites can bring the size of commercial captures to a decline, possibly close to collapse."[148] A 2003 report produced by Will Heyman of Texas A&M and Nicanor Requena of The Nature Conservancy in Belize, along with Eloy Sosa of ECOSUR made the metaphor explicit, arguing, "[O]ne can consider that the protection of reproductive aggregation sites is similar to the protection of a savings account in a bank. If possible, we should capture the interest, not the savings capital." The report went on to say: "This analogy is particularly appropriate when one considers the management of reproductive aggregations—source sites for the reproduction of the majority of the commercially important reef fish in the regions of the MBRS."[149]

In interviews, epistemic community respondents indicated that the choice of economic language to describe the impacts of biodiversity loss and environmental degradation was necessary to persuade these local stakeholders about the importance of environmental management and good practices. Again, respondents indicated that the use of economic language was a strategic choice for some, as it differed with internally held reasons for biodiversity management, which emphasized the holistic rather than the consumptive value of reef ecosystems. Alfredo Arellano Guillermo, then regional director of CONANP, noted that the economic approach was an important component of communicating to local fishermen. "Unfortunately," he said in an interview, "our society is based largely on the issue of costs and compensation for environmental impacts ... if we don't carry out that kind of valuation, the people will not—they might not pay it any mind."[150]

While "as a naturalist or biologist, the value that biodiversity has is for human health," Rosa Loreto, also of CONANP, admitted, "If we look at it from the perspective that the people do, that is, only economic, well it does have its value, right? ... [Because] it's generating economic revenue for them."[151]

Yet some of the epistemic community members expressed genuine concern about the impact of ecological management on low-income populations in ways that suggested the link between conservation and low-income livelihoods was not just a strategic decision. For example, José Manuel Cárdenas Magaña of CONAPESCA, misquoting a poem apocryphally attributed to the fifteenth-century philosopher king Nezahualcoyótl, argued that conservation and ecological management should not come at the expense of the poor:

There's a poem from Nezahualcoyótl that says, more or less: "I love the deer. I love the tapir. I love the singsong of the bird of one hundred voices. But I love most my brother man." In other words, it's important to conserve nature. But it's also important that our coastal communities, our populations have some sustenance. Because how else are we going to manage? Yes, we can't take it all. We have to care for nature. But, "don't touch, don't take, don't grab": that's the ecologist's position. ... I would say that the ecologists have to give some alternatives to the fisherman then, and that part is our responsibility.[152]

Thus, while the scientific network was motivated to conserve fish stocks and the coastal environment in Quintana Roo, its members did not approach this in a top-down manner, but rather with management strategies that used knowledge produced from the lay public in the fishing community. But although epistemic community members referenced ecological and intrinsic values of biodiversity in communicating with federal environmental agencies and fishing cooperatives, they used neoliberal claims almost exclusively to argue to hoteliers that conserving biodiversity made good economic sense. As members pointed out in the Normas Práctica studies and the MARTI initiatives, poor hotel management causes erosion, attendant pollution, and reef sedimentation that could damage hotel infrastructure and degrade the market appeal of coastal landscapes. When beaches are too eroded, hoteliers may find it necessary to construct buffering walls to maintain the long-term structural integrity of the coastal buildings, but at tremendous additional cost. This was clearly laid out in the long-term forecasts of environmental degradation on coastal environments provided by the epistemic community, which emphasized the economic cost of a poor environment. In particular, the MARTI partnership and Normas Prácticas studies framed good environmental practices as economically sound in the long term. In describing Los Amigos's participation in the MARTI program, Merediz Alonso stated: "For the hotels that are currently in operation, what we do is carry out a diagnosis with them, on how to manage energy, water, toxic residues. ... Things that are practical and that help them to save energy, water, money, and that is an element, to answer your question, as to how we approach them. So that they see that [the environment] has an economic value as well."[153]

However, it was clear that epistemic community members saw the use of neoliberal arguments with hoteliers as strictly strategic. In fact, Eloy Sosa of ECOSUR argued that this commodity-based logic was a "kind of blindness": "When you speak to [hoteliers] about environmentally friendly development, something less destructive, what they think is that it's got to be less cabins, material less—less concrete. They look at it from an accounting perspective, right? And this, as I say, is blindness."[154]

Enrique Gálvez of SEMARNAT made a similar argument about communicating to hoteliers, noting that the interconnected nature of coastal biodiversity was only likely to sway their decision making, if it was clear that it brought economic consequences to them: "Those gentlemen that want to do away with the mangrove should understand that if they do away with the mangrove, they're doing away with the coral reef, which is what they want to sell. Or that if they tear out the seagrass near the coast, their fine sand beach is going to be lost."[155]

In this, Sosa's and Gálvez's arguments used language that was very similar to comments made by critical scholars in environmental geography and ecological economics. For example, Kosoy and Corbera also use the rhetoric of impaired sight and limited vision to describe what neoliberal commodification does to our understanding of nature: "[Commodification] consists of itemizing ecosystem services for the purpose of monetary valuation, pricing and exchange, thus obscuring ecosystems' complexity. ... We suggest that this contributes to make human-nature relationships invisible through imposing a single language of valuation."[156] This suggests, as do McCaulay's comments from chapter 1, that the critical literature's concerns about the limits of neoliberalism resonate with people's real-life experiences with the commodification of nature. Neoliberal economics simply cannot capture all of the value and meaning that people ascribe to the environment.

In this case, the epistemic community had mixed success. Its members were considerably successful in persuading environmental policymakers in CONANP, SEMARNAT, and CONAPESCA to adopt new policies, and had some success in persuading fishing cooperatives to change practices.

However, the community had little success in engaging with the governance of coastal hotel construction whether by the hoteliers or the state government of Quintana Roo.

In protected areas management, the institutions implementing MBRS adopted the recommendations issued by the civil society network. CONANP and SEMARNAT adopted the PMS methodology designed by the UNU-INWEH consortium, based on ICZM studies carried out during the late 1990s, as the primary monitoring tool in the Mesoamerican basin.[157] After the MBRS Project concluded in 2007, the federal agencies continued to employ PMS, indicating that its adoption was not contingent on GEF support.[158]

Protected areas management also bore the traces of epistemic community influence. In the Sian Ka'an area, CONANP and SEMARNAT replaced the 1993 plan with one designed with assistance from civil society organizations such as Los Amigos and TNC. Under the new plan, monitoring and protection of the Sian Ka'an Biosphere Reserve was integrated with the Reefs of Sian Ka'an and the Área de Uaymil, and incorporated into what is currently referred to as the "Sian Ka'an Complex": a zone of over 652,000 hectares, or approximately half of the total protected areas coverage in Quintana Roo.[159] In addition, the agencies entered into sponsorship agreements with UNESCO and international corporations, such as Gillette, to purchase sections of coastal wetlands in Sian Ka'an for conservation, monitoring these areas through joint efforts with actors in the epistemic community, namely TNC and Los Amigos.[160]

Similarly at Xcalak, epistemic community members WWF-México, TNC, and URI-CRC successfully drafted a federally accepted management plan, with the approval of CONANP and SEMARNAT for the newly created protected area. This plan included limitations on the quantity of divers (recreational or otherwise) based on ecosystem loading capacity, prohibitions on the use of SCUBA and other types of augmenting fishing equipment, and the creation of zones of no-capture and restricted access for registered cooperatives.[161]

Not all recommendations were incorporated into the policies of the environmental agencies, however. At the time of writing, the adoption of additional federal protected-areas status at sites recommended by the epistemic community, such as Majahual, had not been carried out. CONANP members were concerned that the adoption of protected area status in these areas, though preferred by Los Amigos, would have been too economically costly, given the marginal importance of those zones to reef conservation. As Patricia Santos of CONANP noted, "There are zones where, even if there are corals, the population density is very low. There's just pure rock, sand, seagrass, and one little coral here, another over there, one here, and we can't call that the reef, nor can we call it a coral community. ... And then, when a place is already very altered ... it doesn't merit having a category of protection that requires money, personnel, equipment. ... In other words, it's so deteriorated that it's not worth the trouble to give it a special category of protection."[162] This suggests a further split in the overall consensus within the epistemic community, as both Los Amigos and CONANP are prominent members of the network. Nevertheless, this difference between them about the importance of extending protected area status to those zones did not cause any notable tension within the network, since it was not mentioned outside of one interview with CONANP staff.

The epistemic community also influenced the practices and policies of fisheries management. After the project to monitor spawning sites concluded in 2003, the community identified additional sites meriting protection in Mexico, increasing the recognized number from twenty-seven to thirty-nine.[163] In these sites, SAGARPA and CONAPESCA adopted policies requiring permits for fishing cooperatives, establishing seasonal allowances and limiting the use of fishing boats to those with small outboard motors.[164] CONANP also coordinated with CONAPESCA to manage spawning sites, classifying them as protected areas under environmental law, and banning commercial fishing in them in the interest of maintaining ecosystem health.[165]

Fishing cooperative practices demonstrated some epistemic community influence as well. Throughout the coast, there were some exemplary cases of the reform of fishing practices, at places like Xcalak. After the involvement of epistemic community organizations, the XCC established no-take zones, limited appropriate extractive techniques to low-impact methods, and agreed to protect overall health in the region, all without additional government regulation.[166] At Punta Allen, the cooperatives adopted a voluntary ban on the use of SCUBA equipment for lobster harvesting.[167] In a 2006 CONAPESCA survey of fishing cooperatives, 26.7 percent were identified as carrying out what the federal government described as a high level of sustainable management and extraction, including using low-impact fishing techniques and regulated harvesting; 40 percent carried out moderate action, but stopped short of specifically targeted conservation of stocks whereas 33 percent carried out no discernible management effort.[168]

This is not to say that fisheries management, even among cooperatives working with CONANP and CONAPESCA, is devoid of contention. At the newly created area at Xcalak (Parque Nacional de Arrecife, Xcalak, or PNAX), some local fishermen began to resent what they saw as complicity between former members of the Xcalak Community Committee and external academics and governmental officials to exclude community members from the benefits of using natural resources.[169] For example, despite his initial support for the creation of a National Park at Xcalak, El Papá and other fishermen felt alienated by the actual implementation of the eventual plan in the mid-2000s. One fisherman who did not want to be identified claimed that some of the authority figures in the community were able to use elements of the plan—things like permits to act as a tour guide—to enrich themselves at a cost to less socially connected members. This also corresponded with some of the observations of El Papá. "They didn't consider us in elaborating the plan," he said. "They designed it at the University and signed it there, and only carried some of the authorities from the town to sign it as well, like the president of the cooperative, the delegate, and representatives of the ecological conservation committee, without taking into account their ideas." Thus, despite lay participation in the plan's design, actual implementation through CONANP began to erode the participatory measures that had been there since the 1990s. This suggests, unfortunately, that participatory governance measures of the sort described by McCormick and others can deteriorate if not adequately cared for.

However, El Papá and other fishermen who were critical of the PNAX plan were not opposed to environmental protection per se, but rather to management that was insufficiently democratic, and poorly targeted. El Papá, for instance, objected to the fact that, under the management plan, "boats used for tourism cannot be used for fishing. Since there are low tourist seasons, you have to buy another boat to fish, which requires a lot of capital." Similarly, another Xcalak fisherman who will be identified as Juan Pelota objected to the timing of the seasons for capturing conch, noting that they interfered with a long-standing tradition in Xcalak of using conch in *ceviches*, a pickled seafood dish. But El Papá, Juan Pelota, and other fishermen who were interviewed were clear that conservation was needed, particularly in light of the continued vulnerability of the area to outside incursion and illegal fishing for the tourist market.[170] El Papá observed, "With all my years of experience as a fisherman, I have seen that the species are declining, they're being finished, and we need to conserve certain areas. But the management should be strict, with good vigilance from the authorities ... there are these outsider fishermen who are carrying off species without anybody controlling or punishing them."[171]

As contemporary studies on protected areas management in Mexico have indicated, it is essential that conservation plans include local actors if they are to gain legitimacy.[172] However, the experience of Xcalak indicates that local participation can deteriorate over time, even if institutions were initially designed in an inclusive manner. This suggests that a participatory approach to management is an ongoing practice, and it cannot be assumed that participatory management will necessarily persist over time. Nevertheless, the data indicate that the epistemic community influenced federal policy and practice, as well as local fishing norms, on processes relevant to the MBRS. Federal environmental and agricultural agencies adopted regulations and changed approaches to fit with the recommendations of epistemic community members. Fishermen also changed practices, and recognized the importance of coastal conservation to their own well-being as coastal residents.

State and Hotelier Resistance: Pushback against Environmentalism

While the epistemic community had some success in influencing coastal environmental management, it was nearly undone by concerted opposition from hotel operators and their political allies in the state government. CONANP managers did produce regulations, including establishing sanctions, limiting the amount of recreational divers in reef environments within AMPs, and also established monitoring patrols.[173] However, the cost of comprehensive marine monitoring is extremely high in terms of time and financial resources, and so the federal government has been unable to establish independent verification of compliance with these guidelines. Finally, the recommendations to establish a wider zone of restriction to replace the ZFMT to date have not been enacted.

Fortunately for conservationists, a broader, national campaign on mangrove protection led to some of the most important changes in regulations over coastal expansion. This cannot be attributed solely to actions of the epistemic community however, since this campaign comprised different (although overlapping) sets of actors, and targeted areas besides the MBRS.

In 2001, Vicente Fox appointed Alberto Cárdenas Jiménez as Secretary of the Environment. In 2003, SEMARNAT adopted federal norm NOM-022-SEMARNAT-2003, following the publication of studies on the importance of mangrove swamps to coastal ecosystems. NOM-022 established federal regulations such as barring construction within 100 meters of mangrove zones, except where necessary to restore the function of degraded mangrove zones and maintain the flow of fresh water to the open ocean from inland sources.[174] This policy had clear, positive implications for the management goals of the epistemic community, by restricting legitimate coastal construction.

Over the next four years, opponents of regulation made the removal of this policy into a top priority. After a spirited national campaign by neocorporatist hotelier associations and state governors, including (from Quintana Roo) ACLUVAC, APIR, Grupo Quintana Roo, and then governor Hendricks Díaz, Secretary Cárdenas added section 4.43 to NOM-022, stating that coastal construction and mangrove removal would be permitted, provided developers paid certain "compensation measures," generally measured as a one-time fine of MX$1,000 per hectare cleared, and received permission from the state government.[175]

If the goal was to inhibit the stripping of mangroves, this fine was thoroughly ineffective. Such an inconsequential sum functioned only to provide developers with an excuse for clearing mangrove zones and continuing development.[176] Martín Balám, a Quintana Roo environmental advocate and member of the NGO Simbiosis noted in a 2012 interview that "the problem is that many people prefer to pay fines, since those are the people with money." In addition, attempts to encourage hoteliers to adopt measures to provide municipal services for the spontaneously emerging "support communities," and to place a higher value on maintaining ecological integrity failed to take hold. Domínguez Calderón of CONANP noted that, despite the efforts of the conservationist community, hoteliers seemed to lack the will to invest in the necessary infrastructure for the surrounding low-income communities: "[Hoteliers] are supposed to come with a treatment plan and location for services, for the hotel as well as for communities that form, the support communities. But right now, the tourist developers are only thinking about investing in their own hotel."[177]

In response, the national mangrove network mobilized to call for the restoration of federal protection of mangrove zones. CEMDA, which had been campaigning since the early 2000s to protect local resources from overexploitation had already developed expertise in resisting the destruction of mangrove zones. For instance, in 2000, CEMDA successfully lobbied the Zedillo administration to halt the development of a salt plant proposed by Mitsubishi on San Ignacio Lagoon.[178] By 2004, CEMDA had joined other organizations from the mangrove network, like Greenpeace Mexico, in protests against the continued development of the hotel industry over mangrove zones.[179] That year, Greenpeace, CEMDA, and a "concerned citizens" group protested a visit by then president Fox to La Paz in Baja California Sur. The protestors, mobilized by the sale of 300 hectares of mangrove and apparent plans to construct a tourist complex at La Paz, greeted Fox with shouts of: "Fox, understand, the land is not for sale" ("Fox, entiende, la patria no se vende").[180] This network was clear that, as epistemic community documents argued in the MBRS, destruction of mangroves would lead to a series of highly problematic consequences for coastal residents: it would expose the coast to increased environmental damage, and—crucially—undermine the livelihoods of residents, particularly fishermen. In fact, David Martínez of SEDETUR pointed out that the link between the socioeconomic and environmental motives of different sectors of the anti-hotel movement was crucial in mobilizing resistance against massive tourism in Quintana Roo:

From the point of view that I have, the [resistance to large-scale hotels] does not follow motives that are strictly environmental. It comes from the tradition of the population that has always been fishermen, and that were taken by surprise by touristic activities ... it owes to the fact that they see the nature of the all-inclusive hotels, for example at the Riviera Maya. This is what happens: the tourist arrives, he enters the hotel, and he does not leave from there. So the people who are not investors, who don't have the kind of money to do this type of development say: "So if he arrives, he goes in the hotel, now I can't sell him water, I can't sell him a shirt, I can't sell him anything. So, better if they don't make any hotels."[181]

Thus, conservationists and local community organizations participated together in efforts to restore protection to mangrove zones as ecologically important to coastal resources, as well as critical to the well-being of low-income coastal communities. Federal protection was later restored in 2007 after a national campaign from the mangrove TAN led to congressional approval of federal Article 60 Ter of the LGVS, prohibiting "the removal, filling, transplant, cutting, or any work or activity that affects the integrity of the hydrological flow of the mangrove; of the ecosystem and its zone of influence; of its natural productivity; of the natural loading capacity of the ecosystem for touristic projects; of the zones of shelter, reproduction, refuge, feeding and fish fry."[182]

In Quintana Roo, this resulted in a halt of some of the planned and current development and construction throughout the state.[183] Unsurprisingly, hotelier associations and governors once again began a national campaign to repeal federal protection of mangrove zones. In 2007, Quintana Roo's then governor Felix González Canto led an association of sixteen governors from Baja California and other littoral states, requesting that Calderón's administration once again overturn Article 60 Ter. The hoteliers supported this effort, with Ángel Lemus making his argument about "eating mangrove,"[184] and claiming that Article 60 placed an excessive financial burden on the development potential of coastal states.[185] As Eloy Sosa noted, "[One] of the political processes that is trying deliberately to counter [Article 60 Ter] is the state government. ... It's not just me saying that, the *press* is saying that. The press has realized that there is a group of governors that is intending, let's say, to bend this law, or change this law, and among them is the very same governor [of Quintana Roo].[186] Similarly, Enrique Galvéz of SEMARNAT described a constant lobbying effort by hotel interests to the state and local governments to ease the regulatory burden on the construction of hotels: "[Now] there is the law of flora and wildlife, the [LGVS]. This law impedes the destruction of mangroves by the hotels. And the powerful businessmen are exerting pressure on the local government to give them permits to destroy the mangrove. So, there is a *very* direct conflict that SEMARNAT, and also PROFEPA, are confronting in this case."[187]

To date, Article 60 Ter remains intact. In fact, in 2008, a CONANP staffer based in the Puerto Morelos Protected Area was conducting a reef monitoring exercise from a small speedboat. He gestured at the shoreline of the Riviera Maya, indicating some construction that had been abandoned, or at least held in abeyance over several years. "The law," he said, "put a stop to some of that." However, it is clear that hoteliers are actively engaged in undermining the law, through legal means like lobbying, and quasi-legal ones where possible. For example, after Hurricane Dean struck the Yucatán Peninsula in 2007, large areas of coastal mangrove were destroyed along the coast of Quintana Roo, including at Majahual. By effectively clearing the mangrove, Hurricane Dean gave hoteliers the excuse they needed, and by April of 2008, infrastructural development like paved roads and hotels were already visible, and a passing observer could see how the new roads disrupted the hydrological flow of fresh water from mangrove zones.[188] During a 2012 field trip to monitor the health of mangrove zones in the swamps near Xcalak, Miguel Montalvo, a campesino and employee of Simbiosis decried the problem of illegal activity and its effects on coastal management. "What happens," he said, "is that they tell low-income people to be careful with the mangrove because they are destroying it, but then people with a lot of money disappear entire hectares of mangrove between nighttime and the morning. At least, that's how I see it."[189]

Hoteliers would also simply resort to corruption where necessary. As Adriana Yoloxóchitl Olivera, an environmental advocate and member of the epistemic community noted, hoteliers are demonstrably unconvinced by environmental arguments for conservation in the MBRS region. In describing the post–Hurricane Dean development and Majahual, she observed:

That area of Majahual, as I'm saying, was an area of pure mangrove. Well, where there would be mangroves, they are now filled and cut, filled with stone. And who cared? Who said anything? Sure, the scientists, but so what? They had said that the zone was very fragile, that there should be a zoning plan for minimal growth, low-impact ecotourism. ... In front of Majahual is the biggest reef in Mexico, the Mesoamerican reef. Part of the Mesoamerican reef. But it's not that [the hoteliers] don't know, it's that they don't care.[190]

After the 2012 elections, the fate of coastal mangrove protection became a little more uncertain. The PAN, which had created the environmental legislation that protected mangrove zones, lost the executive branch to the PRI in the same round of elections that saw former quintanarroense governor Félix González Canto elected to the senate. Moreover, Senator González Canto is at the time of writing president of the Federal Tourist Commission. As a result, Quintana Roo's mangrove zones are, according to environmentalists like Armando Elizalde, a diving instructor based in Quintana Roo, "under the jurisdiction of only one party across the board; municipal, state, and federal levels." As Elizalde suggests, "[T]here's no one to turn to for justice if you fall under the state's bull's eye." Further, the MBRS, which was scheduled to enter into a second phase of funding from the GEF and the World Bank has been delayed, due to the inability of the other three states of the basin to reach an agreement with Guatemala for continued regional cooperation. Without support from the GEF, advances in the MBRS Project are likely to remain delayed, and since opponents of federal regulation have now gained a political opportunity to reform Article 60 Ter, it is unclear how much longer the current system of protection will remain in place.

However, the network remains vigilant. In 2008, Greenpeace launched a protest against what they described as the "predatory model" of tourism sought by the state by unfurling a banner over the facade of the Secretariat of Tourism in the Federal District. In a public statement, Greenpeace condemned the fact that "the strategy and the only thing that the Secretariat of Tourism cares about is attracting investment, even at the cost of the important coastal ecosystems like mangroves or sand dunes, which generates strong ecological impacts."[191] At present, RedManglar and other actors in the network are also trying to pressure the federal government to extend additional protection over mangrove zones, by having them listed as "under danger of extinction" through the NOM-059 series of SEMAR-NAT. Thus, while the epistemic community was successful in influencing policy specific to the MBRS, the practical effects of its actions in conserving the region remain located within a broader national debate over mangrove zones and developmental policy.

Conclusion

This chapter supports the argument that socialization strengthens the ability of transnational networks to influence local implementation of biodiversity norms. Further, this chapter undermines the rationale for using neoliberal frames about national development to persuade political and economic actors to change their behavior. Instead, claims that resonate with the interests of local populations seem better suited to changing behavior by mobilizing constituents to challenge environmental policy as problematic on multiple fronts: ecological, social, political, and cultural.

As I have indicated, the epistemic community socialized extensively with federal environmental agencies, particularly CONANP and SEMAR-NAT. In response, these agencies adopted the PMS monitoring strategy and incorporated findings and parameters of the environmental problem as espoused by the network of scientists. CONANP had staffers participating as epistemic community members, gathering information and reports as part of a research network and sharing findings with civil society researchers including Los Amigos, WWF-México, TNC, and others. Similarly, CONAP-ESCA members and fishing cooperative members were also comprehensively socialized with the epistemic community. The fishing management workshops, for example, incorporated knowledge and capacity building exercises among epistemic community members, fishing policymakers in the federal government, and managers from various cooperatives. Like CONANP, CONAPESCA members conducted joint studies of reef environmental processes, although targeted more specifically at fish conservation rather than ecological management per se.

In addition, CONANP and SEMARNAT staffers, like Patricia Santos, described in interviews how the MBRS Project presented new ideas about the integration and interconnectivity of the basin, one of the core principles of the epistemic community. This supports arguments that socialization leads to a willingness of policymakers to accept the claims of the scientists and act accordingly. Santos said, "The MBRS project, to me, it seems like it fulfilled a primary attempt to understand the area, recognize how valuable this barrier reef is at the environmental level and to classify it. ... There are marine currents that come like so, from south to north, that implicate all the richness and biodiversity in this zone."[192]

However, nothing the epistemic community did seemed to matter to the interests of hoteliers or the state government. While the epistemic community members did not socialize with the state government in the same capacity as they did with the federal government, they certainly worked with the hotel industry through the MARTI initiative and the Normas Prácticas reports. Despite the scientific information produced by the epistemic community, hotel developers continued to demonstrate a total lack of interest in conserving coastal mangroves. Instead, hoteliers and the governor's office adamantly campaigned against new federal regulations in 2003, and again in 2007. As Enrique Galvez of SEMARNAT put it: "The mangrove bothers them, because it disturbs the hotel surroundings, or it bothers them because of the mosquitoes. The hotels want to be on the beach. They don't want to be inland. And so—and they want to invest as little as possible—the easiest thing to do, is fill the mangrove.[193]

As in Jamaica, the neoliberal arguments for conservation were not effective precisely because purely economic calculations privileged a perspective on management rooted in short-term, immediate exploitation. In

2008, Alfredo Arellano Guillermo described the challenges of convincing hoteliers to take a long-term view of costs and investment, clarifying the difference in perspectives: "Traditionally, in the case of tourism in coastal development in Mexico, the expectation of a return on investment among the major hotel developers, is a return in six, seven, eight years. In sustainable development, the plan for a return on investment of resources and benefits, we're talking about the long-term, possibly fifteen years. To the way of thinking of the investor, it's a notable difference."[194]

Further, in comments echoing Diana McCauley's observations of the bauxite industry in Jamaica, Yoloxóchitl observed that the economic development promised by this model of growth would benefit only a few, while bringing environmental vulnerability to many.

From the governor to the President of the Republic, they're going to accede to the pressure of businessmen, and put economic interests over the conservation of natural resources. Why? Because right now, apparently, it's better to have an economic gain. Apparently. But that economic gain only benefits very few people. The owners of the hotels, and some few employees that manage it. But the harm it's causing, that's what we're going to be seeing for the future.[195]

Instead, what mattered was the concerted political opposition against the repeal of mangrove protection. To be clear, the knowledge produced by the epistemic community was only one part of a broader universe of knowledge on the link between mangrove zones and coastal ecosystem health. As indicated throughout, local actors in Quintana Roo also held knowledge about the impact of fishing on their daily lives, as well as knowledge about how coastal ecosystems functioned—the relationship of fishermen to fish stocks, the location of fish breeding grounds, the presence of anthropogenic threats, and so on. This combination of scientific and lay knowledge linked ecosystem stability, coral reef health, and coastal integrity against tidal waves and storm energy with the socioeconomic well-being of marginalized populations. Further, since the national mass public, especially coastal residents, saw this connection as integral to life on the coast, NGOs, fishermen, and communities were willing to apply political pressure to state and federal governments to resist challenges by hoteliers and sympathetic state governments.

This difference in perspectives was crucial to epistemic community members in their explanations of why economic arguments did not resonate with hoteliers and pro-tourism state officials. In short, hotel investors and developers had the capacity to extract short-term economic profits quickly enough that the long-term costs of ecological degradation could be safely externalized to future populations of people who were either marginalized or geographically removed. It was not clear how economic logic could overcome the calculation that, as Merediz Alonso, channeling Milton Friedman, put it: "the director of a business has the obligation to seek a return on investment in the short term. That's why they get paid." In short, since large-scale hotel investors were not native to Quintana Roo, they could profit from overexploitation in the short term, while avoiding the long-term effects of environmental degradation. As Merediz Alonso explained in 2012:

Clearing coastal vegetation, which is something really cheap to do, is now making us lose beaches. So, we're spending hundreds of millions of dollars dragging sand from Isla Mujeres and Cozumel to support Cancún and Playa del Carmen. So, an action that was cheap ... has become a major expense for the Mexicans. Those who developed the hotels did their business and left. They sold their hotels, and are happy earning their money, and those who are paying for the broken plates are we, the Mexican taxpayers.[196]

These comments clarify the difficulty of using neoliberal and global capitalist markets for conservation in developing countries. Here, we see how neoliberalism, combined with the mobility of capital, has created a class of political and economic elites who can benefit from resource overexploitation. At the same time, this class is insulated, both politically and geographically, from the social, economic, and environmental effects of resource degradation. The fact that scientific advocacy, tied to local justice concerns about participation and tradition, managed to arrest this process, even if it is only temporary, is a small but notable triumph.

3 Mexico and Biodiversity in the Mesoamerican Biological Corridor

Introduction

Not every advocacy campaign ends in such success as seen in the MBRS Project in chapter 2 and the Cockpit Country project in chapter 1. In 2001, the Mexican government launched a regional project called the Proyecto para la Consolidación del Corredor Biológico Mesoamericano—México (Project for the Consolidation of the Mesoamerican Biological Corridor—Mexico, or CBMMx Project). This project, roughly concurrent with the MBRS efforts, was intended to conserve biodiversity in the peninsular states of Campeche, Yucatán, and Quintana Roo, and in Chiapas. However, whereas the networks involved in the MBRS and the Cockpit Country projects described earlier were successful in influencing the goals and conduct of biodiversity conservation, the network discussed here was less so. Key network goals in the CBMMx Project, like the cartographic definition of the area and control over project design and implementation were taken over by political interests to the dismay of the ecologists involved. Further, marginalized indigenous and campesino populations were initially alienated from the decision-making process, despite promises that the CBMMx Project leaders would strongly encourage local participation. In addition to undermining environmental goals, this frustrated local support so much that some of the communities targeted to receive financial support from the project began actively opposing it by 2007, convinced that it was part of a plan to grab indigenous land for a massive regional infrastructural project.

Why was this project comparatively more difficult for transnational networks to shape? One of the factors that explains why this campaign struggled where the others succeeded is that this network, unlike the others, could not generate an intersubjective consensus on the relevant cause-and-effect relationships between human activity and biodiversity in the region. As a result, the network was unable to present a unified argument about what was important to local biodiversity management, or even how to measure it. While it is difficult in the social sciences to argue why something did not occur, the argument in the epistemic community literature that networks without a knowledge consensus find advocacy more difficult seems borne out in this case.

This chapter also returns to the analysis of the effects of socialization and framing on advocacy. This network generated robust social ties with policymakers in targeted agencies. The network's inability to turn socialization into influence here thus suggests that socialization, if necessary, is an insufficient variable in predicting network success. In other words, it is not enough for networks to have ties to audience members in the policymaker sector if they do not agree on the science.

Further, network members and managers in the CBMMx Project advocated for the project by promoting economic valorization schemes that put a price on resource use. However, while network members emphasized that economic management should be carried out in such a way as to meet the needs of low-income and rural populations, project managers in state governmental agencies, particularly in Quintana Roo, were more interested in linking conservation to large-scale interests in the tourist industry. By 2008, network members felt that local governments had a limited and short-term view of biodiversity conservation in Mexican Mesoamerica. Rural residents in corridor zones were also critical of the project because of the apparent emphasis on turning resources to the interest of economic elites, and a problematic lack of participation by local populations. Without the interest or imagination to make low-income, rural populations more included in project design, managers in the CBMMx were not able to generate local support for this globally designed program. Without this support, the project was delayed, and was viewed with suspicion by precisely those people whom it was intended to help. This was particularly pronounced in *Chiapaneco* areas, where there is a history of antagonism with the state. By underplaying the importance of conservation to the marginalized, the implementation of the project was not oriented toward a management approach consonant with local justice.

This is not to say the project was an unambiguous failure. The CBMMx Project has provided funds to Mexico that have been successfully directed to projects in low-income campesino and indigenous communities in ways that have supported biodiversity conservation and brought benefits to the marginalized. Communities like Kantemó, a small village in the municipality of José María Morelos, have received technical training on biodiversity management and support for ecotourism infrastructure. After 2011, the CBMMx Project was extended to include Tabasco, a state that had previously been unable to receive corridor funds. However, at the local level, ecologists and community groups alike remain skeptical about the social and environmental achievements of the project as it is currently being implemented. These success stories, while admirable, are not representative of a broad level of local legitimacy of the CBMMx Project in Mesoamerica. This chapter thus presents one of several possible examples of the difficulties of transnational advocacy in the developing world.

The Mesoamerican region, part of a transboundary zone connecting seven Central American countries and the southern states of Mexico, is an internationally important site of endemism and biodiversity.[1] The Mexican section of the biological corridor is comprised largely of a karst limestone base, with low-lying wetlands in the states of Quintana Roo, dry forests in Campeche, rainforests in Yucatán state, and temperate mesophile forests in Chiapas.[2] Unique climatological and geomorphological features of this region, including frequent hurricanes, thin subsoil, a near absence of aboveground rivers, and millennia of evolution under these circumstances have contributed to the exceptional biodiversity characterizing the area.[3] Studies of the Yucatán Peninsula have found thousands of different species of plants and hundreds of mammals, birds, reptiles, and amphibians in the region, with as many as nine hundred different plant species and two hundred animal species per hectare, many of them endemic.[4]

However, despite the fact that the GEF and World Bank have officially designated the biological corridor as falling within a region delineated by maps published after 2001, this designation remains contested. In fact, at the time of writing, there are still stakeholders who differ about what the region entails. Scientists are critical about the lack of attention to biodiversity hotspots and ecological relationships, while local communities became increasingly suspicious about the willingness of project managers to respect local claims to traditional resource use. These contestations became a central point in debates about project management, as I will describe.

Land, Agriculture, and Environmental Justice in Mesoamerica

This biodiversity is subject to human pressure from various activities, as local communities, oil exploration, and agroindustry extract benefits from the exploitation of natural resources in the region. Agricultural activity—whether slash-and-burn agricultural cultivation among peasant and indigenous populations, mechanized and commercial agroindustry, or cattle farming—typically requires broad land conversion of pristine forest to monoculture crops, such as the popularly consumed chili peppers. Land clearance also further allows easier access for invasive and opportunist species, including fast-growth plants such as *guarumbo* (or *guarumo*), a tree cultivated by the Maya for its medicinal properties and used in making blowguns.[5]

But while agriculture is environmentally stressful, not all agriculture is equally so. Mechanized farming and cattle farming are problematic not only because of the scale of these operations, but also because they compete with traditional land needs of campesino and indigenous populations in rural Mesoamerica. Cattle farming is particularly harmful, as the thin topsoil and poor vegetative conditions in the Yucatán peninsula require an intensive use of resources, such as fertilizer, to create conditions propitious to cattle.[6] Moreover, cattle farming has had a high level of support from the federal government, which has, through the 1990s, provided subsidies to cattle ranchers for the expansion of farms throughout the Yucatán. After the neoliberal reforms of the early 1990s and Mexico's ratification of NAFTA, direct support for cattle farming declined. Instead, the Mexican government launched an agricultural support program called PROCAMPO, which gave funds to farmers for crop and feed production, which support cattle production indirectly. Since PROCAMPO was administered on the basis of landholding size, it ended up serving as a regressive subsidy, as larger landholders could receive more benefits from the federal government, exacerbating the divide between small and large farmers. Agroindustry and subsistence agriculture exacerbate problems associated with land clearance when practitioners, particularly large landholders, introduce chemical pesticides and biocides that accumulate as toxins in terrestrial and subterraneous aquatic ecosystems.[7]

The neoliberal reforms of the 1990s had another effect on land tenure and equity in Mexico. In 1992, on the path to joining both NAFTA and the nascent WTO (World Trade Organization), Mexico reformed Article 27 of the Constitution to allow *ejidatarios* (holders of communal land, or *ejidos*) to parcelize and sell their land to non-ejido residents. Intended to rationalize land holding and alleviate regulatory pressure on the state, this reform had a mixed impact on ownership rights and *ejidatario* autonomy.[8] Among some ejidos, like those in Tulúm, residents parcelized their land in order to resist suspected government intervention and strengthen local land claims. However, in other ejidos, residents sold land to private buyers for sums that may have seemed large to low-income, agrarian communities, but were far below what ended up being the market value of these properties. In Buenavista, for instance, ejidatarios sold waterfront land to developers for US$600 per hectare that, ten years later, was worth US$140,000 per hectare.[9] In order to explain how low-income landowners could be persuaded to part with viable communally held land, Ulyses Huesca of the National Commission for the Study and Use of Biodiversity (Comisión Nacional para el Conocimiento y Uso de la Biodiversidad, or CONABIO) told the following story in 2011:

Sometimes what happens is that the landowners are men of seventy, eighty years, of ill health, and with children that don't want to work the land. The children of ejidatarios feel like their parents have lost all spirit over the past twenty, thirty years, and they can't see how to improve their economy, so because of this, they don't want to do what their parents did. ... Here is where the investor arrives and says, "I'll buy it." ... In some places, ejidal rights to forty hectares can cost 100,000 or 150,000 pesos, and that for an investor, is nothing.

Once I had to go do a study in Playa del Carmen, because they were going to construct some development. When I got there, the person they carried me to, to show me the land, was a man living in the front in a shack. So I went, and the *señor* said, yes, he was the one that was going to take me to see the land, the forest, and the animals, and while I was walking with him and chatting, I was questioning him. I asked him why he had sold the land, and he answered that now he was old, and that before he used to sow maize and owned sheep, but now he can't manage all that. And the people that wanted to buy the land offered him 500,000 pesos, which for them was not much money, as I was saying. This money, you know is nothing, because you know the cost of living, but for them that live in their small world, it looks like a lot of money, an immensity, and that's why they sell.

To be fair, parcelization could occasionally strengthen land claims of some marginalized groups. For example, Hamilton showed that in some ejidos, women were able to gain more control over land use postreform, if their surrounding community recognized that women could contribute to the local economy.[10] The fact that neoliberal reforms empowered some women in those cases indicates that neoliberalism does not always exacerbate inequities along gender or other lines. Nevertheless, the land reform has created additional vulnerabilities for marginalized populations, since the reforms provided a mechanism through which political-economic elites can capture land for large-scale developmental projects. As indicated earlier, this socioeconomic vulnerability is linked to growing ecological threats.

There are additional challenges that emerge from agricultural and other uses. Land conversion and loss of forests for agriculture and logging also contribute to regional forest fires. Degraded and poorly managed forests tend to accumulate flammable debris, including discarded twigs and shrubbery, which exacerbates the propensity of the spread of fires. This process is in turn worsened by the prevalence of slash-and-burn production among rural populations.[11] Since 2005, the Mesoamerican states of Quintana Roo, Chiapas, and Oaxaca have been three of the top nineteen states in the country affected by forest fires.[12]

Unsustainable logging for firewood and timber production also contributes to biodiversity loss. Timber production tends to be concentrated on a few commercially viable species, such as mahogany and cedar, which are produced for the tourist market and subsequently overharvested. By depleting these species, rural populations can degrade the regenerative capacity of the limestone jungle.[13] Moreover, the demand for these timber products creates incentives for rural populations to develop tree plantations in jungle areas, which has caused problems due to the introduction of invasives in sensitive ecosystems.[14] Hunting for subsistence consumption or for sport among different sectors of the peninsular population may also become problematic if unregulated, particularly when endangered species are targeted.

However, the most significant sources of environmental degradation are industrial in origin. The construction of roads and high-speed throughways in jungle areas causes environmental stress by fragmenting ecosystems and interrupting migratory patterns of land-based fauna.[15] Incidental pollution from vehicle emissions negatively affects the immediate environment of sensitive flora by contributing to the accumulation of toxins in plants. Oil spills and other resultant pollution from petroleum extraction are significant threats to environmental integrity. In fact, until the Deepwater Horizon disaster, the biggest peacetime oil spill occurred under Mexican jurisdiction, when the Ixtoc I well run by the state-run industry PEMEX exploded off the coast of Campeche state, eventually spilling over three million barrels into the Gulf of Mexico.[16] Currently, oil exploration still takes place throughout the states in Mesoamerica, namely Tabasco, Campeche, and Veracruz, creating problems when the toxic material is spilled, or when heavy machinery emits incidental air pollution.[17]

The idea that these ecological threats are a necessary part of "national development" should be questioned. As in Jamaica with bauxite production, the practices of the most heavily supported economic activities worsen, rather than improve, the environmental and economic security of marginalized populations. The disruption caused by mining and drilling for oil can impel the displacement of rural communities, who then migrate and contribute to more extensive patterns of resource use and environmental degradation. In addition, subsidized cattle farming, while ostensibly aimed at improving the livelihoods of agrarian populations in the Yucatán, fractures ecosystems by converting large areas to monocultural pasturelands, and economically displaces traditional and subsistence agricultural practices.[18] Thus, ecological harm is facilitated by a system that also contributes to marginalization of the most vulnerable, or, as Pellow put it: "the exploitation of humans and the environment is a unified practice."[19]

A variety of actors among state and federal agencies are responsible for managing these competing interests. One of the primary agencies in the context of this project, and one targeted in project campaigns, is CONABIO. CONABIO is an intersectorial commission created under the federal government in 1993 with the overarching mandate of coordinating biodiversity management and helping Mexico implement the CBD.[20] CONABIO carries out activities such as conducting inventories of national biodiversity stocks and assessments of the impact of human activity on natural resources, and since 1997 has been delegated as the agency responsible for designing the National Biodiversity Strategy and Action Plan (NBSAP), required by states as signatories to the CBD.[21] When the CBMMx Project was launched, CONABIO was the agency assigned responsibility for disbursing funds for local projects and activities in the areas identified as part of the constituent corridors.[22] Indeed, as described later, CONABIO was a gatekeeper agency in determining which zones would be included as areas covered by the CBMMx Project, and hence subject to GEF funds.

In addition to CONABIO, individual federal agencies participating in natural resource management include SEMARNAT, the Comisión Nacional Forestal (National Forestry Commission, or CONAFOR) and SAGARPA. As described in chapter 2, SEMARNAT's executive agency in CONANP monitors environmental processes in protected areas, including in those near to corridor zones.[23] SAGARPA provides federal resources, such as funds, subsidies, and development permits to states and municipalities for agriculturally based development.[24] CONAFOR, created in 2001, is an administrative agency of SEMARNAT and manages forestry resources, including restoration and conservation activities in corridor zones.[25]

Corridor management also impacts on indigenous rights issues, as the majority of the population of corridor zones in Quintana Roo, Chiapas, and Campeche is indigenous. Most of the land within these zones are organized into ejidos, or communally owned agrarian areas, wherein the low-income population is highly dependent on subsistence and commercial agriculture.[26] In these areas, the Comisión Nacional para el Desarrollo de los Pueblos Indígenas (National Commission for the Development of Indigenous Peoples, or CDI), a federal agency created in 2003, promotes economically oriented projects and activities such as agricultural and artisanal practices.[27] In addition, CDI assists in legal advocacy for indigenous communities, particularly in Chiapas, where ejidos often lack official documentation, don't have legal recognition of land ownership, and are at risk of land appropriation and dispossession.[28] The CDI, however, does not participate formally in the project, but rather acts in an advisory role to SEMARNAT and other land-use management agencies in the state and federal government.

Transnational Mobilization around the Mesoamerican Biological Corridors

The movement toward managing Mesoamerica as interlinked biological corridors began in the industrialized world before turning into a global program involving stakeholders at multiple levels. In the late 1960s, researchers like Harvard biologist E. O. Wilson began rethinking existing approaches to conservation. Wilson and others argued that the ability of species of fauna and flora to thrive depended not only on creating isolated zones of protection, but also on creating additional areas that respected the roaming and migrating habits of vulnerable species. Even when species are placed on protected reserves, fauna and flora become more vulnerable to threats, degradation, and predators if their protected habitat is too small. Consequently, when protected areas are established, care has to be taken to ensure that they do not fragment ecosystems into tiny islands of biodiversity, but that they permit the free movement of migratory species in what were called "biological corridors."[29]

In the 1980s, international wildlife specialists from the University of Florida and the Wildlife Conservation Society (WCS) observed that ecosystem fragmentation was a common problem in protected areas management in Mesoamerica.[30] Concerned about the conservation of migratory species, WCS headed a coalition of actors in 1989 to advocate for more effective management under a project called the Path of the Panther, or Paseo Pantera. The Paseo Pantera, which relied on the biological corridor concepts described by Wilson and contemporary researchers like Reed Noss of the University of Florida, would have been a regional biological corridor between Mexico and Panama. It would allow comparatively safe passage for migratory wildlife between already established protected areas and preserves by regulating human activity in crucial transit zones.[31] Within Mexico, some of the areas identified as important to biodiversity management included the Biosphere Reserve of Calakmul, near the border of Guatemala.[32]

In the early 1990s, the same political opportunity structure that led to regional cooperation for the MBRS Project also provided fertile political ground for a regional biodiversity project in inland Mesoamerica. In the buildup to the 1992 Rio UN Conference on Environment and Development (UNCED), the Central American states and Mexico endorsed the idea of multilateral environmental management through a variety of forums and conventions supported by international institutions including the Central American Commission for Development (CCAD).[33] Although Mexico was not a full member of CCAD, its transboundary forest zone with Guatemala, known as the Mayan Jungle, or Selva Maya, made it essential to the goal of biodiversity management in the region.[34]

In 1993, at the first International Wildlife Management Congress, CCAD, and Mexico discussed ways in which they could improve the regional management of biodiversity. Here, experts on biological corridors, including Dr. Reed Noss who was attending, recommended the adoption of biological corridors in Mesoamerica.[35] In February 1996, the CCAD states and Mexico met at the second intergovernmental Tuxtla Summit (Tuxtla II) in

Costa Rica, and agreed to adopt a project to conserve biological corridors in a statement titled the "Mechanism of Dialogue and Concertation."[36] The Mexican component of this project was the CBMMx Project. After 1996, the government of Mexico began requesting information and research on regional biodiversity from local and transnational experts on biological corridors and on biodiversity in Mesoamerica.[37]

After the Mexican government endorsed the CBMMx Project in 1996, CONABIO took the lead in building a knowledge network with the necessary expertise to design an appropriate response to this international goal. CONABIO was well suited to this task due to its history of working with civil society research organizations in Mesoamerica. For example, when CONABIO began drafting Mexico's NBSAP, the agency recruited over 125 organizations from institutions at a variety of different levels.[38] These included locally active groups Los Amigos de Sian Ka'an, Yum Balám, and Econcienca; regionally active organizations Pronatura and Simbiosis; and transnational environmental NGOs Conservation International, The Nature Conservancy (TNC), and the World Wildlife Fund for Nature (WWF). Further, CONABIO paid for research from academic institutions, like the Intercultural Mayan University of Quintana Roo, the University of Quintana Roo (UQROO), El Colegio de la Frontera Sur (ECOSUR), and the National Autonomous University of Mexico (UNAM) when their purposes overlapped with CONABIO's mandate.[39]

By the late 1990s, these groups had become involved in conducting research on Mesoamerican biodiversity by, among other things, promoting nutrition and health among rural communities in the Yucatán through traditional medicine; monitoring pollution in sensitive ecosystems; and educating local communities about the legal framework of natural resource exploitation.[40] Thus, when CONABIO began holding workshops on the CBMMx Project in 1998, it had tapped into a well-developed conservation network. In Chiapas and Quintana Roo, CONABIO met with environmental NGOs and institutions such as ECOSUR, Pronatura, Los Amigos, and Conservation International.[41] In 1999, CONABIO held an additional workshop in Cancún, with participants from UQROO, UNAM, ECOSUR, and foreign institutions like Oxford University, the University of Central Florida, and the California Academy of Sciences.[42]

One of the outcomes of these workshops was an agreement by CONABIO, the civil society, and the academic organizations to have project management focus on changing behavior in the ejidos of the Yucatán since they were physically closer to the biodiversity that the conservationists identified as globally important.[43] By including ejidos in management, the network hoped to strengthen other elements of conservation, like the identification and siting of ecologically important areas, appropriate regulations, and an appropriate monitoring strategy.

To be clear, the inclusion of indigenous people and ejidatarios did not emerge purely out of the social conscience of the CBMMx Project's planners. In 1998, a transnational group of rural indigenous and campesino communities called the Asociación Coordinadora Indígena y Campesina de Agroforestería Comunitaria Centroamericana (ACICAFOC) launched a counterproposal to the approach derived from the Paseo Pantera.[44] This counterproposal highlighted a growing concern among members of ACICAFOC that the project, as planned, would further disenfranchise marginalized groups by preventing them from using the land in the interest of some global conception of biodiversity.[45] Asserting that indigenous groups should be included in project design, and worried about the possibility of externally driven fortress-style conservation, the group "demanded a conceptual expansion of the [Mesoamerican Biological Corridor] from conservation to a more inclusive vision of sustainable development, which would include all the Central American peoples and cultures depending upon natural resources for their survival."[46] After this pressure, CCAD agreed to include a component in the Mesoamerican Biological Corridor to address the "social and productive" elements of conservation in Mesoamerica. At the 1999 Cancún workshop, CONABIO finalized the Mexican areas chosen in project proposal for the CBMMx Project, and submitted it to the GEF.[47]

By this time, this informal network that consisted of federal agencies, civil society actors, and academics had expanded into a transnational advocacy network. Researchers shared a common policy enterprise, namely the development of managed biological corridors in Mesoamerica, based on their understanding of the important ecological relationships in the area, and built on information exchanges and a shared approach developed after the Paseo Pantera project.[48] After 2000, other organizations joined in the production of policy relevant knowledge, of which a partial list is given in table 3.1. This network, like the MBRS Project epistemic community described in chapter 2, was substantially larger than the table indicates, and a conservative estimate would put the figure at 70 to 120 members. The

Table 3.1
Partial list of TAN organizations

Organization	Individuals	Functions	Science training
Simbiosis SA de CV	Martín Balám	Ecosystem monitoring. Habitat health evaluation. Project development in corridor ejidos.	Biology
	María Luisa Villarreal Sonora	Ecosystem monitoring. Habitat health evaluation. Project development in corridor ejidos.	Biology
Los Amigos de Sian Ka'an	Various	Population monitoring (fauna and flora). Biodiversity monitoring. Project development in ejidos.	Various
The Nature Conservancy	Various	Population monitoring of fauna	Ecology
Conservation International	Various	Project development in corridor ejidos	Various
University of Florida	Reed Noss	Research on biological corridors	Conservation biology
Wildlife Conservation Society	Jim Barborak	Research on biological corridors	Conservation biology
Yum Balám	Various	Project development in corridor ejidos. Monitoring.	Various
Pronatura A.C.	Various	Project development in corridor ejidos. Monitoring.	Various
Econciencia A.C.	Arturo Bayona	Project development in corridor ejidos.	Biology
UQROO	Benito Presas	Population monitoring of fauna and flora. Ecosystem monitoring. Human impact studies.	Biology
	Alberto Perreira	Population monitoring of fauna and flora	Biology
	María Magdalena Vásquez	Population monitoring of fauna, arthropods, mites	Biology
ECOSUR	Various	Population monitoring of fauna, arthropods, mites. Ecosystem monitoring. Human impact studies.	Primarily biology
UNAM	Various	Population monitoring of fauna, arthropods, mites. Ecosystem monitoring. Human impact studies.	Various

CBMMx Project was officially launched in 2000 with the signatures of the World Bank and the government of Mexico.

Like the MBRS network, this TAN sustained itself through a variety of different processes, including shared research, meetings, and other forms of intergroup socialization. CONABIO and the federal government strengthened network ties by requiring member organizations to participate in institutions like state-level advisory councils called Consejos Consultivos Estatales, or CCEs. The CCEs were created to identify areas critical for biodiversity management, evaluate funding requests for conservation pilot projects, and recommend appropriate environmental regulations and zoning policies in corridor zones.[49] Each CCE was staffed by civil society actors from organizations like Pronatura, Econciencia, and the Intercultural Mayan University of Quintana Roo, as well as by state government representatives.[50] The CCEs held several, albeit irregular, meetings a year in each state once the project was officially launched. Since the federal government was in charge of implementing biodiversity, CONABIO held additional annual meetings with federal agencies in environment and agriculture, as well as with TAN member organizations, such as Los Amigos and WWF-México.[51]

Before discussing advocacy and policy preferences, I will note differences between this network and the epistemic communities discussed in the previous two chapters. In contrast to those two cases, the network discussed here did not manage to agree on the science behind human activity and biodiversity loss in the CBMMx Project. Moreover, project stakeholders were well aware that the scientific consensus was not there. For example, a project document produced for the World Bank in 2000 noted that "there is no unified scientific agreement regarding the role of corridors to combine genetic, demographic, and other forces threatening small populations nor is there accord on the relative importance of these threats."[52] Three years into the project in 2004, a technical evaluation of the CBMMx Project similarly observed, "[T]here is still no established baseline [of information]."[53] The evaluation went on: "[T]here are absolutely no shared criteria about the geographic demarcation definition, there are no shared geophysical, nor political-administrative, nor biological, nor ecological, nor land ownership criteria."[54]

As these quotes indicate, a general interest among various stakeholders in conserving biological corridors was complicated by a lack of shared scientific understanding. In fact, the lack of consensus on science reflects the fact that academic researchers disagreed about what comprised important biodiversity and how to measure it. As researcher Felipe Serrano of ECOSUR noted in an office interview in 2008: "A researcher from ECOSUR can have an opinion about the state of biodiversity in some region, or state, and it's not necessarily the same opinion as that of a researcher from a national university. And this has happened, it's happening constantly."[55]

Without a knowledge consensus, this network cannot be considered an epistemic community. This affects expectations of the network's ability to influence policy, since the epistemic community literature suggests that networks with lower levels of scientific agreement have a harder time shaping management. I argue here that the lack of consensus did negatively affect the network's ability to influence policy in some key areas of the advocacy campaign. However, the lack of consensus was not the only determinant of the network's successes and difficulties in this case of transnational advocacy. As I have argued throughout, network influence also depends on the ability of networks to socialize with target audiences and use appropriate framing tools. In order to understand how these affect influence, and at what levels of governance (that is, local, federal, or international), I will examine these characteristics as well.

Formally, the network established strong social ties with policymakers in the federal government, and in particular with CONABIO. To administer the CBMMx Project, the Mexican government established an agency under CONABIO called the National Technical Unit, responsible for drafting annual Plans of Action. In these plans, the National Unit assesses the status of project implementation, makes recommendations for subprojects, issues funds for the purchase of equipment, and conducts progress reports for the World Bank.[56]

Subordinate to the National Unit are two regionally based organizations called Regional Technical Units, organized such that one is responsible for all the peninsular states of Quintana Roo, Campeche, and Yucatán, and the other for Chiapas. These Regional Units work with the aforementioned state-level CCEs, which in addition to serving as sites of information exchange between TAN members, are staffed by governmental representatives at all levels; municipal, state, and federal. Finally, the locally generated policy recommendations are transmitted back to the central administrating body, CONABIO, after being revised by a national supervisory agency called the Consejo Consultivo Nacional or CCN.[57] The CCN, which provides federal oversight of the project, is constituted of federal agencies from the secretariats of environment (SEMARNAT), agriculture (SAGARPA), social development (SEDESOL), transport (SCT), agrarian reform (SRA), education (SEP), health (SSA), and trade (SECOFI), all of which had formally pledged to collaborate in environmental management.[58] Thus, socialization was a formal requirement of the CBMMx Project.

Through these myriad agencies, civil society organizations in the TAN are socialized with policymakers in generating biodiversity-relevant knowledge at each level: at the federal level with CONABIO and the CCN; at the regional level with the UTRs; and at the state level with the CCEs. Both the federally-oriented CCN and the state-based CCEs have formally established seats for civil society actors to participate in project design. On the CCN, members of the transnational organization WWF and faculty members from UNAM and ECOSUR were officially recognized as participants. At the regional level, the UTRs of Chiapas and the Yucatán Peninsula held a series of knowledge-generating workshops between 2005 and 2009 with locally recognized ENGOs and academics to assist in designing locally relevant projects for biodiversity management.[59] These workshops also included plans to train community residents and local leaders to fulfill the goals of the project, including by acting as tour guides and marketing products to the commercial sector.

Moreover, the civil society was encouraged to participate in the goals of the CBMMx Project, particularly in the design of biodiversity management projects. TAN organizations such as Simbiosis, Econciencia, and Pronatura, and others with locally relevant knowledge, could submit requests to support activities such as ecotourism, artisanal development, and sustainable agriculture in corridor zones. Occasionally, network members worked directly with federal policymakers rather than through the CBMMx Project. For example, SEMARNAT, which sought to rationalize ecological zoning through the implementation of subsidized wildlife management units (UMAs), participated in information-gathering seminars with TAN members from Simbiosis, Pronatura, UNAM, ECOSUR, and UQROO, as well as with state environmental agencies.[60] In another example, in 2005, Econciencia worked with CDI to create an ecotourism project in the rural ejido of Kantemó, one of the areas identified as relevant to biological corridor management.[61] Through these various linkages, the network had a robust political opportunity structure through which it could disseminate ideas about conservation and corridor management.

As the network began arguing for new a biodiversity management approach in Mesoamerica, members deliberately emphasized the economic rationale for conservation. They adopted this approach out of what they saw as a necessity in alleviating concerns Mexican policymakers had about international pressure for local conservation in the early 1990s. After the WCS coalition launched the Paseo Pantera initiative, the participating governments in the 1996 Tuxtla II Summit opposed what they saw as a drive for a preservationist, or "no-access" regime of protected areas in the region. Preservationism, they argued, would result in a loss of political support for conservation, as marginalized constituencies (and hence policymakers) would adamantly resist any regulations that prevented the economic exploitation of natural resources.[62] Local communities in particular were worried that this biodiversity-oriented project was insufficiently attuned to their local needs, and would result in expropriation of their land for the benefit of outside actors, as seen in the ACICAFOC campaign.[63] Dzahuindanda Flores, coordinator of a state-level subcommittee of SAGARPA, summarized the concerns held by marginalized communities and their sympathizers about conservation by saying in an interview in 2008, "the problem is one of development." Flores went on: "How can we provide for the people that live in these communities? We can't say to them, 'don't sow, don't cultivate, don't work,' because then they'll tell us, 'ok, then give me something to eat.' We can't do that. But at the same time, we have to correctly manage the resources.[64]

Miguel Montalvo, a resident of an *ejido* in Othón P. Blanco municipality made a similar observation in an interview in 2012. Capturing the tension between the need to conserve natural resources and provide for the well-being of rural populations, Montalvo said: "How are the people in the country going to live? The people sow their corn. They live from this, and the land. The government says 'don't touch,' and if they don't, they have no work—the *campesino* has no work in the city. So what I think is that if the *campesino* can't cut trees, then he can't sow, and if he can't sow, he can't live, so then he has to rob. The way I see it, this is no solution."[65]

Admittedly, the initial Paseo Pantera proposals had, as described by a 2007 review from López and Jímenez from the National University of Costa Rica, "a very strong protectionist-conservationist view."[66] In responding to these concerns, the conservationist network supporting the CBM's push argued that conservation was indeed compatible with development, if policymakers just realized the economic value of natural resources. In 2001, Jim Barborak of WCS, Kenton Miller, and others of the World Resources Institute, and researchers from Mexico's UNAM attended the Congress of the Mesoamerican Society for Biology and Conservation with members from policymaker agencies like SEMARNAT and SAGARPA. At this meeting, Barborak used Miller and the WRI's research to argue that ecological conservation and biological corridor management, if conducted according to scientific knowledge, could improve the socioeconomic well-being of agrarian populations by promoting commercial activities among marginalized and poor populations. Further, since the project would depend on formally recognizing land ownership patterns, incorporating local communities into corridor management could strengthen land tenure claims, particularly among indigenous societies.[67] As a result, conservation could both improve local biodiversity and, as Barborak proposed, "strengthen democratic governance and make possible the participation of the civil society" in determining land use.[68]

However, while there were some economic arguments about the benefits of conservation, it was clear that not all economic activities were compatible with sustainable biodiversity management. For example, while the World Bank documents noted that conservation could help by "increasing economic viability for the diversified and ecologically sustainable Mayan rural economy,"[69] the report from López and Jímenez observed that large industrial practices, like logging and agroindustry, were irreconcilable with both conservation and local autonomy.[70]

In any case, the managers of the project, including the CCAD and the governments of the involved countries, began designing their response to the CBMMx Project initiative to elucidate the economic benefits of conservation. In 2002, the CCAD commissioned Radoslav Barzev of Nicaragua to carry out the first of several economic valorizations of biodiversity management in corridor zones. These valorizations were supposed to be a tool to help policymakers and local populations understand the connection between biodiversity loss and socioeconomic problems by assessing prices of services provided by functional ecosystems.[71] For example, Barzev's valorization argued the following: The underlying causes of biodiversity loss lay in the failure of the market to recognize the economic value of natural resources, a problem widespread among "thousands of individuals acting in a decentralized manner in diverse points."[72] The impacts of biodiversity loss were economic, consisting of the loss of goods such as potable water, tourism, and artisan goods, and ecosystem damage in commercially important zones.[73] Finally, the appropriate policies relevant to the CBM and corridor management were those that acted as a "catalyst for sustainable development," both for local communities and for national economic development.[74] This line of arguments also fits with a 2001 WRI study that used a developmental approach, one focused on property rights and market mechanisms, as a strategy for managing the CBMMx Project.[75] In fairness to the WRI, this study also noted that biodiversity conservation could provide "spiritual" values, but emphasized the use of payment for ecosystem services, a neoliberal mechanism, to encourage conservation.

The Mexican state and federal governments responded positively to the CCAD and network's arguments that biodiversity conservation could be seen as an economic activity. Problematically, the way in which the governments framed the discussion of economics and conservation was based on a developmental model attuned to the interests of prominent economic actors. After the CBMMx Project started, the state governments began including references to corridor management in their sexennial development plans by linking the goals of the CBMMx Project with major economic activities. For example, the Quintana Roo state government drew several connections between the potential importance of sustainable biodiversity to prominent industries, especially to tourism in the Riviera Maya and the foreign export market.[76] Linking conservation to tourism was particularly important since the state government saw tourism as "the axis around which the economy of the state revolves."[77] In their development plans, the state government argued that conserved landscapes inland could serve to diversify the tourist market, sell carbon credits, and produce artisanal goods for sale in the centers of Cancún and other parts of the Riviera Maya.

Certainly, low-income residents can derive much-needed economic revenue from using natural resources and biodiversity. For this reason, the argument that biodiversity conservation can provide economic goods does not necessarily lead to practices that alienate low-income and marginalized communities. But, as scholars of Mesoamerica like Grandia have noted, that depends on careful attention being paid to the scale of economic activity in which biodiversity use is located.[78]

As I argued in chapter 2, marginalized groups are too often not fully incorporated into the benefits of all developmental projects, and may even be further disenfranchised by them. I argued that large-scale tourism, while bringing millions of dollars in foreign revenue to Mexico, fails to share the bulk of its revenue with the fishermen and coastal communities that are displaced by the socioeconomic and geographic changes occasioned by the industry. This supports other studies on Fiji,[79] Ecuador,[80] and elsewhere in Mexico,[81] as well as chapter 1 on Jamaica. In short, the literature on comparative environmental politics is rife with examples showing how large-scale neoliberal programs can generate economic profits, but in a tremendously inequitable way. Nevertheless, it was clear to the local NGOs within the network that, if they wanted to participate in the project, they would have to speak the language of economics chosen by the state. As a result, some NGOs began emphasizing the economic justification for conservation even more—in the case of Simbiosis, reinventing themselves as a business in order to appeal to policymakers:

I don't need to tell you what the government thinks about NGOs. We went to the corridor meetings, and we said, "You have to conserve the forest, and do so legally and sustainably," and they said, "Yeah, yeah, it's those treehugger NGOs again." ... And so we said, "We're going to get certified as a business." And as a business, the next meeting we had with the government was incredible. We arrived, and "Oh, it's those NGOs again." "No, no, no," we said, "We're a business. We're certified as a business." "Business? Oh, perfect." ... And with this in mind, we said we'd better continue presenting ourselves as a business rather than as an NGO.[82]

Advocacy in the Corridors: Success and Failure

The advocacy network did have some success in shaping behavior in zones covered by the CBMMx Project. This success emerged largely through multisectoral efforts between civil society NGOs and political institutions involved in the project, like CONABIO, SEMARNAT, and SAGARPA. As I indicated, the CBMMx Project focused on improving environmental practices in ejidos, identified as the relevant focal areas for project efforts. At the same time, some of the most serious threats to biodiversity were not addressed, because of the immense political support behind them. Cattle farming lost importance as a threat to biodiversity, largely because after the implementation of NAFTA, and the 2000 change in the administration of the federal government, SAGARPA recognized that the thin subsoil and poor plant conditions in the region were simply incompatible with the needs of cattle farming, and thus did not merit additional federal subsidies.[83] Despite universal recognition that oil exploration was tremendously ecologically harmful, no one in the advocacy campaign wanted to tackle the sector. Ulyses Huesca, a member of CONABIO based in Yucatán state succinctly observed that "criticizing PEMEX is like criticizing the Bible, or something like that, right?" This is a particularly telling metaphor in overwhelmingly Catholic Mexico.

Nevertheless, civil society agencies actively promoted new projects in ejidos and rural communities in order to persuade inhabitants that their local economic development would be served best by conservation. These projects focused on small-scale activities in rural communities. To enhance the incentives to change local behavior, they worked with state and federal agencies to access funds and subsidies for new activities, and get support to expand the available market access for sustainably produced goods. These included a project by Econciencia to promote ecotourism in the ejido of Kantemó, where visitors can take a short bicycle ride to a subterranean cave inhabited by dangling, bat-eating serpents. Other projects included a range of artisanal, hunting, agricultural, and tourism projects by NGOs active in the peninsula, like Simbiosis, Yum Balám, and Los Amigos.

Network members admitted that the continued emphasis on the economic benefits of conservation was problematic. "What is needed," said Arturo Bayona of Econciencia, "is a discourse of the soul, rather than of the economy." However, Bayona admitted "at the end of the day, the people are carrying out these projects for economics." He added, "And yes, we can speak about the importance of the environment. That could be a second point. But we know very well that if we don't do it like this, if you don't have [the economic argument], you won't have [environmental management]."[84]

Similarly, María Magdalena of UQROO noted in 2008 that the economic arguments and the distribution of funds for conservation were key in getting local buy-in to the goals of the CBMMx Project: "There are communities here in Quintana Roo that receive some economic support in order to stop them cutting trees down. This support allows them to develop other activities that, at the same time, conserves—activities that are related to the conservation of the forest. In other words, like they're paying the peasants to care for the forest. Well, they have to do it this way, because the peasants don't understand the value of conserving the forest."[85]

It seems a little unfair to accuse rural peasants of "not understanding" the value of the forest, particularly since (despite its problems) peasant and subsistence agriculture is not as serious a threat to biodiversity as oil, cattle, or tourism. Moreover, unlike the actors responsible for those processes, the rural marginalized are more vulnerable to harmful changes in local ecosystems. What this observation suggested is that, after the project began, there were still elements within the scientific network that were skeptical about the use of economic arguments—even those aimed at the interest of low-income populations—as a justification for conservation. Further, drawing an implicit boundary between what rural inhabitants "understand" about conservation and scientific knowledge illustrates how conservationists distinguished between expert knowledge, produced formally, and the embodied knowledge of the lay population.

This is not to say that the economic arguments for conservation or the focus on changing rural behavior were fruitless. After the CBMMx Project was launched, there were some positive changes in behavior among Mexican actors toward biodiversity conservation. Governmental agencies involved in the CBMMx Project were willing to support new initiatives launched by network organizations in corridor zones. Some of these required new outlays and regulatory changes by policymakers. In Quintana Roo, SAGARPA, SEMARNAT, and CONAFOR provided funds for sustainable agricultural development in focal area ejidos within the Sian Ka'an-Calakmul corridor in 2005.[86] In Campeche, these agencies also ran a series of information and awareness-building workshops in ejidal focal areas, to foster local support for government-directed sustainable use projects, as well as to evaluate ecological zoning under the POET system.[87] The federal government through SAGARPA and SEMARNAT approved an ecological certification program to generate market demand for sustainably produced goods in foreign markets.[88]

In 2007, CONABIO and the UTN published a catalog of commodities and services produced in corridor zones for promotion in regional markets.[89] Between 2006 and 2008, the UTR-Chiapas and the UTR-Peninsula participated in a variety of forums linking the CBMMx Project with lucrative markets. These included one held in Chiapas on international tourism in 2006, and one in 2007 between producers of corridor commodities and tourist conglomerates in the Riviera Maya.[90] As indicated, these were oriented around the idea that conservation could become a "win-win-win" strategy, if the economic power of tourism was directed toward sustainable management practices that would be good for indigenous groups, developmental interests, and conservationists alike. At the same time, not all efforts were linked to economic projects. For fire management, federal agents in the National Forestry Commission (CONAFOR) assisted in the creation of forest fire management teams in ejidos in Chiapas and Campeche.[91] All of these projects indicated that state and federal agencies were willing to adopt new practices in response to new information produced by network members. Throughout the Yucatán, for instance, the federal government through SEMARNAT and CONABIO helped local honey producers in communities like Xmaben, Campeche, gain access to organic certification and markets in foreign countries.

However, while state and federal agencies carried out some of the conservationist recommendations under the CBMMx Project, the Mexican government also took steps that undermined the goals of the advocacy campaign. Given the mandate of the GEF project—direct international funds and knowledge to change local behavior in key areas—one of the primary issues that needed to be settled under the project was figuring out which areas actually belonged to the *corredores biológicos*. Between 1989, when the WCS network launched Paseo Pantera, and 2001, when the CBMMx Project started, local and transnational NGOs and policymakers proposed a variety of cartographic definitions of the corridor. As the conservationist network grew over time, the areas that it proposed also changed. All of these changes had important political ramifications, as they affected which zones received investment and support from national governments and international institutions.

The Paseo Pantera, which guided advocacy between 1989 and 1995, focused on a relatively small area, namely the Selva Maya zone in the two states of Campeche and Quintana Roo. At the 1996 Tuxtla Gutiérrez meeting in Chiapas, the participants proposed a total of ten corridors in four states, Campeche, Quintana Roo, Chiapas, and Yucatán, adding to the zones previously identified near Calakmul.[92] In the 1998 Cancún meeting, after the involvement of ACICAFOC, the network participants proposed a total of thirty-one corridors in Mesoamerica, adding the states of Tabasco, Veracruz, and Oaxaca to those four previously considered, bringing the total states they thought relevant to the CBMMx Project to seven.[93] At the final conceptual workshop in Cancún in 1999, these thirty-one proposed corridors were submitted in the final negotiation for the CBMMx Project.[94]

Since the zones that were selected would receive funds and support from the state government, the CBMMx Project institutions and CONABIO, the selection of areas was of particular importance, not only to biodiversity management, but also to the economic well-being of marginalized populations, especially in ejidos and indigenous communities.

However, when the project was launched, the zones accepted by the Mexican government and CONABIO differed noticeably from the recommendations in 1999. All identified corridor zones in the states of Oaxaca and Veracruz, as well as some of those in Yucatán were removed from consideration. Shortly before the launch of the CBMMx Project in 2000, all identified corridor zones in the state of Tabasco were excised, reducing the final number of recognized corridors to five, and the number of included states to four. Eventually, Tabasco was reintroduced to the CBMMx Project program, but that took place only in 2011, a decade after the troubled start of the project. A series of maps illustrating how the outlines of the Mexican component of the biological corridors changed between 1995 and 2000 is available in figures 3.1–3.3.

Unfortunately, the network was unable to generate a consensus that could have presented a unified, scientific argument about which zones should be included in corridor management. As noted earlier, network members were aware of the lack of agreement within the scientific community about the dimensions of biodiversity in the Mexican section of Mesoamerica. That said, local and foreign network members were unhappy with the final selection of project managers, which they saw as scientifically flawed. Notably, this skepticism was not reflected in official World Bank project documents, which asserted that the final selection was based on "biodiversity significance," as well as "social viability, technical feasibility and social and political support."[95] The following quotes from Martín Balám and María Villareal of Simbiosis however, contradict that assessment.

Notably, both Balám and Villareal were invited to participate in the meetings on project design held with representatives from the state and federal government, and the World Bank. In describing how the project managers left municipalities out, they noted that the "logical" thing the managers should have done was to follow a zone that extended from the Sian Ka'an Reserve, that "passes through four marginalized municipalities, which are Lázaro Cárdenas, Solidaridad, Felipe Carrillo Puerto, and Othón P. Blanco. And they didn't do it that way. What they did, was they took all

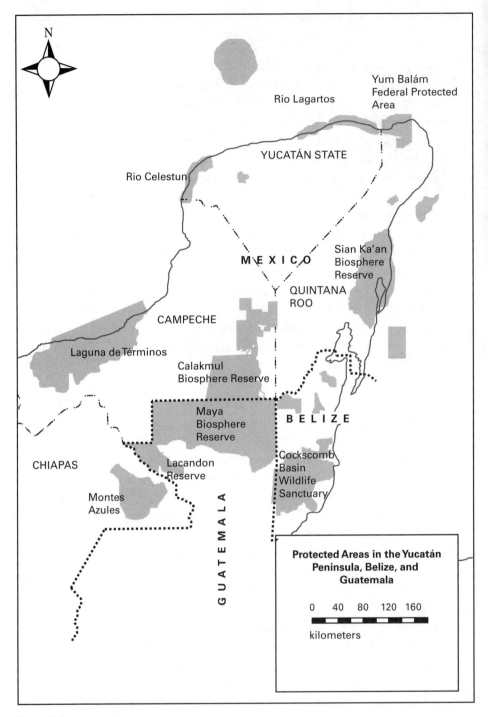

Figure 3.1
1995 map of relevant protected areas to CBMMx Project according to Los Amigos. *Source:* Author's reproduction of map provided by Los Amigos de Sian Ka'an in Juan José Morales, *Introducción a los Ecosistemas de la Península de Yucatán: La Gran Selva Maya* (Cancún, Mexico: Los Amigos de Sian Ka'an, 1995), 159. Used with permission from Los Amigos de Sian Ka'an.

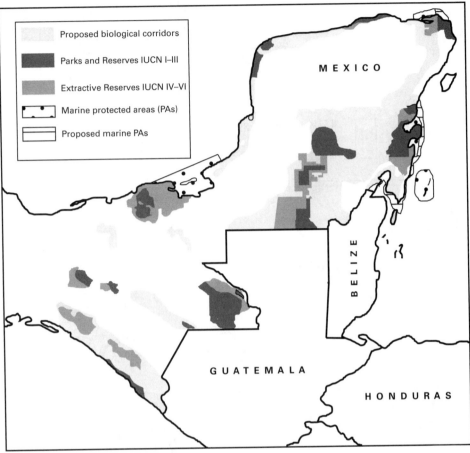

Figure 3.2
1996 proposal from WCS including zones on the west coast of Campeche, Tabasco, the northern third of Quintana Roo. *Source:* Author's reproduction of map in Jocelyn Kaiser, "Bold Corridor Project Confronts Political Reality," *Science* 293, no. 5538 (2001): 2196–2199, 2197.

the non-marginalized municipalities." For Balám and Villareal, the importance of including marginalized communities was also rooted in the fact that those were the areas in which biodiversity was more intact:

What we wanted to include in the corridor, and what was logical was, [*pointing to map*] this is Sian Ka'an, and here is Calakmul. So, we said that ... the corridor should take all that's right here, so Felipe Carrillo Puerto, here is José María Morelos, Solidaridad, here is Othón P. Blanco, which is the biggest municipality we have, and so on. And where there are more forests, better conserved and everything. And more

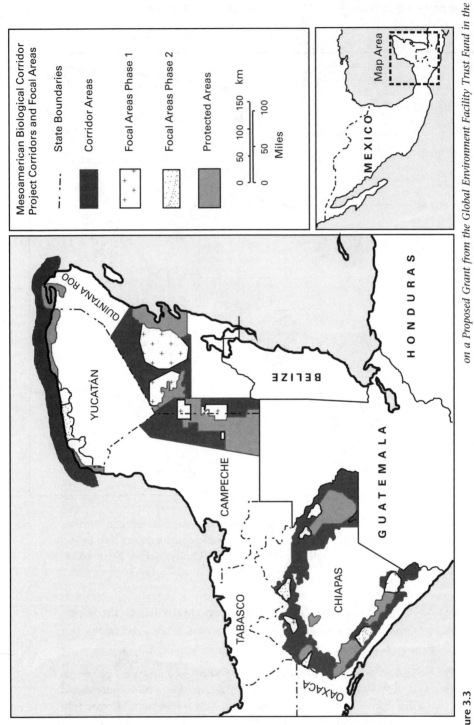

Figure 3.3

2000 CONABIO final selection, having removed zones in West Campeche, the northern third of Quintana Roo, and Tabasco. *Source:* Author's re- on a Proposed Grant from the Global Environment Facility Trust Fund in the Amount of SDR 11.5 Million to Nacional Financiera, S.N.C. for a Mesoamerican Biological Corridor Project, Report No. 23132-ME (Washington, DC:

Mesoamerican Biological Corridor
Project Corridors and Focal Areas

- – · – State Boundaries
- Corridor Areas
- Focal Areas Phase 1
- Focal Areas Phase 2
- Protected Areas

biodiversity than in the rest of the state. But then the decision was to take only Felipe Carrillo Puerto and José María Morelos. And a tiny little piece of Othón P. Blanco. But they basically left the whole municipality out.[96]

Similarly, María Magdalena Vasquez of UQROO was critical about the selection of corridor zones as missing areas that were crucial to proper management. In a 2008 interview, she noted: "There were discussions in which we weren't all in agreement about the project. And right now, there are some important ecological areas in Yucatán for example, that are not connected at all with the rest of the Corredor Biológico Mesoamericano. There are more ecosystems that weren't chosen, and now some people are saying: "What happened?"[97]

In explaining this, network members attributed it to the willingness and ability of governmental policymakers to direct funds to political rather than ecological goals. Respondents like Villareal were clear that "the corridor design had a political function." Villarreal went on: "Because they wanted to focus on Felipe Carrillo Puerto—it's one of the most politically conflicted municipalities of the state ... and José María Morelos. Those two municipalities have been a little bit problematic, politically. So, they were basically thinking that they were going to distribute funds with the money that the Corredor Biológico Mesoamericano project was going to bring in, put in a whole heap of things for the people and all that.[98]

Besides the local concern about the politicization of project design in Mexico, foreign members of the network were concerned with they saw as government led shift of rhetoric to drive the project toward nonenvironmental (read: socioeconomic) goals. This was most pronounced among some of the big international NGOs (BINGOs) that had been involved with the project since its inception as the Paseo Pantera. Notable among these was the Wildlife Conservation Society. For example, after the project was launched, Jim Barborak of WCS noted: "There is a concern that what started out as a science-based project has become populist-based and less guided by ecological principles."[99]

Reed Noss, who also worked on biological corridors for the CBMMx Project, said, "[Around] 1999 or 2000, I was contacted by some people with the World Bank and other agencies, who wanted to include me in some research and workshops related to design of the Mexican part of the corridor. However, when it became clear (through conference calls) that I thought biological considerations should drive corridor location, and that new core conservation areas had to be part of legitimate corridor design, I was un-invited from the project."[100]

These arguments about the proper relationship between the local economy and the environment differ from the language used by Montalvo the ejidatario who, like Flores in SAGARPA and the staff of Simbiosis, explicitly linked biodiversity conservation to the knowledge and autonomy of local communities. For example, Montalvo stated that the expert knowledge held by the government lacked important information about the local ecology that the embodied knowledge of the indigenous possessed. He said, "The state government passes laws, but they don't know the reality, which you get from living in the field, about what are some of these trees. They see a plant, nothing more, and it looks beautiful, and they want to conserve it. They don't know how it produces. We who live there, we know when it's over-populating, or when its population is controlled. We're not destroying the trees. On the contrary, we want to expand their territory for cultivation."[101]

Similarly, Balám of Simbiosis asserted that the scientific perspective of conservation should not erase the needs of local populations who actually lived in the forest and rural areas of Mesoamerica: "We're always focused on looking at how the people can use natural resources. In the jungles and everything. Why? Because normally, what bothers me—I'm a biologist, and María as well—what bothers me is that too often, we biologists are too romantic. We say 'don't touch the jungle or anything,' and we don't take into consideration the people that live in the jungle."[102]

To be clear, both the populations of preservationist-oriented foreign actors and the local use-oriented communities were concerned that the expansion of large-scale economic interests in cattle, oil, or tourism would pose major threats to biodiversity. Where they differed was in how they treated local interest in using resources. For preservationists, the "populism" of appealing to local groups was necessary, if distracting from the real goal of biodiversity conservation (hence the need to "pay" people who did not understand the value of nature). For conservationists in the network, primarily made of local NGOs native to the Yucatán and some policymakers in federal agencies, biodiversity management was something inclusive of the people who lived in and near the resources in question. This disagreement within the network, between actors in local NGOs and Mexican agencies who were concerned about local welfare, and BINGOs and some scientists who had a preservationist view of biodiversity management, prevented a cohesive approach in the conservationist network about the underlying rationale of the CBMMx Project.

To some extent, these differences seem rooted in one of the enduring debates about biodiversity conservation: are people a part of nature, or does nature exist separately from, and hence need to be protected from people? The idea that man is separable from nature is an underlying narrative that justifies the exclusionary approaches to conservation illustrated earlier in my discussion of research from Dowie, Zebich-Knos, Chapin, and others. As feminists like Haraway and other critical theorists have pointed out since the 1980s, the idea that man is separable from nature is not a natural idea, though it is one that may have become hegemonic in conservation circles. Rather, it is an idea that is rooted in a Western desire and belief in the possibility of dominating nature, and that later emerged as a discourse in the American conservation movement, based as it was around the reification of control over land.[103]

Further, the fact that this discourse is rooted in a Western and colonial idea about the pristine and pure state of wilderness may explain why this conservation approach threatens the expropriation of land and control from indigenous communities in its modern manifestations. Unfortunately for the CBMMx Project, this tension between different groups in the network—the BINGOs and some Mexican academics who wanted preservation, and the local NGOs who wanted community welfare—made it difficult to create a management approach that would satisfy all stakeholders.

Besides complicating the selection of corridor zones, the network's inability to generate a consensus created another obstacle to the members' ability to influence governance in Mesoamerica. One of the primary challenges to gathering information on biodiversity loss in the CBMMx Project was the lack of a standardized methodology for ecosystem monitoring. Agencies that studied biodiversity in the region, such as ECOSUR, UQROO, Pronatura, UNAM, and governmental agencies in SEMARNAT and SAGARPA, did so in an uncoordinated manner, focusing on research specific to their areas of expertise and interest, rather than functioning as parts of an integrated monitoring system.[104] Gonzalo Merediz Alonso of Los Amigos, who also worked on the MBRS Project described earlier, unfavorably compared the status of monitoring across the two projects: "I think that in the [MBRS Project], we've had more advances. I think the synoptic methodology, the synoptic monitoring methodology [of the MBRS] is a real advance in this sense. But in this area, we have plenty, plenty of work left for the Corridor. For example, various organizations are working in the area of bird and habitat conservation, and, well, at this moment there just isn't an agreed-upon methodology to study and monitor bird populations."[105]

In 2005, CONABIO attempted to remedy this situation by contracting a study on biodiversity monitoring with the Jorge L. Tamayo Center of Studies in Geography and Geomathics (CentroGeo). CentroGeo, a Geographic Information Science modeling institution in Mexico, was supposed, among other things, to establish a standard series of indicators for biodiversity health and create a baseline analysis of the contemporary state of the environment through an "exhaustive investigation of existing methods."[106] However, in 2009, CentroGeo and the CBMMx Project institutions had still not developed an agreed-upon approach, concluding at the time that there was still no scientific consensus on a standard model of investigation and baseline monitoring.[107]

But the most significant obstacle to the network's desire to shape environmental governance in Mesoamerica was a breakdown in participation by local communities in the project. After the project was launched, policymakers in the state and federal government began implementing it in a way that treated indigenous communities primarily as economic actors to be included within the tourist market, and not as actors with an autonomously derived local economy. As a result, indigenous and campesino communities and their role in conserving biodiversity became part of a neoliberal model of development that reproduced them as possible commodities within elite-driven economic growth. In addition, despite promises to ACICAFOC that the project would be designed with indigenous and campesino participation, the socioeconomic and cultural concerns of local actors were shut out institutionally. Instead, project management became increasingly top-down, and directed by the state and federal agencies for agendas that they set. In so doing, this strategy exposed what Ervine, in discussing the CBMMx Project, described as the "contradiction between the [neoliberal] blueprint's a priori determination of the causes of biodiversity loss and thus permissible project-level interventions, rooted in a market ethos, and the goals of a transformative participatory development."[108] In other words, to use the language of Liza Grandia, the project abandoned its Bolivarian ideal to adopt a bureaucratic reality.[109]

For advocates like Arturo Bayona of Econciencia who were interested in promoting environmental alternatives among marginalized populations, state governments were too narrowly focused on turning conservation projects into commodities for the large-scale tourist market. While promoting rural welfare through incorporation in the tourist market seemed economically rational, it soon became apparent that linking rural communities to this market was more difficult than it seemed. It could not be carried out simply by educating indigenous people about the value that their goods (artisanal products; ecotourism) had to foreigners. Rural communities very rarely had the capacity to participate in this market at a scale that fit with the adopted model.

For example, while some communities could certainly take advantage of support for infrastructure, training as tour guides, and could acquire the permits necessary to benefit from CBMMx Project sponsorship, others were unable to access these resources. Licenciado Tun, the Program Director for Indigenous Projects in the CDI explained, describing the difficulties in creating tourist projects in marginalized zones:

I have tried to educate some communities, some commissions, so that they can work in alternative tourism projects. But I've felt a rejection, like they're not convinced that these projects are worth the effort. What happens is—you have to recognize that these are costly projects. You have to pay for an environmental impact assessment, the EIA is costly. And you have to site the project in an office, they're also going to charge you for the space. We're talking about projects, in the case of alternative tourism, that can cost up to one million Mexican pesos. That's a high sum.[110]

As difficulties mounted, it became clear that the government, especially in the state agencies, was more interested in furthering the large-scale coastal tourist development than investing in marginalized communities for small-scale growth. As key actors in state institutions like SEDETUR failed to demonstrate convincing interest in the small-scale goals of community development, either in infrastructure or other forms of support, Bayona commented: "If we had the support of the state tourism secretariat, it would be easy. But we don't have it. There isn't a center for sustainable tourism in Quintana Roo. The only thing we have is Cancún, Cozumel, because that's where the millions come in."[111]

Bayona was also supported in this observation by Enrique Galvez of SEMARNAT, who noted that "the ecotourism projects are of no interest to the state government," and by an ejidal resident who I will call Alfonso

Bey. In 2008, Galvez explained that the potential return on investment and the economic rationale for developing the rural and marginalized zones of Mexico "doesn't compare with the quantity of resources, the demand, the number of businesses, and the sources of finance there to develop Cancún, Tulúm, Playa del Carmen, Cozumel." He added: "That's a lot of money, it's a tremendous amount in comparison with the few, scanty resources and the little capacity invested in the communities where there are also attractions, and which could possibly be important."[112]

In a 2012 interview conducted with Alfonso Bey while navigating the thickly rooted mangrove swamps near Xcalak, Bey reiterated the points made by Bayona and Galvez, saying this about the project: "[T]he ones that you find on the coastal zone are the only ones that have benefited, but not *ejidos*, no." Bey continued, describing how his ejido was ignored by the CBMMx Project: "They said that they would bring different options for the *ejidos*, good investment ... but this has been going on for many years, and some campesinos are in this project, but it hasn't happened. The resources don't arrive to the *ejidos*. ... Even my *ejido* is inside the *corredor biológico*, and nobody from this project has arrived yet to bring us work or investment."[113] For the civil society members of the network, the increasing emphasis in Mexico on using the project to promote large-scale development confounded the broader goals of biodiversity conservation as it did not do enough to bring sustainable development to poor rural communities.

This was exacerbated by a widespread belief that the international community, particularly through global financial instruments, was going to invest "an indefinite amount of funds in dollars" for resource conservation.[114] In 2004, an external evaluation of the CBMMx Project found that this belief has "replaced the goal of social participation, of the reorientation of public funds, and most importantly, the development of sustainable use projects to benefit the environment and the socioeconomic wellbeing of inhabitants in the focal areas."[115] As observed by Barborak of WCS, some of the later project documents focused on economic development such that "if not for a brief mention of the CBM, you wouldn't know that you were talking about a project whose original goal was contributing to biodiversity conservation in the region."[116] However, when this "indefinite amount of funds" did not materialize, it became more difficult to get local support for a project that implied additional regulations on the use of natural resources.

The Loss of Legitimacy and Local Support for CBMMx Project Initiatives

The mixed and laggardly influence in creating and implementing projects, combined with very low influence in delineating which zones would receive GEF funds exacerbated underlying problems affecting local participation in corridor management. At the local level, Mexican organizations within the network such as Simbiosis, Pronatura, Econciencia, and Los Amigos had, by working with marginalized and indigenous communities in corridor zones and ejidos since the 1980s and 1990s, established a broad base of legitimacy within these communities.[117] In contrast, ejidal residents developed a high level of distrust toward federal and state governments based on a history of indigenous marginalization, linguistic barriers, and problems with land tenure and property rights. One notable exception was the CDI, which, by explicitly advocating for indigenous rights, built up good faith with indigenous communities. For example, during my first period of field research, the CDI was engaged in a regional program throughout the peninsula to bail out indigenous people arrested for environmental crimes. Historically however, tensions between rural and indigenous people in Mexico have occasionally erupted into violence, most dramatically, in the conflicts between governmental agencies and indigenous residents and their sympathizers in Chiapas.[118] Understandably, these political conflicts and historic disenfranchisement have created barriers to cooperation between rural communities and federal and state policymakers.

During the design and early stages of the CBMMx Project, NGOs served as intermediaries between the federal government and local communities, encouraging residents to comply with federal and state environmental regulations, and serving as advocates for indigenous and rural property rights.[119] However, after the launch of the CBMMx Project, civil society network members were increasingly ignored in project administration, despite their formal inclusion in the bodies of the project. As described earlier, one of the conditions of the project, and one of the ways in which civil society members were institutionally given a voice in its management, was the creation of State Advisory Councils (CCEs) and Regional Technical Units (UTRs). However, network members felt increasingly marginalized in the day-to-day management of the project, and became increasingly concerned about the willingness of state policymakers to listen to their input in these institutions. One member of the CCE in Yucatán state stated explicitly:

"Well, if we only get involved at the end of project proposals, we have no way to influence how they're designed and carried out. It's done already. But that *is* what is happening. And that's how the majority of the council members feel, at least in the academic and social sectors. ... Why? Because it's not in our hands to call a meeting. Or set the agenda. [The policymakers] call the meetings; *they* set the agenda."[120]

Unfortunately, the CDI, despite (or because of) its focus on indigenous rights, did not have as direct a role in project design as other agencies. Licenciado Tun commented on this, noting that indigenous groups questioned the low profile of the CDI in informing the conduct of the project:

As I was telling you yesterday, the ones that are directly in charge of the project are the ecologists. And then SEMARNAT. We [at the CDI] aren't completely involved in the CBMMx. We simply give opinions on it, no? ... What we can do to link ourselves more closely with the CBMMx, is have a meeting with SEMARNAT, right? ... But there have been some days that I've left a SEMARNAT meeting in indigenous zones, and they [indigenous people] ask us: "Why doesn't the CDI manage these projects?" And [they ask] because it is in indigenous zones.[121]

Finally, when asked about the growth of environmental restrictions on land management in the Yucatán, Alfonso Bey said the following:

The campesinos are not taken into account. The people who decide are they. ... We who live in the field know what's happening, but the people who don't, don't. There are people in the Maya zone who don't know how to read, so they tell them which color to vote for. There are people in the Maya zone who don't even speak Spanish, so it's difficult to make people listen to them. When they're looking for votes, they reach every last corner, but when they win, you never see them again. They promise a lot of things, but never carry them out.[122]

These problems of participation in land management severely undermined project legitimacy. While the Mexican government was supposed to constitute the state advisory councils as part of the administration of the project, their implementation was laggardly, and the first CCE was launched only in 2003 in Quintana Roo, a full three years after the start of the CBMMx Project.[123] Due to this delay, the World Bank initially refused to release funds to CONABIO, and budgetary documents and interviews reveal that project financing did not begin until 2005.[124] Unfortunately, the government of Mexico had, in an attempt to "sell" the CBMMx Project to peasant populations, persuaded community members and local stakeholders that the CBMMx Project would lead to significant economic revenue, with resources flowing from international funding mechanisms to marginalized communities. Since these funds were unavailable for several years after the predicted start date of the project, and since the network had little to no control over where funds were being disbursed, ejido residents and network organizations began doubting the commitment of corridor agencies to needed local development efforts. The following interviews from Enrique Galvez of SEMARNAT and María Villarreal of Simbiosis respectively illustrate the rising dissatisfaction with the conduct of the CBMMx Project after its launch:

[The CBMMx] was planned for seven years. We've gone through almost seven years now, about six years. But for five years, it didn't operate. The resources were there. The proposal was there. The personnel was there—well, to oversee the political side of it, rather than the practical, applied side. So, the resources weren't in operation, practically nothing was done. It was stagnating.[125]

[The] government thought the CBMMx would be some World Bank program, an international program, that was going to bring in funds to this zone, because the political decision was to focus on this zone. But it didn't turn out that way ... We heard our colleagues saying, "They're just paying for consultants, and consultants, and consultants, and they're not carrying out the projects they said they would." ... And we began to see conflicts. And what happened is, we got to a point where the CBMMx lost all credibility. And we saw various meetings where only two people attended. They invited everybody in the zone, all the businesses and everything, but nobody came. ... There were large expectations for the project, and it didn't meet the expectations. Even the NGOs began to dissent.[126]

This loss of legitimacy was such that, in corridor zones of Chiapas, ejido residents became convinced that the CBMMx Project was part of the Puebla Panama Project, a federal government plan to seize communally held lands and ejidos for the launch of a regional industrialization project.[127] Concurrently with the CBM, the governments of Mexico and Central America had planned the Puebla-Panama Project (Proyecto Puebla Panamá, or PPP), a multibillion-dollar program, funded by the Inter-American Development Bank (IDB), to further integrate the states' economies. Officially, the PPP was targeted at meeting eight goals, including sustainable development and human development. However, the vast majority of funds—some 85 percent—were committed to transportation and energy.

Almost as soon as the PPP was launched in 2001, it entered into trouble. Believing that the PPP would commit its wealth of resources to large infrastructure such as large dams, highways, and airports that would benefit developers and transform the landscape, indigenous groups mobilized in protest what they feared would be land grabs.[128] In 2002, a transnational coalition of Mayans and rural campesinos from Mexico and Guatemala held a press conference to denounce a hydroelectric dam project on the Usumacinta River, along the border of the two countries.[129] This dam, which the Fox administration championed as a key part of the PPP, would have flooded between 800 square kilometers to 1,315 square kilometers of Maya territory, one third of which was in Mexico.[130] It would have provided 2 percent of Mexico's energy needs, and submerged historic Maya cities that had been recently discovered, such as Piedras Negras, and hectares of agricultural land.[131] Just as Khagram described in India, or McCormick in Brazil, this dam project and the context of the PPP in which it was embedded, was based on a developmental discourse that saw modernization defined in a specific way: billions of dollars spent on large infrastructure, like monuments to a specific model of liberal capitalism.

Further, the response of the Mexican government and the IDB to protests against the dam have inspired more distrust against regional and international governance programs in Mesoamerica. Historically, the Usumacinta has been a major part of the Mayan civilization, as it played a key role in providing transportation and water. While it had significant cultural and ecological importance to the Maya, the Mexican government had been planning to construct a dam on Usumacinta since the 1980s, as part of the "big dam regime" that, according to Khagram, emerged after the 1950s.[132] This regime, supported by international agencies like the World Bank and the Inter-American Development Bank as well as the implementing national governments, constituted a hegemonic normative approach to the governance of hydroelectric dams and riparian management. This approach was oriented around the idea that environmental governance, like all forms of governance, was to be constructed around a worldview based on industrial modernization and neoliberal capitalism. As occurred in India and Brazil, indigenous groups in Mexico and Guatemala resisted the dam for virtually identical reasons: awareness that this large-scale infrastructure would displace the most vulnerable in the interest of the political elite. This opposition, in conjunction with the civil war in Guatemala, terminated the project in its first planning stages in 1987.

But the Mexican government under Salinas again tried to dam the Usumacinta in 1992 on the way to NAFTA, before it collapsed again under protests, and revived it again under Fox, as part of the PPP. As Grandia describes, the supporters of the dam in the Mexican government and international institutions had established a pattern of keeping the project and others like it alive, by shuffling them around whenever opposition emerged.

[In] 2002 I had the opportunity to ask an IDB/Guatemala representative about their plans to fund a controversial hydroelectric dam along the Usumacinta River that would flood thousands of hectares of national parks in Mexico and Guatemala (including very high biodiversity regions of the Sierra Lacandón Park in northern Petén). He cleverly replied that there would be no funding from the IDB office in Guatemala, but did not rule out the possibility of Mexico office funding the same project.[133]

Making matters worse, despite the opposition to the PPP by local NGOs and indigenous groups, some of the big international NGOs (BINGOs) in conservation signed on to the project in the early 2000s. For instance, Alfonso Romo, then president of pharmaceutical conglomerate Grupo Pulsar, worked on the PPP with President Fox, while serving on the board of Conservation International (CI).[134] Problematically, CI and the World Conservation Society (WCS) were also two of the primary international organizations involved in the CBM. Given the collaboration between BINGOs and the government in the increasingly top-down CBMMx Project, and their apparent insistence on advancing the goals of the PPP in other institutions, it is not surprising that indigenous and campesino populations saw the CBMMx Project as "a veiled mechanism, to ease the way for conditions favorable to the implementation of the Plan Puebla Panamá in a supposed strategy against the culture and rights of the indigenous people."[135]

Whether the CBMMx Project would lead to state-led capitalist exploitation, or top-down preservation according to the indigenous and campesino groups was irrelevant. In either of those seemingly plausible scenarios, the CBMMx Project and the PPP, both advanced by similar groups, seemingly threatened access to land and the use of resources. Due to mounting political difficulties, over one hundred CBMMx subprojects, including training workshops and ecosystem studies, were canceled in Chiapas and the peninsula between 2005 and 2007. Since ejidos began resisting the government-led efforts to implement the project, the administrative goals had to be changed after 2007. Then, project managers in CONABIO and the network agreed to abandon the previous ideal of focusing on ecologically important focal areas, in order to focus on implementation in those remaining communities that were more likely to "have a good disposition toward the project."[136] Despite the hopes of conservationists, scientific networks did not have a great deal of influence over the actual conduct of the CBMMx Project.

Conclusion

In this case, an environmentally oriented TAN emerged in the 1990s to advocate for increased biodiversity protection in Mesoamerica through the adoption of biological corridors, administered and managed by governmental policymakers and the civil society. However, the eventual implementation of the project fell far short of what the network wanted. Network members were critical of the selection of corridor zones, the emphasis by the state government on using conservation to meet the needs of the tourist industry, and their ability to participate in decision making. In fact, Magdalena Vásquez of UQROO, commenting on the effect of the network on the project, said: "We've influenced nothing."

In fairness to the network, that overstates the setbacks that the conservationists experienced. The government of Mexico and the international agencies did adopt the idea of biological corridors, which came initially from non-Mexican organizations and academics within the CBM network. Federal agencies did launch some sustainable conservation projects supporting ecotourism and market access for things like artisanal products and honey (of which Galvez of SEMARNAT was particularly proud). However, while the project was supposed to be a "win-win-win-win-win-win-win,"[137] for all stakeholders, it fell short of the mark. Environmentalists were discouraged by the ecological coverage of the project. Indigenous and rural groups (and their supporters) were dissatisfied with the participation of marginalized communities. Governmental officials and project managers within the CBMMx Project were irritated at persistent local opposition and laggardly implementation of conservationist mechanisms.

So what explains the lower level of network influence in this case, when compared to the others? Jamaica's relatively influential epistemic community could be explained as due to advocacy taking place in a comparatively democratic country with a more autonomous civil society. But the MBRS Project also took place in the Mesoamerican part of Mexico, and with many of the same actors in the federal government and the NGO community. In order to explain, we have to turn again to Davis Cross's discussion of civil society influence as something that operates on different levels of governance, and with different actors.

First, the network's inability to generate a consensus contributed to its lack of influence over the selection of Mexican zones in the CBMMx Project. This outcome does fit with the epistemic community literature predicting a lower chance of success when scientists have a disagreement about the parameters of a problem. When contrasted with the MBRS Project, in which an epistemic community was able to set the terms of managing a defined region, this conclusion seems additionally plausible.

Second, the network lost influence over the framing of the CBMMx Project. While network members expressed an interest in conserving biodiversity for its scientific or ecological value (among the preservationists) or its cultural and subsistence value to marginalized groups, the actual conduct of the project emphasized the commodification of goods for inclusion in large-scale tourist markets. Notably, network members themselves adopted this frame in the conduct of the project. This suggests that influence is a two-way street: policymakers and other actors, just like advocacy networks, have their own preferences about taking action, and will try to frame the discourse in which policies are debated to legitimate these preferences. As indicated here, the neoliberal framing of the CBMMx Project privileged those activities taken for the economic elite.

This approach manifested in the primary obstacle to network influence: the breakdown in participatory mechanisms for the mass public. The suspicion of marginalized groups of the CBMMx Project, and their belief that it was associated with the despised PPP, combined with their visible absence from the decision-making process to lead to local opposition to and alienation from the CBMMx Project shortly after it launched. This alienation between the indigenous and campesino populations from decision making exacerbated ongoing tensions between low-income rural people and environmental authorities. In explaining the work of the CDI in liberating imprisoned indigenous people, Licenciado Tun was clear that environmental criminality was rooted in poverty and difficulties among the indigenous in participating fully in the political system: "It's a vicious circle that we're combatting. It's the need of the people that makes them cut trees illegally, and hunt illegally. This need provokes them into committing a federal crime. ... There are environmental crimes, there are crimes like robbery. There are even familial crimes, because of the fact that they can't bear the stress of feeding their children. Because they can't get any money."

Third, this shows the limits of socialization as a means of generating influence. Under the auspices of the project, network members formally socialized with policymakers at the state and federal level. However, to the extent that socialization strengthens a shared understanding of a problem, this understanding was one centered on a neoliberal capitalist perspective. In other words, NGOs and civil society members were given access to participate in the project, but under the assumption that they would speak in the language of neoliberal economics. Thus, socialization may just as well lead to a change in perspective held by an advocacy network, as a change in perspective from their target audiences.

4   Egypt and the Migratory Soaring Birds Project

Introduction

At first glance, Egypt in the post-revolution era has a variety of sociopolitical challenges against which the importance of environmental governance
pales in comparison. When thinking about pressing issues like growing
governmental autocracy, shuttering of the civil society, rising insecurity
among women, and economic inequality, it is difficult to see why issues
like bird conservation and land management matter. However, as indicated
throughout this book, environmental advocacy in developing countries is
often rooted in much more than esoteric appeals to save intrinsically valuable species. For marginalized people, environmental activism and policy
matter, because they determine who can have access to land and water, and
how they are allowed to use natural resources. Even in Egypt, environmental advocacy is one of the ways in which the civil society tries to participate
in the political system.[1]

Indeed, scholars on environmental rights like Hiskes argue that without
rights to environmental goods like clean air, water, and soil, people will
be unable to fully access their civil and political rights. Further, as Hiskes
and the literature on environmental justice point out, environmental rights
and environmental justice also has an important procedural dimension:
that is, environmental justice requires that attention be paid to how much
different people participate in decision making, and not just the outcome
of these decisions. To quote the second Principle of Environmental Justice
from the multinational People of Color Environmental Summit: "environmental justice demands that public policy be based on mutual respect and
justice for all peoples, free from any form of discrimination or bias."[2] In
order to make public environmental policy nondiscriminatory, and hence

justice-oriented, it is necessary to reform a political system such that the mass public has a voice and a means of participation. Thus, as Hiskes says about environmental rights, "the overall effect of their implementation would be to increase participation and therefore democratic discussion."[3] In practice then, environmental advocacy in developing countries is often isomorphic with struggles for democratization. In this regard, Egypt is very similar to other authoritarian or post-transitional states like Brazil and post-Soviet countries, in which greater demands for public participation have been manifested in pressures for new environmental regulations.[4]

This matters because, as the previous three chapters argue, one of the cognitive resources that transnational networks need to influence policymaking is socialization with target audiences. When networks have socialization, as well as a scientific consensus and a framework grounding conservation norms with the beliefs of local populations, they are likely to shape environmental policymaking. Socialization affects influence because it encourages the mutual ownership of knowledge. As the experiences of networks in Jamaica and Mexico here show, target audiences may well believe the claims of knowledge networks holding a consensus, but still resist environmental reform if they have not been socialized in the production of this knowledge.

However, it is not clear here how the open or closed nature of a political system affects the propensity of state policymakers to socialize with civil society experts. First, in Jamaica, only one agency in the Ministry of Agriculture was willing to socialize with the advocacy network, despite the fact that Jamaica is the most democratic and politically open of the countries studied. Second, the epistemic community in chapter 2 and the advocacy network in chapter 3 generated strong social ties with Mexican federal secretariats in environment and agriculture, as well as agencies in protected areas and fisheries. This took place despite Mexico's history of one-party corporatism and bureaucratic autocracy from which they only started transitioning in 2000. Further, as this chapter later shows, in the 1980s Egypt under Mubarak created substantial political opportunity structures through which the civil society influenced protected areas and marine management. If autocratic Egypt could promote civil society influence over protected areas in the 1980s, that suggests that autocracy is not a necessary barrier to socialization between experts and policymakers.

Does this mean that political openness leads to fewer political opportunity structures for socialization? This is not an implausible argument. As politically closed states tend to co-opt civil society groups, knowledge networks in autocratic states may have greater access to policy. Further, as Lee Kuan Yew intimated in 1994, authoritarian regimes may be less unwieldy at policymaking than democracies, which are constitutionally obligated to listen to different voices.[5] Former president George W. Bush himself seemed to agree with this statement in 2000, when he commented on tax policy in the United States, saying "If this were a dictatorship, it'd be a heck of a lot easier, just so long as I'm the dictator." Given these arguments, it seems plausible to assume that if autocratic regimes engage with experts in cognitively complex issue areas, they may respond more dynamically to new information than open, pluralistic regimes that have to continually balance competing interests. Certainly, as Sowers and Teets point out, autocratic states like Egypt and China can and have ceded autonomy over some policy areas to civil society groups. In those cases, this was motivated by a desire to ease the regulatory burden on the state, and a belief in the expertise and efficiency of recognized groups in areas like environmental management or health education.[6]

In this chapter, I discuss how Egypt's authoritarian regime has responded to environmental advocacy in protected areas through the implementation of a GEF-funded project titled the Project for Mainstreaming Conservation of Migratory Soaring Birds into Key Productive Sectors along the Rift Valley/ Red Sea Flyway (hereafter, the MSB project). The research suggests that it is possible for authoritarian systems to respond effectively to information from the civil society in complex areas like the environment.

Unfortunately, this chapter also finds that, while authoritarian regimes may have certain advantages in environmental policymaking in theory, these advantages are likely to be temporary. Effective environmental policymaking depends on a continued interest in incorporating new information, even if this challenges vested interests. As this book has shown so far, managing scarce natural resources is, like everything else in politics, highly contentious, and likely to become more so over time, as resources become more scarce. Inevitably, elites and the marginalized will have divergent preferences over environmental policy, and when this happens, autocratic regimes that do not build robust structures for civil society engagement will find it too easy to ignore new information.

The network discussed here tried to conserve an area known as the Rift Valley/Red Sea Flyway, part of the larger migration route known as the African-Eurasian Flyway. The flyway can be imagined as an aerial corridor taken by migratory birds traveling from European states north of the Mediterranean Sea through the eastern coast of the African continent, passing through the airspace of several countries, including Egypt.[7] This area is a crucial zone for global populations of migratory soaring birds, as for some species, between 50 percent and 100 percent of their global population traverses it.[8] Like the Northern Bald Ibis, several of these birds are listed on the World Conservation Union (IUCN) Red List of Threatened Species.[9]

This makes conservation of the flyway and the status of these birds very important. The fact that most or all of the world's population passes through this area means mismanagement in relatively small geographic zones could have global ramifications for conservation. In addition, some of these migratory birds are apex predators. Declines in their populations could signal unforeseen problems in sensitive ecosystems.[10] For example, migratory birds have to stop and recuperate at the wetlands scattered throughout northern and eastern Africa. When researchers find corpses of birds scattered around wetlands, this could be an indicator that the ecosystems' integrity has been compromised, and points to unacknowledged ecological threats.[11]

These birds are so vulnerable precisely because they have to migrate. In order to conserve energy on the transcontinental route, migratory soaring birds fly by soaring and gliding on hot air thermals, flapping as little as possible, primarily on ascent. Because hot air thermals are formed primarily over level ground, rather than over large bodies of water and mountain ranges, migratory soaring birds have very restricted migratory paths, and are funneled through identifiable "bottlenecks" (see figure 4.1). These bottlenecks provide spectacular bird-watching possibilities, and expose the birds to human interference within a compressed timeframe.[12]

Since these birds rely on thermals, they often travel at very low altitudes, easily within shotgun or rifle range.[13] In some instances, birds fly low enough that trappers need only construct large nets to capture them.[14] When hunters use lead shot, discarded lead pellets can accumulate in rest areas, leading to heavy metal poisoning in the local flora.[15] Even well-meaning but uninformed tourists may disturb exhausted and undernourished birds by traveling too close to rest areas, leading to further stress and hence

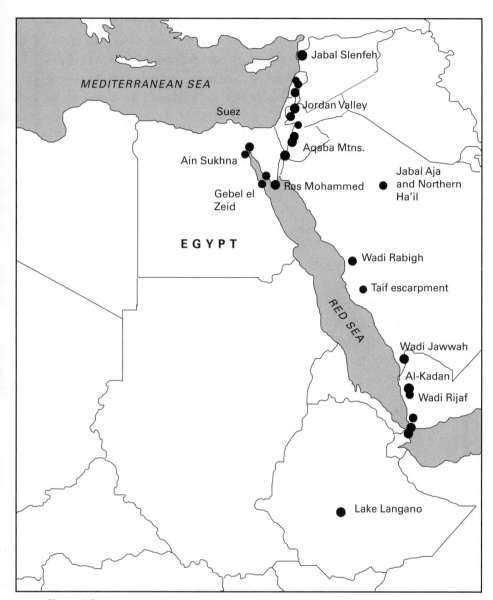

Figure 4.1

Map of Middle East and North African bird bottleneck sites. *Source:* Author's reproduction of map provided in R. F. Porter, *Soaring Bird Migration in the Middle East and North East Africa: The Bottleneck Sites* (Cambridge, UK: Birdlife International, 2005), 6.

death. One of the birders involved in the advocacy campaign described here commented on the effect of desert bikers on resting places in Sharm el Sheikh in the Sinai Peninsula: "[The] biggest majority of the storks from Eastern Europe fly through this point, and have a resting place at a sewage farm in Sharm el Sheikh. All these bikers going through the sewage farms are scaring the birds away. They can't rest, they have to fly further south, some of them are exhausted, more of them will die."[16]

Tourism and urban development in flyway zones in the Sinai Peninsula and along the Red Sea coast has also exposed birds to toxic chemicals. Hotel operators who do not dispose of waste properly can pollute the bodies of water that birds need to rehydrate after their journey. When waste is dumped into open-air pits, birds searching for water sometimes mistake them for freshwater.[17] Pesticides, rodenticides, and poisoned bait, aimed at pests such as the feral dogs plaguing agricultural areas, may also kill or harm some species of predatory or carrion birds. These stresses are, in addition to coastal overdevelopment, causing rapid declines in healthy coral reefs in Egypt's coastal zones.

Finally, the construction of wind farms along the flyway may create hazards for birds that become trapped in power lines, or collide with wind turbines. The same wind conditions that are most conducive to energy generation are also propitious for soaring birds, which either risk collisions or have to detour from the flyway, again increasing the chance of exhaustion and death.[18]

Political Authoritarianism, Institutional Distortion, and Tourism in Egypt

As in all other cases studied in this book, these anthropogenic threats are not just problematic from an environmental standpoint, but they also create hardships for some of the marginalized communities in Egypt. On one hand, it is clear that the activities of lower-income Bedouin populations who reside in the desert of the Sinai Peninsula and along the Red Sea Coast can contribute to the stresses described earlier. Bedouin tribal groups, most of whom are semi-nomadic, do engage in trapping and hunting of birds.[19] On the other hand, prominent economic sectors, particularly in tourism, not only contribute the primary sources of stress on desert biodiversity management, but also displace Bedouin communities.

In some cases, this displacement is indirect. Waste disposal from tourist sites or excessive water usage reduce the utility of subterranean and groundwater supplies, on which Bedouin communities depend for subsistence and agriculture.[20] On occasion, this is more direct, as occurred in 1999 when the Egyptian government bulldozed Bedouin camps to develop the Sinai for tourism.[21] As the next section explains, coastal tourism has become over the past two decades a major source of revenue and interest to the military and political elite. As powerful players have become more invested in promoting large-scale development along the Red Sea and Sinai coastlines, it has become harder for Bedouin or nonpolitically connected communities to make use of resources like land, or even ply their trade as tour guides or hosts to visitors. Consequently, the growth of large-scale tourism has, as in Mexico, created new environmental stresses as well as difficulties for the socioeconomic well-being of marginalized populations.

The management of these processes falls under the purview of a range of different governmental authorities. Direct environmental management is the jurisdiction of the Ministry of State for Environmental Affairs (MSEA) and its executive agency, the Egyptian Environmental Affairs Agency (EEAA). Formally, the EEAA's authority over natural resource management is concentrated in the Nature Conservation Sector (NCS).[22] The NCS is the focal point for the Convention on Biological Diversity (CBD) and other multilateral environmental agreements (MEAs) relevant to the management of migratory birds and transitory habitats. These include the Convention on Migratory Species (CMS) and the Ramsar Convention on the protection of wetlands, all of which were invoked as relevant to the GEF Project.[23] NCS authority is further delegated to a National Biodiversity Unit and a Protectorates Division.[24]

The Biodiversity Unit is charged with conducting national biodiversity inventories, and with implementing the Convention on Biological Diversity (CBD) by drafting a *National Biodiversity Strategy and Action Plan* (NBSAP).[25] Since some of the areas important for bird management are found within the network of protected areas, and under environmental Law 102/1983, the Protectorates Division has some authority to determine entry conditions, regulate hunting permits, and appoint rangers to staff and monitor established areas.[26]

In addition, the Protectorates Division is tasked with coordinating management of protected areas with Egypt's governorates, of which there have been twenty-nine since 2009.[27] Three in particular are important to migratory soaring bird and flyway management: the North Sinai, the South Sinai and the Red Sea governorates, although migrating birds have been found as far inland as Helwan. Some of the key protected areas addressed in these governorates are: the Red Sea Islands in the Red Sea governorate; Ras Mohammed and Sant Katherin (also written as Saint Katherine and Saint Catherine) National Parks in the South Sinai governorate; and Zaranik in the North Sinai governorate. Governors manage local pollution standards, monitor waste management, and have oversight over development projects in their jurisdiction. To coordinate with the NCS, governors work through Environmental Management Units established in each governorate.[28]

While natural resource agencies are legally key players in balancing Egypt's environmental and tourist management, authority in this and other areas has been shaped by a complex web of relationships involving the military and security apparatus, personal ties, and economic vested interests. This distortion of Egyptian regulatory institutions means the legal apparatus does not give a clear picture of how authority operates in the state.

A disjuncture between the institutional division of power and the actual exercise of power is, of course, not restricted to Egypt. In fact, as Gandhi points out, although nondemocratic states may often share similar institutions, they may exercise power in qualitatively different ways.[29] For example, although Nigeria, Mexico, and Egypt were all presidential states under authoritarian rule, political institutions played very different roles in each system. Under the Partido Revolucionario Institucional (PRI), Mexico was a bureaucratic-authoritarian state with real power invested in the party, rather than in individual leaders, as memorably turned into satire by the film *La Ley de Herodes*.[30] In Nigeria, the political elite exercised power in a presidential system under neopatrimonial rule, where kinship ties and elite relationships determined policy.[31] Finally, in Egypt, despite the decades-long rule of Mubarak, the post-transition process suggests that at least at the end, the regime was not a personalist system as Koehler asserted in 2008, but a military one-party state.[32] Anderson illustrates the strength and institutional continuity of the military after the downfall of Mubarak by describing the regime's control over the departure of Morsi and its penetration into the domestic economy, emphasizing that "the military [will] not allow its institutional prerogatives to be substantially eroded."[33]

This involvement of the military in Egypt's political economy and natural resource use is particularly apparent in the management of large-scale tourism. The military and security apparatus became involved in occupying and developing the Sinai Peninsula after the 1981 withdrawal of Israel. Since then, the military has used formal and informal institutions to curb the de jure authority of other agencies and the civil society to influence policy.

In order to create a buffer zone against future Israeli occupation, and to take advantage of the new legal and administrative vacuum in the peninsula, the Mubarak regime began investing heavily in tourism, settlements, and other kinds of economic activity and infrastructure. Under the virtually permanent state of emergency under Mubarak, the military "retained use-rights to large tracts of land" in the Sinai (as well as near the border with the Sudan) with the authority to restrict at will the mobility of researchers, academics, and tourists in the interest of security.[34] In 1991, with support from the United States Agency for International Development (USAID), the government created the Tourist Development Authority (TDA) to spur development by parceling and selling land in the Sinai and along the Red Sea to investors. This large-scale sand-and-sea tourism represented a change from the previous model emphasizing Egypt's cultural history, and was meant to create a lucrative market for Egypt's natural resources.

Under Mubarak, Egypt did engage in some measures to liberalize the political economy. For example, in the 1990s Mubarak presided over a series of privatization reforms, by selling off state-owned enterprises, and reducing direct state control in some sectors. However, while this privatization did lead to more economic competition in the tourist industry, this limited competition took place not under a functional free market system, but between crony capitalists in the business elite and the military apparatus who viewed the autonomous private sector as a threat to their interests.[35] This limited liberalization, which brought with it rising unemployment and cuts in social welfare, has continued to concentrate decision-making authority over land management in the hands of the elite, although the elite is now more socially diverse.

The growing lucrativeness of tourism meant that economic and political elites who wanted to control this sector had more incentive to do so. The government's investment in tourism made the sector grow tremendously over the next two decades, most of which took place along the Red Sea and Sinai Peninsula. Between 1993 and 2011, tourist visits to Egypt grew from 1.1 million to 11.5 million, with a corresponding growth of revenue from US$1.9 billion to US$9.5 billion.[36] Of 5 million tourists visiting Egypt annually in 2003, approximately 2.1 million of these participate in coastal tourism in the Red Sea.[37] When measured in terms of constructed hotel space, the Red Sea and the South Sinai governorates have 28 percent and 24 percent of the total share of Egyptian tourism respectively. The North Sinai governorate is less important to tourism, with the lowest share of hotel rooms at 0.5 percent as of 2000.[38]

Even here, the security apparatus gained several formal and informal footholds in this sector. The Ministry of Defense and Military Production designed the land use maps that the TDA used to distribute coastal allotments. Moreover, Sowers indicates that many of these lands were sold at extremely low prices to ex-military and security personnel.[39] Similarly, Joya describes how the military, engaged in coastal development and tourist expansion, has become an economic class of its own with undisclosed and therefore unaccountable millions of dollars in revenue.[40] Although governorates are also technically responsible for shaping management in tourist zones, governors are appointed by the president, rather than elected by the mass public, directing accountability toward the executive branch. Further, the military has historically held additional informal authority over natural resource management. Under former air force commander turned president Mubarak, significant numbers of executive appointees to natural resource management agencies came from the state security apparatus, regardless of training or scientific background.[41] Those apparatchiks who were closer to Mubarak had greater access to valuable political positions.

Even the declaration of protected areas is complicated by relationships between the executive branch and the agencies responsible for enforcing environmental policy. In 1997, the prime minister's office fixed the number and location of all current and proposed protected areas in Egypt through the creation of a Land Utilization Map.[42] This map currently describes twenty-seven existing and thirteen planned protected areas, comprising the forty sites to be declared in 2017 on the Land Utilization Map, effectively limiting the ability of new information to spur dynamic responses to the need for protected areas.[43]

This political system through which the Mubarak regime shaped natural resource management until 2011 is described by Adly as "embedded cronyism."[44] It differs markedly from the postcorporatist Mexican system and the patron-clientelist Jamaican system. The importance of personal relationships and the centralization of land use authority in Egypt has been greater than those of the centralized, erstwhile bureaucratic-authoritarian Mexican government, and the comparatively politically open Jamaican system. At the same time, the institutional stability of military officers and their discipline of the system in the post-transition era shows that the state is not a purely personalist regime. Clearly, institutional relationships within the military also influence how power operates in this autocratic system. As a result, the formal division of authority and institutional jurisdiction in the Egyptian system gives a distorted view of the real allocation of power and authority. Personalism, cronyism, and the military command structure combine to make the management of political resources highly arbitrary.

But regardless of how the competition over political power takes place within the regime, as will be indicated further on, there are far greater restrictions on autonomous mass-public political expressions in Egypt than in the previous two countries studied. While it is too early to tell how former general and current president Abdel Fattah al-Sisi will exercise power, the post-transitional regime is institutionally very similar in key ways to that of Mubarak. A former military officer has taken control of a state in which civil liberties have been restricted, and in which the military has developed formal and informal networks of power in tourism and other politically important sectors. While al-Sisi has made some changes, such as ending the emergency law established by Mubarak, it is likely that tourist management will be shaped by path dependency and continued (perhaps strengthened) military control for the foreseeable future. It is within this context of de facto centralization and personalistic structures of authority that the Project for Mainstreaming Conservation of Migratory Soaring Birds developed.

Transnational Mobilization around the Rift Valley/Red Sea Flyway

The emergence of the MSB project followed the same essential pattern as the previous three cases: concern about the management of globally important biodiversity developed among a set of core, transnationally organized civil society actors who, in the process of mobilizing support for management among target audiences, developed a common policy enterprise.

Again, identifiable ENGOs were crucial to the development of a nucleus of concerned actors (see table 4.1).

Concern about the bird flyways in the Red Sea and Rift Valley region developed among a transnational network of birders in the 1970s. In 1972, ornithologist R. E. Moreau compiled studies to map out the routes of the

Table 4.1

List of TAN members in the MSB project

Organization	Individuals	Functions	Science training
Birdlife International	Graham Tucker	Threat assessment. Species monitoring.	Ornithology
	Richard Porter	Species monitoring	Ornithology
	Sherif Baha el Din (also NCE)		Ornithology
	Mindy Baha el Din (also NCE)	Species monitoring	Ornithology
Cairo University	Mohammed Kassas (also NCE)	Protected areas ecology. Biodiversity studies.	Botany
NCE	Hala Barakat		Ornithology
	Mary Megalli	Species and habitat monitoring	Ornithology
	John Grainger (also EgyBirdGroup)	Species and habitat monitoring	Ornithology
	Mohammed Amin	Species and habitat monitoring	Ornithology
EgyBirdGroup	István Moldován	Ranger training. Habitat monitoring. Species monitoring.	Ornithology
	Tom Coles	Species and habitat monitoring	Ornithology
	Nick Williams	Species and habitat monitoring	Ornithology
	Dick Hoek	Species and habitat monitoring	Ornithology
	Alaa El-Din	Habitat monitoring. Protected areas management.	Ranger
	Gudrun Hilgerloh	Habitat monitoring	Ornithology

African-Eurasian flyway.[45] The African-Eurasian Flyway was identified at the time as one of the three globally important routes for migratory birds, the other two occurring in the Americas and in the Palaearctic-South Asian Flyway. This study was later cited as a foundational project by other ENGOs, such as Birdlife International, that became concerned about depleting populations of migratory soaring birds in the 1980s and 1990s.[46]

In the early 1990s, Birdlife and other transnational stakeholders in migratory soaring bird management, such as the World Conservation Union (IUCN) and Wetlands International, began conducting research and sharing information to identify emerging threats and problems with the integrity of the flyway. Between 1991 and 1992, Birdlife and Wetlands International, then known as the International Waterfowl and Wetlands Research Bureau, held a series of international workshops to conduct threat analyses and map the geographic dimensions of the African-Eurasian Flyway.[47] Between 1992 and 1995, Birdlife and Wetlands International developed a series of projects to protect bird species in the European section of the flyway, and since the 1990s, Wetlands International has been developing "Implementation Priorities" for the African-Eurasian Waterbird Agreement (AEWA), including recommendations on local bird conservation.[48]

At the same time, Birdlife began establishing contacts with domestic sources of expertise in Middle Eastern and North African (MENA) flyway countries, such as Egypt. Creating a governance system in the MENA region was a crucial step, since conservation efforts in Europe could be undone by mismanagement along other points of the flyway. The contacts between Birdlife and domestic experts developed around the same time that local actors in Egypt began independently studying management and population patterns of migratory soaring birds. In Egypt, a group of researchers had created the Egyptian Ornithological Society in the 1980s. Though small and short-lived, the group counted among its members Egyptian experts on birding, such as Sherif Baha el Din and Moustafa Fouda.[49] Sherif became affiliated with Birdlife in 1989, when he married Mindy Rosenzweig, an American ornithologist hired by Birdlife to work in Cairo. In 1990, Birdlife hired Sherif Baha el Din to be the official Birdlife Affiliate in Egypt, assigning him the responsibility of conducting research on mapping and species identification of birds in Egypt.[50] Therefore, by 1990, a TAN consisting of Egyptian and non-Egyptian researchers had emerged, and began studying challenges to conservation of migratory soaring bird populations.

In the middle to late 1990s, the TAN found multiple opportunities in the international political arena to influence the agenda of regional bird conservation. During that period, governments in the region sought to demonstrate compliance with MEAs relating to biodiversity and endangered species management. In 1995, governments that were members of the 1979 Convention on Migratory Species (CMS) negotiated an MEA under the CMS called the African-Eurasian Waterbird Agreement. AEWA was an agreement created explicitly to improve management of the birds that used the flyway. Under this agreement, the member governments used the research on bird migration conducted between 1991 and 1995 from Birdlife, Wetlands International, the WWF, and the IUCN, to promote improved regional management of migratory birds and habitats among neighboring countries in the flyway zone.[51] In 1997, the Egyptian government explicitly linked AEWA to its efforts to carry out the Convention on Biological Diversity.[52]

As member governments began planning the management and monitoring processes to carry out AEWA, they drafted Action Plans, created with input from the network of ENGOs, to use in situ conservation to protect waterbirds. In the Action Plans, member governments reiterated some of the same concerns generated by TAN organizations Wetlands and Birdlife. For example, echoing the concerns of the ENGOs, the Action Plans highlighted the significance of the flyway for global species and ecosystems, and discussed the need to ban or phase out environmentally harmful activities such as the use of lead shot; illegal taking of birds; human disturbances in resting sites; and the use of poisoned bait.[53] After AEWA entered into force in 1999, members of Birdlife, Wetlands International, the IUCN, and the WWF became officially involved with the international institution, by serving on AEWA's Technical Committee, and participating as observers in the Meetings of the Parties (MOPs).[54]

During the late 1990s, Birdlife International took steps that strengthened the connections between the transnational pool of knowledge and local experts in the various countries involved in regional bird conservation. For example, between 1997 and 2003, Birdlife and the United Nations Development Programme (UNDP) launched a project to identify Important Bird Areas (IBAs) in Africa. Under Birdlife's definition, IBAs are defined as those areas in which at least 1 percent of a global population of migratory birds pass through, or areas that function as bottlenecks.[55] In Egypt, Sherif Baha el Din carried out the identification of IBAs, finding a total of thirty-four, most of which were also identified as sensitive and ecologically important wetlands (see figure 4.2).[56] As in the AEWA study, this report highlighted the geophysical parameters of the flyway, illustrated the importance of bird habitats, and identified specific anthropogenic threats to migratory soaring birds including: tourist development, pollution, agriculture, and unregulated persecution.[57]

By the end of the 1990s, reports and studies generated for AEWA, the IBA program, and domestic studies indicated that the existing management structure was insufficient to protect these birds and their habitats from these anthropogenic threats. In order to address this problem, Birdlife

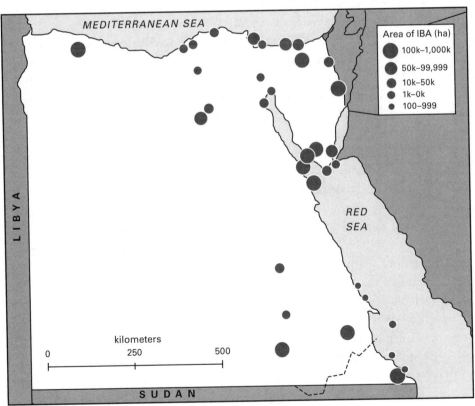

Figure 4.2
Map of BLI registered Important Bird Areas. *Source:* Author's reproduction of map in Sherif Baha el Din, *Directory of Important Bird Areas in Egypt* (Cairo: Birdlife International, 1999), 242, http://www.birdlife.org/datazone/userfiles/file/IBAs/AfricaCntryPDFs/Egypt.pdf, accessed June 10, 2015.

began developing an additional project to improve management of all migratory soaring birds and habitats in the flyway region. In 2003, Birdlife began drafting a proposal for a GEF-funded effort.[58]

As conceptualized, the project Birdlife was planning was intended to focus on those countries with poor environmental governance, but which were critical to the effective management of migratory soaring birds in the African-Eurasian Flyway. These were Djibouti, Egypt, Eritrea, Ethiopia, Jordan, Lebanon, Saudi Arabia, Sudan, Syria, Yemen, and territories controlled by the Palestinian Authority.[59] The part of the flyway covered by these countries was called the Rift Valley/Red Sea Flyway. Like AEWA, the planned project initially took a site-specific approach to the in situ conservation of IBAs,[60] and was linked to other biodiversity related MEAs, such as the CBD and the Ramsar Convention.[61]

In order to clarify the needs of the project, Birdlife recruited local and transnational experts to conduct a threat assessment on bird management in 2004. Building on research conducted by Baha el Din in Egypt, and local expertise in other countries, this assessment reiterated the need for improved legislation and environmental regulation in the Red Sea/Rift Valley countries. Further, the assessment, synthesized by Graham Tucker of Birdlife, identified as significant regional threats some of the same concerns brought up earlier in the AEWA studies and the IBA studies, namely unregulated hunting, tourism, and improper waste disposal.[62]

The project proposal was finalized under the GEF in 2005. In order to create a targeted management approach, Birdlife ornithologists Graham Tucker and Richard Porter conducted a study that year on the species of migratory soaring birds primarily dependent on the flyway. This study identified thirty-seven vulnerable species, and the health of these species then became the primary indicator for the success of regional bird conservation under the proposed GEF-funded project.[63]

Generally, Birdlife's modus operandi is to delegate management authority and funds garnered from GEF projects to local, affiliated ENGOs. However, whereas countries such as Lebanon had civil society ENGOs that were approved to work independently on migratory bird issues, Egypt did not. In order to keep Egypt involved in the Birdlife-developed project, the MSEA/EEAA was made the implementing agency, with the understanding that a domestic ENGO would be incorporated later, become an official Birdlife Affiliate, and function as the implementing agency of the MSB project.[64]

To this end, Mindy and Sherif Baha el Din, along with associates from the Egyptian Academy of Scientific Research and Technology and Cairo University created Nature Conservation Egypt (NCE) as an ENGO in 2005.

NCE became an official Birdlife Affiliate, and after 2006, resident birders from Egypt and countries such as the United States, Romania, and the UK joined the organization to advocate for improved migratory soaring bird and habitat management. The network grew further with the creation of an email list called EgyBirdGroup, established by Romanian ornithologist István Moldován, also an NCE member. Under this email list, members of NCE could share reports and information on birds with researchers from around the world who were interested in Egyptian birding. The EgyBird-Group network was crucial to the knowledge pool available to the TAN, as some of the ornithologists participating in the EgyBirdGroup mailing list included Tom Coles and Nick Williams, both of whom were recognized global experts on Sooty Falcons (*Falco concolor*), one of the indicator soaring birds addressed by the project.[65]

This network built on foundational research conducted in the 1970s and concretized between 1991 and 2003, demonstrating the importance of the flyway to globally endangered migratory soaring birds, identifying key migratory soaring birds to be covered by management efforts, and highlighting the threats faced in each flyway country. Like the other networks identified in the research, the size of the TAN is larger than is suggested in the provided table. The EgyBirdGroup alone counts 185 members, but most of these actors were not a core part of the network. During the period of field research, most of the emails on the list (which included exchanges of draft reports, discussions of threats to birds, and requests for hospitality for visiting researchers), were sent by around fifteen of the EgyBirdGroup members. An approximation of the core network actively involved in advocacy suggests that it counts between thirty and forty members, larger than the Jamaican Cockpit Country epistemic community, but smaller than the networks active in Mexico.

The link between transnational and Egyptian knowledge was facilitated by the Baha el Dins, as well as through Moldován's creation of the Egy-BirdGroup mailing list. In addition, transnational researchers conducting field surveys of migratory birds had to work with locally based expertise in remote, desert sites. For example, Alaa el-Din, a ranger in the Red Sea Protectorate, and István Moldován who conducted research near Hurghada, also in the Red Sea area, were contact points for Birdlife researchers. Among the non-Egyptians who made use of this network were the British ornithologists John Grainger and Nick Williams, and researchers from other organizations, such as Dick Hoek of WWF. Notably, the Egyptian network was not maintained by a comparable level of regular meetings and formalized processes as occurred in the other networks, especially the network involved in the MBRS Project.

While the network was based in part on knowledge produced in Egypt, it had little connection to a lay population, particularly when compared to the networks in the Mexican and Jamaican cases that depended on lay mobilization for their conservation efforts. The Egyptian network was comprised specifically of specialists, either trained formally as ornithologists, or as rangers through the Egyptian government or other research institution. In part, this lack of connection to local nonexperts in the Rift Valley/Red Sea Flyway was due to the very low population density in desert areas, even though Bedouins and other tribal people lived off the land. The end result was a network whose access to environmental knowledge and subsequent knowledge claims were not grounded in the local justice narratives of desert dwellers. This is despite the fact that, as a staffer at the EEAA explained, land management and natural resource use is crucial to the subsistence and livelihood of people who live near protected areas, like Lake Burullus on the Mediterranean: "The people of Burullus are very simple people, and they like to get their food from out of the lake over there, and from the sea. And so, they don't care what we [in the EEAA] do. Unless he gets a benefit from out of it. Other things, no. He's not going to support you [in conservation] because day by day, whatever he gets from the nature, he sells it in the market, and from this money he eats, and feeds his kids. And he's going to kill you, if you stop him."[66]

Unfortunately, the lack of lay involvement in conservation under the MSB project meant the network was unable to establish a base of support in the mass public. This was problematic for the network's goals of influencing policy, since the network in this case faced substantial obstacles in communicating their shared information to policymakers, due to Egypt's autocratic centralization, embedded cronyism, and domestically weak civil society. Further, the network could not generate a knowledge consensus on the science behind biodiversity loss in the Red Sea/Rift Valley Flyway, all of which disadvantaged the network's advocacy goals.

One of the primary issues addressed by this chapter is whether political centralization and autocracy are conducive to greater socialization or not. As described earlier, the Egyptian political system is highly closed, with decision-making authority over natural resources dispersed among formal and informal relationships shaped by the state security apparatus. Formally, there is minimal scope for the exchange of ideas and information between the civil society and policymakers, and every interview respondent, in the civil society and in policymaker agencies, has observed that there is no institutional "mechanism"[67] for communication between the government and ENGOs. While Egypt has a few dozen ENGOs, most of which are based in Cairo,[68] they have little autonomy under the Egyptian legal system. Unsurprisingly, this suggests that autocracy has a chilling effect on the ability of nonstate actors to influence environmental policymaking.

However, the Egyptian system was not always hostile to social ties between the civil society and policymakers. Historically, transnational networks of experts have had some success in influencing natural resource management in Egypt precisely because of personal ties to policymakers. After the 1972 Stockholm Conference (UNCHE), and prior to the creation of the EEAA/MSEA in 1982, the Egyptian government found itself in need of scientific environmental knowledge. UNCHE marked the first international conference explicitly targeted at environmental governance, and in its wake, governments felt some pressure to at least appear as if they were going to do something about the environment. During this period, academics from the National Academy were able to exercise significant influence on policymaking in Egypt, particularly in a protected areas management.[69] As the renowned Egyptian botanist, and former president of the IUCN, Mohammed Kassas explained, the need for information on conservation, and the lack of a clear governmental program meant the scientific community had privileged access to shaping protected areas management:

[The] history is this: before 1980, before 1982, all environmental concerns were in two groups. One is the national MAB [Man and Biosphere] committee. And this national committee belongs to the ministry of higher education, so [it was based] within universities. ... So the link there was very close, between the scientific groups as represented in the MAB national committee, and the government ... And this group of scientists in the MAB commission set out the first proposal for an organization for the environment. And this group also produced a statement for nature conservation in Egypt, including identifying a list of sites to be protected. All this was preparatory for 1982. This was the scientific community very much involved, very much concerned with the environment, including nature conservation.[70]

Because of this period of involvement by civil society scientists in the production of policy relevant knowledge, and the cultivation of personal ties between researchers and policymakers, scientists had measurable impact on environmental governance in Egypt, at least until the 1980s. For example, Egyptian governmental support for the marine oil pollution regime in the Mediterranean Sea was facilitated by the willingness of policymakers to endorse suggestions and findings from scientists like Mohammed Kassas. During this time, the domestic civil society had comparatively freer rein to socialize with foreign researchers, which helped the Egyptian scientists gain access to cutting-edge knowledge about pollution and environmental mitigation.[71]

This process whereby an autocratic system creates political opportunities for technical experts to influence policy is not uncommon. Teets writes about "consultative authoritarianism" in China, where policymakers retain control of the political system, but grant sufficient autonomy to experts in areas they feel insufficiently prepared to manage.[72] Described by Sowers as "embedded autonomy," this system operated in Egypt through the 1980s and early 1990s, as environmentalists like Kassas and el-Din convinced the state to adopt reforms in managing protected areas and marine management.[73]

But after the 1990s, the formerly attentive regime began limiting the sphere of access for the civil society. Whereas top leadership posts in the environmental agencies had gone to technical experts before, by the 2000s, Mubarak had started turning more to his associates in the security apparatus and employing cronyism in the management of Egypt's affairs. Mubarak's antipathy to independent experts was also repeated in other branches influenced by the military apparatus. In illustrating the growing split between the political elite and technical experts in the civil society, a 2008 cable released by WikiLeaks in 2011 describes a government whose "increasing opposition to dialogue with academia is symptomatic of its social and intellectual decline."[74] The military in particular became "increasingly intolerant of intellectual freedom," such that, under defense minister Tantawi, military personnel who seemed too independent from the political apparatus were sanctioned. This combined with the closing of the political space for civil society autonomy. As one example, the 2002 parliamentary Law 84 permits the dissolution of NGOs by executive order, and criminalized any association between domestic civil society and transnational NGOs without prior permission from the government.[75] Further, the closing of this space occurred alongside a reduction of autonomy and authority in environmental regulatory agencies.

The isolation of the civil society from environmental policymaking was exacerbated by a growing alienation of the environmental agencies (MSEA/EEAA and the NCS) from other branches of government. At the time of writing, civil society TAN members were able to formally establish ties with policymakers in the NCS. For example, the current director of the Nature Conservation Sector is Moustafa Fouda, former member of the Egyptian Ornithological Society and erstwhile colleague of Sherif Baha el Din. Sherif himself was in the employ of the MSEA/EEAA as a technical consultant to the NCS and scientific advisor to the Zaranik Protected Area in the North Sinai, making the Baha el Dins and Moustafa Fouda potential points of connection between the civil society and policymakers in the NCS.

However, these social links were sharply limited, as first, there was little communication between other members of the TAN and Fouda or other policymakers, and second, what links were present were described in interviews as ad hoc. Mohammed Kassas himself commented on this, saying: "I think that maybe people like Moustafa Fouda get advice on scientific matters on an individual basis, not in any organized manner. There is no science advisory committee for these protected areas. It is not accessorized."[76]

The isolation of the NCS in environmental policymaking further complicates the communication between the civil society and the Egyptian government. First, as described earlier, environmental authority over protectorates rests with the center and the security apparatus through institutions such as personal ties and the power of the governorates.[77] As one EEAA staffer described, this was manifested by increasing oversight by elites in the military and tourism ministries over environmental regulations. Second, at the time of writing, the NCS was still chronically underfunded, and did not have the authority to independently carry out essential functions, such as allocating resources, hiring staff, and setting priorities for management in established protectorates, whether IBAs or otherwise. The Sant Katherin National Park and Ras Mohammed in the South Sinai governorate generate revenue through user access fees. However, these fees are not collected and managed by the Protectorates Division of the NCS, but rather are submitted to a centrally controlled Environment Protection Fund under the executive branch.[78] Parks and protected areas in Ras Mohammed,

Sant Katherin, and the Red Sea Islands generate approximately 96 percent of revenue from protected areas, yet receive only a fraction in return as maintenance and upkeep.[79] Since the executive branch has discretion over how these funds are managed, and can direct them to areas outside the Protectorates Division, the NCS is essentially subsidizing other functions of the government.[80]

Finally, the network was unable to generate a scientific consensus on the causes, consequences, and extent of the challenges facing migratory soaring bird populations. As indicated in the previous chapters and the literature, knowledge consensus is a defining feature of epistemic communities. But despite sharing a common interest in conserving flyway zones, members of this network did not generate an intersubjective consensus on the causal relationship between human activity and depletion of bird populations. There was no clear agreement on how to disaggregate and measure the relative contribution of each kind of anthropogenic activity to bird mortality rates at a regional or domestic level, and in some cases, disagreement about whether observed mortalities were the result of human activity. In a 2005 assessment of bottleneck sites, Birdlife ornithologist Richard Porter noted: "Whilst the main threats to soaring birds on migration have been studied elsewhere in the world, there is a serious lack of quantitative data for the Middle East. For example it is known that the shooting of raptors for the stuffed-bird trade is a common practice in Syria but there is no information on the numbers involved."[81]

The finding of substantial uncertainty was reiterated throughout the development of the MSB project. In 2005, the final project proposal for the MSB project noted the "lack of quantitative information"[82] that could give a clear picture of the effect of specific activities, such as tourism and hunting to migratory soaring bird populations. The report continued, observing that "beliefs about what threatens [migratory soaring birds] during migration may not be supported by evidence."[83] In 2007, the German Development Bank commissioned an investigation of the potential impact of wind farms on migratory soaring bird populations in Gebel el Zeit in the Red Sea governorate. Like the Porter report, this study concluded that clear, uncontested, and scientifically valid data on the likely impact of wind turbines on migratory soaring bird populations was not available.[84] In 2008, the EgyBirdGroup circulated multiple reports of mass mortalities of migrating White Storks near reservoirs in Sharm el Sheikh, a tourist destination in the South Sinai governorate. After tracing the messages and discussion of the online group, it was clear that there was no scientific consensus on the likely cause of death. Among the hypotheses that members advanced to explain the mass death were: anthropogenic causes such as consumption of polluted water and human persecution; and natural phenomena, such as bacteria, bird flu, and exhaustion.[85] The correlation between the number of observed storks and actual site mortality was also debated, as one birder noted that the arid climate at Sharm el Sheikh desiccates and preserves bird corpses, possibly leading to the overcounting of bird deaths from one event.

Policymakers and Economic Language: Advocacy and Tourism in Egypt

The network active in Egypt therefore faced several obstacles to environmental advocacy in the Rift Valley/Red Sea. Network members did not share a consensus, and they were stymied from communicating by Egypt's increasingly politically diffident system. Not surprisingly, network members turned to economic language here as well, in an attempt to speak in a way they thought policymakers would understand. For example, in 2003, Birdlife asserted that effective management would be possible once policymakers recognized the economic value of conservation to the primary developmental sectors in participating countries.[86] As Mary Megalli of NCE and Tahr Issa in the Protectorates Division of the NCS respectively observed:

You can't go to [policymakers] and talk about conservation. You have to insert it in other things, like ecotourism and so on, to make it sound like development.[87]

... the decision makers understand only the economics. They don't believe in biology or in the importance of some—you can talk about only money, and the importance of it, and how much they are going to lose. So, we have to work for the importance of biodiversity this way, so they can understand. And I think most of it—not most—a *lot* of people understand now, especially in the tourism part.[88]

As the project got underway, the network began to focus on including biodiversity conservation in the tourist program of the government. This marked a change from the previous goals of the project. Whereas the initial goal was to create new protected areas for bird conservation, between 2005 and 2009, Birdlife and the UNDP decided that a site-specific approach focusing on protected areas management would have been ineffective. The primary weakness of using in situ conservation as the primary mechanism, was that migratory soaring birds had too much variation in their flight patterns and resting arrangements to be sure that managing statically defined areas would protect them.[89] As a result, the network adopted a "double-mainstreaming" effort, where they would advise the Egyptian government how to include the goals of migratory soaring bird conservation in key development sectors. Since unregulated tourism was a major threat to bird conservation, one effort focused on making tourist development projects in the Red Sea governorate more flyway friendly.

Although shifting away from exclusively focusing on site-specific conservation, the improved management of protected areas remained an important goal of the TAN.[90] Of the thirty-four IBAs identified in Egypt, fifteen are in currently existing protected areas, and three lie within future proposed areas to be established by 2017.[91] A functional protected areas management regime is therefore crucial to migratory soaring bird conservation. Since only six of the identified protected areas were identified as "receiving adequate protection"[92] in 2000, TAN members advocated for reform of protectorate management, albeit in an ad hoc manner. For example, István Moldován of NCE and EgyBirdGroup participated occasionally in the training of rangers in Red Sea protectorate management in order to persuade the governmental employees to adopt monitoring and management techniques that would help conserve birds and their habitats.[93]

Besides seeking improvements in protectorate management, the TAN used its knowledge base and affiliation with organizations like USAID to promote the greening of tourism. As described, the Red Sea and Sinai governorates are important areas for both tourism and bird conservation. The Red Sea governorate has nine of the IBAs identified in Baha el Din's study, while the North and South Sinai governorates have five each.[94] As this book has shown, those governorates are also crucial areas for large scale tourism. TAN efforts focused on mainstreaming migratory soaring bird concerns into ongoing projects in these areas, largely by promoting ecotourism organized around migratory soaring bird-watching. For example, Birdlife's Middle East Advisor Richard Porter argued in studies used in planning the GEF MBS project that policymakers in the TDA, NCS, and governorates could regulate tourist incursions into bird habitats and resting areas by promoting greater awareness of bird sensitivity among visitors.[95] Doing so would also help promote greater commercial interest in conservation, since tourists who learned about birds would presumably be interested in paying for things like bird-watching tours.

One of the subsequent tourist projects in the Red Sea is the Livelihood and Income from the Environment (LIFE) project, a USAID-funded effort to assist the Tourist Development Authority (TDA) to develop sustainable tourism.[96] As part of this effort, Birdlife funded a manual compiled by Sherif Baha el Din promoting eco-friendly bird-watching in the Wadi el Gamal National Park on the Red Sea coast.[97]

Ecotourism, if supported by the government, would not only contribute to national economic revenue generation and biodiversity conservation, but would also supposedly contribute additional benefits to marginalized populations, primarily of nomads and Bedouins. With the expected growing demand for low-impact tourism and bird-watching, Bedouins would find employment as tour guides, giving them space to contribute local knowledge and expertise to protected areas management. Since tourists would be paying for these services through user access fees, this would mean an important source of revenue for desert people.

This was an important conceptual step in building support for improving governance. Ideally, giving local, marginalized populations a source of revenue from conservation would help alleviate some of the stressors caused by environmentally unfriendly habits, such as unregulated hunting and excessive pesticide use, while including disenfranchised people in a governance program from which they had historically been excluded.[98] At the same time, the idea of including marginalized people in the tourist industry is one that still bases conservation mechanisms on the economic interests of the elite, whether in the crony-capitalist- or military-controlled tourist sector. To the extent that Bedouins and other tribal groups were considered, it was as possible components in the tourist industry, rather than as end users in their own right.

Finally, the TAN sought to incorporate migratory soaring bird concerns into Egypt's energy sector, by using migration patterns to inform programs like the construction of wind farms. In 2006, the Egyptian government planned to construct wind farms funded by the German Development Bank in Gebel el Zeit, an area in the Red Sea governorate that was also identified as an IBA.[99] This farm was intended to contribute a significant amount of energy to the power grid of Egypt—potentially in excess of 3,000 megawatts. As part of the planning effort, the German Development Bank commissioned a feasibility study from a team of ornithologists, led by a German specialist in migrating birds, Gudrun Hilgerloh, from Johannes

Gutenberg University, and followed up with a later review in 2007.[100] Hil-gerloh, who had been exchanging information on the EgyBirdGroup list, divided the proposed construction area into three zones, and argued that construction should be limited to the northernmost zone of the planned area, the area least likely to lead to substantial losses in bird populations.[101] This link between the bird-oriented TAN and the government's energy program marked one of the main ways in which the network gained access to policymaking and environmental planning around bird conservation.

Military Control and Failed Environmental Advocacy in Egypt

While network members may have been occasionally included in ranger training, the network had minimal success in influencing the overall reform of protectorates. Interviews with former protectorates managers indicate that such collaborations between the civil society and the government was undersupported at best, and discouraged at worst. As one former Red Sea protectorates manager said: "If you follow the governmental system, you have to communicate to the higher level of management. You are not allowed to communicate with journalists, for instance. You are not allowed to communicate with people, or elected officials."[102]

In addition, the general system of protectorate management is complicated by the fact that the NCS remains marginalized within the MSEA/ EEAA. As described, this means that the ostensible policymaking authorities on protectorate management are limited in their ability to set management priorities in protected areas, regardless of civil society participation.

Since the late 2000s, the government of Egypt has taken some steps toward reforming protectorates management, and improving the autonomy of the NCS. In 2008, the government submitted a proposal for a GEF-funded project, slated to begin in June of 2010, to improve protected areas management relevant to IBAs and migrating birds covered by the MSB project.[103] As part of this reform effort, the government has endorsed the delegation of further authority and autonomy to the NCS, a key step to improving policy, and necessary to close existing institutional gaps.[104]

However, the historic implementation of protected areas management in Egypt shows a considerable gap between legislation and practice. As observed by a prominent Egyptian biologist from the UNESCO Man and Biosphere program,[105] and a former director of Red Sea protectorates respectively, formally passed policies may go unfulfilled:

[The law] says that each nature reserve must have a Board of Directors. No Board of Directors has been appointed until now for any one of the twenty-seven. Only a Director. Number two; it says that the Ministry must designate a buffer area around the natural reserve—this has not been done yet—in which the Ministry has authority to control activities that will ... affect the nature reserve. So, according to that law, which is not implemented, you can't have a factory, which will send air or water which is polluted, to the natural reserve. You shouldn't do that, if you apply that law to the letter. But it hasn't been implemented.[106]

In Egypt, you can find a lot of protected areas, you know. They have everything, you know. They have the infrastructure, they have the management plan, but they don't have the mentality, the good mentality of the managers. Some of them are not even—they don't know why these protected areas are established.[107]

As noted, members of the TAN, particularly Sherif Baha el Din, had some input in the design of formal ecotourism projects and worked to include issues pertinent to migratory soaring birds in tourist development in the Red Sea area. However, TAN members indicated that their ability to participate in tourism planning was ephemeral at best. In particular, respondents indicated that the only way to get full state support for conservation would rely on network members projecting improbably large and rapid returns on ecotourism activities, like bird-watching. Failing this, the project risked a loss of institutional support.[108] This was especially problematic, given that, as described in interviews, commitment to improved management tended to fade when initial impetus—such as funding generated from USAID and LIFE projects—ended.[109] Another former protectorates ranger, who will be identified pseudonymously only as Ahmed, described some of the difficulties in getting institutional support from the Egyptian government that would outlast the flow of foreign funds: "Another problem with these funded projects—I think they're great when the project is still funded, because they're constantly putting in money. As soon as they leave, all the money coming in, is gone. There's no way to maintain what is established."[110]

Further, despite the LIFE project's inclusion of migratory soaring bird concerns in management, the Egyptian Tourism Federation, a public-private partnership between the Ministry of Tourism and hoteliers, did not mention these birds in their ecotourism plans in the Red Sea coast.[111] Finally, the problem with ecotourism implementation in Egypt is that policymakers and managers may use the term "ecotourism" to refer to a broad array of practices, even those that are contrary to the spirit of environmentally sustainable management. For network members and staffers in the EEAA, this was due to the fact that the large-scale tourist model preferred by the Egyptian elite was not conducive to the low-impact activities that conservationists hoped to inculcate in the industry. If anything, the environmental tools proposed by the network were being co-opted to greenwash the tourist industry, with minimal change in behavior. For example, Mary Megalli of EgyBirdGroup noted that the adoption of ecotourism projects around bird-watching was not translated into meaningful change:

[The] birds of the western Paleoarctic, so many of them migrate here. It's one of the easiest places to find birds that you can't find elsewhere. Along with eastern-western Paleoarctic birds. So, bird-watching tourism, it's been picked up on by the tourism people, and often even in brochures in hotels, or brochures made by the government, they'll mention bird-watching as an activity, along with riding four-wheelers in the desert. But, having mentioned it, they usually don't have a clue what to do about it. They haven't considered the fact that if you offer bird-watching, then you shouldn't have a thousand storks die at Sharm al Sheikh. It's just a catchword.[112]

Similarly, staffers at EEAA noted in interviews and in studies on ecotourism in Egypt that sustainable tourism was, at best, being poorly implemented. The following quotes come from a former protectorates manager from the South Sinai governorate and a study on biodiversity capacity building conducted by the MSEA/EEAA respectively:

[All] the hotels in Sharm say that they have an ecotourism. Because the people come and enjoy the open air, the nature. But over there is not completely—it's not ecotourism. Ecotourism is going in your virgin places and trying to not hurt that virginity, and using whatever minimum resources. ... But you go over there, one guest over there in Sharm uses about 2, 3 cubic meters of water daily, and about, let us say, 10, 20 kilowatts of electricity. So, it's not ecotourism.[113]

While "ecotourism" has become a fashionable term used in the development realm, its practical implementations have been of variable quality.[114]

The primary success in the TAN's efforts to influence biodiversity conservation and mainstream migratory soaring bird concern occurred with energy management in the Red Sea. The German Development Bank responded favorably to Hilgerloh's suggestion, banning construction in the southern three zones, and committing to search for alternative sites for future construction in Egypt.[115] In that case, the recommendations of the civil society became practice. However, this did not show the TAN's influence on the Egyptian government, but rather on a German institution with which the network had established social ties. While undoubtedly important for conservation, this case of success does not suggest that the civil society had influence in the design and implementation of governmental policymaking.

Conclusion

Formally, the effort of the TAN to "mainstream" concern about migratory soaring birds in various sectors in Egypt was successful. As indicated, concerns about migratory soaring bird conservation and habitat management were incorporated into existing plans for protected areas management, including bilateral tourist development projects in the Red Sea, national biodiversity management objectives, and energy management plans.

However, the TAN remained dissatisfied with the actual institutional response and implementation of migratory soaring bird management. First, while the Egyptian government was willing to formally recognize migratory soaring bird concerns as an issue, its response to new information generated by the TAN was hampered by centralization and institutional distortions in natural resource management. The Protectorates Division and the NCS continued to suffer from a lack of resources and low institutional autonomy. The long-term commitment of the MSEA/EEAA to migratory soaring bird mainstreaming, beyond verbal inclusion in project documents was not considered meaningful by TAN interview respondents.

Second, with few exceptions, the TAN remained excluded from the policy decision process. Although the NCS maintained some ties with members of the migratory soaring bird TAN, including Sherif Baha el Din and Mindy el Din, this communication did not extend to the rest of the NCE, or the migratory soaring bird-oriented network. Despite the formal inclusion of the NCE NGO in the MSEA/EEAA's efforts, interview respondents were unanimous in stating that the NCE had no formal input into the implementation of the project, the allocation of resources, or the priorities set in management. The one sector that evinced TAN success was in wind farm construction, and that occurred primarily because ornithologists were able to influence the German Development Bank, the funding agency behind wind farm construction in Gebel el Zeit, not due to any success in persuading Egyptian policymakers directly. At the local management level, members of the TAN occasionally were able to make contact with park rangers in, for example, Red Sea protectorates and Sant Katherin for training sessions and information exchange, but these successes were unorganized, and unsystematic.

Third, while the networks in Jamaica and the SAM were able to tap into mass public support for conservation, the Egyptian network was unable to do so. Much as occurred in the CBMMx Project, this can be explained in part by the focus of the project on linking conservation to the interests of the elite class, rather than the lay public. As with the CBMMx Project, this network was unable to reframe the discourse on conservation toward local justice, although in this case, there is no evidence that they tried. This represented a lost opportunity for the conservationist movement since, as Megalli described, conservation does not resonate with the mass public, outside the privileged few who have access to formal education: "[Frankly], as you've seen, nature conservation, if you made a list of the concerns of local people, the public, if you listed one hundred things, nature conservation would be on the bottom. They don't even know it exists."[116]

Of all factors, the low level of socialization between the network and target audiences was the most significant obstacle to influence. In this case, the exclusion of the migratory soaring bird TAN from de facto project management, and the lack of support from the MSEA/EEAA presented a barrier to the network's efforts. As suggested, the personalist, autocratic Egyptian natural-resource management regime undermined socialization between the network and policymakers, as well as between the network and the mass public, and even the network's ability to generate policy-relevant knowledge.

However, this failure to mobilize locals should not all be attributed to the elite-driven conservationist movement. The Egyptian government's clear willingness to use force to control the civil society under Mubarak, and now Sisi, would make any sort of civil society mobilization difficult. But the counter-Mubarak mobilization in Tahrir Square suggests that it is not impossible. Given the centralization of control over land use in the hands of a political-economic elite, tourism and its attendant environmental problems is an area badly in need of democratic reform.

5   Institutions and Regime Design

Introduction

As scholars of global environmental governance are well aware, nonstate actors can influence how states respond to international problems such as biodiversity loss and ozone depletion. Of course, nonstate actors, unlike states, have to rely on cognitive and persuasive power rather than economic or military resources. As I have argued so far, the epistemic community literature shows that transnational advocacy networks of individuals who share a consensus on the causal relationships and rationales for action in a complex issue area are more likely to influence decision making because their arguments are more likely to be taken seriously by target audiences. Moreover, when networks can ground their claims in local understanding of norms and justice, they will have a better chance of persuading local communities to support their arguments.

However, while scholars agree that nonstate actors matter to environmental governance, they do not always agree why. For rationalists, nonstate actors matter because they can contribute to a knowledge base for rational decision making by clarifying material cause-and-effect relationships. For example, in describing how nonstate actors affect environmental regime design, rationalists point out that, as proselytizers, the civil society can foster a state's interest in doing something about an emerging problem.[1] As sources of expertise and knowledge, they may supplement a state's capacity to respond to emerging problems. Finally, by contributing to monitoring and reporting, the civil society may enhance the contractual environment of regimes by ensuring the recording of infractions. While potentially important to the conduct of regimes, their inclusion in institutions from this perspective is purely functional, and constrained by the parameters set by states.[2]

In the cognitivist tradition, I argue that nonstate actors matter when they shape the norms of behavior to which states and other actors are bound. Norms, or ideas about appropriate behavior in a given issue area, are crucial in explaining political and social behavior. Norms shape how actors think about their identity, how they understand their reality, and how they evaluate the "rightness" of social action in ways that a materialist approach cannot explain. Moreover, the importance of norms in shaping behavior is likely to increase in contemporary environmental governance as the international society faces the challenge of regime complexity. Regime complexity creates additional uncertainty about states' obligations in the international arena, and this uncertainty gives nonstate actors additional room to influence norms of appropriate behavior and thus affect international relations.

As Young and others have written, regime complexity is a function of the sheer growth in the number of international institutions in the modern era. Here, I use the term "institution" in its broad theoretical sense, to refer not just to "relatively stable sets of related constitutive, regulative, and procedural norms and rules" in the international system.[3] Rather, the universe of institutions includes formally established organizations, like the Global Environment Facility (GEF), as well as treaties, their respective protocols, and soft law expectations. The growth in international institutions means that they are increasingly made of rules, norms, and principles that interplay in various ways.[4] Using Young's typology, we can describe these interactions as falling into four (not necessarily exclusive) categories. Institutions may be *embedded* in "broader principles and practices" that constitute a deep structure of shared understandings among actors.[5] For example, all international institutions are embedded in the broader norm of state sovereignty. More concretely, Ruggie describes the function of global financial institutions as constituted in part by the embedded principles of economic liberalism.[6] Institutions may be *nested* as specific arrangements within a broader regime to regulate a particular topic. Protocols to multilateral agreements would fall into this category. They may be *clustered*, when functionally different institutions are combined into an institutional package. For example, the regimes over marine oil pollution, deep seabed minerals, and fishing rights are combined into the law of the seas. Finally, they may *overlap*, where regimes that "were formed for different purposes and largely without reference to one another intersect on a de facto basis."[7] To Young's typology, we can add another kind of interplay from Betts. Regimes may be *parallel* to one another, where "obligations in similar areas may or may not contradict one another."[8]

As the international society continues to create international institutions to respond to the problems of governance, more institutions are likely to experience interplay of one kind or another. As a result, scholars of international environmental politics have ceased to describe governance as something carried out by individual regimes. Rather, international environmental governance is shaped by *regime complexes*. A *regime complex* is an "array of partially overlapping and nonhierarchical institutions governing a particular issue area ... marked by the existence of several legal agreements that are created and maintained in distinct fora."[9] For example, Jungcurt,[10] Rosendal,[11] and Orsini, Morin, and Young[12] all write about the emergence of a regime complex in plant genetic resources (PGR). As they explain, PGR falls under a series of overlapping institutions, including the WTO TRIPS Agreement, the International Undertaking on Plant Varieties, and the Convention on Biological Diversity's Access and Benefit Sharing Protocol (ABS Protocol). Besides the regime complex on PGR, scholars have written about regime complexes in climate change[13] and in nonenvironmental issue areas like refugee management.[14]

The challenge that regime complexity poses is that as institutional interplay increases, it becomes more difficult to tell what an actor's international obligations are in any given area. This is the essential difficulty of regime complexity, also described by UNEP and scholars as institutional *multiplicity*.[15] Because institutions are not hierarchically ordered, overlapping regimes with potentially conflicting rules lead to a lack of clarity about the appropriateness of certain policies. For example, the often-contentious international negotiations about the rules of the regime complex on PGR make it clear that some states and nonstate actors, including indigenous rights groups and some developing nations, feel that the intellectual property protection requirements of the WTO TRIPS Agreement gives too much control over genetic material to pharmaceutical corporations in rich countries. Conversely others, including GMO-producing states and pharmaceutical companies, feel the Access and Benefit Sharing Protocol of the Convention on Biological Diversity (CBD) does not give adequate protection to the intellectual property rights promised in TRIPS.[16] Since it is unclear whether TRIPS supersedes the ABS Protocol or vice versa, the differences between the rule structure of TRIPS and that of the ABS mean there is some ambiguity among the principal stakeholders of PGR about governance issues, including whether the WTO, Convention on Biological Diversity (CBD), or some other organization like the Food and Agricultural Organization (FAO) is the appropriate forum in which to regulate PGR.

The rise of regime complexity also makes it more challenging to determine whether individual environmental regimes are effective. In general, studies of individual regimes argue that properly designed institutions can provide financial incentives to laggardly actors, clarify appropriate rules, and specify requirements for compliance, encouraging states to take needed action where they otherwise would not.[17] When this happens, institutions can meaningfully shape international outcomes. Institutions may be considered "effective," even if the behavioral change they cause in states stops short of some ideal metric of compliance.[18] From this perspective, the international regime, consisting of the actions, expectations, rules and negotiations of states, comprises the "basic unit of analysis."[19]

However, in regime complexes, institutions may overlap in ways that are either synergistic or disruptive.[20] If regimes are effective when they persuade states to take action where they otherwise would not, we could plausibly create some measure of effectiveness by testing whether a regime's goals are being translated into action by member states. But if compliance with one institution undermines the goals of another overlapping institution, it is not clear that we can study regimes in isolation in order to find instances of effectiveness in global governance. Thus, the effectiveness of regime complexes will be shrouded in conceptual ambiguity.

This ambiguity is enhanced by the contingent nature of regime interplay. First, regime overlap is not a necessary function of the rules and structures of separate institutions, but occurs only when key actors believe that the "norms, rules, and procedures" of previously distinct institutions are interrelated at an operative or normative level.[21] There is some inherent subjectivity in the fact that regime overlap emerges from a subjective understanding of political behavior. In other words, a regime complex is not called into existence by scholars who need an analytic tool to describe international politics: "What creates a regime complex is not the subject itself or the related rules and their impacts, but the perceptions of actors regarding these matters. A regime complex can emerge as a result of change in the understanding of the problem without any formal institutional change. Perceptions draw the boundaries of the complex."[22]

Second, the subjectivity inherent in determining *when* institutions overlap means there is additional subjectivity and uncertainty about *how* institutions overlap. Occasionally, regime overlap and emerging complexes can lead to rule convergence and synergy, as has occurred in global trade.[23] In this case, the various international and regional institutions that have been created to regulate trade have shown a great deal of agreement on core principles and underlying procedures in areas like the movement of capital and transboundary tariffs. While the morality of the shift toward trade liberalism has been criticized, it is clear that the trade regime complex has fostered cooperation and policy agreement among states. This complex is characterized by fairly effective governance. But institutional overlap is just as likely to lead to disruption and rule uncertainty, as has occurred in PGR, climate change, and forestry governance.[24] If actors determine subjectively whether rules in one set of institutions pertain to activities in another overlapping set, they may also determine the scope and meaning of this overlap—that is, whether the overlap is synergistic or disruptive. Conceptually, this means there is no necessary relationship between the emergence of regime complexes and whether or not complexes lead to effective governance.[25]

It is in this space of ambiguity, agnosticism, and perception that nonstate actors shape how regime complexes function. In PGR, the creation over two decades of new institutions containing rules on governing genetic material (from the FAO Undertaking, to the Convention on Biological Diversity, to the WTO TRIPs Agreement, and now to the Nagoya Protocol on Access and Benefit Sharing) was the cause of institutional overlap. But, as Alter and Meunier point out, institutions can be "discovered" to overlap not only when states debate rules in international forums, but also when states attempt to translate new international obligations into implementable policy.[26]

At the level of local implementation, state and nonstate actors may invoke additional international institutions as bearing on an emerging issue area, in order to strengthen favorable policy claims, or undermine problematic ones. For example, as India began carrying out World Bank-funded dam construction projects in the 1990s, nonstate advocacy networks tried to invoke the International Labor Organization's Convention 169 on the rights of indigenous people to shape how the government carried out resettlement in areas affected by dam-related flooding.[27] By referencing global norms about indigenous rights, these networks were able during the 1990s to set limits on the size of large dams in India and Brazil, and reform World Bank practices in funding developmental projects. In other words, nonstate actors may also foster rule uncertainty and regime overlap in order to create space to negotiate the meanings of international norms and obligations at the level of domestic policy.

While Orsini, Morin, and Young among others study the effect of regime complexity on international cooperation,[28] international protected areas governance constitutes a distinct area of study, and one in which nonstate actors are more likely to have influence. The primary goal of protected areas institutions (like the Ramsar Convention and the CBD) is not the synchronization of at-the-border politics, as is the case in climate change and the trade of PGR. Rather, it rests on convincing states to enact domestic politics that do not (for the most part) have an external effect on the movement of goods or pollution between states.

In fact, that has been one of the main challenges of protected areas management under global biodiversity institutions. Less-developed countries (in which most of the world's biodiversity remains) have since the 1970s raised objections about being held globally responsible for managing biodiversity in their borders.[29] The growth of international environmentalism in the post-1970s has placed conservation in areas like the Amazon rainforest on the global agenda, making domestic policy now a matter of international attention. Currently, institutions like the CBD, the Ramsar Convention, and other conservation-oriented regimes are constituted around a set of international expectations about state behavior over domestic natural resource management. These expectations may be fairly broad, consisting primarily of exhortatory declarations that states do something about biodiversity loss, or they may be more targeted, calling on states to apply regulations to save specific species of global concern. International conservation thus depends on developed and developing countries negotiating these expectations to find cooperative solutions to the problem of global biodiversity loss.

However, as the comparative literature on environmental politics makes clear, protected areas conservation in developing countries is not only a matter of debate between LDC governments and the industrialized world, but also is often fiercely contested at the local level within LDCs. From Brazil[30] to Ecuador[31] to India,[32] local communities, governmental policymakers, industrialists, and NGOs in developing countries have disagreed, often violently (and occasionally fatally) over how protected areas are to be managed. Who defines protected areas? Who gets to participate in managing them? Who pays for management? What does "good" management look like? These are not esoteric questions: their answers have had real impacts on the lives of people, and governments have too often answered them by removing people from their land. Therefore, sorting out rule uncertainty and regime complexity in the conduct of institutions that deal with protected areas regimes will depend heavily on resolving local preferences, and not just on creating international cooperative agreements among member states.

To be clear, the fact that this space for nonstate actor negotiation exists in theory does not mean it will necessarily emerge in practice. If nonstate actors are to influence regime complexity, they will depend on access to participation at both the international level of rule negotiation, and domestically at the level of policy implementation. Thus, democratic states with robust participatory mechanisms are more likely to lead to greater civil society influence on environmental policy as these states are more likely to have the space through which civil society actors can engage in policy advocacy. This comports not only with cross-national studies on domestic environmental policy across different states, but also with studies on states that have transitioned into democracy, as in the cases of post-Soviet nations in Eastern Europe.[33] As a result, the importance of nonstate actors and norm interpretation on regime complexity in conservation means "viewing cooperation [under regimes] in terms of states ... may be highly misleading,"[34] or at best, provide only a partial look at how international conservation works.

The potential effect of nonstate actors also means that what is considered "effective" environmental governance is contested through different scales. In protected areas regimes, local actors and communities who are intimately involved with the process of rule implementation may have different ideas about how nature is to be "imagined" (what comprises important ecosystems and what is to be done with them) than national governments, transnational nongovernmental organizations (NGOs), or international secretariats. In these cases, states may be unable to translate rules into policy because the norms that underlie them do not fit with local ideas about appropriate action. When this happens, regime implementation and conservation may either be undermined by resistance at the local level, or have to be carried out through state coercion.

In order to explain how local contestations and nonstate actor preferences affect regime complexity, I studied four cases of globally relevant protected-areas management projects carried out in developing countries. These cases reflect the importance and wonder of endemic biodiversity in delicate, threatened ecosystems, and the reality of a world in which biodiversity is under increasing threat from human action. First, I covered the Project for Sustainable Conservation of Globally Important Caribbean Bird Habitats carried out in Jamaica's Cockpit Country. Cockpit Country comprises a mountainous area in the northwestern section of the island, inhabited by rural farmers and low-income communities, and threatened by bauxite mining. Second, I discussed the Proyecto para la Conservación y Uso Sostenible del Sistema Arrecifal Mesoamericano (MBRS Project) carried out in Mexico. The MBRS is a coastal and marine ecosystem off the eastern coast of the Yucatán Peninsula where large-scale coastal tourism has been expanding since the 1970s. The MBRS is also populated along the coast by small-scale fishermen, and low-income indigenous communities. Third, I introduced another case in Mexico, the Proyecto del Corredor Biológico Mesoamericano—México (CBMMx Project). Like the MBRS Project, the CBMMx Project concerned Mexico's southern states, but focused inland, where the expansion of cattle farming and unregulated agriculture posed the primary threats to biodiversity. Like the MBRS, communities that live in the CBMMx Project are largely low-income and indigenous. Finally, I studied the Project for Sustainable Conservation of Migratory Soaring Birds carried out in Egypt, which was designed to conserve sensitive ecosystems along the Rift Valley/Red Sea region.

All of these projects were established pursuant to the CBD and financed by the GEF. In comparing these cases, I found that TANs shaped regime complexity by influencing how these governments negotiated and understood the rules of various institutions that applied to their conservation efforts. In determining whether a regime complex existed, I examined policy documents and position papers and recorded arguments by state and nonstate actors to see which international obligations they invoked as pertinent to the project. If important actors (stakeholders, institutions involved in project management, policymakers, and epistemic community members) cited institutional obligations as a reason for action, I included those institutions in tracing the regime complex in which the state was located. I also tested to see whether these actors perceived of a rule conflict by studying their policy positions and rationales for action. As I discovered, while governmental actors, scientists, industry leaders, and local communities sometimes agreed in principle that new protected areas should be created, the language and global norms they invoked did not always correspond and, as a result, neither did their policy preferences. Using Young's and Betts's typologies, I describe the intersection between the various regimes invoked by actors as *embedded, clustered, nested, overlapping,* or *parallel.*

In each country, stakeholders invoked different international institutions relevant to protected areas governance, and most of the ecologically focused ones were nested within the CBD. Although the CBD is a "broad, thin regime,"[35] it does provide some capacity and guidelines to member states to conserve biodiversity and manage protected areas. The primary capacity-building institution within the biodiversity regime is the GEF, administered financially and technically by the World Bank, the United Nations Development Programme (UNDP), and the United Nations Environment Programme (UNEP). The GEF was created specifically to transfer funds, resources, and technical expertise to developing countries (LDCs), under the rationale that most of the terrestrial biodiversity exists within the jurisdiction of LDCs, and that urgent action within these countries is central to effective conservation of biodiversity.[36] In the projects studied, the GEF provided substantial funds to the participating states in the amounts of: US$2,000,000 to Birdlife Jamaica for the Project for Sustainable Conservation in Cockpit Country,[37] US$14,840,000 to Nacional Financiera in Mexico for the MBRS and CBMMx Projects,[38] US$680,000 directly to the MSEA/EEAA as the implementing partner, and another US$1,100,000 through the Red Sea Governatorate Project for MSB double-mainstreaming efforts in Egypt.[39]

While the GEF and the CBD institutions do contribute to generating concern among parties, and have established mechanisms for capacity building, these institutions have very low rule specificity. The GEF has made ratification of the CBD a condition for receiving funds for the ongoing projects discussed in the research, thus establishing rules and incentives for compliance. However, the substantive obligations of the CBD are vague enough to allow parties sufficient scope to equivocate in practice while formally complying with the procedural requirements of the treaty, as monitoring and the actual content of domestic implementation are left to the discretion of states.[40] In each case, local and transnational contestations over implementation have played a key role in constituting and making sense of the regime complexes in which each project was embedded.

Jamaica and Cockpit Country Management

The first case discusses conservation efforts in Jamaica's Cockpit Country, a highly biodiverse region of rainforests and niche microhabitats, formed by conical limestone hills and depressions that resemble the cockfighting pits that give the area its name. Cockpit Country does not have a legally fixed border, which makes contestations over what Cockpit Country "is" and what it is "for" crucial in figuring out how it is to be managed. For Jamaica, there are four institutions on protected areas management that have been nested within the CBD. These are (1) the Convention for the Protection and Development of the Marine Environment of the Wider Caribbean Region (Cartagena Convention),[41] (2) its 1990 protocol on specially protected areas and wildlife (SPAW Protocol),[42] and (3) the Ramsar Convention. These institutions act parallel to one another within the broader biodiversity regime and they share a general interest in conserving protected areas, but do not have normative or operational procedures that intersect in the context of the Cockpit Country. A diagram showing the regime complex pertinent to Cockpit Country conservation is shown in figure 5.1.

These institutions have all played a minor role in the governance of Cockpit Country. For example, the Ramsar Convention calls on member states like Jamaica to conserve wetlands of global importance. In 2007, the National Environmental Protection Agency (NEPA) reported that a Ramsar site, the Black River Lower Morass, had its origin in Cockpit Country. For NEPA and the GEF,[43] while this raised the importance of Cockpit Country to downstream conservation, it did not imply specific rules for management in the Cockpit itself, as it neither is a littoral ecosystem, nor does it have wetlands. The Cartagena Convention, drafted in 1983, was established subsequent to the 1979 Caribbean Environment Programme (CEP-UNEP), one of UNEP's Regional Seas Programmes, and establishes general obligations for "Contracting Parties" to conserve and sustainably manage marine

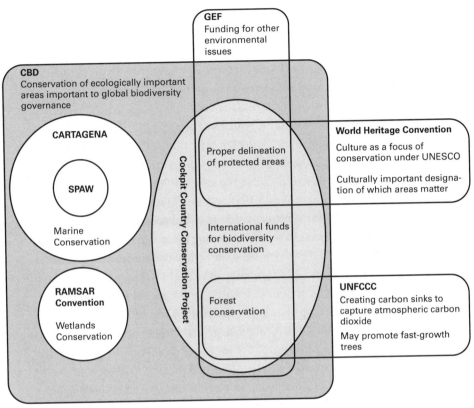

Figure 5.1
The Cockpit Country regime complex.

ecosystems in the Caribbean Sea,[44] and limit land-based sources of marine pollution.[45] Since the 1980s, Meetings of the Parties (MOPs) and the SPAW Protocol of the Convention have explicitly stated that marine management may depend on inland conservation.[46]

In 1999, when a transnational network of advocates lobbied the World Bank to fund conservation in Cockpit Country, some of their members used Jamaica's obligations under Cartagena and SPAW to justify their conservationist push.[47] After the project was adopted, Ann Haynes-Sutton of the Jamaica Environmental Trust, one of the organizing NGOs affiliated with the GEF project, did the same in a 2004 study on in Jamaica's protected areas management system.[48] But beyond raising a general interest in conservation, these institutions have not had any clear effect on how state and nonstate actors understand their international obligations to manage Cockpit Country. The institutions have not established clear regulatory parameters for managing Cockpit Country, nor have they identified species of concern. At most, they have raised the profile of the region.

Problematically, a disruptive overlap between these ecologically oriented institutions and the World Heritage Convention has led to local norm contestation and rule ambiguity about conservation in Cockpit Country. As described in chapter 2, Jamaican members of the transnational epistemic community have been calling since the early 1990s for the declaration of the Cockpit Country as a World Heritage site. The rationale for invoking the World Heritage Convention is that it establishes some guidelines for managing protected areas in ways that could strengthen the protected areas framework of Jamaica. For example, under UNESCO guidelines, zones that are designated as World Heritage sites have to be registered as potential sites under the Convention, under which governments then have to create a legal delineation of boundaries, protecting registered zones "against development and change that might negatively impact the integrity and/ or authenticity of the property."[49] For local stakeholders worried about the Jamaican government's commitment to protecting the Cockpit from bauxite mining, the World Heritage designation would give an additional layer of bureaucratic defense. Moreover, as some stakeholders have commented, World Heritage status brings with it prestige that could be parlayed into investments and funds from the international society, or into advertising in tourism. For example, Article 13 of the Convention specifically states that parties can seek international assistance to protect, conserve, or rehabilitate successfully nominated areas, which implies access to international funds. Similarly, Simon Mitchell of the University of the West Indies (UWI) noted about the Cockpit Country in 2013: "World Heritage is something we really want, because that puts it out there as something very important to protect, and people will recognize that."[50]

During the entire lifespan of the project, local governmental actors and other stakeholders continued to bring the World Heritage Convention to bear on management of the Cockpit Country. Between 2001 and 2013, epistemic community members called on the government of Jamaica in national policy debates, and in international conferences like the 2001

13th International Congress of Speleology to ratify the Convention and declare the site a World Heritage area.

On one hand, for conservationists, the World Heritage Convention has potentially important synergistic overlaps with the biodiversity regime. The potential increase in prestige, and the clarification of Cockpit Country's legal boundaries were both goals that the epistemic community, conservationist policymakers, and local communities agreed upon. On the other hand, the World Heritage Convention (WHC) emphasizes the importance of culture to determining and managing protected areas in a way that differs from the ecological emphasis of the Convention on Biological Diversity and the various protected areas regimes nested within it. Articles 1 and 2 of the WHC, and Annex 3 of its 2013 Operational Guidelines are clear that the kinds of areas that should be included in the WHC are those that demonstrate cultural importance, not just importance to nature and science.[51] While this does not necessarily bring the WHC into conflict with the ecological goals of the biodiversity regime, local stakeholders in Jamaica have interpreted the cultural and ecological goals of the various international institutions in mutually incompatible ways in planning for Cockpit Country management.

For Maroons who have lived in the area since the early anti-colonial and anti-slavery struggles, culture was crucial to their understanding of the land and what they knew as Cockpit Country. Since the 1990s, when the possibility of bauxite mining was first raised, Maroon leaders have reiterated the cultural importance of Cockpit Country in interviews with academics and researchers on conservation, noting the importance of history in delineating the area. Recently, in a 2013 interview, a Maroon stated that the region known as Cockpit Country was defined specifically by anticolonial struggles:

The Maroons them from Clarendon straight back through Maroon Town, Accompong, has shown clearly [that] ... even from 1690, the whole of the section right there was Cockpit Country ... because the Cockpit Country is where warfare arise from, right? I feel clearly within myself and other people views as well, that there should be no mining in or around Cockpit Country, because even in these areas from Maroon Town straight to Accompong ... the whole of them place ... was the battle field for the Maroons. It was Cockpit Country and is still Cockpit Country. So we really would like to see no mining in those regions because it is going mess up all of our heritage.[52]

As a result, for these communities, the region was marked by borders determined through battles fought against the British in the Maroon Wars. In referencing their postcolonial struggles, the Maroons also made continual reference to another international institution—namely, a treaty signed with the British at the end of the guerilla struggles. To the descendants of those who signed it, the story of this treaty has been passed down through oral recollections as a sacred "blood oath" guaranteeing the Maroons perpetual sovereignty over land in Cockpit Country.[53]

By the late 2000s, when the Ministry of Agriculture agreed under continual political pressure to protect Cockpit Country against mining, the cultural claims of Maroon leaders had become folded in to the policy arguments of the Cockpit Country Stakeholders Group (CCSG). The organizations within the CCSG included groups who had been invoking the WHC since 1999, members of the epistemic community, Jamaican supporters locally and in the diaspora, and various transnational advocates. In advocating for protection of Cockpit Country, the CCSG drew up a map based on boundaries derived in part from ecological relationships, but also informed by the colonial-era road system and the location of Maroon battles (see figure 1.4).

However, these culturally informed borders did not entirely fit with what scientists, including some in the epistemic community, understood to be the ecologically defined borders of Cockpit Country. In 2009, an ad hoc working group comprising scientists from governmental agencies like the Forestry Department, NEPA, Jamaica's National Heritage Trust, and the Office of the Prime Minister as well as epistemic community organizations Windsor Research Centre and the Nature Conservancy, drafted a National Ecological Gap Assessment Report (NEGAR). The NEGAR, required by the CBD, was intended to create an ecological map of the protected areas governance structure and gaps in coverage in Jamaica. As part of the NEGAR, the working group mapped Cockpit Country according to what they understood as the ecological characteristics of the region, and it soon became clear that the two maps—NEGAR and CCSG—were different (see figure 5.2).

In 2013, the Center for Environmental Management at UWI held a series of public consultations with the major stakeholders in Cockpit Country policymaking to determine what the boundaries of the protected zone should be. These included government officials from the JBI and the Ministry of Agriculture, members of Maroon communities, and scientists from UWI

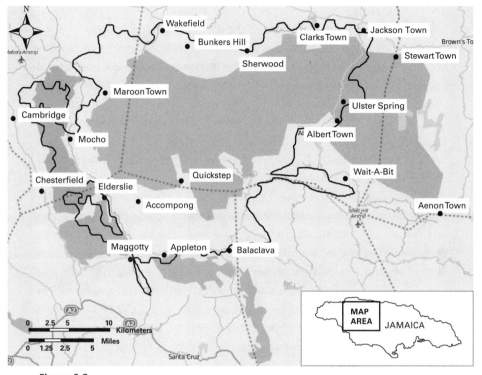

Figure 5.2
NEGAR boundary of Cockpit Country. *Source:* Author's reproduction of map taken from Dale Webber and Claudel Noel, *Public Consultations on Defining the Boundaries of the Cockpit Country*, technical report prepared for the Centre for Environmental Management of the University of the West Indies (Kingston: Centre for Environmental Management 2013), 181.

and advocacy organizations. While some members of the epistemic community, like Mike Schwartz of the Windsor Research Centre, saw the possibility of a compromise position between the NEGAR and CCSG borders, not everyone agreed. The Forestry Department, which had been a critical ally and participant in the early conservationist advocacy of the epistemic community deemed the CCSG borders "unacceptable," and saw the NEGAR boundaries as "ideal." The Forestry Department's stated objection to using the CCSG borders was based on fears that, if cultural claims were used to define the region, their conservationist goals would be taken over by the Maroons who "stated that they own the entire Cockpit Country [and] also believed that they can do whatever they want with the forest resources."[54] Within the Jamaican government, the Ministry of Environment and the Ministry of Tourism—both of which joined the Forestry Department in opposing mining in the area—similarly sided with the NEGAR borders and against the CCSG. In contrast, NGOs and Maroons in the CCSG vastly preferred the CCSG version which was informed by cultural arguments and the history of the Maroon Wars. By 2013, it was clear that differing understandings at the local level about the appropriateness of cultural heritage on one hand, and biodiversity on the other, led to a tension among stakeholders in Cockpit Country conservation.

Even as the overlap between the WHC and CBD has led to rule ambiguity and contestation among conservationists, the efforts of local actors to invoke the climate change regime could lead to additional regime complexity in the near future. Within the UN system, there are a variety of institutions that are aimed at incentivizing developing states like Jamaica to reduce deforestation and land degradation. Land and forest loss is important to the climate regime complex because healthy forests and land tend to absorb more carbon than they emit, making them function as "carbon sinks" in climate discussions. The more land and forests that are cut down or degraded, the less ability the earth has to absorb anthropogenic carbon dioxide. Among the international mechanisms are programs like the Clean Development Mechanism under the Kyoto Protocol, and the conservation programs to reduce emissions from deforestation and degradation (known as REDD+) under the UN. These provide capacity building and investments to developing countries so that they reduce the loss of forest cover through activities like logging and mining, in exchange for generating carbon credits that other actors can use to offset their own carbon production.

In 2011, the Planning Institute of Jamaica (PIOJ) submitted a report to the Forest Carbon Partnership Facility, indicating an interest in attracting REDD+ support to manage Cockpit Country. That year as well, Peter Edwards of NOAA conducted an economic valuation of the Cockpit Country for the Windsor Research Centre to demonstrate the potential value of carbon storage in the region. Using IPCC data, Edwards claimed that Cockpit Country contributed over US$10 million per year in removing atmospheric carbon, and encouraged the government of Jamaica to participate in REDD+, with the intent of generating revenue and protecting the area.

However, NGOs should be cautious about bringing additional institutions in climate change to bear on an already complex situation. Studies of other developing countries that have participated in REDD+ and similar institutions show that managing areas as carbon sinks can disrupt the goals of other, overlapping protected areas institutions. For example, in Tanzania, Mexico, Brazil, and Costa Rica, the requirements of REDD+ that governments set aside and regulate land under the goals of the climate regime has led to concerns among indigenous groups who have feared being dispossessed by a state with which they have a history of mutual hostility.[55] In addition, the carbon-capture approach of REDD+ has led to incentives among those governments to promote fast-growing trees as carbon sinks, even if doing so displaces native fauna for alien species.[56] Thus, if local and state actors do bring the climate change regime complex to bear on protected areas management here, the end result could be a regime complex with greater disruptive overlap, as I will discuss in one of the cases in Mexico.

Mexico and the Mesoamerican Reef System

As in Jamaica, Mexico's conservation efforts are linked to a regime complex consisting of institutions in protected areas, cultural conservation, and climate change. Due to Mexico's regional importance to Latin America and its sizable indigenous population, stakeholders have also invoked international institutions pertaining to regional political integration and indigenous rights. In contrast to Jamaica, the overlap between the cultural institutions of UNESCO and the World Heritage Convention with the environmental institutions of the CBD and other conservation agreements have not led to similar levels of contestation over appropriate policy in either of the two projects. This suggests again that the kind of institutional overlap—whether synergistic or disruptive—cannot be objectively determined simply by identifying the institutions that overlap. Rather, institutional overlap is determined by subjective understandings among actors. Again, this is not to say that there is no contestation over policy: in the MBRS Project, hoteliers and local policymakers in Quintana Roo state have vigorously opposed additional conservationist measures, while local communities in the CBMMx Project opposed the project throughout the late 2000s.

In Mexico's MBRS Project, the institutions nested within the biodiversity regime are (1) the Cartagena Convention, (2) its SPAW Protocol, (3) its Protocol Concerning Pollution from Land-Based Sources and Activities (LBS Protocol), (4) The Ramsar Convention, (5) The Tulúm Declaration, (6) the Centroamerican Commission on Environment and Development (CCAD), and (7) the Caribbean Environment Programme of the UNEP (CEP-UNEP). A diagram showing the regime complex pertinent to MBRS conservation is shown in figure 5.3.

In contrast to Jamaica, these institutions have a higher level of rule specificity bearing on protected areas management in the MBRS. The Cartagena Convention, ratified by Mexico in 1985, links marine management in the Caribbean Sea, part of which includes Mexico's territorial waters in the Mesoamerican basin, to the broader goals of global biodiversity conservation. This concern in turn was reinforced by the 1999 adoption of a

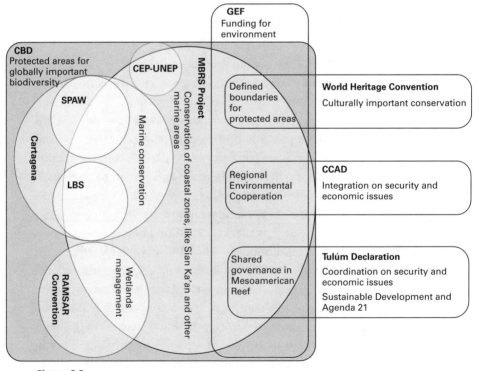

Figure 5.3
The MBRS Project regime complex.

Protocol Concerning Pollution from Land-Based Sources and Activities (LBS Protocol) to the Cartagena Convention. The LBS Protocol requires states to cooperate bilaterally or regionally to limit transboundary marine pollution,[57] to hold regular meetings of the parties[58] and to report to UNEP on the implementation of the agreement.[59] Like the MBRS Project, the LBS Protocol is concerned with limiting terrestrial sources of marine pollution.

The 1997 Tulúm Declaration specifically cited the Mesoamerican basin as a region requiring urgent cooperative action for biodiversity governance among states.[60] The Declaration further linked sustainable development and Agenda 21 to the conservation of the reef ecosystem as a site of globally important biodiversity, a buffer zone against coastal erosion, and relevant to tourist development.[61]

The CCAD and CEP-UNEP also raise the profile of the Mesoamerican reef. CCAD asserted in 1996 that the regional governments of Central American countries and Mexico should cooperate for improved, multilateral environmental management, particularly for transboundary ecosystems like the basin. The LBS Protocol and the CEP-UNEP further enhance the capacity of states to respond to problems associated with coastal environmental degradation. The CEP-UNEP functions as a standing scientific body for the Protocol. It has published information on the causes and types of marine pollution in the Wider Caribbean Region, including forty-eight technical reports since 1989. In 1994, it concluded a technical report highlighting the contribution of sedimentation, hydrocarbons, sewage, and agricultural runoff to marine environmental degradation, all of which pertain to marine management off the coast of Quintana Roo.[62] In addition, the organization maintains highly technical information sources for parties, such as databases on marine litter, protected areas management, and surveys on pollution loading in the Mesoamerican basin.[63]

The SPAW Protocol and the Ramsar Convention have also established additional rules that clarify the importance of conservation in the MBRS to global governance. Articles 5 and 11 of the SPAW Protocol call on parties to take specific conservation measures, including the prohibition of activities harming the kinds of coastal mangroves and seagrasses found in the MBRS Project.[64] As a signatory to Ramsar, Mexico is required to identify wetlands of international importance, designate them as such in a centrally recognized list,[65] and create domestically established measures for conservation of the area.[66] As of 2010, several of the areas involved in the MBRS Project have become Ramsar sites, including the Sian Ka'an Reserve (declared 2003), and National Parks at Xcalak (2003), Puerto Morelos (2004), Banco Chinchorro (2004), and Cozumel (2005).

There are institutions that overlap with these biodiversity instruments, but they have not done so in a disruptive way. Like Jamaica, Mexico is a member of the World Heritage Convention, but Mexico has gone further than Jamaica has by implementing the WHC and declaring some areas World Heritage sites. One of these, the Sian Ka'an Biosphere Reserve, is virtually in the middle of the zone covered by the MBRS Project. While the Jamaican case was marked by debates over the use of cultural or scientific borders to manage protected areas, these debates have not emerged in the inclusion of Sian Ka'an. In short, proponents of conservation had no apparent difficulty in reconciling the cultural element of protected areas management under the WHC with the ecological elements of the overlapping biodiversity regime complex.

Mexico and the Corredor Biológico Mesoamericano

In the CBMMx Project, the implications of implementing different environmental regimes have led to more apparent disruption in the emergent complex. Like the MBRS, the nested environmental institutions bearing on the CBMMx Project provide more rule specificity than that in Jamaica. These rules have emerged through institutions like (1) the Action Plan of the Tuxtla Gutiérrez II Summit, (2) the Ramsar Convention, and (3) the CCAD. As indicated earlier, many of these are shared with the regime complex relevant to the MBRS Project. A diagram showing the regime complex pertinent to CBMMx Project conservation is shown in figure 5.4.

Like the MBRS Project, the efforts toward managing the CBMMx Project emerged in the background of regional efforts to coordinate environmental management, including the 1996 Tuxtla II Summit, a multilateral meeting to coordinate security, trade, and environmental governance in Mesoamerica. Subsequent to this summit, the Central American states and Mexico issued the Tuxtla Declaration, which called on states to promote the establishment of the Mesoamerican Biological Corridor, or Corredor Biológico Mesoamericano. First, the Tuxtla Declaration enhanced the level of concern around the eventual CBMMx Project; it linked regional environmental cooperation to the broader goals of regionalism and interdependence in

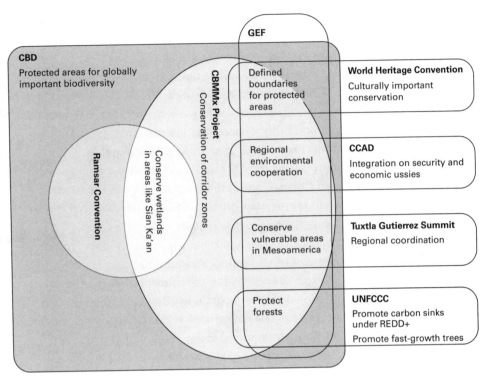

Figure 5.4
The CBMMx Project regime complex.

matters of trade, transboundary crime, and social development.[67] Second, the CCAD, established to promote regional integration in Central America and Mexico, linked coordinated environmental management to both regional development and economic, social, and ecological sustainability.[68]

As in the MBRS Project, the Ramsar Convention identifies specific sites in the CBMMx Project as meriting protection, specifically the Sian Ka'an Biosphere Reserve. The Tuxtla Declaration indicates which areas are to be managed by signatory parties to the Declaration by defining the Mesoamerican Biological Corridor as the area running from the neovolcanic zone in Mexico to Panama. Although this zone was not well defined, it nevertheless included areas in the southern states of Mexico that eventually were subsumed in the CBMMx Project.

Further, as in the MBRS, the overlap between the biodiversity institutions and the cultural institutions of the WHC is synergistic. World Heritage sites within the CBMMx Project zone, like Calakmul and (again) Sian Ka'an, have been included without the contestation seen in Jamaica. In 2009, the World Conservation Union (IUCN), one of the major pushers for the CBD, described the use of the WHC as a conservation tool in Mesoamerica and Mexico as the "best marketing idea in conservation."[69]

As in Jamaica, policymakers and local actors were attracted to the climate change regime by the possibility of accessing international funds as participants. In 2009, agents from federal agencies SEMARNAT and CONABIO, along with representatives from the CBMMx Project, created a proposal for REDD+ participation in Chiapas, one of the states involved in the CBMMx Project. However, while the overlap between the climate change regime complex is still only potentially disruptive in Jamaica's regime complex, it is already proving problematic to several stakeholders in the CBMMx Project.

In 2010, the government of California entered into an agreement with the government of Chiapas (as well as the government of Acre in Brazil) to implement a jurisdictional REDD+ program to offset California's carbon emissions by promoting "the restoration and reforestation of degraded lands and forests, and through improved forest management practices."[70] As a jurisdictional program, Chiapas would generate carbon credits through statewide efforts, including changes in land use policies and financial incentives to save forests. These carbon credits could then theoretically be sold to California to offset that state's greenhouse gas emissions. The Chiapaneco statewide effort distinguishes this program from other carbon offset schemes that depend on agreements with local communities, and that have been criticized for allowing leakage in areas not covered by REDD. The state government of Chiapas included the REDD+ efforts in their 2013–2018 developmental plan, pledging in a statement from its Ministry of Environment and Natural Health to adjust its legal land management framework in order to address climate change, economic growth, and the quality of life in marginalized (largely indigenous) communities.[71]

However, despite the hopeful statements from the Chiapaneco government and the state of California, community members within Chiapas, who were otherwise in favor of land conservation, treated the proposed REDD+ program with skepticism, if not outright hostility. This skepticism is unsurprising, given the well-documented history of violent conflict between peasant and indigenous Chiapanecos/as and the federal government over land, particularly in the Zapatista uprising.[72] Local communities worried that the proposed state reforms under REDD+ would replace traditional agricultural practices with tree husbandry practices that came from outsiders, for the benefit of outsiders. In a 2013 letter to California's Governor Brown, a group of Mexican NGOs and community-based organizations from Chiapas (among them Zapatistas and Friends of the Earth-Mexico) sharply criticized the deal between the Chiapaneco government and California. Titled "Mother Earth Is Not for Sale," the letter condemned what its authors saw as a clear threat to parcelize and commodify traditionally held land to alleviate California's responsibility to curb its own emissions. Further, they cited practices under REDD+ as promoting poor environmentalism, by promoting alien species (including Pine and African Oil Palm) in native forested areas in order to gain carbon credits that could be purchased as indulgences by consumers in the industrialized world. The group saw REDD+'s promotion of new management practices in forested rural areas as adding insult to injury, stating: "Indigenous people are made responsible for the success of REDD+, while at the same time peasant farmers' production systems are criminalized accusing them of causing climate change."[73]

As mentioned before, these local and indigenous struggles over REDD+ and the carbon credit market are not uncommon to conservation issues in developing countries. Indeed, as other cases in Mexico, Brazil, Costa Rica, and Tanzania (among others) show, the overlap between REDD+ and conservation is particularly problematic, given the tendency of the carbon credit mechanism to marginalize existing agricultural practices and privilege the parcelization and commodification of land. Even for those who are less concerned about the impact of these changing norms on local land rights and indigenous culture, an environmental regime that rests on the alienation of local constituents is not likely to succeed. While REDD+ can work in practice, projects created under its framework should be designed with far more local participation to avoid the kinds of conflictive overlaps seen here, and in other developing countries, such as Papua New Guinea and others mentioned in this book.[74]

At present, the Chiapaneco statewide project is still in the planning stages and, to be fair, the REDD Working Group from California has been clear that the government of California should only partner with Chiapas if indigenous rights and livelihoods are protected in the conduct of REDD+.[75] However, since local opposition has already lead to the 2013 cancellation of an earlier REDD+ program in Chiapas, it is clear that integrating the goals of the climate change regime complex with the goals of local conservation is not going to be free from conflict.

Egypt and the Management of Migratory Soaring Birds

The final case studied here took place in Egypt. Whereas the previous cases involved some synergistic and disruptive overlap among different international institutions, protected areas management in Egypt was comparatively free of the rule ambiguity found in other regime complexes. In this case, a TAN emerged in the late 1990s concerned about an area referred to as the Rift Valley/Red Sea Flyway, part of the larger migration route known as the African-Eurasian Flyway. This area comprises an aerial corridor that migratory birds take when traveling from states north of the Mediterranean Sea through the eastern coast of the African continent.

In the early 1990s, Birdlife and other transnational stakeholders in MSB management, such as the IUCN and Wetlands International, began conducting research and sharing information to identify emerging threats and problems with the integrity of the flyway. In the mid to late 1990s, the efforts of the emerging TAN found purchase in the international political arena, as governments in the region sought to demonstrate compliance with MEAs relating to biodiversity and endangered species management. In 1995, parties to the 1979 Convention on Migratory Species negotiated an MEA subordinate to the CMS called the African-Eurasian Waterbird Agreement (AEWA). In AEWA, the parties used the research on bird migration conducted between 1991 and 1995 from Birdlife, Wetlands International, the WWF, and the IUCN to promote improved regional management of migratory birds and habitats among neighboring countries in the flyway zone.[76]

By the end of the 1990s, Birdlife began drafting a proposal for a GEF-funded effort to begin in 2003.[77] As conceptualized, the project was intended to focus on those countries with poor environmental governance but that were critical to the effective management of migratory soaring birds in the African-Eurasian Flyway. These countries included Djibouti, Egypt, Eritrea, Ethiopia, Jordan, Lebanon, Saudi Arabia, Sudan, Syria, Yemen, and territories controlled by the Palestinian Authority.[78] The section of the flyway involving these countries' airspaces was referred to as the Rift Valley/Red Sea Flyway.

The institutions under the biodiversity regime that apply to Egyptian management and the Rift Valley/Red Sea Flyway Project show a much higher degree of rule specificity than in the previous cases. The multilateral environmental agreements (MEAs) that Egypt signed that are relevant to the MSB project are (1) the Ramsar Convention, (2) its Protocol to Amend the Convention on Wetlands of International Importance Especially as Waterfowl Habitat, (3) the African Convention on the Conservation of Nature and Natural Resources, (4) the Convention on Migratory Species (CMS), (5) the African-Eurasian Waterbird Agreement (AEWA), (6) the Protocol Concerning Specially Protected Areas and Biological Diversity in the Mediterranean (under the Barcelona Convention), and (7) the Protocol Concerning the Conservation of Biological Diversity and the Establishment of Network of Protected Areas in the Red Sea and Gulf of Aden (under the Jeddah Convention). A diagram showing the regime complex pertinent to Rift Valley/Red Sea Flyway conservation is shown in figure 5.5.

In 1998, UNEP and the secretariats of the CBD, the CMS, the Ramsar Convention, CITES, and the WHC commissioned the WCMC to undertake a study that would make it easier for states to report on their activities to those institutions, without having to duplicate their reporting efforts.[79] Subsequent to this study, UNEP-WCMC held workshops on harmonizing conservation goals and reporting requirements in 2000[80] and 2004[81] with the secretariats of the following MEAs: the CBD, CMS, Ramsar Convention, and AEWA, all of which were cited by the MSB project documents as relevant to biodiversity management in the flyway. These workshops asserted a common interest in biodiversity management among these treaties, explicitly linking the goals of the CBD with migratory bird management under the CMS and AEWA, and with wetlands conservation under Ramsar. In regards to the Rift Valley/Red Sea Flyway project, several of the ecosystems used by migratory soaring birds as resting points, particularly in the North Sinai, are wetlands, and several resting areas are important to migratory waterfowls. The Protocol Concerning Special Protected Areas of the Barcelona Convention (henceforth the Protocol Concerning Protected Areas) and the Protocol Concerning the Conservation of Biological Diversity and the Establishment of Network of Protected Areas in the Red Sea and the Gulf of Aden (henceforth the Protocol Concerning Biological Diversity in the Red Sea) further bear on conservation in the flyway by citing Red Sea conservation as necessary to global governance.[82]

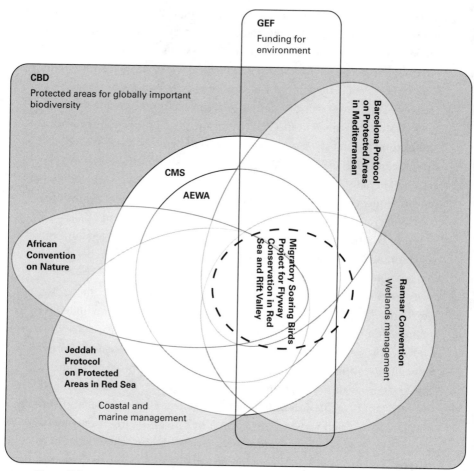

Figure 5.5
The Rift Valley/Red Sea Flyway regime complex.

As the Egyptian project focuses more strongly on migratory species than the projects in Jamaica or Mexico, the CMS and its subsidiary AEWA are institutions nested within the biodiversity regime that affect Red Sea Flyway governance.[83] The CMS lists species to be conserved in Appendices I and II to the Convention, which require parties to endeavor to "provide immediate protection" and "conclude Agreements covering the conservation" of migratory species respectively.[84] Some of the species adopted in the CMS include the Steppe Eagle (*Aquila heliaca*), the Dalmatian Pelican

(*Pelecanus crispus*), and the White Stork (*Ciconia ciconia*), all of which were listed as crucial species in a 2005 study on migratory soaring birds for the MSB project.[85] By the early 2000s, the Appendices singled out several of the migratory soaring bird species that traversed the Rift Valley/Red Sea region of Egypt and East Africa as meriting additional attention from parties.[86]

In 2007, the CMS members drafted an Action Plan calling on parties to protect birds in the African-Eurasian Flyway zone, including recommendations that, "where possible," parties ban exposed poison bait, prevent the disturbance of rest sites, and create protected areas in identified zones; in Egypt, these zones were sites identified by the locally active NGO Birdlife in the early 2000s.[87] More generally, COPs to the CMS have illustrated certain anthropogenic activities as problematic for migratory species, as did COP-7, which passed a resolution calling on parties to assess the impact of wind turbines on migratory birds.[88]

As with the CMS, AEWA identifies particular species whose conservation is of global concern; these include falcons and birds of prey listed in the MSB project. AEWA also lists some crucial zones identified by Egyptian NGOs and state policymakers as relevant to the Rift Valley/Red Sea Flyway Project.[89]

The Ramsar Convention highlights key areas within the Rift Valley/Red Sea Flyway to be targeted for conservation. Lake Bardawil in the Sinai Peninsula (declared 1988), for example, is also identified as a Birdlife Important Bird Area (IBA).[90] The African Convention on the Conservation of Nature calls on ratifying states to ban the hunting and killing without prior approval of several endangered species, including storks, pelicans, cranes, and vultures, all of which are covered by the MSB project.[91] In addition, the Protocol Concerning Protected Areas calls on parties to protect, conserve, and manage endangered species and their habitats, which also includes species like the Dalmatian Pelican (*Pelecanus crispus*) that are identified in the MSB project.[92]

In this case, the institutions that state and local actors have invoked as relevant to protected areas management in Egypt exhibit a much higher level of rule clarity and synergistic overlap than in the previous three cases. The institutions that affect governance here do not have rules that stakeholders have interpreted in contested ways. Instead, by sharing the names of species (in the CMS, AEWA, and African Convention) and areas (in Ramsar, AEWA, and the Protocol Concerning Protected Areas) to be conserved, these institutions have established a very coherent international framework for conservation along the Rift Valley/Red Sea Flyway.

As noted, Egypt's synergistic interplay in regard to Red Sea governance compares favorably to that of Mexico and Jamaica. In Jamaica, competing ideas over whether conservation should be culturally or ecologically driven has led to disagreements among policymakers and advocates who share the goal of conserving Cockpit Country. This has played out in the context of the competing norms of the World Heritage Convention and the biodiversity institutions. In Mexico, while the cultural debates have been less problematic, the fact that state policymakers have sought to apply a governance mechanism derived from the climate regime complex has led to consternation among local communities and NGOs. In the CBMMx Project, those who oppose the use of the climate regime-complex approach are worried that the goals of capturing carbon do not fit well with local ideas about biodiversity conservation and indigenous rights. In those cases, the presence of additional international institutions has been interpreted as a basis for norm contestation over local management in Jamaica and Mexico, and has hampered local cooperation in conservation and governance. However, as the following makes clear, synergistic interplay and rule clarity among international institutions has not led to improved governance in Egypt. In fact, of the three countries, it has performed the worst on translating international conservation goals into real policy change on the ground. Further, as these cases have shown, understanding how these countries have performed in their respective regime complexes requires an examination of nonstate actor perceptions.

Variation in Project Outcomes: A Qualitative Assessment

A qualitative analysis of project performance indicates that despite the synergistic interplay of multiple international institutions, Egypt proved the most reluctant implementer of global biodiversity conservation goals. Conservation, to the extent that it occurs, is largely epiphenomenal. For example, the Ramsar site Lake Bardawil is listed as a protected area, but is so isolated from human activity, that conservation from anthropogenic stress is virtually guaranteed, no matter what the state does. In contrast, areas that do experience higher traffic like the Sinai Peninsula and the Red Sea tourist zones have a much lower quality of environmental management.

With widespread problems like poor waste management and unsustainable water use, local environments in Egyptian protected areas have shown remarkable levels of degradation (see chapter 4).

Moreover, rather than using GEF funds to meet the project's goals of building local capacity for governance, Egyptian officials captured project resources, making them disappear into an opaque bureaucracy. Civil society agencies like local affiliates of Birdlife International and other NGO members who were supposed to be included in managing the project universally complained in interviews that they were excluded from participating in local efforts, and had no idea where or how GEF funds were being allocated. Worse, as Sowers has described, the Egyptian government's long-standing practice of isolating and enervating its primary biodiversity management agency, the Nature Conservation Sector (NCS), has alienated the civil society from participating in environmental policymaking by weakening a potential ally to conservationist NGOs.[93]

Synergistic interplay has not necessarily led to effective governance in Mexico either. As described earlier, in the CBMMx Project, the interplay between the biodiversity regimes and the climate change regime complex has led to some rule ambiguity about managing local forests. Further, some of the local conflicts emerging in Chiapas are precisely due to the fact that local communities and the state government disagree about whether carbon storage and carbon sink management should inform land conservation. Those tensions, which led to protests against REDD+, have certainly been influenced by disruptive overlap between the biodiversity and climate change regime complexes. However, not all of the conflict under the CBMMx Project is due to such disruptive regime overlap. In the areas outside Chiapas, the climate change regime has not been invoked. The nonconservation regimes that have been invoked, namely in the WHC, have not stimulated arguments over land management in the way that they have in Jamaica. Instead, the conflict that has emerged in the CBMMx Project has done so because of norm contestations about the importance and definition of biodiversity between the transnational advocacy network, Mexican policymakers, and CBMMx Project managers. In short, the transnational advocacy network of experts that participated in early stages of project design has been highly critical of the areas that the project covered. Local conservationist NGOs have continually criticized the abandonment of ecologically crucial zones under the project, and bemoaned what they have described as the politicization of zone selection.

As the maps in chapter 3 show, the areas identified as relevant to the CBMMx Project changed noticeably between 1995 and 2001, when the project was finally launched. In 2006, five years after the project launched, the World Resources Institute called again for project management to include zones in the states of Yucatán and Tabasco, on the basis of their importance to local biodiversity. To this date, those additional zones remain uncovered by GEF funds and the CBD's project. As members of the TAN indicated, the inability of the network to generate an intersubjective consensus undermined their ability to create a coherent argument for including ecologically important (as opposed to politically salient) zones in the project

Further, since the areas that the CBMMx Project covers do not fit with local ideas about the social and environmental dimensions of appropriate conservation, local resistance has proven a long-standing problem for the project. Resentment about exclusion from project design and implementation, as well as fears about the perceived political nature of fund allocation, contributed to a de facto withdrawal of participation from the civil society between 2001 and 2007. As a result, project implementation stagnated, necessitating a restart after 2007. Synergistic overlap in this case did not forestall local contestation and challenges to environmental governance.

This is not to say that synergistic overlap is meaningless. In the MBRS Project, synergistic overlap supported effective governance by clarifying areas of importance to Mesoamerican reef management and building capacity among member states to conserve areas such as the Sian Ka'an Biosphere Reserve. In the MBRS Project, the Mexican government and the GEF took their understanding of what comprised the MBRS directly from civil society studies conducted in the 1990s, particularly those from WWF-México and Los Amigos de Sian Ka'an. Furthermore, the Mexican government and its federal environmental agencies adopted a monitoring methodology that the epistemic community developed based on the scientists' understanding of the relevant processes and threats to biodiversity in the MBRS region. The state also adopted new regulations governing the extraction of fish species and the management of protected areas through legislation like Article 60 Ter and NOM-059, which protected coastal mangroves from being cleared for hotel construction.

Finally, these new ideas about MBRS biodiversity were mutually supportive of claims made by local community members who wanted their livelihoods as fishermen protected from the resource overexploitation that characterizes hotel development. This support proved crucial after 2007, when hoteliers and state governments began a concerted push against new federal regulation, arguing that economic development and poverty could only be addressed by allowing hoteliers to continue business as usual. To date, federal regulation has remained in place with support from local communities, who view environmental regulation as a bulwark against the over-exploitation of natural resources. As Raúl Gómez, a fisherman from Xcalak argued, tourism was less of a boon for development, and more a threat to local management of natural resources: "It's not a good thing to clear away all the mangroves. It will promote more tourism, but it will affect nature and our work as fishermen."[94]

As described, this improved governance took place under a regime complex constituted by various international biodiversity institutions and the World Heritage Convention. Synergy certainly contributed to improved management in this case, but the case in Jamaica makes it clear that synergistic interplay is not necessary for improved biodiversity management: the type of interplay does not predict that states will change their behavior to conform to international expectations about environmental governance.

In Jamaica, normative conflicts over the role of culture or ecology have not prevented the government from implementing significant reforms to protect biodiversity from bauxite mining, the major threat identified under the GEF project. In 2007, under mounting political pressure, Agricultural Minister Clarke issued a hold on mining and prospecting leases, pending a definition of Cockpit Country's legal borders. After parliamentary elections, the Ministry of Agriculture asserted that Cockpit Country, as defined by the advocacy coalition, would be permanently off limits to mining. Policymakers and epistemic community members attributed this to the mobilization and concerted activism of the local community, and the final GEF report on the project described the outcome of the moratorium as due to the "most successful advocacy work."[95] However, until there is a formal agreement on what biodiversity "means" in Cockpit Country, the protected status will remain tenuous.

Conclusion

In the context of biodiversity management, what comprises "appropriate behavior" is very often negotiated not at the international level between states and institutions, but transnationally and locally among nonstate actors. While international institutions such as the CBD, GEF, the CMS, AEWA, and the Ramsar Convention may have contributed to state willingness to launch biodiversity projects, the state and transnational networks engaged in occasionally acrimonious contestations over the geophysical dimensions of appropriate management. The debates in Mexico between the civil society and governments over the inclusion of corridor zones in the CBMMx Project demonstrate this, as do the debates in Jamaica between the civil society, the government, and bauxite agencies over the size of Cockpit Country. Government commitment to declaring protected areas and issuing management plans would have meant very little for biodiversity governance if these areas were not carefully selected or if the plans were not adequately designed to meet local needs, or both.[96]

What these cases tell us is that nonstate actor preferences and norms have a constitutive effect on regime complexity. First, as the literature indicates, and as I have argued here, regimes may be "discovered" to overlap at the level of implementation. When the obligations of one international treaty are translated into domestic policy, local actors may invoke other treaties to support or challenge the legitimacy of emerging policy. For example, local actors in Mexico used the World Heritage Convention to support the conservationist program of the GEF and the Convention on Biological Diversity in areas like Sian Ka'an. Conversely, Jamaican stakeholders used the language of culture and the possibility of a World Heritage site in Cockpit Country to argue that conservation should be applied to a larger area than the one proposed by the scientists who emphasized the ecological goals of the CBD. This observation that regime complexes emerge from local actor contestation is also borne out by contemporary studies in issue areas like PGR and maritime piracy, where nonstate actors like businesses invoke international rules in an attempt to buttress their claims and satisfy their domestic interests.[97]

Second, as these examples make clear, while nonstate and subnational actors have materially informed interests, cultural and other normative understandings matter tremendously in explaining how they see the world and hence, construct their preferences. For example, anti-conservationist mining interests in Jamaica and tourist operations in Mexico were explicitly concerned about their economic bottom line in opposing new environmental regulations. But the Maroons' claim to land in Cockpit Country (and what they meant by "Cockpit Country") cannot be understood independent of their anti-colonial and anti-slavery narratives. Historical myth and narrative is not something that is materially defined, but created subjectively in human society. This subjective element in determining preferences means that whether or not regime overlap is disruptive or synergistic is not something inherent to the rules of regimes, or restricted to material cost–benefit calculations. Rather, it emerges as well from the normative understandings of different actors about their social reality and its attendant rules and policy implications. This is why the overlap between the World Heritage Convention and the Convention on Biological Diversity—so problematic in Jamaica—was uncontroversial in the MBRS and CBMMx Projects. Perceptions and norms matter.

Third, whether or not a regime complex is seen as synergistic has no clear effect on its problem-solving nature. The Egyptian MSB project, while linked to a regime complex with a high degree of mutually supporting rules, performed far worse than the Jamaican Cockpit Country project. While Orsini, Morin, and Young indicate that complexity may enhance problem solving, this seems to apply only to regimes that depend more on international cooperation among states, and at-the-border regulation. Protected areas regimes, however, depend much more on the relationships between nonstate actors and the state apparatus; that is where interpretation over treaty implementation becomes much more salient. This reinforces a normative element in the constitution regime complexity and effectiveness. Perception matters in "coupling and the decoupling of different regimes,"[98] as well as whether or not regimes are effective.

This research argues that norms have a constitutive effect on international relations. Norms can determine whether regime complexes emerge, whether they overlap in synergistic or disruptive ways, and whether local policies that emerge from them are effective. As such, my argument about how regime complexes function in global environmental governance moves away from a rationalist understanding of international institutions.[99] As I have noted, this is particularly likely to emerge in areas of governance that depend on turning global norms into explicitly domestic policy, in which cross-border coordination is not relevant. There are myriad international regimes that affect this kind of behavior, some of which I have mentioned here, like the Ramsar Convention, the Convention on Migratory Species, the REDD+ institutions in the climate change regime, and regional agreements like the Cartagena Convention. There are also others, including a whole array of regional agreements, and international MEAs, like the Convention on International Trade of Endangered Species (CITES).

Institutions certainly matter for material reasons; the provision of technical and financial capacity through the GEF, UNEP, and secretariats of various MEAs was important in supporting the GEF project in Cockpit Country, the MBRS Project, the CBMMx Project, and the MSB project. Regardless of political will and commitment, monitoring the isolated and rugged terrain of Cockpit Country, the marine ecosystems off the coast of the Yucatán, and the desert migrating spots in the Rift Valley/Red Sea Flyway can be prohibitively expensive to developing countries. In interviews and conversations with staffers from the Forestry Department in Jamaica, CONANP in Mexico, and the Egyptian NCS, the challenge of scarce resources and mounting responsibilities was a constant refrain. As rationalists would argue, material conditions do matter, and institutions that can provide the right kinds of material incentives can help states cooperate and build effective mechanisms for global environmental governance. However, ignoring how norms affect global environmental governance overlooks an important part of understanding how the global civil society shapes the interpretation and conduct of international governance.

6 Conclusion: Grounding Global Conservation in Local Norms

Science, Socialization, and Environmental Justice: Conservation in Developing Countries

Over the past few decades, inspired by global institutions like the 1972 Stockholm Declaration, the 1992 Agenda 21, and the 1993 Convention on Biological Diversity, transnational networks of environmental advocates have lobbied governments to help change how people conserve the Earth's resources. As I have argued here, these transnational networks matter to the implementation of international conservationist regimes. They can help ground the norms underlying regimes in participating states. When they are successful, they can have more of an impact on the willingness of local actors to comply and carry out the obligations of regimes than just the internationally designed elements of the regime itself. Moreover, as environmental governance becomes increasingly characterized by regime complexity, transnational networks can influence how states understand their international obligations, by making normative claims about how to deal with rule ambiguity. In making these arguments, I linked the literature on comparative environmental politics with the constructivist school of international relations.

However, my case studies are clear that this advocacy is not always successful. Encouraging examples of biodiversity projects in Jamaica's Cockpit Country and along the eastern coast of Quintana Roo state in Mexico show how advocacy networks can persuade policymakers and the mass public to adopt new behaviors to conserve globally important biodiversity. Conversely, case studies of similar efforts in Egypt and along the Yucatán Peninsula show how political opposition and scientific disagreements can stymie advocacy campaigns and projects. Even the successful cases covered here faced setbacks when economically powerful actors and some political elites opposed new environmental regulations. Moreover, these challenges emerged despite the efforts of multilateral environmental institutions and financial organizations like the Global Environmental Fund, the World Bank, UNEP, and the Convention on Biological Diversity to build capacity and will for conservation in recipient states.

In this, my research joins other studies showing the uphill, sometimes successful but occasionally failed struggles of transnational advocacy to influence environmental policy in developing countries like Ecuador[1] and Brazil.[2] So for scholars of transnational advocacy, policymakers, and members of advocacy networks, the fact that environmental advocacy has mixed success raises important questions: When are transnational networks more effective? What cognitive or material factors contribute to their ability to offer interpretations of reality that are accepted by policymakers? How are networks constrained by domestic politics of the state that is the subject of transnational advocacy campaigns?

In answering these questions, I relied heavily on the epistemic community literature.[3] As I show here, the epistemic communities literature fills in an important part of the puzzle. This literature argues that networks of experts who generate a scientific consensus on the causal dimensions of an emerging problem area are more likely to influence the behavior of governments and other key actors.[4] In addition, studies on the politics and sociology of turning information into policy argue that networks who socialize with policymakers in the production of knowledge claims are likely to have more influence over policymaking that those who do not.[5] That is, socialization increases the influence of transnational advocacy networks. Finally, I argue that networks who situate arguments about conservation in local understandings about resource access and environmental justice are far more likely to shape behavior than those who link conservation to national claims about economic development.

This last argument about the importance of local justice vis-à-vis national economic development differs from previous writing on the participation of developing countries in global environmental governance. Academics such as Marian Miller and Lawrence Susskind argued that the relationship between LDC government and the environment is conditioned by the workings of the global political economy. This includes factors such as global history of development and industrialization, the worsening environmental North–South split in the years after UNCED, and LDC concerns about the inequitable distribution of global wealth and ownership of capital.[6] LDCs are highly indebted, yet rely heavily on the production of primary goods, which means that LDC efforts to "catch up" with the process of industrialization launched in the developed world depend on the immediate overexploitation of natural resources. In order to ensure that LDC governments will take environmentally friendly action, it may seem that international institutions, states, and transnational networks have to link environmental management to the interests of economic development. However, as I illustrate here, arguments relying on an economic valorization of environmental management are potentially counterproductive, in that they reify an epistemology that is likely to be harmful to the interests of sustainable, long-term management. Thus, I conclude that the use of local justice frames strengthens arguments for conservation by mobilizing local actors against resource exploitation.

I argue further that linking environmental claims to justice can guard against one of the challenges to conservation described by Chapin,[7] Dowie,[8] Zebich-Knos,[9] and others. Policy-relevant knowledge should be produced in a participatory way so that those people who live near to and depend on biodiversity are not marginalized by exclusionary or "fortress" approaches to conservation. As such, I conclude that environmentally just and sustainable conservation is found between exploitation and preservation.

I developed this argument by studying transnational advocacy aimed at building support for international conservation regimes in Jamaica, Mexico, and Egypt. In Jamaica, a transnational network emerged in the 1990s, concerned about biodiversity loss among globally important bird populations residing in Cockpit Country, a mountainous rainforest region in the northwestern section of the island. The transnational network generated an intersubjective consensus on the causal dimensions of biodiversity loss. The network then participated in the design and implementation of the Project for Sustainable Conservation of Globally Important Bird Habitats, a regional GEF-funded project simultaneously carried out in the Dominican Republic and the Bahamas. The primary threats identified were bauxite mining and decentralized agricultural activity. The network campaigned to persuade (1) agricultural policymakers in the Forestry Department, (2) mining policymakers in the Ministry of Agriculture and the Jamaica Bauxite Institute (JBI), and (3) protected areas policymakers in the Ministry of

Environment and the National Environment Protection Agency (NEPA) to improve their environmental management practices.

While the network managed to generate a knowledge consensus on the cause-and-effect relationship between human activity and environmental degradation, they were able to socialize only with the Forestry Department, but not the Ministry of Agriculture, the JBI, or NEPA. The network did, however, use neoliberal arguments about the economic value of conservation to national development in order to persuade the JBI and the Ministry of Agriculture to regulate mining in Cockpit Country.

Initially, the network only succeeded in influencing the behavior of the Forestry Department. The network's scientific arguments and its members' claims that biodiversity conservation had long-term economic benefits to tourism and coastal development did not change the calculus of the JBI and the Ministry of Agriculture. Instead, both of these agencies continued to prefer the short-term exploitation of Cockpit Country by mining companies. Only when the network's claims were included in local demands about the cultural, historic, and subsistence importance of Cockpit Country to rural people was advocacy successful. Once these links were made, local communities were willing to mobilize to defend Cockpit Country from the government of Jamaica's clear interest in mining the region for bauxite ore. Like Pellow,[10] McCormick,[11] and Mohai, Pellow, and Timmons Roberts,[12] I argue that justice framing is a crucial tool in sustaining environmental movements. Scientific consensus, even when held by publicly recognized experts, is not sufficient to create influence.

I built on this argument in chapter 2 by discussing a case of transnational advocacy in the Mesoamerican Barrier Reef System (MBRS). In the 1990s, an epistemic community emerged to advocate for biodiversity management conservation in the MBRS, which included the coast of Quintana Roo state in Mexico. This advocacy centered on Mexico's implementation of the Proyecto para el Sistema Arrecifal Mesoamericano, funded by the GEF as relevant to the Convention on Biological Diversity. Here, the network again generated an intersubjective consensus on the relationship between the major anthropogenic threats—fishing, tourism, and coastal development—and biodiversity loss.

In order to carry out this project, the network had to engage with the practices and policies of a variety of different actors in Mexico. These consisted of (1) protected areas policymakers in la Secretaría de Manejo Ambiental y

Recursos Naturales (SEMARNAT) and la Comisión Nacional de Áreas Naturales Protegidas (CONANP), (2) fishing policymakers in la Comisión Nacional de Pesquería (CONAPESCA) and la Secretaría de Agricultura, Ganadería, Desarrollo Rural, y Pesquería (SAGARPA), (3) civil society quintanarroense fishing cooperatives, (4) tourism policymakers in the quintanarroense state government, and (5) transnational hotelier associations.

The network managed to socialize with all actors, although to a lesser degree with the quintanarroense state government. After the initial advocacy campaign, SEMARNAT, CONANP, SAGARPA, CONAPESCA, and the fishing cooperatives all supported new protections for coastal ecosystems. But despite this support, and the network's attempt to persuade hoteliers of the economic rationality of conservation, neither the hoteliers nor their allies in the state government were receptive toward new regulations and policies of the late 2000s. Instead, they argued that development was something that needed to happen at a cost to biodiversity. They attempted to repeal new environmental regulations, most notably in Article 60 Ter and NOM-059, but have had their changes held at bay by a mass public concerned about being exposed to increasing environmental vulnerabilities, and being dispossessed of resources necessary for subsistence and tradition.

Notably, this conservation movement, which included scientists, fishermen, and local community groups, was skeptical about the developmental model propounded by the state. The benefits of large-scale tourism were too concentrated in the hands of a political economic elite, and the ecological costs too heavily borne by the marginalized for tourist-driven development to seem attractive to rural, low-income people. Arguments that tourism would bring "development" to poor communities simply did not resonate with the lived experiences of many coastal communities in and outside of tourist zones. As the literature shows, this imbalance between the costs and benefits of environmental use between the marginalized and the privileged is at the heart of environmental justice.[13] Like the anti-dam movements discussed by Khagram[14] and McCormick,[15] locals rejected the state's ideas about what development should be precisely because of this perceived imbalance. As a result, the continued willingness of the hotel lobby to build in the face of a shared science shows that consensus, though it mattered, was not enough to generate uniform agreement among key actors about the value of conservation.

But the following chapter demonstrated that, even if insufficient, knowledge consensus is a crucial part of environmental advocacy. Chapter 3 discusses a project funded by the GEF to conserve the Mesoamerican Biological Corridor in Mexico. In this project, an advocacy network tried to promote conservation among various actors, including (1) policymakers in the federal biodiversity agency la Comisión Nacional de la Biodiversidad (CONABIO), (2) agricultural management in la Secretaría de la Ganadería, Agricultura, Desarrollo Rural, Pesca y Alimentación (SAGARPA), (3) protected areas managers in SEMARNAT and CONANP, and (4) state and municipal governments.

Although the network established robust social links with CONABIO, SEMARNAT, and SAGARPA, they could not generate a consensus on important parameters of the project. When the project was finally launched, scientists within the network objected to what they saw as the politicization of what should have been ecological principles. This exacerbated a breakdown of communication among local communities, national governments, and scientific networks, which led to distrust and stagnation of the project's goals. Thus, even where networks can socialize with target audiences, political actors can exploit an absence of clear scientific agreement to resist unfavorable policy implications of new information. Socialization is also not sufficient for influence, if not joined with other kinds of cognitive power.

However, chapter 4 on Egypt shows why socialization is necessary by illustrating what happens in its absence. In this case, a network attempted to advocate for environmental reform affecting the Rift Valley/Red Sea Flyway, a region along the Red Sea coast and the Sinai Peninsula. To do so, the network had to engage with actors including (1) the Ministry of State of Environmental Affairs (MSEA) and the Egyptian Environmental Affairs Agency (EEAA), (2) the Nature Conservation Sector (NCS), (3) the governorates of the North Sinai, the South Sinai, and the Red Sea, and (4) the Tourism Development Authority (TDA).

The network did not generate an intersubjective consensus. More problematically, network members were institutionally discouraged from socializing with target audiences, as sometimes happens in autocratic systems. Instead, closed decision making, governmental antipathy to the civil society, and political cronyism hampered the free flow of knowledge from experts to decision makers by isolating civil society experts, and marginalizing the environmental agencies most likely to be receptive to ecological arguments. Further, this took place in a system in which tourist development was an integral part of the interests of the military and cronyist economic elite.

As a result, the network had far less influence over the conduct of the project and the implementation of global biodiversity conservation than even the network involved in the Mesoamerican Biological Corridor project. In Egypt, the government captured project funds and failed to meaningfully change the management of protected areas, tourism, and coastal development. While the network members and environmental advocates in the Mesoamerican Biological Corridor were dissatisfied with what members saw as persistent problems with project implementation, they were qualitatively better off than their counterparts in the Egyptian case. In Mexico, network members may not have had as much influence as they wanted, but they did have regular institutional access to policymakers through the State Consultative Councils (CCEs) after 2007, as well as through other formal mechanisms. They were critical about the selection of corridor zones, but NGOs like Simbiosis and Econciencia did introduce new projects with state support in targeted zones like Kantemó. Although the transnational biological corridor network was less effective than the epistemic communities in Jamaica and the MBRS, it was far more effective than the one in Egypt.

Implications for Theory and Practice

The cases show that a scientific consensus is important to successful advocacy. Consensus functions as expected, to limit competing arguments and to legitimate the claims of activists. In all cases where networks demonstrated success in influencing policy, namely in Jamaica and the MBRS Project in Mexico, advocacy networks shared a causal consensus on the processes relevant to environmental management. Where they could not, in the Corredor Biológico Mesoamericano—México (CBMMx Project), federal political patronage interests overrode network preferences for biodiversity management.

Since consensus matters, a question relevant to the study of transnational environmental advocacy is: When are epistemic communities likely to emerge within broader networks? Can scientific consensus be, if not deliberately engineered, at least fostered? I argue that policymakers and scientists can take deliberate steps to increase the likelihood that environmental advocates produce authoritative and consensually held scientific knowledge.

As the Egyptian case shows, generating a knowledge consensus is much more difficult when scientists face serious technical obstacles to gathering information. Chapter 4 describes, for example, an unmistakable disagreement within the network about the causes of mass deaths of birds in desert areas like Sharm el Sheikh. One of the primary reasons given for this breakdown was the lack of support for gathering data in an inhospitable desert. As a participant observer I can attest that studying desert birds may necessitate scrambling up crumbling dirt cliffs, traversing sand dunes, and combing through manmade and animal refuse for minute signs of bird spoor in stunning desert heat. Conducting research in mosquito-plagued mangrove swamps, or hacking through mountainous rainforest in Jamaica and Mexico is also physically demanding, especially without proper equipment. As a 2005 study on bird bottlenecks by Porter described: "To undertake a comprehensive count at any site would require a commitment to watch for an entire season for at least eight hours per day. Two observers present for all of the time would be essential and up to four when there are large numbers passing. They would need to be capable of total concentration for searching for high flying birds against a brilliant blue sky, for counting large and wheeling flocks and, of course, tricky identification."[16]

In order for researchers in the civil society and policymaker sector to get the information they need to make credible, intersubjectively held claims about environmental science, they need sufficient resources, support, and autonomy. Policymakers have served this role in several instances in the developed and developing world. The United States does this through the National Science Foundation (NSF), as does the federal government of Mexico through the Universidad Nacional Autónoma de México (UNAM) and the Centro de Investigaciones de Quintana Roo (CIQRO), predecessor of el Colegio de la Frontera Sur (ECOSUR). In fact, as chapter 2 illustrated, ECOSUR was one of the primary research organizations of the epistemic community active in the Mesoamerican reef system. Similarly, the government of Jamaica, through a project carried out by the Canadian International Development Agency (CIDA) and Jamaica's Forestry Department provided funds for bird monitoring training, which the epistemic community members used to generate knowledge in their campaign. In addition, Haas's study of the EPA's role in providing technical support in ozone science[17] has been joined by Moser's research on the Maine and Hawaiian governments' sponsorship of research on sea-level rise[18] to show how committed policymaker agencies can help researchers generate high-quality scientific knowledge. In contrast, in post-1990s Egypt, the government apparently lost interest in providing this kind of support, a fact lamented by Mohammed Kassas in an interview in 2008: "In Egypt, like in the rest of the world, scientists would be willing to do research if they had funds. Scientists, for instance in Egyptian universities, have no university funds that will support large-scale research projects. And large-scale research projects need to be supported, either by EEAA, or supported by bilateral aid programs, like joint American-Egyptian universities."[19]

As Sowers makes clear (supported by a comparison with Haas's earlier work on scientific networks in Egypt) this state of affairs represents an unfortunate break from one characterized by previous autonomy and support for civil society experts.[20] Under "embedded autonomy" (or Teets's "consultative authoritarianism"[21]) autocratic leaders can certainly make space for scientists to conduct policy-relevant research. In doing so, they may provide the technical support researchers need to generate usable information, and create an understanding about an environmental problem, but there is no guarantee that this will last.

At the same time, access to institutional funds may be necessary, but insufficient in building a scientific consensus. One possible step researchers can take is to narrow their research agenda such that scientists have a commonly shared baseline for understanding emerging problems. The experience of the epistemic community involved in international negotiations on the ozone layer is particularly instructive in this regard. After the negotiation of the framework Vienna Convention on the ozone layer, Mostafa Tolba, who was adamant about deriving a binding agreement, used UNEP's offices to commission studies on ozone depletion from transnational scientific working groups.

Scientists within these groups focused their research on seven particular ozone-depleting substances (ODS) out of dozens in use at the time, and adopted a program focused on a chlorine-loading model of the stratosphere, abandoning previous attempts to track the rate of ozone depletion with the rate of change of ODS emissions. As Litfin noted, this comprised a truncated view of the environmental problem.[22] However, these choices were driven by the social necessity of getting an agreement among experts to address an emerging problem. These choices worked. As Litfin and Haas describe, this program fostered a core set of agreed-upon principles and arguments called the Würzburg Consensus, which then strengthened the arguments made by pusher states for a strong regulatory protocol.[23]

Similarly, a more recent study by Burger and others on the U.S. Department of Energy's (DOE) decision to close its management of nuclear test sites at Amchitka Island in Alaska was made possible only with a scientific consensus held by the DOE, the state government of Alaska, and other stakeholders.[24] This consensus was only possible when a network of recognized experts agreed upon a Science Plan, comprising an accepted methodology and specified parameters for assessing environmental harm and improvement.

In the cases studied here, the networks that developed a standardized or restricted research agenda similarly developed a scientific consensus on relevant causal processes. In Jamaica, the Nature Conservancy (TNC) and the Windsor Research Center (WRC) developed a shared methodology, which was then later shared with other ENGOs, such as the Southern Trelawny Environment Association (STEA) and the Forestry Department. In Mexico, the reef monitoring methodology used by the network was developed over a period of several years, by the International Coral Reef Initiative (ICRI) workshops in the mid-1990s, and the Atlantic Gulf Reef Rapid Assessment (AGRRA) initiative from 1998 onward, before the MBRS Project was formally created. The methodology was later formally adopted as a component of the project under the Programa de Monitoreo Sinóptico (PMS) in 2002. As these cases indicate, the ability of networks to develop a scientific consensus depends as much on social choices about who participates, and how, as well as the technical training of recognized experts.

In contrast, the transnational advocacy network in the Mexican CBMMx Project did not start trying to generate a shared methodology until after the launch of the project, after federal policymakers had already asserted their preferences over project management. The lack of a shared research program prevented the network from generating a shared conceptualization of, and hence knowledge consensus on, biodiversity loss in the CBMMx Project.

As of the time of writing, the network still had not developed a commonly held methodology on understanding biodiversity loss in Mexican Mesoamerica. Now that the second phase of the project has been launched, the CBMMx Project TAN should foster and generate an intersubjective consensus through a shared understanding of biodiversity. If the TAN demonstrated a scientific consensus on the importance of additional areas to biodiversity conservation in Mesoamerica, the network would have an additional cognitive tool to lobby for additional funds from the GEF, as well as to undermine competing arguments for limited biodiversity protection.

The research also shows that institutions such as the GEF can and should play a formative role in fostering a knowledge consensus. First, as occurred with Mostafa Tolba's influence over the ozone scientific network's focus on limited ozone-depleting substances, international institutions can, under the mandate of gathering useful policy-relevant information, constrain the research agenda taken by transnational networks. By doing so, institutions may encourage the adoption of a standardized approach to understanding environmental problems among scientists.

Second, the GEF should ensure that local and transnational networks of experts have sufficient resources to ensure that scientific knowledge is credible. In Egypt's case, an effective, direct transfer of resources to Nature Conservation Egypt (NCE)—instead of having funds mediated by the Egyptian government—would have aided the network in conducting research, overcoming the gaps in the current state of knowledge. Moreover, international institutions engaging directly with domestic NGOs would obviate the need of scientific experts to depend on antipathetic state agencies. Again, by facilitating consensus, international environmental organizations would improve the chance that networks of experts would influence environmental management and contribute to effective reform. Of course, this may be easier said than done when trying to get an autocratic state to buy in to global governance mechanisms.

Networks will also need to take advantage of the opportunities available to socialize with policymakers and other target audiences. In describing how global environmental assessments become influential, Clark, Mitchell, and Cash argue that "the process by which information is generated and delivered affects the potential of that information process to influence outcomes."[25] Actors who are socialized in the generation of information and knowledge associated with an emerging problem are therefore more likely to adopt the normative implications associated with that knowledge and consider the conclusions relevant to their own interests. As my research shows, networks that do generate a consensus, but are unable to socialize with policymakers and others will have more difficulty in persuading those target audiences to take action. Despite the scientific credibility of the network, Jamaican policymakers in the bauxite mining sector were resistant to arguments for comprehensive protection of sensitive ecosystems in Cockpit Country, and consensus in the MBRS Project was insufficient to overcome environmental recalcitrance by the quintanarroense government and transnational hoteliers.

While it would be easy to say that scientific networks should therefore make sure to build social ties with policymakers and target audiences, they will be constrained by the availability of opportunity structures in political systems. I suggest that increasing political openness—a measure of democracy—will improve the chances that transnational networks would influence policy in target countries. Hiskes, for example, argues that full participation in environmental policymaking is only possible in a pluralist democracy.[26]

This is not to suggest that institutional democracy will necessarily lead to political opportunity structures through which networks can socialize with policymakers. The civil society had more success socializing with a greater number of natural resource managers in Mexico than in Jamaica, even while Mexico has a more recent history with autocracy, only transitioning away from a bureaucratic-authoritarian model in 2000. One possible explanation is that increased centralization improves the likelihood that powerful political elites will socialize with civil society researchers in the production of policy-relevant knowledge. Autocratic policymakers may desire more control over, and hence involvement with the production of policy-relevant knowledge. By doing so, they may be more likely to perceive such knowledge as legitimate, and share perspectives with civil society actors.

At a certain point, however, autocracy and centralization calcifies the state and diminishes the ability of civil society researchers to gain necessary access to policymakers. In extreme cases, state leaders can place loyalists in positions of scientific authority to guarantee that they never have to hear bad news. Romania's Ceausescu managed this quite well, when he appointed his wife as chair of the National Council of Science and Technology.[27] The literature on comparative environmental politics does indicate that democracy, in general, leads to better opportunities for socialization, but my cases support Hochstetler's point that access can be uneven within and across cases, even in liberalizing countries.[28]

Theoretical and Practical Implications

This research clarifies the importance of taking a multilevel approach to understanding how epistemic communities and knowledge networks influence global environmental governance. While authors such as Betsill and Corell restrict the study of network influence to focus on the impact of advocacy on international environmental negotiations,[29] it is clear that biodiversity management is shaped by the actions and practices not only of policymakers, but also of transnational corporations, networks, nonstate governance structures such as the International Organization of Standards ISO 14000 series, and local, community-based organizations (CBOs).[30] After all, the advocacy campaigns on biodiversity governance discussed here occurred after the Convention on Biological Diversity (CBD) was negotiated, and independently of recent negotiations on the Cartagena Protocol on Biosafety and the Nagoya Protocol on Access and Benefit Sharing. Studying the effect of epistemic communities on environmental management requires paying attention to the impact of networks not only on national policymakers, but also on subnational actors and other transnational interests, including transnational capital holders. This is of particular interest to environmental governance in less-developed countries, as managing environmental problems in these political systems depends less on coordination among states, and more on the domestic implementation and internalization of environmental norms among different sectors.

Expanding the parameters of global environmental management to consider multiple sources and levels of political action further gives a clearer picture of how and when knowledge deployed by networks exerts influence on governance. As indicated throughout, framing matters, although not in the way commonly theorized by supporters of the neoliberal model. Epistemic communities were successful in Jamaica and Mexico when they reframed biodiversity loss as part of a broader problem of ecosystem integrity, local sustainability, and autonomy over the local use of natural resources to policymakers and actors. These frames strengthened arguments for local participation in environmental management, as well as an approach that focused on the interests of marginalized groups. As works by Carruthers, Hiskes, Pellow, and others indicate, these are crucial elements in environmental justice. Conversely, epistemic communities and TANs were unable to translate knowledge into action when they framed biodiversity loss as relevant to the interests of global capitalism.

What this suggests is that the choice of which frames are relevant to understanding a politically contested issue area is more than just a rhetorical exercise. Different frames or discourses privilege different courses of action, and by extension different constellations of political actors. While epistemic communities and knowledge networks attempt to influence the interests of policymakers, local actors, and transnational capitalists, these target audiences do not necessarily have isomorphic goals. This means that epistemic communities and knowledge networks should be careful about how they frame knowledge claims, as the improper choice of frames by networks could validate political interests that are more likely to be inimical to the policy preferences of advocates.

Frames provide a reason or narrative for action. If the narrative is one that privileges commodification, then alternate approaches will be delegitimized. As I argue throughout, the danger of framing conservation as an issue of neoliberal economics is that it discredits cultural and emotional reasons for taking action, undermining local support. If policymakers or conservationists wish to do so, that is their prerogative, but they should recognize that neoliberal framing is a normative decision. There is nothing inevitable about treating the environment as a tool of capitalism.

At the same time, scientific networks should be careful about framing conservation as a "pure" scientific endeavor. Conservation for conservation's sake is just as likely to alienate local actors who would, under a preservationist approach, be just as excluded from using natural resources. This is as incompatible with an environmental justice approach as is overexploitation. While networks should use scientific consensus to exercise influence, the ability of a scientific consensus to shape policy may be attenuated or strengthened by the social relationships of knowledge production, and by the power dynamics implied by accepted problem frames.

I have used the MBRS Project to illustrate how frames affect policy rationalization and outcomes. In that case, a network generated a consensus and socialized with state policymakers and hoteliers, but the neoliberal developmental model informing coastal development pointed inexorably to the continued expansion of large-scale tourism in the state. For the conservationists in the network, large-scale tourism was the most pressing threat to environmental sustainability along the coast, other than climate change. Indeed, the research indicates that arguments linking biodiversity to national economic development via transnational capitalism had little success. As indicated throughout, transnational capitalism is intimately connected with environmental degradation. Jamaican biodiversity in Cockpit Country was threatened by transnational aluminum production; Mexican coastal and terrestrial biodiversity in the Mesoamerican region was threatened by transnational tourism; Egyptian biodiversity in the Red Sea region was threatened by transnational tourism and energy; and in all cases, these stated interests benefited from a privileged relationship with the state.

As shown, networks used neoliberal economic arguments, but failed to convince mining managers in Jamaica, hoteliers and *quintanarroense* state officials in the Mexican reef region, Mexican federal land-use managers in Mesoamerica, and land use managers in Egypt to adopt environmental reforms. Conversely, ecological sustainability arguments, which did not depend on privileging the interests of transnational capitalism, were adopted in Jamaica by the Forestry Department, and in Mexico by SEMARNAT, CONANP, and fishing cooperatives. Again, this success was manifested by changes in environmental behavior, and the adoption of sustainable management practices.

What this means is that arguments by the GEF and other international environmental institutions to use neoliberal versions of "biodiversity mainstreaming" to counter overexploitation will play into the economic interests of elites who benefit from the neoliberal paradigm. This is contrary to the goals of sustainable development. Economic frames that privilege the worldview of transnational capitalism advance elite preferences for natural resource use to the detriment of local populations, and further mean that concern for substantive environmental reform is likely to be transient. At the end of the day, transnational elites do not have a comparative cultural, emotional, or historic attachment to sustained natural resource management to that held by local actors, preferring instead to maximize short-term economic exploitation. To use Lorde's aphorism, "the master's tools will never dismantle the master's house."[31] Viris Pingue in Jamaica's Cockpit Country repeatedly referred to the bauxite interests as "foreigners" who wished to exploit natural resources. Interviews with Alfredo Arellano, chair of the National Reef Committee in the MBRS Project, and Ildefonso Palermo, member of the Quintana Roo Comité Consultivo Estatal in the CBMMx Project, similarly illustrate conceptual problems with the way in which the holders of transnational capital approach the use of natural resources:

Traditionally, in the case of tourism in coastal development in Mexico, the expectation of a return on investment among the major hotel developers, is a return in six, seven, eight years. In sustainable development, the plan for a return on investment of resources and benefits, we're talking about the long-term, possibly fifteen years. To the way of thinking of the investor, it's a notable difference. ... Unfortunately, with globalization, the hotel chains—Spanish, Italian and German—are looking for the exploitation of short-term resources. ... And this brings more than environmental impacts, this also has social impacts.[32]

You're going to have very destructive actions in the name of development. Very negative. ... Because they talk about nature as if it were segmented or fragmented, where you have nature on one side and man on another. ... So you utilize nature to the maximum because, after all, under this idea, the short term is going to predominate, and of course, profit. Immediate profit. A return on investment as soon as possible. This is pure business.[33]

This book joins the literature on environmental justice that is skeptical about the ability of modern neoliberalism to promote environmental sustainability. As Faber and McCarthy argue: "With the ascendancy of neoliberalism, globalization, and the growing concentration of corporate power over all spheres of life, the ability of the movement to solve the ecological crisis is undermined."[34]

Consequently, sustainable biodiversity management is better served by a policy framework that empowers local actors as the primary stakeholders. This is qualitatively different from the stated goals of biodiversity mainstreaming as described by the GEF, which calls for linking sustainable biodiversity management policies to elite economic interests "where the primary focus has previously been on production, economic activity, and development, rather than on biodiversity conservation losses or gains."[35]

First, the successful adoption of frames that privilege and empower local interests through narratives of justice increases the possibility that transnational knowledge networks will gain political allies in the campaign for improved environmental management. As indicated in Jamaica, local communities in Cockpit Country mobilized in support of the biodiversity conservation goals of the Project for Sustainable Conservation of Globally Important Bird Habitats, lobbying ardently for a moratorium on bauxite mining through the CCSG. Similarly, locally based fishing cooperatives in Mexico were highly supportive of the MBRS Project and the sustainable use of marine resources promoted by the transnational network. Pellow, Khagram, McCormick, and many others similarly describe how coalitions of experts joined local activists to resist harmful environmental policies that were carried out in the name of a particular model of development. In those cases, local actors, concerned about how transnational capitalism would degrade their long-term planes for using resources, provided political support to scientific networks that were advocating for conservation.

Second, taking a management approach that focuses on empowering local actors minimizes the possibility of local resistance against natural resource conservation policies. If local actors feel alienated from the goals of environmental management, as occurred in the CBMMx Project, they could effectively withdraw from and undermine conservation efforts. In short, local support grounds transnational norms in a specific political context, described as "norm localization" by Acharya.[36] As McCormick describes, the importance of framing is that it "connects activist experiences with a social justice perspective meant to initiate and sustain movements."[37] The fact that justice framing can sustain movements is an important reason why it should be considered by scientific networks.

Promoting Environmental Justice in Developing Countries

Given these constraints on the efficacy of scientific knowledge, namely the need to attain socialization and consensus and to empower local actors, the following section gives specific recommendations to the GEF and to networks to improve the influence of transnational knowledge-based communities over global environmental governance. These recommendations focus on enhancing the impact of knowledge networks on the domestic implementation of MEAs and environmental norms. As such, while drawn from these specific cases, they are relevant to environmental issue areas characterized by similar relationships between international obligations and domestic practices. Moreover, these arguments support the existing research on the importance of using science to empower activism in countries like Brazil,[38] India,[39] and Zimbabwe.[40]

As knowledge consensus is insufficient, international organizations should also promote substantive socialization between governmental agencies and civil society networks of experts in generating policy-relevant knowledge. This should be carried out by credibly threatening to withhold project funds unless state agencies effectively integrate local experts into planning and management strategies. While the GEF did include mechanisms for civil society-government interaction in its biodiversity management projects, insufficient attention was paid to the quality of civil society participation, particularly in Egypt.

In that case, the GEF funded a project in which the network of civil society advocates universally asserted that there was no substantive communication between experts and natural resource managers in the government. In fact, during the development of the MSB project, project partners in Birdlife International recognized that there was no domestic civil society ENGO that could act as an implementing agency. While Nature Conservation Egypt was established shortly after the design of the MSB project, as described in chapter 5, the organization was given only a formal role in project participation, with no authority over agenda setting and project design.

However, as seen in the case of the CBMMx Project, the GEF can exercise leverage to persuade governments to take a more active role in ensuring civil society participation. As described in chapter 4, the threat issued by the World Bank to withdraw GEF funds persuaded the Mexican state governments and the federal agency la Comisión Nacional de la Biodiversidad (CONABIO) to finally create the Consejos Consultivos Estatales (CCEs), institutionalizing them as forums of participation for civil society experts. At best, projects that lack effective expert participation are likely to lead to inefficiently spent resources. At worst, given the centralization of power in Egypt (a government characterized by embedded cronyism), this is likely to perpetuate harmful patterns of resource use by empowering environmentally antipathetic actors. The GEF should therefore refuse to transfer additional funds to autocratic countries for conservation projects unless these concerns are meaningfully addressed, and should take a similar stance in countries characterized by analogous relationships between the state and environmentally exploitative actors. While the Mubarak regime is no longer in power, this does not necessarily mean that the cloistered political system will liberalize to empower environmental activism without prodding from external economic actors.

Technocracy or Democracy?

As a final note, critical theorists observe that the privilege accorded to scientific inquiry may lead to technocratic policymaking. This is problematic when science delegitimates local participation, and hence local democracy, especially when the networks carrying transnational claims and norms to the developing world are rooted in Northern countries. Moreover, as the preceding policy suggestions indicate, transnational networks may be empowered or facilitated by international financial institutions like the GEF and the World Bank, which have been amply criticized as embodying Northern, capitalist interests. As indicated throughout the discussion, the transnational networks active in environmental advocacy in Jamaica, Mexico, and Egypt are based, at least in part, in ENGOs, academic institutions, and scientific communities from the United States, the UK, and continental Europe.

Even though the language used by the networks is based on scientific, ostensibly universalist epistemologies, the preponderance of Northern actors in transnational networks is still problematic. Authors such as Kütting and Lipschultz critique the authority accorded to scientific inquiry as a rationalist epistemology for undermining worldviews based on, for example, cultural or emotional epistemologies.[41] Additionally problematic, science is validated in ways that tend not to acknowledge the fact that scientific inquiry itself is driven by normative biases.

However, this research indicates that concerns about the anti-democratic nature of transnational scientific advocacy can be addressed. In practice, domestic policymaking and resource management in developing countries is often nondemocratic, even where policymakers claim a public mandate to engage in development. Khagram[42] and Moog Rodrigues[43] illustrate cases of popularly elected governments in India and Brazil, where natural resource management policy created tremendous costs for marginalized rural populations. In those cases, scientists pushed for more participatory environmental policy.

A similar logic adheres in the cases described here. While Egypt cannot plausibly make the claim to be a representative government, Jamaica and Mexico, especially after 2000, are administered by governments that can credibly base their legitimacy on their electoral support by the mass public. Nevertheless, the erstwhile stances taken by these government officials over natural resource management have clearly negative consequences for local populations. Bauxite mining in the Cockpit Country, if it took place, would have resulted in the loss of economic livelihood among Maroons and agricultural populations who resided in areas of bauxite deposits. Indeed, as the research indicates, bauxite companies were allegedly seeking to relocate residents, before public outcry and a responsive administration halted bauxite expansionist plans. Similarly, the ongoing concern among coastal fishing populations in Quintana Roo was that hoteliers continuing the pattern of large-scale resort construction would damage marine ecosystems to the extent that subsistence fishing would become impossible.

Consequently, recognizing that transnational knowledge networks can and do use environmental justice principles to sometimes oppose the transnational and domestic forces that marginalize local populations can alleviate concerns of critical theorists about antidemocratic tendencies of scientists. Indeed, as suggested here, transnational knowledge networks are likely to meet their environmental policy goals when they adopt frameworks and strategies that empower local populations and improve their autonomy over natural resource management. Environmental justice is not just a rhetorical tool. It can be an important mobilization framework, and one that has proven political power. Mohai and others note "there is not a consensus among environmentalists on whether broadening environmentalism to include justice is always a good idea."[44] But it is clear that conservationists and environmental advocates ignore justice at a significant cost.

Notes

Introduction

1. Timothy Swanson, *Global Action for Biodiversity: An International Framework for Implementing the Convention on Biological Diversity* (New York: Earthscan, 1997); G. Kristin Rosendal, *The Convention on Biological Diversity and Developing Countries* (New York: Springer Science & Business Media, 2000); G. Kristin Rosendal and Peter Schei, "Convention on Biological Diversity: From National Conservation to Global Responsibility," in *International Environmental Agreements: An Introduction*, ed. Steinar Andresen, Elin Lerum Boasson, and Geir Hønneland (New York: Routledge, 2012), 119–133.

2. Oran Young, Leslie King, and Heike Schroeder, eds., *Institutions and Environmental Change: Principal Findings, Applications, and Research Frontiers* (Cambridge: MIT Press, 2008).

3. United Nations Convention on Biological Diversity, 1992, Article 2, http://www.cbd.int/convention/text/default.shtml, accessed July 22, 2013.

4. See inter alia, Marc Williams, "The Third World and Global Environmental Negotiations: Interests, Institutions and Ideas," *Global Environmental Politics* 5 (2005): 48–69; Adil Najam, "Dynamics of the Southern Collective: Developing Countries in Desertification Negotiations," *Global Environmental Politics* 4 (2004): 128–154; Susan Sell, "North–South Environmental Bargaining: Ozone, Climate Change and Biodiversity" (*Global Governance* 2 (1996): 97–118, 110. See in particular, Marian Miller, *The Third World in Global Environmental Politics* (Boulder: Lynne Reinner Publishers, 1995), for a discussion of the Third World as a negotiating bloc in global biodiversity governance.

5. Millennium Ecosystem Assessment 2005, *Ecosystems and Human Well-Being*, Synthesis Report (Washington, DC: World Resources Institute, 2005), 4.

6. Secretariat of the Convention on Biological Diversity, *Global Biodiversity Outlook 3* (Montreal: Convention on Biological Diversity, 2010), 9.

7. United Nations, 2012, *Millennium Development Goals Report 2012* (New York: UN Publications), 49–52; Millennium Ecosystem Assessment 2005, *Ecosystems and Human Well-Being*.

8. Millennium Ecosystem Assessment 2005, *Ecosystems and Well-Being*, 5.

9. See K. J. Mulongoy and S. P. Chape, eds., "Protected Areas and Biodiversity," in *An Overview of Key Issues* (Montreal: CBD Secretariat and UNEP-WCMC, 2004), 9–10.

10. Ibid.

11. David G. Victor, "Toward Effective International Cooperation on Climate Change: Numbers, Interests, and Institutions," *Global Environmental Politics* 6, no. 3 (2006): 90–103.

12. See Ronald B. Mitchell, "Evaluating the Performance of Environmental Institutions: What to Evaluate and How to Evaluate It?" in Young, King, and Schroeder, eds., *Institutions and Environmental Change*.

13. Victor Galaz, Per Olsson, Thomas Hahn, Carl Folke, and Uno Svedin, "The Problem of Fit among Biophysical Systems, Environmental and Resource Regimes, and Broader Governance Systems: Insights and Emerging Challenges," in Young, King, and Schroeder, eds., *Institutions and Environmental Change*.

14. Sanjeev Khagram, *Dams and Development: Transnational Struggles for Water and Power* (Ithaca: Cornell University Press, 2004).

15. Sabrina McCormick, *Mobilizing Science: Movements, Participation, and the Remaking of Knowledge* (Philadelphia: Temple University Press, 2009).

16. See Paul Wapner, *Environmental Activism and World Civic Politics* (Ithaca: SUNY Press, 1996).

17. Margaret Keck and Kathryn Sikkink, *Activists Beyond Borders* (Ithaca: Cornell University Press, 1998).

18. Peter Haas, "Introduction: Epistemic Communities and International Policy Coordination," *International Organization* 46 (1992): 1–35.

19. Michelle M. Betsill and Elisabeth Corell, "NGO Influence in International Environmental Negotiations," *Global Environmental Politics* 1, no. 4 (2001): 65–85.

20. Scholars in the reflectivist tradition work in fields including constructivism, feminism, and critical theory. Important texts in this approach include Audie Klotz, *Norms in International Relations: The Struggle Against Apartheid* (Ithaca: Cornell University Press, 1995); Audie Klotz, "Transnational Activism and Global Transformations: The Anti-Apartheid and Abolitionist Experiences," *European Journal of International Relations* 8, no. 1 (2002): 49–76; Thomas Risse-Kappen, "Ideas Do Not Float Freely: Transnational Coalitions, Domestic Structures, and the End of the Cold War," *International Organization* 48 (1994): 185–214; John G. Ruggie, "International

Regimes, Transactions, and Change: Embedded Liberalism in the Postwar Economic System," *International Organization* 36, no. 2 (1982): 379–415; Alexander Wendt, "Anarchy Is What States Make of It," *International Organization* 46, no. 2 (1992); Alexander Wendt, *Social Theory of International Politics* (New York: Cambridge University Press, 1999).

21. Scholars in the rationalist tradition work primarily in the fields of realism, neo-realism, and institutional liberalism. Important texts in this approach include Robert O. Keohane, "International Institutions: Two Approaches," *International Studies Quarterly* 32, no. 4 (1988): 381–386; John Mearsheimer, *The Tragedy of Great Power Politics* (New York: W. W. Norton, 2001); John Mearsheimer, "The False Promise of International Institutions," *International Security* 19, no. 3 (1994): 5–49; Hans Morgenthau Kenneth, *Politics Among Nations* (New York: Knopf, 1948); Kenneth Waltz, *Theory of International Politics* (New York: McGraw Hill Publishers, 1979).

22. Keck and Sikkink, *Activists Beyond Borders*, 2. As networks oriented around a shared purpose, one not based on national loyalties, TANs challenge the primacy of the sovereign nation-state as the primary organizing principle of relevant action in international politics. Some scholars such as Lucy Ford, however, are critical of the idea that the global civil society represents a fundamental change in the ordering of power and preferences in global governance. Rather, they argue, the global civil society reproduces the same divisions of labor and international hierarchy; see Lucy Ford, "Challenging Global Environmental Governance: Social Movement Agency and Global Civil Society," *Global Environmental Politics* 3, no. 2 (2003): 120–134.

23. See in particular, Karen Litfin, *Ozone Discourses: Science and Politics in Global Environmental Cooperation* (New York: Cambridge University Press, 1994), 15; Steven Lukes's "third face of power" indicates that power is exercised by an actor A when A convinced B to take action contrary to B's objective interests. Steven Lukes, *Power: A Radical View* (London: Macmillan, 1974). Such a use of power and argumentation would be manipulative, whereas my claim that networks can teach other actors to think differently about their interests refers to a persuasive use of power and argumentation. Under persuasion, it is not the case that B would take action contrary to its objective interests, since what your interests are is socially determined.

24. Clark et al. illustrate this iterated conception of influence in William C. Clark, Ronald B. Mitchell, and David W. Cash, "Evaluating the Influence of Global Environmental Assessments," in *Global Environmental Assessments: Information and Influence*, ed. Roland B. Mitchell, William C. Clark, David W. Cash, and Nancy M. Dickson (Cambridge, MA: MIT Press, 2006), 11.

25. See Risse-Kappen, "Ideas Do Not Float Freely"; Brian Frederking, *Resolving Security Dilemmas: A Constructivist Explanation of the INF Treaty* (Burlington, VT: Ashgate, 2000).

26. See Klotz, *Norms in International Relations*; Klotz, "Transnational Activism and Global Transformations."

27. Radoslav Dimitrov, "Hostage to Norms: States, Institutions and Global Forest Politics," *Global Environmental Politics*, 5 (2005): 1–24.

28. See Richard Price and Nina Tannenwald, "Norms and Deterrence: The Nuclear and Chemical Weapons Taboos," in *The Culture of National Security*, ed. Peter Katzenstein (New York: Columbia University Press, 1996), 114–152.

29. María Guadalupe Moog Rodrigues, *Global Environmentalism and Local Politics: Transnational Advocacy Networks in Brazil, Ecuador, and India* (Albany: SUNY Press, 2004).

30. Tora Skodvin and Steinar Andresen, "Non-state Influence in the International Whaling Convention, 1970–1990," *Global Environmental Politics* 3 (2004): 61–86.

31. Khagram, *Dams and Development*; Ralph B. Levering, "Brokering the Law of the Sea Treaty," in *Transnational Social Movements and Global Politics*, ed. Jackie Smith, Charles Chatfield, and Ron Pagnucco (Syracuse: Syracuse University Press, 1997), 225–242. See also the discussion of environmental TANs in Keck and Sikkink, *Activists Beyond Borders*, chap. 4.

32. See Wapner, *Environmental Activism and World Civic Politics*, for a discussion of the various levels of engagement (both at the state and substate levels) of global civil society actors, such as TANs.

33. Peter Haas, "Do Regimes Matter?: Epistemic Communities and Mediterranean Pollution Control," *International Organization* 43 (1989): 377–403; Haas, "Introduction"; Steven Bernstein, *The Compromise of Liberal Environmentalism* (New York: Columbia University Press, 2001); Radoslav Dimitrov, "Knowledge, Power and Interests in Environmental Regime Formation," *International Studies Quarterly* 47 (2003): 123–150.

34. See also Klotz, "Transnational Activism and Global Transformations": "... scientific expertise and [purely] principled ideas are not the same ... epistemic communities are not moral movements" (52).

35. See for example John Ruggie's book on the spread of "embedded liberalism" in international markets in the post-World War II era for an example of an economic epistemic community. Ruggie, *Constructing World Polity* (New York: Routledge, 1998).

36. Mai'a K. Davis Cross, "Rethinking Epistemic Communities Twenty Years Later," *Review of International Studies* 39, no. 1 (2013): 137–160, 155.

37. Cross, "Rethinking Epistemic Communities," 157.

38. See Steinar Andresen, Tora Skodvin, and Arild Underdal *Science and Politics in International Environmental Regimes* (New York: Manchester University Press, 2000); Dimitrov, "Knowledge, Power and Interests in Environmental Regime Formation"; Keck and Sikkink, *Activists Beyond Borders*. For more critical takes on this perception

of science's authority, see McCormick, *Mobilizing Science*; and Tim Forsyth, *Critical Political Ecology: The Politics of Environmental Science* (New York: Routledge, 2002).

39. Mark A. Levy, "European Acid Rain: The Power of Tote-Board Diplomacy," in *Institutions for the Earth: Sources of Effective International Environmental Protection*, ed. Peter M. Haas, Robert O. Keohane, and Mark A. Levy (Cambridge, MA: MIT Press, 1993), 75–132; Jørgen Wettestad, "Acid Lessons? LRTAP Implementation and Effectiveness," *Global Environmental Change* 7, no. 3 (1997): 235–249.

40. Peter Haas, *Saving the Mediterranean* (New York: Columbia University Press, 1990); Haas, "Do Regimes Matter?"

41. Peter Haas, ed., "Banning Chlorofluorocarbons: Epistemic Community Efforts to Protect Stratospheric Ozone," in *Knowledge, Power and International Policy Coordination* (Columbia: University of South Carolina Press, 1992), 187–224.

42. Cross, "Rethinking Epistemic Communities."

43. Sabrina McCormick, *Mobilizing Science: Movements, Participation, and the Remaking of Knowledge* (Philadelphia, PA: Temple University Press, 2009).

44. Amitav Acharya, "How Ideas Spread: Whose Norms Matter? Norm Localization and Institutional Change in Asian Regionalism," *International Organization* 58 (2004): 239–275.

45. Bernstein, *The Compromise of Liberal Environmentalism*.

46. Doug McAdam, John D. McCarthy, and Mayer N. Zald, *Comparative Perspectives on Social Movements* (New York: Cambridge University Press, 1996).

47. Ronald B. Mitchell, William C. Clark, and David Cash, "Information and Influence," in Mitchell et al., eds., *Global Environmental Assessments*, 310.

48. Bernstein, *The Compromise of Liberal Environmentalism*.

49. Karen Bakker, "The Limits of 'Neoliberal Natures': Debating Green Neoliberalism," *Progress in Human Geography* 34, no. 6 (2010): 715–735; Noel Castree, "Commentary," *Environment and Planning A* 38, no. 1 (2006): 1–6.

50. Bakker, "The Limits of 'Neoliberal Natures,'" 723–724.

51. Maaria Curlier and Steinar Andresen, "International Trade in Endangered Species: The CITES Regime," in *Environmental Regime Effectiveness*, ed. Edward L. Miles, Steinar Andresen, Elaine M. Carlin, Jon Birger Skjærseth, Arild Underdal, and Jørgen Wettestad (Cambridge, MA: MIT Press), 357–378, 367.

52. Stephen R. Carpenter, Ruth DeFries, Thomas Dietz, Harold A. Mooney, Stephen Polasky, Walter V. Reid, and Robert J. Scholes, "Millennium Ecosystem Assessment: Research Needs," *Science* 314 (2006): 257–258; Brendan Fisher Kerry Turner, Matthew Zylstra, Roy Brouwer, Rudolf de Groot, Stephen Farber, Paul Ferraro, Rhys

Green, David Hadley, Julian Harlow, Paul Jefferiss, Chris Kirkby, Paul Morling, Shaun Mowatt, Robin Naidoo, Jouni Paavola, Bernardo Strassburg, Doug Yu, and Andrew Balmford, "Ecosystem Services and Economic Theory: Integration for Policy Relevant Research," *Ecological Applications*, 18, no. 8 (2008): 2050–2067; David Pimentel, Christa Wilson, Christine McCullum, Rachel Huang, Paulette Dwen, Jessica Flack, Quynh Tran, Tamara Saltman, and Barbara Cliff, "Economic and Environmental Benefits of Biodiversity," *BioScience* 47, no. 11 (1997): 747–757; Robert T. Watson, "Turning Science into Policy: Challenges and Experiences from the Science-Policy Interface," *Philosophical Transactions of the Royal Society* 360, no. 1454 (2005): 471–477.

53. CBD COP-10, Decision X/2. See also Caroline Peterson and Brian Huntley, *Mainstreaming Biodiversity in Production Landscapes* (Washington, DC: Global Environment Facility, 2005), 3.

54. I am using Bakker's typology of "neoliberalism" here, to describe two components of a multivariate process that operate at different geographic scales. See Bakker, "The Limits of 'Neoliberal Natures'"; Castree, "Commentary."

55. Carpenter et al., Millennium Ecosystem Assessment; Nicolás Kosoy and Esteve Cordera, "Payments for Ecosystem Services as Commodity Fetishism," *Ecological Economics* 69, no. 6 (2010): 1228–1236; National Research Council, *Valuing Ecosystem Services: Toward Better Environmental Decision-Making* (Washington, DC: National Academies Press, 2004); Richard B. Norgaard, Ecosystem Services: From Eye-opening Metaphor to Complexity Blinder, *Ecological Economics* 63, no. 4 (2010): 1219–1227.

56. Dana R. Fisher and Jessica F. Green, "Understanding Disenfranchisement: Civil Society and Developing Countries' Influence and Participation in Global Governance for Sustainable Development," *Global Environmental Politics* 4 (2004): 65–84, 68; Najam, "Dynamics of the Southern Collective"; Jordi Diez and O. P. Dwivedi, *Global Environmental Challenges: Perspectives from the Global South* (Toronto, Ontario: University of Toronto Press, 2008); J. Timmons Roberts and Bradley Parks, *A Climate of Injustice: Global Inequality, North–South Politics, and Climate Policy* (Cambridge, MA: MIT Press, 2006).

57. The production of CFCs is historically concentrated in the United States, which produced about half of global CFCs in the 1970s. Other major producers were the UK; France; Germany; Italy; and the Netherlands. See Peter Haas et al., eds., *Institutions for the Earth*, 29. There are also some natural sources of atmospheric chlorine. NASA identifies volcanic eruptions as contributing to this factor, but notes that anthropogenic sources comprises at least 80 percent of chlorine in the atmosphere. NASA Observatory, *World of Change: Antarctic Ozone Hole*, 2011, http://earthobservatory.nasa.gov/Features/WorldOfChange/ozone.php, accessed August 2015.

58. Lawrence Susskind, *Environmental Diplomacy: Negotiating More Effective Global Agreements* (New York: Oxford University Press, 1994), 19. This situation is neither

ecologically nor politically sustainable in the long term. The 1987 World Conference on Environment and Development (WCED) Report noted the interplay of global markets and the comparative disadvantage of LDCs in the international capital markets by observing that "economic policies of some major industrial countries had depressed and destabilized the international economy, which aggravated these pressures on developing countries," cited in Bernstein, *The Compromise of Liberal Environmentalism*, 65.

59. Roberts and Parks, *A Climate of Injustice*.

60. See Bernstein, *The Compromise of Liberal Environmentalism*; Miller, *The Third World in Global Environmental Politics*.

61. Margaret Biswas and Asit K. Biswas, "Environment and Sustained Development in the Third World: A Review of the Past Decade," *Third World Quarterly* 4, no. 3 (1982): 479–491, 484.

62. JoAnn Carmin and Julian Agyeman, eds., *Environmental Inequalities Beyond Borders: Local Perspectives on Global Injustices* (Cambridge, MA: MIT Press, 2011); Gabriela Kütting, "Environmental Justice," *Global Environmental Politics* 4, no. 1 (2004): 115–121; David Naguib Pellow, *Resisting Global Toxics: Transnational Movements for Environmental Justice* (Cambridge, MA: MIT Press, 2007).

63. As Pellow, *Resisting Global Toxics*, and others note, it is difficult to parse the relationships among poverty, race, ethnicity, and gender, particularly since these are all interrelated at both global and local levels.

64. Ibid. See also Peter Newell, "Race, Class, and the Global Politics of Environmental Inequality," *Global Environmental Politics* 5, no. 3 (2005): 70–94.

65. Sanjeev Ali and Mary Ackley, "Foreign Investment and Environmental Justice in an Island Economy: Mining, Bottled Water, and Corporate Social Responsibility in Fiji," in Carmin and Agyeman, eds., *Environmental Inequalities Beyond Borders*, 67–84.

66. UN Division for the Advancement of Women (UNDAW), "Women and Water." Report published to promote the goals of the Beijing Declaration and the Platform for Action, 2005, http://www.tinyurl.com/undaw, accessed May 2015.

67. David Carruthers, ed., *Environmental Justice in Latin America: Problems, Promise, and Practice* (Cambridge, MA: MIT Press, 2008).

68. Richard Hiskes, *The Human Right to a Green Future: Environmental Rights and Intergenerational Justice* (New York: Cambridge University Press, 2009).

69. Bryan G. Norton and Douglas Noonan, "Ecology and Valuation: Big Changes Needed," *Ecological Economics* 63, no. 4 (2007): 664–675, 665. See also Bakker, "The Limits of 'Neoliberal Natures'"; Erik Gómez-Baggethun, Rudolf de Groot, Pedro L. Thomas, and Carlos Montes, "The History of Ecosystem Services in Economic Theory and Practice: From Early Notions to Markets and Payment Schemes," *Ecologi-*

cal Economics 69, no. 6 (2009): 1209–1218; Kosoy and Cordera, "Payments for Ecosystem Services."

70. Stephen R. Carpenter, Harold A. Mooney, John Agard, Doris Capistrano, Ruth S. DeFries, Sandra Díaz, Thomas Dietz, Anantha K. Duraiappah, Alfred Oteng-Yeboah, "Science for Managing Ecosystem Services: Beyond the Millennium Ecosystem Assessment," *Proceedings of the National Academy of Science* 106, no. 5 (2009): 1305–1312; Millennium Ecosystem Assessment 2005, *Ecosystems and Human Well-Being*.

71. For approaches critical of the idea of science as impartial, see Litfin, *Ozone Discourses*, 24; Andrew Karvonen and Ralf Brand, "Technical Expertise, Sustainability, and the Politics of Specialized Knowledge," in *Environmental Governance: Power and Knowledge in a Local-Global World*, ed. Gabriela Kutting and Ronnie D. Lipschultz (New York: Routledge, 2009), 38–59. These critical approaches are concerned about the authority accorded to scientific knowledge, particularly since doing so privileges one value set at the expense of others.

72. McCormick, *Mobilizing Science*.

73. Karvonen and Brand, "Technical Expertise, Sustainability."

74. Forsyth, *Critical Political Ecology*.

75. Donna Haraway, "Situated Knowledges: The Science Question in Feminism and the Privileging of Partial Perspective," *Feminist Studies* 14, no. 3 (1988): 575–599.

76. Ibid.

77. Helen Longino, *Science as Social Knowledge: Values and Objectivity in Scientific Inquiry* (Princeton, NJ: Princeton University Press, 1990).

78. Forsyth, *Critical Political Ecology*.

79. McCormick, *Mobilizing Science*, 30.

80. Ibid.

81. Forsyth, *Critical Political Ecology*; Haraway, "Situated Knowledges"; McCormick, *Mobilizing Science*; Litfin, *Ozone Discourses*.

82. Forsyth, *Critical Political Ecology*, 185.

83. Carol Cohn, "Sex and Death in the Rational World of Defense Intellectuals," *Signs*, 22, no. 4 (1987): 687–718.

84. Paul Mohai, David Pellow, and J. Timmons Roberts, "Environmental Justice," *Annual Review of Environment and Resources* 34 (2009): 405–430, 407.

85. Alison Phipps, "I Can't Do with Whinging Women! Feminism and the Habitus of 'Women in Science' Activists," *Women's Studies International Forum* 29, no. 2 (2006): 125–135.

86. Mark Dowie, "Conservation Refugees: When Protecting Nature Means Kicking People Out," *Orion Magazine*, May 2005, http://www.orionmagazine.org/index.php/ articles/article/161, accessed May 2015; Mac Chapin, "A Challenge to Conservationists," *World Watch Magazine*, Nov./Dec. 2004, http://tinyurl.com/challenge -conservation, accessed May 2014.

87. Dowie, "Conservation Refugees."

88. Saskia Vermeylen and Gordon Walker, "Environmental Justice, Values, and Biological Diversity: The San and the Hoodia Benefit-Sharing Agreement," in Carmin and Agyeman, eds., *Environmental Inequalities Beyond Borders*, 105–128.

89. Ibid., 121.

90. McCormick, *Mobilizing Science*.

91. Ibid., 70.

92. Quoted in Chapin, "A Challenge to Conservationists," 21.

93. See Hiskes, *The Human Right to a Green Future*.

94. McCormick, *Mobilizing Science*, passim.

95. Karvonen and Brand, "Technical Expertise, Sustainability," 54.

96. McCormick, *Mobilizing Science*; Pellow, *Resisting Global Toxics*.

97. Michele Zebich-Knos, "Ecotourism, Park Systems, and Environmental Justice in Latin America," in Carruthers, ed., *Environmental Justice in Latin America*, 185–211.

98. See Rodrigues, *Global Environmentalism and Local Politics*; Mitchell, Clark, and Cash, "Information and Influence."

99. Clark, Mitchell, and Cash, "Evaluating the Influence of Global Environmental Assessments," 14. See also Karen Litfin, "Environment, Wealth and Authority: Global Climate Change and Emerging Modes of Legitimation," *International Studies Review* 2, no. 2 (2000): 119–148, 130, where Litfin argues that knowledge generation and internalization is a fundamentally social process.

100. David Snow, E. Burke Rochford Jr., Steven K. Worden, and Robert D. Benford, "Frame Alignment Processes, Micromobilization, and Movement Participation," *American Sociological Review* 51, no. 4 (1986): 464–481, 464; Mario Diani, "Linking Mobilization Frames and Political Opportunities: Insights from Regional Populism in Italy," *American Sociological Review* 61 (1996): 1053–1069.

101. The idea that the frames adopted by a social advocacy network function to provide an internally consistent rationale for action is mentioned in sociological studies of social movements, for example in Diani, "Linking Mobilization Frames and Political Opportunities"; David Snow et al., "Frame Alignment Processes"; as well as in previously mentioned political science studies of transnational social

movements by Sanjeev Khagram, Moog Rodrigues and María Guadalupe, and Margaret Keck and Kathryn Sikkink.

102. Regina Axelrod, "Democracy and the Global Nuclear Renaissance: From the Czech Republic to Fukushima," in *The Global Environment: Institutions, Law, and Policy*, 4th ed., ed. Regina Axelrod and Stacy VanDeveer (Washington, DC: CQ Press, 2014), 305–329.

103. Tom Perrault, "Popular Protest and Unpopular Policies: State Restructuring, Resource Conflict, and Social Justice in Bolivia," in Carruthers, ed., *Environmental Justice in Latin America*, 239–262, 247.

104. Kathryn Hochstetler, "Democracy and the Environment in Latin America and Eastern Europe," in *Comparative Environmental Politics: Theory, Practice, and Prospects*, ed. Paul Steinberg and Stacy VanDeveer (Cambridge, MA: MIT Press, 2012), 199–229.

105. Liliana Botcheva, "Focus and Effectiveness of Environmental Activism in Eastern Europe: A Comparative Study of Environmental Movements in Bulgaria, Hungary, Slovakia, and Romania," *Journal of Environment and Development* 5, no. 3 (1996): 292–308. Compare Botcheva's work with Hochstetler, "Democracy and the Environment in Latin America and Eastern Europe"; Axelrod, "Democracy and the Global Nuclear Renaissance."

106. Keck and Sikkink, *Activists Beyond Borders*.

107. See Andresen et al., *Science and Politics in International Environmental Regimes*, passim; Litfin, Ozone *Discourses*.

108. Jessica C. Teets, *Civil Society under Authoritarianism: The China Model* (New York: Cambridge University Press, 2014).

109. Jeannie Sowers, "Nature Reserves and Authoritarian Rule in Egypt: Embedded Autonomy Revisited," *The Journal of Environment & Development* 16, no. 4 (2007): 375–397. See also Sowers, *Environmental Politics in Egypt: Activists, Experts and the State* (New York: Routledge, 2013).

110. Khagram, *Dams and Development*, 22; Adam Przeworski and Fernando Limongi, "Political Regimes and Economic Growth," *Journal of Economic Perspectives* 7, no. 3 (1993): 51–69, 54.

111. See Andresen et al., *Science and Politics in International Environmental Regimes*, 10 and passim; Litfin *Ozone Discourses*.

112. Rodrigues, *Global Environmentalism and Local Politics*.

113. Max Stephenson Jr. and Lisa A. Schweitzer, "Learning from the Quest for Environmental Justice in the Niger River Delta," in Carmin and Agyeman, eds., *Environmental Inequalities Beyond Borders*, 45–66.

114. Ibid., 61.

115. Kate O'Neill, "The Comparative Study of Environmental Movements," in Steinberg and VanDeveer, eds., *Comparative Environmental Politics*, 115–142.

116. Betsill and Corell, "NGO Influence in International Environmental Negotiations." The comparative literature on environmental policymaking is large, and includes the volumes and texts mentioned throughout this chapter, such as Carmin and Agyeman, eds., *Environmental Inequalities Beyond Borders*; Carruthers, ed., *Environmental Justice in Latin America*; Steinberg and VanDeveer, eds., *Comparative Environmental Politics*.

117. Mark Beeson, "The Coming of Environmental Authoritarianism," *Environmental Politics* 19, no. 2 (2010): 276–294; Joanna Lewis and Kelly Sims Gallagher, "Energy and Environment in China: Achievements and Enduring Challenges," in Axelrod and VanDeveer, eds., *The Global Environment*.

118. Mostafa Tolba, quoted in "UNEP Executive Directors Panel at GEG Forum—June 2009," posted by GEG Project, 2010. https://vimeo.com/6340518, accessed May 2015.

119. Oran Young, "Institutional Linkages in International Society: Polar Perspectives," *Global Governance* 22, no. 1 (1996): 1–23; Amandine Orsini, Jean-Frédéric Morin, and Oran Young, "Regime Complexes: A Buzz, a Boom, or a Boost for Global Governance?" *Global Governance* 19 (2013): 27–39; Kal Raustiala and David G. Victor, "The Regime Complex for Plant Genetic Resources," *International Organization* 58, no. 2 (2004): 277–309; Karen J. Alter and Sophie Meunier, "The Politics of International Regime Complexity," *Perspectives on Politics* 7, no. 1 (2009): 13–24; Young, King, and Schroeder, eds., *Institutions and Environmental Change*; Sebastian Oberthür and Olav Schram Stokke, *Managing Institutional Complexity: Regime Interplay and Global Environmental Change* (Cambridge, MA: MIT Press, 2011).

120. As Kütting notes, the mainstream international relations literature, which focuses on treaty implementation, is generally silent on the role of environmental justice (Kütting, "Environmental Justice"). For an exception, see Roberts and Parks, *A Climate of Injustice*.

121. Edward L. Miles, Steinar Andresen, Elain M. Carlin, Jon Birger Skjærseth, Arild Underdal, and Jørgen Wettestad, eds., *Environmental Regime Effectiveness: Confronting Theory with Evidence* (Cambridge, MA: MIT Press, 2002); Oran Young, *Effectiveness of International Environmental Regimes: Causal Connections and Behavioral Mechanisms* (Cambridge, MA: MIT Press, 1999).

122. Young, *Effectiveness of International Environmental Regimes*.

123. CBD COP-10, Decision X/2; Gómez-Baggethun et al., "The History of Ecosystem Services"; Norton and Noonan, "Ecology and Valuation"; Millenium Ecosystem

Assessment 2005, *Ecosystems and Human Well-Being*; Peterson and Huntley, *Mainstreaming Biodiversity*.

124. Carmin and Agyeman, eds., *Environmental Inequalities Beyond Borders*; Alastair Iles, "Mapping Environmental Justice in Technology Flows: Computer Waste Impacts in Asia," *Global Environmental Politics* 4, no. 4 (2004): 76–107; Khagram, *Dams and Development*; Pellow, *Resisting Global Toxics*; David Schlosberg and David Carruthers, "Indigenous Struggles, Environmental Justice, and Community Capabilities," *Global Environmental Politics* 10, no. 4 (2010): 12–35. For a review of the literature, see Kütting, "Environmental Justice."

1   Jamaica and the Conservation of Globally Important Bird Habitats

1. Kathryn Hochstetler and Margaret Keck, *Greening Brazil: Environmental Activism in State and Society* (Durham, NC: Duke University Press, 2007).

2. Michele Zebich-Knos, "Ecotourism, Park Systems, and Environmental Justice in Latin America," in *Environmental Justice in Latin America: Problems, Promise, and Practice*, ed. David Carruthers (Cambridge, MA: MIT Press, 2008), 185–212.

3. Carruthers, ed., *Environmental Justice in Latin America*.

4. David Pellow, *Resisting Global Toxics: Transnational Movements for Environmental Justice* (Cambridge, MA: MIT Press, 2007).

5. JoAnn Carmin and Julian Agyeman, eds., *Environmental Inequalities Beyond Borders: Local Perspectives on Global Injustices* (Cambridge, MA: MIT Press: 2011).

6. G. Kristin Rosendal, *The Convention on Biological Diversity and Developing Countries* (London: Kluwer Academic Publishers, 2000).

7. Kristin Rosendal and Peter Johan Schei, "Convention on Biological Diversity: From National Conservation to Global Responsibility," in *International Environmental Agreements: An Introduction*, ed. Steinar Andresen, Elin Lerum Boasson, and Geir Hønneland (New York: Routledge, 2012), 119–133.

8. Timothy Swanson, *Global Action for Biodiversity: An International Framework for Implementing the Convention on Biological Diversity* (New York: Routledge, 2013).

9. Sanjeev Khagram, James V. Riker, and Kathryn Sikkink, eds., *Restructuring World Politics: Transnational Social Movements, Networks, and Norms* (Minneapolis: University of Minnesota Press, 2002).

10. Susan Koenig, with Ann Haynes-Sutton, George Proctor, and Peter Vogel, *Cockpit Country Conservation Report: Biodiversity Assessment* (Kingston: NRCA, 2000), ii.

11. World Bank, *Jamaica Cockpit Country Conservation Project*, project proposal for GEF (Washington, DC: World Bank, 1999), 1; National Environmental Protection

Agency (NEPA), *National Biodiversity Strategy and Action Plan* (Kingston: NEPA, 2003), passim—hereafter, referred to as NBSAP; The Nature Conservancy, *Jamaica National Biodiversity Strategy and Action Plan: National Implementation Support Partnership* (Kingston: TNC, 2003), 1.

12. Cockpit Country provides approximately 42 percent of Jamaica's national yam output. Balfour Spence, *GEF Cockpit Country Conservation Project: Land Management Report* (Kingston: NRCA, 1999), 15.

13. Werner Zips, "Laws in Competition: Traditional Maroon Authorities within Legal Pluralism in Jamaica," *The Journal of Legal Pluralism and Unofficial Law* 28, nos. 37–38 (1996): 279–305; Werner Zips, "'We Are Landowners': Territorial Autonomy and Land Tenure in the Jamaican Maroon Community of Accompong," *The Journal of Legal Pluralism and Unofficial Law* 30, no. 40 (1998): 89–121.

14. Mining Commissioner Clinton Thompson, author interview conducted July 14, 2011. Mike Schwartz, member of epistemic community organization the Windsor Research Center (WRC), author interviews conducted June 5, 2006, and August 12, 2011.

15. Mike Schwartz, author interviews conducted June 5, 2006, and August 12, 2011. Data confirmed by comparing maps produced by epistemic community organizations from 2006 to 2011.

16. *Jamaica Gleaner*, December 27, 2006.

17. Paige West, *Conservation Is Our Government Now: The Politics of Ecology in Papua New Guinea* (Durham, NC: Duke University Press, 2006).

18. Emma Cervone, *Long Live Atahualpa: Indigenous Politics, Justice, and Democracy in the Northern Andes* (Durham, NC: Duke University Press, 2012).

19. Suzana Sawyer, *Crude Chronicles: Indigenous Politics, Multinational Oil, and Neoliberalism in Ecuador* (Durham, NC: Duke University Press, 2004).

20. George Henderson and Marvin Waterstone, eds., *Geographic Thought: A Praxis Perspective* (New York: Routledge, 2009).

21. "Small-scale" agriculture refers to farming carried out on agricultural plots of ten hectares or less and the majority of agriculture in the area is practiced on plots of four hectares or less. Spence, *GEF Cockpit Country Conservation Project*, passim; ENACT Programme, *Policy on Strategic Environmental Assessment* (draft) (Kingston: Government of Jamaica, 2003), 15. Logging is not generally a result of industrial, large-scale activity, but rather is carried out on a small scale, with teams of three to four individuals working with chainsaws, and transporting materials manually through the area. Spence, *GEF Cockpit Country Conservation Project*, 17–18; Forestry Department, *National Forest Management and Conservation Plan* (Kingston: Forestry Department, 2001), 40.

22. The eastern and southeastern buffer zones provide approximately 42 percent of Jamaica's national yam output, and of a total fifteen million yam sticks produced nationally per annum, an estimated six million are produced in Cockpit Country. See inter alia, Spence, *GEF Cockpit Country Conservation Project*, 15.

23. Forestry Department, *National Forest Management and Conservation Plan*.

24. See inter alia, Spence, *GEF Cockpit Country Conservation Project*; ENACT Programme, *Policy on Strategic Environmental Assessment*, 19; "Jamaica: Toward a Watershed Policy," *Green Paper* no. 2/99 (Kingston: NRCA, 1999), 5–6.

25. Spence, *GEF Cockpit Country Conservation Project*, 17.

26. The Nature Conservancy, *Cockpit Country Conservation Action Plan: A Summary*, (Kingston: TNC, 2006), Appendix D; United Nations Environment Programme (UNEP) and Global Environment Facility (GEF), *Sustainable Conservation of Globally Important Caribbean Bird Habitats: Strengthening a Regional Network for a Shared Resource*, Project number GF/2713-03 (Washington, DC: Global Environment Facility, 2003), 55, https://www.thegef.org/gef/project_list, accessed October 2005; also NEPA, *NBSAP*, passim; Forestry Department, *Forestry Policy 2001* (Kingston: Forestry Department, 2001).

27. See inter alia, Steve Bass and Tighe Geoghan, "Incentives for Watershed Management in Jamaica: Results of a Brief Diagnostic," *CANARI Technical Reports* 314 (Kingston: CANARI, 2007), 7; NEPA, *NBSAP*, passim.

28. See, inter alia, Sawyer, *Crude Chronicles*; Hochstetler and Keck, *Greening Brazil*; Carruthers, ed., *Environmental Justice in Latin America*. For a specific study of Jamaica, note Norman Girvan, *Foreign Capital and Economic Underdevelopment in Jamaica* (Kingston: University of the West Indies Press, 1971).

29. Tony Weis, "Beyond Peasant Deforestation: Environment and Development in Rural Jamaica," *Global Environmental Change* 10 (2000): 299–305, 302; David Barker and David J. Miller, "Farming on the Fringe," in *Environment and Development in the Caribbean: Geographical Perspectives*, ed. D. Barker and D. F. M. McGregor (Kingston: UWI Press, 1995), 271–292, 281. Several farmers owned more than one plot, with a modal class of three plots per farmer, cited in this 1995 study.

30. Spence, *GEF Cockpit Country Conservation Project*, 40.

31. See inter alia, Spence, *GEF Cockpit Country Conservation Project*, 93; Barker and Miller, "Farming on the Fringe," 282; Karyl Walker, "Cockpit Country Worry," *Sunday Observer*, November 19, 2006; Kayenne Taylor, "Report on the Legal Imperatives and Implications of the Cockpit Country Conservation Project," report produced for the World Bank (Kingston: n.p., 1999), 93.

32. Girvan, *Foreign Capital and Economic Underdevelopment in Jamaica*, 21–22.

33. Although this figure is the contribution of mining in all sectors, bauxite and alumnia mining make up 99 percent of the total revenues of the mining sector. See the NRCA reports prepared by Dennis Morrison and Michael Mitchell, *Sector Assessment Reports—Mining* (Kingston: NRCA, 1999), 2–3; STATIN, "Economic Statistics: Volume of Production in the Mining Sector 2006–2008," http://statinja.gov.jm/ProMining.aspx, accessed August 2015.

34. USGS 2006, 10.11.

35. Sawyer, *Crude Chronicles*. For Fiji, see Saleem H. Ali and Mary A. Ackley, "Foreign Investment and Environmental Justice in an Island Economy: Mining, Bottled Water, and Corporate Social Responsibility in Fiji," in Carmin and Agyeman, eds., *Environmental Inequalities Beyond Borders*, 67–84.

36. Walter Rodney, *How Europe Underdeveloped Africa* (Dar es-Salaam: Bogle-L'Ouverture Publications, 1972).

37. Girvan, *Foreign Capital and Economic Underdevelopment in Jamaica.*

38. Eduardo Galeano, *The Open Veins of Latin America* (Mexico City: Siglo XXI Editores, 1971). To be sure, Galeano later expressed regret at the prose and phrasing of his book.

39. Carlene Edie, "Domestic Politics and External Relations in Jamaica under Michael Manley, 1972–1980," *Studies in Comparative International Development* 21, no. 1 (1986): 71–94; William Jesse Biddle and John D. Stephens, "Dependent Development and Foreign Policy: The Case of Jamaica," *International Studies Quarterly* 33 (1989): 411–434.

40. Edie, "Domestic Politics and External Relations." See also Ann Genova, "Nigeria's Nationalization of British Petroleum," *International Journal of African Historical Studies* 43, no. 1 (2010): 115–136, for a discussion on Nigeria's nationalization policies and rhetoric around domestic control of oil.

41. Jay Mandle, *Persistent Underdevelopment: Change and Economic Modernization in the West Indies* (Amsterdam: Overseas Publishers Association, 1996).

42. Morrison and Mitchell, *Sector Assessment Reports—Mining*, 2–3.

43. Jamaica Information Service, "The Jamaica Bauxite Institute," http://jis.gov.jm/agencies/jamaica-bauxite-institute-jbi/, accessed August 2015

44. Carib Cement, *2005 Annual Report*, http://www.caribcement.com/files/cms/CCCL_Annual_Report_2005.pdf, accessed December 2008; former NRCA staff member, author interviews not for attribution, notes taken from telephone interview.

45. "Jamaica Hopes to Harvest Titanium from Red Mud," *Jamaica Gleaner*, February 13, 2015.

46. NEPA, *NBSAP*; Morrison and Mitchell, *Sector Assessment Reports—Mining*.

47. NEPA, *NBSAP*, 27–28; Mick Day, "Karst Terrains: Environmental Changes and Human Impact," *Catena Supplement* 25 (1993): 109–125, 121.

48. UNEP, *Global Environmental Facility Project Document*, 56.

49. Kimberly John, author interviews conducted July 12, 2006, transcript of audio-cassette recording.

50. "Are Jamaica's Red Mud Lakes Safe?" *Jamaica Gleaner*, October 10, 2010.

51. "Dust, Stench, and Claim of Impotence," *Jamaica Observer*, February 11, 2007.

52. Lenford Bailey, quoted in "Dust, Stench, and Claim of Impotence," *Jamaica Observer*.

53. Ali and Ackley, "Foreign Investment and Environmental Justice in an Island Economy," 67.

54. Peter Newell, "Race, Class, and the Global Politics of Environmental Inequality," *Global Environmental Politics*, 5, no. 3 (2005): 70–94, 70.

55. Mike Schwartz, personal communication, January 22, 2008.

56. Viris Pingue, local yam farmer in Cockpit Country, author interviews conducted July 14, 2011, transcript of digital voice recording.

57. The environmental portfolio has been transferred to various other ministries since its inception. In 1992, the portfolio was created in the Ministry of Tourism and the Environment. In 2000 the portfolio of Environment was shifted to the Ministry of Land and Environment; in 2001, as the Ministry of Local Government and the Environment; in 2007 as the Ministry of Health and the Environment. Throughout the chapter, the Ministry will be referred to as the Ministry of Environment for consistency. Information from author interview with Jean Jo Bellamy, from notes taken from telephone interview conducted August 1, 2007; author interview with Franklin McDonald, from notes taken from telephone interview conducted August 29, 2007; C. Easton and Associates, *ENACT Jamaica Case Study: A Governance Model in Capacity Enhancement for Sustainable Development* (Kingston: ENACT Programme, 2004).

58. Between 1994 and 2008, the Department of Mining was a part of the Ministry of Agriculture (1994–1997), Ministry of Mining and Energy (1997–2002), Ministry of Land and Environment (2002–2005), Ministry of Agriculture (2006–2007), Ministry of Agriculture and Lands (2007–June 2008), and the Ministry of Mining and Tele-communications (2008–present). Mines and Geology Division, *Background Information* (2015), http://www.mgd.gov.jm/background.html, accessed August 2015.

59. See the Forest Act, Act 17 of 1996, http://faolex.fao.org/docs/pdf/jam7934.pdf, accessed August 2015. See also later modifications to this act that expanded the role of the Forestry Department to manage species and biodiversity: Forestry Depart-

ment, *The Forest Regulations, 2001* (Kingston: Forestry Department, 2001) and *Forest Policy 2001.*

60. Morrison and Mitchell, *Sector Assessment Reports—Mining*; NEPA, *NBSAP*, 14.

61. Ivette Torres, *The Mineral Industry of Jamaica* (1998), http://minerals.usgs.gov/minerals/pubs/country/1998/9515098.pdf, accessed November 17, 2015. Also Shanti Persaud, author interviews conducted July 3, 2006, taken from handwritten notes.

62. Shanti Persaud, author interviews conducted July 3, 2006, taken from handwritten notes. See also Morrison and Mitchell, *Sector Assessment Reports—Mining*, 14.

63. L. Alan Eyre, "The Cockpit Country: A World Heritage Site?" in *Environment and Development in the Caribbean: Geographical Perspectives*, ed. David Barker and Duncan F. McGregor (Kingston: UWI Press, 1995), 259–270, 261.

64. Mike Schwartz and Susan Koenig, author interviews conducted July 30, 2006, transcript of audiocassette recording. Also, Catherine Levy, author interview conducted June 30, 2006, taken from handwritten notes of telephone interview; Catherine Levy, *Tribute to Audrey Downer: 1918–2007* (2008), http://www.jamaicachm.org.jm/Article/PDF/August2008.pdf, accessed December 2008; John Fletcher, author questionnaire, received December 9, 2008, from transcript of typed responses.

65. University of the West Indies, *Amazona Parrots* (2008), http://www.mona.uwi.edu/lifesciences/parrot.htm, accessed December 2008; Susan Koenig, author interviews conducted July 30, 2006, transcript of audiocassette recording.

66. Mike Schwartz and Susan Koenig, author interviews conducted July 30, 2006, transcript of audiocassette recording. At the time, Koenig was also planning to carry out a project to study parrot populations in Dominica; John Fletcher, author questionnaire, received December 9, 2008, taken from written responses.

67. The Nature Conservancy had considerable assets, claiming over US$4 billion in total assets for the fiscal year ending in 2005. The Nature Conservancy, *Consolidated Financial Statements*, http://www.nature.org/aboutus/annualreport/files/arfinancials2005.pdf, accessed December 2006; The Nature Conservancy, *About Us*, http://www.nature.org/aboutus/, accessed December 2006; Kimberly John, author interviews conducted July 12, 2006; Ann Haynes-Sutton, author questionnaire received September 27, 2006.

68. World Bank, *Jamaica Cockpit Country Conservation Project*, 1–5; Koenig et al., *Cockpit Country Conservation Project*; Susan Koenig, author interview conducted August 3, 2007, taken from audiocassette recording; Adam Rhodes, "Bauxite vs. the Cockpit Country," *Farquharson Forum—A Guest Column* (2006).

69. Rhodes, "Bauxite vs. the Cockpit Country"; Convention on Biological Diversity (CBD), Articles 7 and 8, http://www.cbd.int/convention/convention.shtml, accessed August 2015.

70. Windsor Research Centre, *Cockpit Country Fact Sheet* (2008), http://www
.cockpitcountry.org/factsheet.html, accessed December 2008. The findings of these
reports and the maps proposed by the community were cited in, inter alia: Susan
Koenig and Mike Schwartz, author interviews conducted August 3, 2007, taken from
audiocassette recording. See also The Nature Conservancy, *Cockpit Country Conservation Action Plan: A Summary* (Kingston: TNC, 2006); Adam Rhodes, "2006, Bauxite vs.
the Cockpit Country."

71. UNEP, *Global Environment Facility Project Document*, 97; Spence, *Cockpit Country
Conservation Project*.

72. Spence, *GEF Cockpit Country Conservation Project*, 3; Koenig et al., *Cockpit Country
Conservation Report*, 12, fig. 3.1. The map produced for this biodiversity assessment
was cited on the WRC website, and provided by the TNC to the author during field
research.

73. Koenig et al., *Cockpit Country Conservation Report*, 10.

74. UNEP, *Global Environmental Facility Project Document*, 49; CBD, Articles 7 and 8.

75. See UNEP, *Global Environment Facility Project Document*, 1.

76. UNEP, *Global Environmental Facility Project Document*, 51–52.

77. Mick Day and Susan Koenig, "Monitoring Practices in Central American and the
Caribbean," *Acta Carsologica* 30, no. 1 (2002): 123–134; Dayne Buddo, author interviews conducted July 20, 2006, transcript of audiocassette recording. The Jamaica
Clearing House Mechanism (CHM) is a quasi-state organization in the National History Division of the Institute of Jamaica, created in 2002 in order to fulfill Jamaica's
obligations as a signatory to the Convention on Biological Diversity with a mandate
to conduct sourcing and standardization of data and methodology among researchers, and facilitate the exchange of information among scientists. The CHM also
helps identify gaps in knowledge about the state of the environment, and can solicit
information from scientific authorities. NEPA, *NBSAP*, 43; Forestry Department,
National Implementation Support Partnership (Kingston, c. 2000), 10.

78. Southern Trelawny Environmental Agency (STEA), *Cockpit Country Biodiversity
Manual* (Albert Town, Jamaica: STEA, c. 2003), 8; Kimberly John, author interviews
conducted July 12, 2006, transcript of audiocassette recording.

79. Koenig et al, *Cockpit Country Conservation Report*, 30.

80. Dayne Buddo, author interview conducted July 20, 2006, transcript of audiocassette recording. Emphasis based on author interpretation of phrasing of respondent.

81. David Snow et al., "Frame Alignment Processes, Micromobilization, and Move-
ment Participation," *American Sociological Review* 51 (1986): 464–481, 464. See also
Margaret Keck and Kathryn Sikkink, *Activists Beyond Borders: Advocacy Networks in
International Politics* (Ithaca: Cornell University Press, 1998), 2–3. Taken from the lit-

erature on social movement organizations (SMOs), the concept of frame alignment explains the internal dynamics within networks converging on a shared set of norms. See also Mario Diani, "Linking Mobilization Frames and Political Opportunities: Insights from Regional Populism in Italy," *American Sociological Review* 61 (1996): 1053–1069, 1058.

82. Susan Koenig, author interviews conducted August 1–6, 2006, transcript of audiocassette recording. Also based on Mick Day, author interviews conducted August 1–6, 2006; Dayne Buddo, author interview conducted July 20, 2006; Mike Schwartz, author interviews conducted August 1–6, 2006; and Marilyn Headley, author interviews conducted July 6, 2006. While conducting field research in the Cockpit Country, the author engaged in trust building with the members of the WRC. During this time, the WRC was engaged in collecting and categorizing species of snakes and frogs for taxonomy and population monitoring. In particular, the TNC Parks-in-Peril (PiP) Project, commissioned by the World Bank, played a key role in this norm transmission.

83. World Bank, *Jamaica Cockpit Country Conservation Project*, 1; Kenneth Bilby, *Cockpit Country Conservation Project: Social Component—Maroon Component* (Kingston: NRCA, 1999), passim.

84. Bilby, *Cockpit Country Conservation Project*. See also Peter Haas, *Institutions for the Earth: Sources of Effective International Environmental Protection* (Cambridge, MA: MIT Press, 2001); and Haas, "Policy Knowledge: Epistemic Communities," *International Encyclopedia of the Social and Behavioral Sciences*, ed. Neil Smelser and Paul Bates (Oxford: Elsevier, 2001), 11578–11586, for a discussion on the conceptual separation of epistemic communities from other kinds of social networks due to the production of the former of scientific knowledge and research.

85. See The Nature Conservancy, *Cockpit Country Conservation Action Plan*, References and Acknowledgments; UNEP, *Global Environment Facility Project Document*, 54.

86. Diana McCaulay, author interviews conducted August 1, 2011, taken from transcript of digital voice recording.

87. For a historic review, see Patrick Bryan, *The Jamaican People: 1880–1902* (Kingston: UWI Press, 2000). For an anthropological discussion of whiteness and authority among Jamaican migrants, see Nancy Foner, *Jamaica Farewell: Jamaican Migrants in London* (Berkeley: University of California Press, 1978). And see how Una Marson addresses social authority in her poetry in collections like *Heights and Depths* (Kingston: self-published, available in National Library of Jamaica, 1931).

88. Catherine Hall, *Civilising Subjects: Metropole and Colony in the English Imagination 1830–1867* (Chicago: University of Chicago Press, 2002). For another take on this, see Daniel Bergner's book, *In the Land of Magic Soldiers: A Story of White and Black in West Africa* (New York: Macmillan, 2004). In this book, Bergner describes how black

Sierra Leonean soldiers publicly longed for the return of white, British rule, with the hope that the rational, civilized British would return "order" to the country plagued by civil war.

89. Tim Forsyth, *Critical Political Ecology: The Politics of Environmental Science* (New York: Routledge, 2003), 185.

90. Spence, *GEF Cockpit Country Conservation Project,* 34.

91. Dayne Buddo, author interview conducted July 20, 2006, transcript of audiocassette recording.

92. Spence, *GEF Cockpit Country Conservation Project,* 21; Taylor, "Report on the Legal Imperatives and Implications of the Cockpit Country Conservation Project," 94–95; Marilyn Headley, author interview conducted July 6, 2006, transcript of audiocassette recording.

93. Marilyn Headley, author interviews conducted July 6, 2006, transcript of audiocassette recording.

94. Shanti Persaud, author interviews conducted July 3, 2006, taken from handwritten notes.

95. Mick Day, author questionnaire conducted September 24, 2006.

96. The Forestry Department, *National Forest Management and Conservation Plan,* 12.

97. Hugh Dixon, author interviews conducted July 31, 2006, transcript of audiocassette recording.

98. Ann Haynes-Sutton, author questionnaire received September 24, 2006, transcript of typed responses.

99. Mike Schwartz, author interviews conducted August 1–6, 2006, transcript of audiocassette recording.

100. Susan Koenig, author interviews conducted August 1–6, 2006, 2006, transcript of audiocassette recording.

101. Forsyth, *Critical Political Ecology.* See also Sabrina McCormick, *Mobilizing Science: Movements, Participation, and the Remaking of Knowledge* (Philadelphia: Temple University Press, 2009); and Donna Haraway, "Situated Knowledges: The Science Question in Feminism and the Privilege of Partial Perspective," *Feminist Studies,* 14, no. 3 (1988): 575–599.

102. Mark Dowie, "Conservation Refugees," *Orion* 24, no. 6 (2005): 16–27.

103. Andrew Karvonen and Ralf Brand, "Technical Expertise, Sustainability and the Politics of Specialized Knowledge," in *Environmental Governance: Power and Knowledge in a Local-Global World,* ed. Gabriela Kütting and Ronnie Lipschultz (New York: Routledge, 2009).

104. The Nature Conservancy, *Cockpit Country Conservation Action Plan*, passim and Appendix C.

105. STEA, *Biodiversity Manual*, 15.

106. UWI researcher, author interviews not for attribution, transcript of audiocassette recording.

107. Koenig et al., *Cockpit Country Conservation Report*, 23, fig. 3.8.

108. Spence, *GEF Cockpit Country Conservation Project*, fig. 6.

109. Dayne Buddo, author interviews conducted July 20, 2006, transcript of audiocassette recording.

110. UWI researcher, author interviews not for attribution, transcript of audiocassette recording.

111. O. B. Evelyn and R. Camirand, "Forest Cover and Deforestation in Jamaica: An Analysis of Forest Cover Estimates over Time," *International Forestry Review* 5 (2003): 354–363, 355; Barker and Miller, "Farming on the Fringe," passim.

112. Barker and Miller, "Farming on the Fringe," 283.

113. Forestry Department, *National Conservation and Management Plan*, 23–24.

114. See a survey of the rates of deforestation in Evelyn and Camirand, "Forest Cover and Deforestation in Jamaica"; Forestry Department, *National Forest Conservation and Management Plan*, 23–24; Spence, *GEF Cockpit Country Management Report*, 19.

115. Kevin Porter, author interviews conducted August 2006, taken from handwritten notes; respondent staff member in the Forestry Department, author interviews conducted August 2006, taken from handwritten notes; Susan Koenig, author interviews conducted August 1–6, 2006, taken from handwritten notes, and transcript of audiocassette recording.

116. Forestry Department, *National Forest Conservation and Management Plan*, 45; Hugh Dixon, author interviews conducted July 31, 2006, transcript of audiocassette recording; Owen Evelyn, author interviews conducted June 23, 2006, transcript of audiocassette recording.

117. Forestry Department, *National Forest Conservation and Management Plan*, 45; Hugh Dixon, author interviews conducted July 31, 2006, transcript of audiocassette recording; Owen Evelyn, author interviews conducted June 23, 2006, transcript of audiocassette recording.

118. In the terminology of the Forestry Department, these were referred to as "Critical Emphasis Areas." See Forestry Department, *National Forest Conservation and Management Plan*, 34; Susan Koenig, author interviews conducted August 2005, taken from handwritten notes.

119. The Nature Conservancy, *Forest Conservation: What We Do* (2015), http://www
.nature.org/ourinitiatives/habitats/forests/howwework/what-we-do-protecting
-restoring-and-managing-forests.xml, accessed August 2015; Kimberly John, author
interview conducted July 12, 2006; Ann Haynes-Sutton, author questionnaire
received September 27, 2006.

120. See the text of the Forest Act, 9, section E.10. See also UNEP/GEF, *Sustainable
Conservation of Globally Important Caribbean Bird Habitats*, 54; The Nature Conservancy, *Cockpit Country Conservation Action Plan*, 3.

121. Craig Thomas, *Bureaucratic Landscapes: Interagency Cooperation and the Preservation of Biodiversity* (Cambridge, MA: MIT Press, 2002).

122. Peter Haas, "Banning Chlorofluorocarbons: Epistemic Community Efforts to
Protect Stratospheric Ozone," *International Organization* 46, no. 1 (1992): 187–224;
Karen Litfin, *Ozone Discourses: Science and Politics in Global Environmental Cooperation*
(New York: Cambridge University Press, 1994). Both authors discuss this, although
Litfin is more critical about the effect of this relationship on the implications of the
value neutrality of science.

123. Owen Evelyn, author interviews conducted June 23, 2006, transcript of audiocassette recording.

124. See CBD, Article 6.

125. Susan Koenig, author interviews conducted August 3, 2006, transcript of
audiocassette recording.

126. Mike Schwartz, author interviews conducted August 3, 2006, transcript of
audiocassette recording.

127. These points made in interviews with the following: former NRCA official
(unattributed), author interviews conducted August 2007, notes taken from telephone interview; Mike Schwartz, author interviews conducted August 3, 2006, taken
from transcript of audiocassette recording; Yolanda Mittoo, author interviews conducted August 2005, taken from handwritten notes; Donna Blake, author interviews
conducted June 28, 2006, taken from audiocassette recording.

128. John Doe, author interview conducted August 2006, transcript of audiocassette
recording.

129. "Piñero's Pear Tree Bottom Hotel Could Be in Trouble," *Jamaica Observer*,
Wednesday, May 17, 2006.

130. Author questionnaire, Mike Schwartz, January 14, 2007, taken from typed
responses; Peter Vogel, *NBSAP Sector Assessment Report—Terrestrial Fauna* (Kingston:
NEPA, 1999); Ann Haynes-Sutton, *NBSAP Sector Assessment Report—Terrestrial Flora*
(Kingston: NEPA, 1999); Diana McCaulay, author questionnaire received January 18,
2007, taken from typed responses.

131. Susan Koenig, author interviews conducted August 3, 2006, transcript of audiocassette recording.

132. Mike Schwartz, author questionnaire received January 7, 2007, taken from handwritten notes; Diana McCaulay, author questionnaire, received January 18, 2007; Jamaica Environmental Trust, "Cockpit Country Press Release" (2006).

133. Forestry Department, *National Forest Management and Conservation Plan*, 95. The Mining Act of Jamaica, 1947, amended 1988, requires that mining companies "restore all mined lands to at least the level of agricultural or pastoral productivity or of suitability for afforestation, which existed before mining." Cited in NEPA, *NBSAP*, 16.

134. Morrison and Mitchell, *Sector Assessment Reports*—Mining, 20.

135. Susan Koenig, *Cockpit Country Conservation Report*, 52, in *Jamaica National Forest Management and Conservation Plan: Roundtable Meeting of Partners in Development* (Kingston: Forestry Department, 2000), Appendix 11, 1–2, author's note stating that grass has in fact been the primary reclamation crop used in mining restoration.

136. STEA, *Biodiversity Manual*, 15.

137. George Proctor, quoted at the 2005 Strategies Workshop on the Cockpit Country Parks-in-Peril Project, in Bridgette B. Barrett, *Strategies Workshop Report*, prepared for The Nature Conservancy (Kingston: TNC, 2005), 5.

138. Viris Pingue, author interviews conducted July 14, 2011, transcript of digital voice recording.

139. Forestry Department, *Forest Policy 2001*, II-2; Forestry Department, *National Forest Conservation and Management Plan*, 66.

140. Marilyn Headley, author interviews conducted June 23, 2006, transcript of audiocassette recording.

141. JAMPRO, *The Importance of the Tourism Mega-Cluster in the National Export Strategy* (from Conference on Global Tourism Growth: A Challenge for SMEs, 2005), http://www.oecd.org/dataoecd/27/5/36886099.pdf, accessed October 2007, 2.

142. The Nature Conservancy *Cockpit Country Parks in Peril: Water Valuation Study Update* (Kingston: TNC, 2005), 2.

143. Dayne Buddo, author interview conducted July 20, 2006, transcript of audiocassette recording.

144. Kimberly John, author interview conducted July 12, 2006, transcript of audiocassette recording.

145. For this study, TNC received a grant of $13,000 of technical support from USAID and Development Alternatives Inc. The Nature Conservancy, *Cockpit Country Parks in Peril*, 1.

146. Ibid., 2.

147. Hugh Dixon, author interview conducted July 31, 2006, transcript of audiocassette recording.

148. Mike Schwartz, author interview conducted August 3, 2006, transcript of audiocassette recording.

149. Owen Evelyn, author interview conducted June 23, 2006, transcript of audiocassette recording.

150. The Nature Conservancy, *Jamaica National Biodiversity Strategy and Action Plan: National Implementation Support Partnership* (Kingston: TNC, 2004), 8–11; Patrick Yugorsky and Ann Sutton, *Categorization of Protected Areas in Jamaica* (Kingston: TNC, 2004), 3; Sacha Reneé-Todd, *A Framework to Manage Jamaica's Protected Areas* (2006; prepared for the Protected Areas Systems Master Plan), 3; Convention on Biological Diversity, 2004, *COP 7 Decision VII/28: Protected Areas (Articles 8 (a)–(e))* §31.

151. See inter alia NEPA, *NBSAP* passim; David Barker, "Yam Farmers on the Forest Edge of Cockpit Country: Aspects of Resource Use and Sustainability," in *Resource Sustainability and Caribbean Development: Geographical Perspectives*, ed. D. F. M. McGregor, D. Barker, and S. Lloyd Evans (Kingston: UWI Press, 1998), 357–371.

152. Yugorsky and Sutton, *Categorization of Protected Areas in Jamaica*, passim; Sacha-Renée Todd, *A Framework to Manage Jamaica's Protected Areas*, passim. By one study, tourists visiting the BJCMNP spend US$2.5 million in the area per year. According to one study, if the Park were to implement access fees, there would be a further gain of US$420,000 per annum, making it a model for developing ecotourism as a means for environmental protection and sustainable development (see ENACT, *Policy on Strategic Environmental Assessment*, 20).

153. Yugorsky and Sutton, *Categorization of Protected Areas in Jamaica*, 17.

154. Douglas Webster and Marcela Daye, *Sector Assessment Reports—Tourism* (Kingston: NRCA, 1999).

155. Barker, "Yam Farmers on the Forest Edge of Cockpit Country"; David J. Miller, "Invasion of the Cockpits: Patterns of Encroachment into the Wet Limestone Rainforest of Cockpit Country, Jamaica," in *Resource Sustainability and Caribbean Development: Geographical Perspectives*, ed. D. F. M. McGregor, D. Barker, and S. Lloyd Evans (Kingston: UWI Press, 1998), 373–389, passim.

156. Spence, *GEF Cockpit Country Conservation Project*, 40–41.

157. Ibid., 22–23; Koenig et al., *Cockpit Country Conservation Report*, 68.

158. Forestry Department, *National Forest Management and Conservation Plan*, 97.

159. John Doe, author interview, August 2006 taken from transcript of audiocassette recording.

160. NEPA, *NBSAP*, 15; Forestry Department, *The Forestry Act*, 8; *Forestry Policy: 2001*, II-1; Forestry Department, *National Forest Management and Conservation Plan*, passim.

161. Marilyn Headley, author interviews conducted July 6, 2006, transcript of audiocassette recording.

162. Ibid.

163. *Jamaica Observer*, Sunday, November 19, 2006.

164. Donna Blake, senior director of the Forestry Department, author interviews conducted June 28, 2006, transcript of audiocassette recording on file with author.

165. Diana McCaulay, member of epistemic community organization the Jamaican Environmental Trust, author interview conducted August 1, 2011.

166. "Cockpit Country Worry," *Jamaica Observer*, Sunday, November 19, 2006.

167. "No Plans to Mine Cockpit Country," *Jamaica Observer*, Sunday, December 10, 2006.

168. "Cockpit Country Worry."

169. "Cockpit Row Boils: Environmentalists Eye Court Action after Gov't Grants Prospecting Licence to Bauxite Firms," *Jamaica Observer*, December 15, 2006; Peter Espeut, "Commentary," *Jamaica Gleaner*, December 20, 2006; Parris Lyew-Ayee, "No Plans to Mine in the Cockpit Country," press release for Jamaica Bauxite Institute (2006).

170. Jamaica Environmental Trust, *Bauxite Mining Poses Major Threat to Cockpit Country Wildlife and Watershed*, press release for Cockpit Country Stakeholders' Group (2006); Jamaica Environment Advocacy Network, "Petition to Save Cockpit Country," petition created for Cockpit Country Stakeholders' Group (2006); Wendy Lee, author questionnaire received February 13, 2007.

171. Mike Schwartz, personal communication, January 2007.

172. "No Plans to Mine Cockpit Country.

173. Pingue, author interview conducted July 23, 2011.

174. Ibid.

175. Diana McCaulay, author interview conducted August 1, 2011.

176. Nigel Varty, *Terminal Evaluation of the UNEP/GEF Project "Sustainable Conservation of Globally Important Caribbean Bird Habitats: Strengthening a Regional Network for a Shared Resource"* (Washington, DC: GEF, 2007), 28.

177. "Davis Suggests Management System for Cockpit Country," *Jamaica Gleaner*, December 27, 2006.

178. Diana McCaulay, author interview conducted August 1, 2011.

2 Tourism, Development, and the Mesoamerican Barrier Reef

1. "Van empresarios contra manglares de QR," *El Universal Estados*, Sunday, January 21, 2007; "Promueven industriales veto a reformas en ley de la vida silvestre, denuncian ONG," *La Jornada*, Wednesday, January 24, 2007.

2. Diario Oficial de la Federación, *Ley General de la Vida Silvestre* (Diario Oficial de la Federación: October 14, 2008), Article 60 Ter. See also "Manglares, refugio de especies comerciales importantes" in *La Jornada*, Monday, February 25, 2008; "Increpan regidores del Verde Ecologista a García Pliego" in *Novedades*, Friday, February 2, 2007.

3. The reef system within the Mesoamerican basin measures 1,000 kilometers in length, making it the second largest continuous reef system in the world, second to the Australian Great Barrier Reef. Gabriela G. Nava Martinez Lorenzo Álvarez Filip, and Roberto Hernández Landa, *Reporte del Programa de Monitoreo Arrecifal: Parque Nacional Arrecifes de Cozumel 2004–2005* (Cozumel: CONANP, 2006), 2; Unidad Coordinadora del Proyecto (UCP), *Políticas de Desarrollo Sustentable de los Recursos Pesqueros, Turismo y Áreas Marinas Protegidas Transfronterizas en el Sistema Arrecifal Mesoamericano* (Belize City: Unidad Coordinadora del Proyecto, 2004), 1.

4. M. García-Salgado, T. Camarena Luhrs, G. Gold-Bouchot, M. Vazquez, G. Galland, G. Nava Martinez, G. Alarcón, and V. Ceja Moreno, *Línea Base del Estado del Sistema Arrefical Mesoamericano* (Belize City: Unidad Coordinadora del Proyecto, 2006), 6.

5. A. Hernández, F. A. Rodríguez-Zaragoza, M. C. García, J. M. Castro, and J. Medina-Flores, *Hacia el manejo sostenible de los recursos pesqueros de Banco Chinchorro* (Cancún: WWF-México, 2008), 5; Unidad Coordinadora del Proyecto (UCP), *Manual—Guía Común para la Evaluación de Estudios de Impacto Ambiental de Proyectos Turísticos en la Zona Comprendida por el SAM* (Belize City: Unidad Coordinadora del Proyecto, 2003), 69; Mar Caribe roundtable, *Ficha Técnica para la Evaluación de los Sitios Prioritarios para la Conservación de los Ambientes Costeros y Oceánicos del SAM*, http://www.conabio.gob.mx/gap/images/2/29/78_Humedales_Costeros_Arrecife_Xcalak _Majahual.pdf, 1–5, accessed August 24, 2015.

6. World Wildlife Fund (WWF-México), *How to Profit by Practicing Sustainable Fishing: Lobster Fishing Practice Guidelines for the Mesoamerican Reef* (Belize City: ICRAN/WWF-México, 2007), 5.

7. García-Salgado et al., *Línea Base del Estado del Sistema Arrefical Mesoamericano*, 100.

8. CODISSA, *Censo Pesquero y Acuícola del Estado de Quintana Roo* (Mexico City: SAGARPA, 2008).

9. Ibid.

10. Comité Técnico Estatal de Evaluación, *Informe de Evaluación Estatal: Programa de Acuacultura y Pesca* (Quintana Roo: SAGARPA, 2006), 56; CCAD, *Documento de Evaluación*, Anexo 4, 2001, 4.

11. Comité Técnico Estatal de Evaluación, *Informe de Evaluación Estatal*, 56; WWF-México, *Best Fishing Practices in Coral Reefs: Methods for Collecting Ecological Data that Support the Ecosystem-Based Fisheries Management* (Cancún: WWF-México, 2008), 20.

12. WWF-México, *MAR Strategic Plan: 2004–2009*, 24; WWF-México, *Best Fishing Practices in Coral Reefs*, 20.

13. WWF-México, *Best Fishing Practices in Coral Reefs*, 20.

14. Albert Franquesa, author interview conducted February 2008, taken from transcript of digital voice recording, translated from Spanish.

15. Graciela Pérez Villegas and Eurosia Carrascal, "El Desarrollo Turístico en Cancún, Quintana Roo y sus Consecuencias sobre la Cubierta Vegetal," *Investigaciones Geográficas, Boletín del Instituto de Geografía, UNAM* 43 (1999): 145–166, 149; David Martínez, author interviews conducted April 29, 2008; María del Consuelo Méndez Sosa, "Desarrollo Económico en Cancún a Partir del Sector Hotelero," produced for La Confederación Nacional Turística, http://claroline.ucaribe.edu.mx/claroline/ claroline/backends/download.php?url=L1ZpZXJuZXNfMzFfZGVfT2N0dWJyZS9kZX NhcnJvbGxvX2Vjb25vbWljb19lbl9jYW5jdW4ucGRm&cidReset=true&cidReq= PTS02, accessed August 24, 2015.

16. Secretaría de Turismo de Quintana Roo (SEDETUR), *Indicadores Turísticos del Estado de Quintana Roo: Enero 2008* (2014), http://sedetur.qroo.gob.mx/estadisticas/ indicadores/Indicadores%20Turisticos%20%202008.pdf, accessed August 24, 2015; Alfredo Arellano Guillermo, "La Reserva de la Biosfera Sian Ka'an en el Contexto del Desarrollo Regional," *Revista de Medio Ambiente, Turismo y Sustentabilidad* 1, no. 1 (2005): 1–6, 2.

17. Wendy Wolford, "Environmental Justice and Agricultural Development in the Brazilian *Cerrado*," in *Environmental Justice in Latin America: Problems, Promise, and Practice*, ed. David Carruthers (Cambridge, MA: MIT Press, 2008), 213–238.

18. Quoted in ibid., 214.

19. Kathryn Hochstetler and Margaret Keck, *Greening Brazil: Environmental Activism in State and Society* (Durham, NC: Duke University Press, 2007).

20. Nelson A. Reed, *The Caste War of Yucatán* (Redwood City, CA: Stanford University Press, 2001).

21. Oriol Pi-Sunyer and R. Brooke Thomas, "Tourism, Environmentalism and Cultural Survival in Quintana Roo," in *Life and Death Matters: Human Rights and the Environment at the End of the Millennium*, ed. Barbara Rose Johnston (Walnut Creek, CA: AltaMira Press, 1997), 187–212.

22. Oriol Pi-Sunyer and R. Brooke Thomas, "Tourism and the Transformation of Daily Life Along the Riviera Maya of Quintana Roo, Mexico," *Journal of Latin American and Caribbean Anthropology* 20, no. 1 (2015): 87–109, 90.

23. Ibid., 90.

24. Albert Franquesa, author interviews conducted February 2008, taken from transcript of digital voice recording, translated from Spanish.

25. David Martínez, author interview conducted April 29, 2008, taken from transcript of digital voice recording. The revenue stream for this period is estimated to fall between US$2,771 million and US$3,319 million per year; SEDTUR, *Indicadores Turísticos*. By another measure, tourism in Cancún brings approximately 25 percent of the GDP of Mexico. See Peter F. Sale, Ernesto A. Chávez, Bruce G. Hatcher, Colin Mayfield, and Jan J. H. Ciborowski, *Guidelines for Developing a Regional Monitoring and Environmental Information System: Final Report to the World Bank* (INWEH/UNU, c. 2000), 24.

26. Cynthia Enloe, *Bananas, Beaches, and Bases: Making Feminist Sense of International Politics*, 2nd ed. (Berkeley: University of California Press, 2014).

27. Comité Técnico Estatal de Evaluación, *Informe de Evaluación Estatal*, 9. Also, taken from discussions with José Manuel Cárdenas Magaña, author interviews conducted May 12–15, 2008.

28. Los Amigos de Sian Ka'an, *Normas Prácticas para el Desarrollo Turístico de la Zona Costera de Quintana Roo, México* (Narragansett: University of Rhode Island, Coastal Resources Center, 1998), passim; M. García Salgado et al., *Línea Base del Estado del Sistema Arrecifal Mesoamericano*, 109–110; WWF-México, *Draft WWF MAR Strategic Action Plan* (Cancún: WWF-México, 2008), 70; Juan José Dominguez Calderón, author interview conducted January 24, 2008, taken from transcript of audiocassette recording.

29. Bessy Aspra de Lupiac et al., *Threat and Root Cause Analysis* (draft), presented for Conservation and Sustainable Use of the Mesoamerican Barrier Reef System, 1999, 10; CCAD, *Documento de Evaluación*, 4–5.

30. See Los Amigos de Sian Ka'an, *Normas Prácticas para el Desarrollo Turístico de la Zona Costera de Quintana Roo*; CCAD, *Documento de Evaluación*, 4–5; UCP, *Manual*, 62, 70.

31. WWF-México, *How to Profit by Practicing Sustainable Fishing*, 3.

32. Enloe, *Bananas, Beaches, and Bases*, 55.

33. Pi-Sunyer and Thomas, "Tourism, Environmentalism and Cultural Survival in Quintana Roo," 46.

34. P. C. Almada-Villela, P. F. Sale, G. Gold Bouchot, and B. Kjerfve, *Manual de Métodos para el Programa de Monitoreo Sinóptoco del SAM* (Belize City: Unidad Coordina-

dora del Proyecto, 2003), 136; Aspra de Lupiac et al., *Threat and Root Cause Analysis*, 8; UCP, *Diseño e Implementación del Foro de Turismo Sustenible del SAM* (SAM: Belize City, 2003), 3; UCP, *Manual*, 63–64; M. García Salgado et al., *Línea Base del Estado del Sistema Arrecifal Mesoamericano*, 6. Also based on conversations with park managers at Puerto Morelos National Park.

35. Albert Franquesa, author interview conducted February 2008, taken from transcript of digital voice recording, translated from Spanish.

36. Luis Alfonso Argüelles Suárez, *Diagnóstico y Programas del Corredor de Sian Ka'an-Calakmul*. CBM-M (National Forestry Commission [CONAFOR], 2005), 8.

37. Aspra de Lupiac et al., *Threat and Root Cause Analysis*, 6; CCAD, *Documento de Evaluación*, 2. According to interviews with Los Amigos staffers, sewage treatment in Quintana Roo is poorly administered, and in Cancún, approximately half of the volume of liquid waste is not treated prior to disposal. Gonzalo Merediz Alonso, author interviews conducted February 2008.

38. Ludger Brenner and Adrián Guillermo Aguila, "Luxury Tourism and Regional Economic Development in Mexico," *The Professional Geography* 54, no. 4 (2002): 500–520; James Barsimantov, Alex Racelis, Grenville Barnes, and Maria DiGiano, "Tenure, Tourism and Timber in Quintana Roo, Mexico: Land Tenure Changes in Forest *Ejidos* after Agrarian Reforms," *International Journal of the Commons* 4, no. 1 (2010): 293–318.

39. "Exigen con valla humana mantener acceso public a una playa en Cancún," *La Jornada*, Sunday, September 21, 2014.

40. Quoted in Ibid.

41. M. Bianet Castellanos, *A Return to Servitude: Maya Migration and the Tourist Trade in Cancún* (Minneapolis: University of Minnesota Press, 2010); Lindsey Carte, Mason McWatters, Erin Daley, and Rebecca Torres, "Experiencing Agricultural Failure: Internal Migration, Tourism, and Local Perceptions of Regional Change in the Yucatán," *Geoforum* 41, no. 5 (2010): 700–710; Gobierno del Estado de Quintana Roo, c. 2011, Plan Quintana Roo 2011–2016 (Gobierno del Estado de Quintana Roo).

42. Gonzalo Merediz Alonso, author interview conducted June 2012, taken from transcript of digital voice recording, translated from Spanish.

43. See the literature mentioned throughout: Carruthers, ed., *Environmental Justice in Latin America*; JoAnn Carmin and Julian Agyeman, *Environmental Inequalities Beyond Borders: Local Perspectives on Global Injustices* (Cambridge, MA: MIT Press, 2011), and several others.

44. "Condena la CIDH crimen de ambientalista en Guerrero," *Proceso 1962*, June 14, 2012, translated from Spanish.

45. See CONABIO, Apéndice: Proceso de Formulación de la Estrategia, *Estrategia Nacional para la Biodiversidad* (Mexico City: CONABIO, 2000), 79; Federation of Mexican States, *Ley Orgánica de la Administración Pública Federal*, 2003, Article 32.

46. Prior to SEMARNAP's creation, environmental management was scattered across various specialized agencies. Interview, SEMARNAT official, not for attribution, 2008; SEMARNAT, *Programa Regional de Educación para la Sustentabilidad en Áreas Naturales Protegidas* (SEMARNAT, 2008), 24.

47. NOM-059-ECOL-1994 and NOM-059-ECOL-2001 indicate that SEMARNAT has the authority to protect species recognized as integral to Mexico's ecology, as well as species under threat, in the interest of maintaining national biodiversity. These regulations are available in the Diario Oficial de la Federación, March 6, 2002. SEMARNAT, *¿Qué hacemos?*, 2009, http://www.semarnat.gob.mx/queessemarnat/Pages/quehacemos.aspx, accessed January 2009; SEMARNAT, *Reglamento de la Ley General de Equilibrio Ecológico y Protección al Ambiente* (Mexico City: Diario Oficial de la Federación, 2003); CONABIO, Apéndice, 77–78.

48. SEMARNAT, "Antecedentes," *SEMARNAT Conocemos*, 2015, http://www.semarnat.gob.mx/conocenos/antecedentes, accessed August 24, 2015.

49. Alfredo Arellano Guillermo, author interview conducted March 2008, taken from transcript of audiocassette recording; José Juan Dominguez Calderón, author interview conducted January 24, 2008, taken from transcript of audiocassette recording; CONANP, "Áreas Protegidas Decretadas," *Qué Hacemos*, 2015, http://www.conanp.gob.mx/que_hacemos/, accessed August 24, 2015. CONANP comes from the Spanish name of the agency, which is *la Comisión Nacional de Áreas Naturales Protegidas*. UCP, *Manual*, 32.

50. José Manuel Cárdenas Magaña, author interviews conducted May 12–15, 2008, taken from transcript of digital voice recording. CONAPESCA, "Misión y Visión", *Conócenos*, 2014, http://www.conapesca.sagarpa.gob.mx/wb/cona/cona_mision_y_vision_acerca, accessed August 24, 2015. CONAPESCA comes from the name of the agency in Spanish, *la Comisión Nacional de Acuacultura y Pesca*.

51. José Manuel Cárdenas Magaña, author interviews conducted May 12–15, 2008.

52. Ibid.; Hernández et al., *Hacia el manejo sostenible de los recursos pesqueros de Banco Chinchorro*, 11; Comité Técnico Estatal de Evaluación, *Informe de Evaluación Estatal*, 13–14.

53. David Martínez, author interview conducted April 29, 2008, taken from transcript of digital voice recording.

54. SEDETUR, "Quiénes Somos," *Conócenos*, 2015, http://sedetur.qroo.gob.mx/index.php/conocenos/quienes-somos, accessed August 24, 2015; David Martínez, author interview conducted April 29, 2008, taken from transcript of digital voice recording, translated from Spanish.

55. Gustavo Olivares, author interviews conducted April 9 and April 10, 2008.

56. Álvaro Hernández Gil, author interview conducted May 15, 2008, taken from transcript of digital voice recording.

57. See chart of surveyed cooperatives for state research published in Comité Técnico Estatal de Evaluación, *Informe de Evaluación Estatal*, 47. See also references to differences in size and practices of cooperatives in CONANP, *Programa de Conservación y Manejo: Reserva De La Biósfera Sian Ka'an, Reserva De La Biósfera Arrecifes De Sian Ka'an Y Área De Protección De Flora Y Fauna Uaymil* (Mexico City: CONANP, 2007), 24–25; Hernández et al., *Hacia el manejo sostenible de los recursos pesqueros de Banco Chinchorro*, 11.

58. David Martínez, author interview conducted April 29, 2008.

59. Gustavo Duncan, *Más Que Plata o Plomo: El Poder Político del Narcotráfico en Colombia y México* (Bogotá: Editorial Debate, 2014).

60. "Narcos dañan manglares en las costas," *El Diario de Sinaloa*, Monday, May 20, 2013; "Encuentran narco laboratorio en un manglar," *La Policíaca*, Wednesday, June 11, 2014.

61. CONANP, *Programa de Conservación y Manejo*, 4–5.

62. Beth R. Chung, "A Community Strategy for Coastal Zone Management of Xcalak, Mexico," *Community-Based Land Use Planning in Conservation Areas: Lessons from Local Participatory Processes that Seek to Balance Economic Uses with Ecosystem Protection*. América Verde Training Manual No. 3 (Arlington, VA: América Verde Publications, The Nature Conservancy, 1999), 3–4.

63. El Papá, author interview conducted July 2012, taken from transcript of digital voice recording, translated from Spanish.

64. J. C. Bezaury, C. L. Sántos, J. McCann, C. Molina Islas, J. Carranza, P. Rubinoff, G. Townsend, D. Robadue, and L. Hale, "Participatory Coastal and Marine Management in Quintana Roo, Mexico," proceedings from the International Tropical Marine Ecosystems Management Symposium, http://www.crc.uri.edu/download/CM_ITMEMSfinalFY99.pdf, accessed August 24, 2015, 6–7; CONANP, *Programa de Manejo, Parque Nacional Arrecifes de Xcalak* (Mexico City: CONANP, 2004), 8–9.

65. CONANP, *Programa de Manejo*, 2; Bezaury et al., "Participatory Coastal and Marine Management in Quintana Roo, Mexico"; CONANP, *Programa de Manejo*, 8–9.

66. CONANP, *Programa de Conservación y Manejo*, 5.

67. Ibid.; The declaration of the Área de Uaymil took place in the Diario Oficial de la Federación (DOF), November 17, 1994; UCP, *Manual*, 28–29.

68. UCP, *Manual*, 28–29.

69. CONANP, *Programa de Conservación y Manejo*, 12–13.

70. Bezaury et al., "Participatory Coastal and Marine Management in Quintana Roo, Mexico," 4–5; CONANP, *Programa de Manejo*, 7. See a general description and critique of Mesoamerican environmental protection in UCP, *Reporte de Avance No. 1* (2001), 6; and World Bank, *Regional (Belize, Guatemala, Honduras, Mexico): Conservation and Sustainable Use of the Mesoamerican Barrier Reef System* (Washington, DC: World Bank, 2000), 8.

71. WWF-México, *Best Fishing Practices in Coral Reefs*, 5–6.

72. Álvaro Hernández Gil, author interview conducted May 15, 2008, taken from transcript of digital voice recording; WWF-México, *Best Fishing Practices in Coral Reefs*, 5–6.

73. This concept that the Barrier Reef System was second in size only to the Great Barrier Reef of Australia was mentioned independently in almost every interview conducted with epistemic community members and policymakers in the process of field research, as well as cited in documents including the UCP, *Plan Operativo Anual Periódo: Julio 2002–Junio 2003* (Belize City: Unidad Coordinadora del Proyecto, 2002), 1, among others.

74. WWF-México, *MAR Strategic Plan 2004–2009*, 10; Gonzalo Merediz Alonso, author interview conducted February 2008; ICRI, Declaration from ICRI Regional Workshop for the Tropical Americas, held Cancún, June 14–22, 2002.

75. UCP, *Políticas de Desarrollo Sustentable* (2004), 2. Original text reads: "... para impulsar el desarrollo regional por la senda de la sustentabilidad económica, social y ecológica." The CCAD is an agency of the Sistema de la Integración Centroamericana (SICA), whose mission stressing the integration of environment and development is available on its website at http://www.sica.int/sica/propositos.aspx?IdEnt=4 01&Idm=1&IdmStyle=1, accessed August 24, 2015.

76. Adela Vázquez Trejo, "La cooperación acerca de la cuestión ambiental en Centroamérica," *Co/incidencias*, no. 2 (July–Dec. 2005): 35–43, 41; UCP, *Políticas de Desarrollo Sustentable* (2004), 3; UCP, *Plan Operativo Anual Período: Julio 2001—Junio 2002* (Belize City: Unidad Coordinadora del Proyecto, 2001), 1.

77. Bezaury et al., "Participatory Coastal and Marine Management in Quintana Roo, Mexico."

78. Ibid.

79. Atlantic and Gulf Rapid Assessment (AGRRA), http://www.agrra.org/index.html, AGRRA Methods Workshop, held in Miami in 1998. List of participants available at http://www.agrra.org/workshops/attend.html. AGRRA is a civil society network interested in developing strategies for post-crisis rapid-response coral reef monitoring in the Caribbean Sea. See also the AGRRA Methods Workshop, held in Akumal, Mexico, May 17–21, 1999.

80. Aspra de Lupiac et al., *Threat and Root Cause Analysis*.

81. A list of participants of the AGRRA workshops was accessed in March 2009, http://www.agrra.org/workshops/finalrep.html#Appendix%201. See further lists of participants for shared members at: Aspra de Lupiac et al., *Threat and Root Cause Analysis*, 15–16; World Bank, *Regional (Belize, Guatemala, Honduras, Mexico): Conservation and Sustainable Use of the Mesoamerican Barrier Reef System—Submission for Work Program Inclusion* (Office Memorandum prepared for GEF Secretariat), 16.

82. Participants at these workshops included agencies involved in the CCAD project, such as members of Los Amigos, TNC, and the Belizean Coastal Zone Management Authority and Institute (CZMA/I). See WWW-México, *MAR Strategic Plan 2004–2009*, 11; Philip A. Kramer and Patricia Richards Kramer, *Ecoregional Conservation Planning for the Mesoamerican Caribbean Reef* (WWF-Centroamerica, 2002), 27; Aspra de Lupiac et al., *Threat and Root Cause Analysis*, 3.

83. See Appendix A and Appendix B in Kramer and Kramer, *Ecoregional Conservation Planning for the Mesoamerican Caribbean Reef*, also maps beginning p. 54. WWF-México, *Draft WWF MAR Strategic Action Plan*, passim.

84. Álvaro Hernández Gil, author interview conducted May 15, 2008, taken from transcript of digital voice recording; World Bank/SAM/CCAD, *Conservación y Uso Sostenible del Sistema Arrecifal Mesoamericano: Revisión de Medio Término* (Belize City: IBRD/SAM/CCAD, 2004), 1; UCP, *Reporte de Avance No. 1*, 1; UCP, *Plan Operativo Anual: Período: Julio 2001–Julio 2002* (Belize City: Unidad Coordinadora del Proyecto, 2001), passim.

85. UCP, *Términos de Referencia para los Grupos de Trabajo Técnico* (Belize City: Unidad Coordinadora del Proyecto, c. 2000), 1–3.

86. CCAD, *Documento de Evaluación*, 7. Alfredo Arellano Guillermo, author interview conducted March 2008, transcript M. García-Salgado et al.; *Línea Base del Estado del Sistema Arrefical Mesoamericano*.

87. M. García-Salgado et al., *Línea Base del Estado del Sistema Arrecifal Mesoamericano*, 138; Juan José Domínguez Calderón, author interview conducted January 24, 2008. Currently, ECOSUR monitors reef health at Punta Allen and Xcalak as an official *Agencia de Apoyo* to CONANP in the context of implementing the SAM. Taken from interviews with Eloy Sosa, Felipe Serrano, Laura Carrillo, and Rosa Loreto Viruel between January and June 2008.

88. Daniel J. Ponce-Taylor, Cynthia A. Arochi Zendejas, and Andrew Cameron, *Global Vision Internacional (GVI) en Mexico: una nueva fórmula de turismo alternativo en Quintana Roo* (Mexico City: Global Vision International, 2006).

89. This function of mangrove zones was mentioned recently in the Mexican Chamber of Congress in *Diario de los Debates*; in a study conducted on ecosystem health for the MBRS Project in M. García-Salgado et al., *Línea Base del Estado del*

Sistema Arrefical Mesoamericano, 109, and in interviews with respondents from the epistemic community, including Álvaro Hernández Gil, Patricia Santos, and Gonzalo Merediz Alonso.

90. World Rainforest Movement, *Mangroves: Local Livelihoods v. Corporate Profits* (Montevideo, Uruguay: World Rainforest Movement, 2002).

91. World Rainforest Movement, *Mangroves*, 57.

92. Deforestación de Manglar San Blas, Nayarit, México. *Environmental Justice Atlas.* http://ejatlas.org/conflict/deforestacion-de-manglar-san-blas-nayarit-mexico, accessed June 13, 2014.

93. *Diario de los Debates,* 67; Albert de Jesús Navarrete and José Juan Oliva Rivera, "Litter Production of *Rhizophora Mangle* at Bacalar Chico, Southern Quintana Roo, Mexico," *Universidad y Ciencia* 18, no. 30 (2002): 79–85.

94. AIDA-CEMDA, Joint Submission UPR Mexico, 2013.

95. On the importance of participation in environmental policymaking, see Michele Zebich-Knos, "Ecotourism, Park Systems, and Environmental Justice in Latin America," in Carruthers, ed., *Environmental Justice in Latin America*; Andrew Karvonen and Ralf Brand, "Technical Expertise, Sustainability, and the Politics of Specialized Knowledge," in *Environmental Governance: Power and Knowledge in a Local-Global World*, ed. Gabriela Kütting and Ronnie Lipschultz (New York: Routledge, 2009), 38–59; and Richard Hiskes, *The Human Right to a Green Future: Environmental Rights and Intergenerational Justice* (New York: Cambridge University Press, 2009).

96. Exequiel Ezcurra, author interview conducted May 2009, taken from handwritten notes of telephone interview.

97. This quote taken from Sabrina McCormick, *Mobilizing Science: Movements, Participation, and the Remaking of Knowledge* (Philadelphia: Temple University Press, 2009). See also Donna Haraway, "Situated Knowledges: The Science Question in Feminism and the Privileging of Partial Perspective," *Feminist Studies* 14, no. 3 (1988): 575–599; Karvonen and Brand, "Technical Expertise, Sustainability, and the Politics of Specialized Knowledge."

98. World Bank, *Regional (Belize, Guatemala, Honduras, Mexico): Conservation and Sustainable Use of the Mesoamerican Barrier Reef System*, passim.

99. UCP, *Políticas de Desarrollo Sustentable de los Recursos Pesqueros, Turismo y Áreas Marinas Protegidas Transfronterizas* (2004), 13–14.

100. Los Amigos de Sian Ka'an, *Normas Prácticas para el Desarrollo Turístico de la Zona Costera de Quintana Roo, México*, 15.

101. Ibid., 11.

102. WWF-México, *Best Fishing Practices in Coral Reefs*, 11.

103. Álvaro Hernández Gil, author interview conducted May 15, 2008, transcript of digital voice recording, translated from Spanish.

104. José Juan Dominguez Calderón, author interview conducted January 24, 2008, taken from transcript of audiocassette recording, taken from transcript of audiocassette recording, translated from Spanish.

105. Gonzalo Merediz Alonso, author interview conducted February 2008, taken from transcript of audiocassette recording, translated from Spanish. This sentiment would be repeated in a study produced by Gonzalo Merediz Alonso, director of Los Amigos, in his chapter in *Sustainable Management of Groundwater in Mexico: Proceedings from a Workshop*, ed. Laura Holliday, Luis Marin, and Henry Vaux (Washington, DC: National Academies Press, 2007), 97–102.

106. UCP, *Manual de Métodos para la Elaboración de Programas de Uso Público en Áreas Protegidas de la Región del Sistema Arrecifal Mesoamericano* (SAM: Belize City, 2005), 35.

107. Secretaría de Economía, *Fideicomiso Fomento Económico Quintana Roo 2025 Cluster Pesca y Acuacultura* (Chetumal, Quintana Roo: Secretaría de Economía, 2009).

108. Rosa María Loreto Viruel, author interview conducted April 18, 2008, taken from transcript of digital voice recording, translated from Spanish.

109. Gonzalo Merediz Alonso, author interview conducted June 2012, taken from transcript of digital voice recording, translated from Spanish.

110. Enrique Galvez, author interview conducted February 2008, taken from transcript of digital voice recording, translated from Spanish; David Martinez, author interview conducted April 29, 2008; Bezaury et al., "Participatory Coastal and Marine Management in Quintana Roo, Mexico," 1.

111. Eloy Sosa, author interview conducted February 2008, taken from transcript of digital voice recording, translated from Spanish.

112. Álvaro Hernández Gil, author interview conducted May 15, 2008, taken from transcript of digital voice recording, translated from Spanish.

113. Eloy Sosa, author interview conducted February 2008, taken from transcript of digital voice recording, translated from Spanish.

114. Kramer and Kramer, *Ecoregional Conservation Planning for the Mesoamerican Caribbean Reef*, 35.

115. M. García-Salgado, et al., *Línea Base del Estado del Sistema Arrecifal Mesoamericano*, passim.

116. Ibid., 120–153, especially 151–153.

117. The Quintana Roo delegation of CONAPESCA provided figures of population changes over time, noting a general tendency to decrease over time in Comité Téc-

nico Estatal de Evaluación, *Informe de Evaluación Estatal*. Specific charts referencing these figures are sampled in this chapter. See also World Bank, *Regional (Belize, Guatemala, Honduras, Mexico): Conservation and Sustainable Use of the Mesoamerican Barrier Reef System*, 5, discussing the increasingly visible decline in catch sizes and biomass among commercially harvested fish in the reef region.

118. José Juan Domínguez Calderón, author interview conducted January 24, 2008, taken from transcript of audiocassette recording, translated from Spanish.

119. Álvaro Hernández Gil, author interview conducted May 15, 2008, taken from transcript of digital voice recording, translated from Spanish.

120. Will Heyman and Nicanor Requena, *Informe Final de la Consultoría: Sitio de las Agregaciones Reproductivas de Peces in la Zona del SAM: Recomendaciones para su Monitoreo y Manejo* (Belize City: Unidad Coordinadora del Proyecto, 2003), passim.

121. Enrique Galvez, author interview conducted February 2008.

122. UCP, *Principios de Manejo para las Áreas Marinas Protegidas: Manual* (Belize City: Unidad Coordinadora del Proyecto, 2003). Developed through a workshop titled *Capacitación en los Principios de Manejo para las Áreas Marinas Protegidas en la Región del Sistema Arrecifal Mesoamericano (SAM)*, or Training in Management Principles for Marine Protected Areas in the Region of the Mesoamerican Reef System (author's translation).

123. See a list of participants in the WWF MAR workshops in WWF-México, *How to Profit by Practicing Sustainable Fishing*, 42.

124. Referenced in interviews with José Manuel Cárdenas Magaña, Álvaro Hernández Gil, and Gonzalo Merediz Alonso. See also WWF-México, *Best Fishing Practices in Coral Reefs*, 13–14. Including local actors, such as fishing cooperatives, in environmental management is recognized as a good governance practice by Jeffrey McNeely of the World Conservation Union in a 1992 article advocating for sustainable biodiversity governance, "The Biodiversity Crisis: Challenges for Research and Management," in *Conservation of Biodiversity for Sustainable Development*, ed. O. T. Sandlund et al. (Oxford: Oxford University Press, 1992), 21–22.

125. WWF-México, *Best Fishing Practices in Coral Reefs*, 14–15.

126. Ibid., 13–14; WWF-México, *How to Profit by Practicing Sustainable Fishing*, passim; Álvaro Hernández Gil, author interview conducted May 15, 2008.

127. Karvonen and Brand, "Technical Expertise, Sustainability, and the Politics of Specialized Knowledge," 54.

128. Los Amigos de Sian Ka'an, *Normas Prácticas para el Desarrollo Turístico de la Zona Costera de Quintana Roo, México*; Gonzalo Merediz Alonso, author interview conducted February 2008; Albert Franquesa, author interview conducted February 2008.

129. Gonzalo Merediz Alonso, author interview conducted February 2008.

130. Aspra de Lupiac et al., *Threat and Root Cause Analysis*, 2.

131. CCAD, *Documento de Evaluación*, 2 states: "In pristine areas exist wetlands, lagoons, beds of seagrass and coastal mangrove forests; these sustain an exceptionally high biodiversity and provide an important habitat for threatened species" (translated from Spanish).

132. Ibid., 9.

133. See P. C. Almada-Villela et al., *Manual de Métodos*, passim; UCP, *Reporte de Avance No. 2*, 11–12; UCP, *Reporte de Avance Técnico y Financiero Reporte No. 4: Enero–Junio 2003* (Belize City: Unidad Coordinadora del Proyecto, 2003), 4.

134. UCP, *Reporte de Avance No. 1*, 11; UCP, *Reporte de Avance Técnico y Financiero No. 4*, 5; World Bank, *Regional (Belize, Guatemala, Honduras, Mexico): Conservation and Sustainable Use of the Mesoamerican Barrier Reef System*, Annex 2, 2.

135. Amigos de Sian Ka'an, *Normas Prácticas para el Desarrollo Turístico de la Zona Costera de Quintana Roo, México*, 28–29.

136. Ibid. The inefficiency of this zone to prevent coastal degradation and erosion was also mentioned in interviews with epistemic community members in Los Amigos.

137. As stated by Felipe Serrano of ECOSUR in interview conducted March 2008, translated from Spanish. This point of view that the epistemic community members would use their access in designing and reforming management plans to advance their ecological understanding was further referenced in interviews with the following: Gonzalo Merediz Alonso, author interview conducted February 2008; Álvaro Hernández Gil, author interview conducted May 15, 2008, taken from transcript of digital voice recording; Eloy Sosa, author interview conducted February 2008. The contribution of ECOSUR and other organizations to the management plans of SEMARNAT and CONANP were also cited in Rosa María Loreto Viruel, author interview conducted April 18, 2008; Kramer and Kramer, *Ecoregional Conservation Planning for the Mesoamerican Caribbean Reef*, 112.

138. UCP, *Principios de Manejo para las Áreas Marinas Protegidas*, 26; CONANP, *Informes de Logros 2003*, 32, http://www.conanp.gob.mx/contenido/pdf/logros_2003 .pdf, accessed August 24, 2015; UCP, *Diseño e Implementación del Foro de Turismo Sustenible del SAM*, 46–48.

139. Álvaro Hernández Gil, author interview conducted May 15, 2008, taken from transcript of digital voice recording.

140. Patricia Santos, author interview conducted May 15, 2008, taken from transcript of audiocassette recording, translated from Spanish.

141. WWF-México, *How to Profit by Practicing Sustainable Fishing*.

142. Key to this effort was a 2002 workshop in Belize, attended by scientists of the four countries, and transnational organizations such as TNC. See Will Heyman and Nicanor Requena, *Informe Final de la Consultoría: Sitios de las agregaciones reproductivas de peces en la zona del SAM: Recomendaciones para su monitoreo y manejo* (Belize City: Unidad Coordinadora del Proyecto, 2003), 4.

143. Heyman and Requena, *Informe Final de la Consultoría*, 11–13; UCP, *Reporte de Avance Técnico y Financiero Reporte No. 4*, 13; Álvaro Hernández Gil, author interview conducted May 15, 2008; Eloy Sosa, author interviews conducted February 2008.

144. WWF-México, *Best Fishing Practices in Coral Reefs*, 14–15.

145. Eloy Sosa, author interviews conducted February 2008, taken from transcript of digital voice recording, translated from Spanish.

146. WWF-México, *How to Profit by Practicing Sustainable Fishing*; WWF-México, *Best Fishing Practices in Coral Reefs*.

147. WWF-México, *How to Profit by Practicing Sustainable Fishing*, 5.

148. UCP, *Reporte de Avance Técnico y Financiero. Reporte No. 3. Período: Julio 2002—Diciembre 2002* (Belize City: Unidad Coordinadora del Proyecto, 2002), 17, translated from Spanish.

149. Heyman and Requena, *Informe Final de la Consultoría*, 13; emphasis added.

150. Alfredo Arrellano Guillermo, author interviews conducted March 2008, taken from transcript of digital voice recording, translated from Spanish.

151. Rosa María Loreto Viruel, author interviews conducted April 18, 2008, taken from transcript of digital voice recording, translated from Spanish.

152. José Manuel Cárdenas Magaña, author interviews conducted May 12–15, 2008, taken from transcript of digital voice recording, translated from Spanish.

153. Gonzalo Merediz Alonso, author interviews conducted February 2008.

154. Eloy Sosa, author interviews conducted February 2008.

155. Enrique Galvez, author interviews conducted February 2008.

156. Nicolás Kosoy and Esteve Corbera, "Payments for Ecosystem Services as Commodity Fetishism," *Ecological Economics* 69 (2010): 1228–1236, 1231–1232.

157. UCP, *Reporte de Avance Técnico y Financiero Reporte No. 6* (2003): 9; UCP, *Reporte de Avance Técnico y Financiero. Reporte No. 8* (2005), 10–12, shows 100 percent compliance of PMS methodology in the sites of the MBRS Project by 2005.

158. José Manuel Cárdenas Magaña, author interviews conducted May 12–15, 2008; Enrique Galvéz, author interviews conducted February 2008; María Carmén García,

author interview conducted March, 2008; Gustavo Olivares, author interviews conducted April 9–10, 2008; SEMARNAT official, author interviews conducted May 2008, not for attribution.

159. CONANP, *Programa de Conservación y Manejo*, 3.

160. See The Nature Conservancy, *The Caribbean Conservation Results: July 2007–June 2008*; International Corporate Wetlands Restoration Partnership (ICWRP), press release for wetlands management in Sian Ka'an, Mexico City (2004).

161. CONANP, *Programa de Manejo: Parque Nacional Arrecifes de Xcalak, México*, passim, especially section 10, treating the administrative rules of the AMP, 86–107.

162. Patricia Santos, author interview conducted May 15, 2008.

163. A. Medina-Quej et al., *La Agregación del Mero* Epinephelus Striatus *en "El Blanquizal" en la Costa Sur de Quintana Roo, México* (Chetumal, Quintana Roo: ECOSUR, 2002); Álvaro Hernández Gil, author interview conducted May 15, 2008; José Manuel Cárdenas Magaña, author interviews conducted May 12–15, 2008; Heyman et al., *Informe Final de la Consultoría*, v. Reports generated by epistemic community members indicate that spawning aggregation sites may have existed in the northern third of the state, but have long been collapsed due to overexploitation. See Ibid., 4.

164. Comité Técnico Estatal de Evaluación, *Informe de Evaluación Estatal*.

165. CONANP, *Programa de Conservación y Manejo: Reserva de la Biósfera Sian Ka'an, Reserva de la Biósfera Arrecifes de Sian Ka'an y Área de Protección Flora y Fauna Uaymil* (Mexico City: CONANP, 2007).

166. Chung, "A Community Strategy for Coastal Zone Management of Xcalak, Mexico," 5.

167. SAM/FMAM/CCAD, *Informe de Revisión de Medio Término 9 al 21 de marzo* (2004), 18.

168. Comité Técnico Estatal de Evaluación, *Informe de Evaluación Estatal*, 52.

169. David M. Hoffman, "Institutional Legitimacy and Co-Management of a Marine Protected Area: Implementation Lessons from the Case of Xcalak Reefs National Park, Mexico," *Human Organization* 68, no. 1 (2009): 39–54.

170. Ibid.

171. El Papá, author interviews conducted July 2012, taken from transcript of digital voice recording, translated from Spanish.

172. Martha Bonilla-Moheno and Eduardo García-Frapolli, "Conservation in Context: A Comparison of Conservation Perspectives in a Mexican Protected Area," *Sustainability* 4, no. 9 (2012): 2317–2333.

173. CONANP, *Programa de Conservación y Manejo*.

174. See NOM-022-SEMARNAT-2003, particularly section 4.

175. Ibid., section 4.43, allowing construction "as long as, in the preliminary report or in the event of an environmental impact, compensation measures are established to benefit the wetlands, and the corresponding authorization to change the land use designation is obtained." Translated from Spanish.

176. Exequiel Ezcurra, author interview conducted May 2009, taken from handwritten notes of telephone interview.

177. José Juan Domínguez Calderón, author interviews conducted January 24, 2008, taken from transcript of audiocassette recording, translated from Spanish.

178. "Mexican Advocates Save Whale Breeding Grounds," *Environmental Law Alliance Worldwide Impact*, October 2000.

179. "200 Hectáreas menos de manglares en La Paz," *Teorem Ambiental*, December 5, 2005.

180. "Reciben a Fox con protestas en La Paz por venta de manglares," *La Jornada*, Tuesday, September 27, 2005.

181. David Martínez, author interviews conducted April 29, 2008, taken from transcript of digital voice recording, translated from Spanish.

182. Diario Oficial de la Federación, *Ley General de la Vida Silvestre* (DOF October 14, 2008), Article 60 Ter. See also "Manglares, refugio de especies comerciales importantes," *La Jornada*; "Increpan regidores del Verde Ecologista a García Pliego," *Novedades*.

183. Enrique Galvez, author interviews conducted February 2008; Eloy Sosa, author interviews conducted February 2008; Respaldo de SCJN a humedales será fundamental para Q. Roo," *Periódico de Quintana Roo*, Wednesday, August 19, 2009.

184. Quote taken from APIR president Miguel Ángel Lemus, cited in "Promueven industriales veto a reformas en ley de vida silvestre, denuncian ONG," *La Jornada*, Wednesday, February 24, 2007, translated from Spanish. In addition, various accounts of hotelier mobilization and state support presented in interviews with epistemic community members, and in the following: "Defienden por internet el recurso natural," *Novedades Quintana Roo*, Wednesday, February 6, 2008; "Van empresarios contra manglares de QR," *El Universal Estados*.

185. "Increpan regidores del Verde Ecologista a García Pliego," *Novedades*. Also taken from interviews with epistemic community members.

186. Eloy Sosa, author interviews conducted February 2008, taken from digital voice recording, translated from Spanish.

187. Enrique Galvéz, author interviews conducted February 2008, taken from transcript of digital voice recording, translated from Spanish.

188. Observed through firsthand observation of Majahual during April 2008, in conjunction with interviews with members of SCPP Andrés Quintana Roo and Abril Navarro.

189. Miguel Montalvo, author interviews conducted July 2012, taken from transcript of digital voice recording, translated from Spanish.

190. Adriana Yoloxóchitl Olivera Gómez, author interviews conducted March 2008, taken from transcript of audiocassette recording, translated from Spanish.

191. "Protesta Greenpeace contra 'turismo depredador,'" *El Universal*, Thursday September 25, 2008.

192. Patricia Santos, author interview conducted May 15, 2008, taken from transcript of digital voice recording, translated from Spanish.

193. Enrique Galvez, author interview conducted February 2008, taken from transcript of digital voice recording, translated from Spanish.

194. Alfredo Arrellano Guillermo, author interview conducted March 2008, taken from transcript of digital voice recording, translated from Spanish.

195. Adriana Yoloxóchitl Olivera Gómez, author interview conducted March 2008, taken from transcript of audiocassette recording, translated from Spanish.

196. Gonzalo Merediz Alonso, author interview conducted June 2012, taken from transcript of digital voice recording, translated from Spanish.

3 Mexico and Biodiversity in the Mesoamerican Biological Corridor

1. World Bank, *Mexico: Mesoamerican Biological Corridor* (World Bank project document, 2000), Annex 3, 1; Comisión Nacional de la Biodiversidad [CONABIO], "El Corredor Biológico Mesoamericano," *Biodiversitas* 7, no. 47 (2003), 2; Comisión Centroamericana de Ambiente y Desarrollo [CCAD], *El Corredor Biológico Mesoamericano: Un plataforma para el desarrollo regional* (CCAD: Serie Técnica 01, 2002), 7.

2. Jorge L. Tamayo, *Primera fase del Sistema de Evaluación y Monitoreo para el Corredor Biológico Mesoamericano—México (Componente de Geomática): Informe Final* (Mexico City: Centro de Investigación en Geografía y Geomática, 2005), 10.

3. World Bank, *Mexico: Mesoamerican Biological Corridor*, 3.

4. Corredor Biológico Mesoamericano [CBM], *Biodiversidad Total y Endémica de Mesoamerica* (2000); Comisión Centroamericana de Ambiente y Desarrollo [CCAD], *Corredor Biológico Mesoamericano: Del Paseo Pantera a un modelo de desarrollo sustentable* (CCAD: Costa Rica, 2000); World Bank, *Mexico: Mesoamerican Biological Corridor*, 2; Tamayo, *Primera Fase del Sistema de Evaluación*, 10.

5. UNEP, *Establecimiento de un Programa para la Consolidación del Corredor Biológico Mesoamericano* (CCAD/PNUD, 1999), 5; Juan José Morales Barbosa, *La Gran Selva Maya* (from the series *Sian Ka'an: Introducción a los Ecosistemas de la Península de Yucatán*, Cancún, Q. Roo: Amigos de Sian Ka'an, 1995), 151.

6. CCAD-PNUD/GEF, *Proyecto Para La Consolidación del Corredor Biológico Mesoamericano* (CBM: Managua, 2002), 52.

7. World Bank, *Mexico: Mesoamerican Biological Corridor*, Annex V, 7–11.

8. Willem Assies, "Land Tenure and Tenure Regimes in Mexico: An Overview," *Journal of Agrarian Change* 8, no. 1 (2008): 33–63.

9. James Barsimantov, Alex Racelis, Grenville Barnes, and Maria DiGiano, "Tenure, Tourism, and Timber in Quintana Roo, Mexico: Land Tenure Changes in Forest Ejidos after Agrarian Reforms," *International Journal of the Commons*, 4, no. 1 (2010): 293–318.

10. Sarah Hamilton, "Neoliberalism, Gender, and Property Rights in Rural Mexico," *Latin American Research Review* (2002): 119–143.

11. UNEP, *Establecimiento de un Programa para la Consolidación del Corredor Biológico Mesoamericano*, 25; USAID, *Assessment of Tropical Forest and Biodiversity Conservation in Mexico* (FAA SECTIONS 118–119 Report, 2008), 52.

12. USAID, *Assessment of Tropical Forest and Biodiversity Conservation in Mexico*, 51.

13. Kenton Miller, Elsa Chang, and Nels Johnson, *Defining Common Ground for the Mesoamerican Biological Corridor* (Washington, DC: World Resources Institute, 2001), 23.

14. CCAD-PNUD/GEF, *Proyecto Para La Consolidación del Corredor Biológico Mesoamericano*, 65; Timothy J. Synott, "Evaluación de las plantaciones forestales en el área Sian Ka'an-Calakmul," *Corredor Biológico Mesoamericano/México: Serie Conocimiento* (CONABIO: Tlalpan, México, 2007), 13–17.

15. UNEP, *Establecimiento de un Programa para la Consolidación del Corredor Biológico Mesoamericano*, 5; Enrique Galvez, author interviews conducted March 2008; Alexander López and Alicia Jímenez, *Latin America Assessment Environmental Conflict and Cooperation: The Mesoamerican Biological Corridor as a Mechanism for Transboundary Cooperation*, Report of the Regional Consultation, July 4–5, 2006 (UNEP: Mexico City, 2007), 10.

16. "Mexicans Still Haunted by 1979 Ixtoc Spill," *BBC News*, June, 14, 2010. http://www.bbc.com/news/10307105, accessed August 25, 2015.

17. CCAD-PNUD/GEF, *Proyecto Para La Consolidación del Corredor Biológico Mesoamericano*, 10.

18. Comisión Nacional para el Desarrollo de los Pueblos Indígenas [CDI], *Consulta a los Pueblos Indígenas Sobre sus Formas y Aspiraciones de Desarrollo: Informe Final* (Comisión Nacional para el Desarrollo de los Pueblos Indígenas: México, DF, 2004), 32. María Esther Ayala, "La Apicultura de la Península de Yucatán: Un Acercamiento Desde la Ecología Humana" (master's thesis, Centro de Investigaciones y Estudios Avanzados [CINVESTAV], 2001), 27.

19. David Pellow, *Resisting Global Toxics: Transnational Movements for Environmental Justice* (Cambridge: MIT Press, 2007), 5.

20. World Bank, *Mexico: Mesoamerican Biological Corridor*, 13.

21. CONABIO, *Estrategia Nacional sobre Biodiversidad de México* (SEMARNAT: Mexico City, 2000). CONABIO completed this in 2000, drawing from a three-year coordinated, multisectoral study.

22. Comisión Nacional del Uso y Conocimiento de la Biodiversidad [CONABIO], *Manual de Operaciones* (Mexico City: SEMARNAT, 2001), 8.40.

23. Interview with Alfredo Arellano Guillermo, March 2008, taken from transcript of audiocassette recording; José Juan Dominguez Calderón, author interview conducted January 24, 2008, taken from transcript of audiocassette recording; CONANP, *Qué es la CONANP?* 2006, http://www.conanp.gob.mx/qienes.html, accessed January 2009; Unidad Coordinadora del Proyecto, *Manual—Guía Común para la Evaluación de EIAs de Proyectos Turísticos* (Belize City: MBRS, 2003), 32.

24. Dzahuindanda Flores, author interviews conducted May 12, 2008.

25. See CONAFOR, *¿Qué es Conafor?* (2015), http://www.conafor.gob.mx/web/nosotros/que-es-conafor/, accessed August 25, 2015.

26. Global Environment Facility [GEF], "Trust Fund Grant Agreement," GEF Trust Fund Grant Number 024371 (2000), http://tinyurl.com/geftrustfundgrantcbm, accessed August 26, 2015, preamble; Corredor Biológico Mesoamericano, *Mexico Mesoamerican Biological Corridor Indigenous Peoples Development Plan* (CBMMx Project, c. 2000), 3.

27. Comisión Nacional para el Desarrollo de los Pueblos Indígenas (CDI), *Ley de la CDI* (2009), http://www.cdi.gob.mx/index.php?option=com_content&task=view&id=5&Itemid=8, accessed October 2009; CDI, *Consulta a los Pueblos Indígenas Sobre sus Formas y Aspiraciones de Desarrollo*; CDI official, interviews conducted March 2008; CDI, *Quienes Somos* (2009), http://www.cdi.gob.mx/index.php?option=com_content&task=view&id=2&Itemid=4, accessed October 2009; CDI, *Lineamientos del Proyecto Manejo y Conservación de Recursos Naturales en Zonas Indígenas* (CDI Project Document for Proyecto MCRNZI 07 revisado con DGEC y DGAJ_ 16_ 07_07, 2007).

28. GEF "Trust Fund Grant Agreement," 6, Section 3.03(a)–3.03(b).

29. Cited in Jocelyn Kaiser, "Bold Corridor Project Confronts Political Reality," *Science* 293, no. 5538 (2001): 2196–2199, 2197, http://www.sciencemag.org/cgi/reprint/sci;293/5538/2196.pdf, accessed August 26, 2015. "Biological corridors" are defined as zones running between existing protected areas, managed under environmental regulations to alleviate anthropogenic stresses on important biodiversity. This definition is taken from a variety of the project documents associated with the CBMMx Project; see, e.g., World Bank, *Project Appraisal Document on a Proposed Grant from the Global Environment Facility Trust Fund in the Amount of SDR 11.5 Million to Nacional Financiera, S.N.C. for a Mesoamerican Biological Corridor Project*, Report No. 23132-ME (Washington, DC: World Bank, 2000), 5.

30. Reed F. Noss, "Corridors in Real Landscapes: A Response to Simberloff and Cox," *Conservation Biology* 1, no. 2 (August 1987): 159–164; CCAD-PNUD/GEF, *Proyecto Para La Consolidación del Corredor Biológico Mesoamericano*, 14.

31. Adela Vázquez Trejo, "La cooperación acerca de la cuestión ambiental en Centroamérica," *Co/incidencias*, no. 2 (July–Dec. 2005): 40; Miller et al., *Defining Common Ground for the Mesoamerican Biological Corridor*; Kaiser, "Bold Corridor Project Confronts Political Reality."

32. Miller et al., *Defining Common Ground for the Mesoamerican Biological Corridor*, 3.

33. CCAD-PNUD/GEF, "Proyecto para la Consolidación del Corredor Biológico Mesoamericano" (Managua: Proyecto Corredor Biológico Mesoamericano, 2002), 12. See also the CONABIO website, http://www.biodiversidad.gob.mx/planeta/internacional/ccad.html, accessed August 26, 2015.

34. López and Jímenez, *Latin America Assessment Environmental Conflict and Cooperation*, 27; Morales, *La Gran Selva Maya*, passim.

35. Reed Noss, author correspondence via email, October 2009; *Newsletter of the Mesoamerican Biodiversity Legal Project* (1993), http://www.ciesin.org/docs/008-594/008-594.html, accessed August 26, 2015.

36. Miller et al., *Defining Common Ground for the Mesoamerican Biological Corridor*, 35; *Declaración Conjunta: Tuxtla II*, 1996, http://tinyurl.com/tuxtladeclaration, accessed August 26, 2015, Article 1; World Bank, *Mexico: Mesoamerican Biological Corridor*, 4; CONABIO, El Corredor Biológico Mesoamericano. According to design documents for the CBMMx Project, Mexico represented an "essential building block for the Mesoamerican Biological Corridor." World Bank, *Mexico: Mesoamerican Biological Corridor*, 5.

37. World Bank, *Project Appraisal Document*, 26.

38. CONABIO, *Estrategia Nacional sobre Biodiversidad de México*, 63–66.

39. One of the earlier studies was carried out in the Sian Ka'an forests by María Magdalena Vázquez of UQROO, titled "Estudio de la fauna edáfica en una selva baja

inundable de la reserva de la biosfera de Sian Ka'an, Q. Roo," final report for SNIB-CONABIO project no. B051 (Mexico City: Universidad de Quintana Roo, 1997). As indicated in chapter 2, Sian Ka'an later became a central point of interest for emerging transnational coalitions around marine biodiversity. María Magdalena Vázquez, *Fauna Edáfica de las Selvas Tropicales de Quintana Roo* (Chetumal: Universidad de Quintana Roo, 2001).

40. Several of these projects were funded by the GEF Small Grants Programme (SGP) between 1998 and 2013, including activities taken by Yum Balám, Los Amigos, and Pronatura. Over four hundred biodiversity conservation projects by local ENGOs have been funded by the GEF since 1994, and can be identified by a search at the GEF SPG website, https://sgp.undp.org/index.php?option=com_sgpprojects&view=projects&Itemid=154, accessed August 26, 2015.

41. CCAD-PNUD/GEF, *Proyecto Para La Consolidación del Corredor Biológico Mesoamericano*, 10.

42. Reed Noss, author correspondence via email, October 2009; World Bank, *Mexico: Mesoamerican Biological Corridor*, 24; Marcela Morales, author interview February 2008, taken from transcript of digital voice recording.

43. CCAD-PNUD/GEF, *Proyecto para la Consolidación del Corredor Biológico Mesoamericano*, 47; World Bank, *Project Appraisal Document*, 6.

44. Liza Grandia, "Between Bolivar and Bureaucracy: The Mesoamerican Biological Corridor," *Conservation and Society* 5, no. 4 (2007): 478–503, 490; Margaret Buck Holland, "Mesoamerican Biological Corridor," in *Climate and Conservation: Landscape and Seascape Science, Planning, and Action*, ed. Jodi Hilty, Charles C. Chester, and Molly S. Cross (Washington, DC: Island Press, 2012), 56–66.

45. Grandia, "Between Bolivar and Bureaucracy."

46. Ibid, 490.

47. World Bank, *Project Appraisal Document*.

48. See discussions about transnational advocacy networks in Margaret Keck and Kathryn Sikkink, *Activists Beyond Borders* (Ithaca: Cornell University Press, 1998); Sanjeev Khagram, *Restructuring World Politics* (Minneapolis: University of Minnesota Press, 2002); María Guadalupe Moog Rodrigues, *Global Environmentalism and Local Politics: Transnational Advocacy Networks in Brazil, Ecuador, and India* (Albany: SUNY Press, 2004).

49. World Bank, *Project Appraisal Document*, 13; PADEP A.C., *Evaluación Técnica del Corredor Biológico Mesoamericano—México: Reporte Final* (Mexico City: PADEP, 2004), 10.

50. CONABIO, *Manual de Operaciones*, 4.6; Ildefonso Palermo, author interview conducted March 2008.

51. CBMMx Project, *Donacion TF-024371—Proyecto "Corredor Biológico Mesoamericano —México" Plan De Adquisiciones Y Contrataciones (PAC) Contratos Sujetos A Examen Posterior Del Banco* (2009), http://www-wds.worldbank.org/external/default/WDS ContentServer/WDSP/IB/2008/01/28/000333038_20080128025407/Rendered/PDF/ 422180PROP0SPA101091101071Ver1Final.pdf, accessed August 26, 2015.

52. World Bank, *Mexico: Mesoamerican Biological Corridor*, 24.

53. PADEP A.C., *Evaluación Técnica del CBMMx*, 13–14, translated from Spanish.

54. Ibid.

55. Felipe Serrano, author interviews conducted March 2008, taken from transcript of digital voice recording, translated from Spanish.

56. World Bank, *Project Appraisal Document*, 12; World Bank, Implementation Letter for GEF Trust Fund Agreement.

57. World Bank, *Project Appraisal Document*, 14–15; CONABIO, *Manual de Operaciones*, 3.5; CONABIO, Retos, Perspectivas Y Estrategias Del CBMM En La Península De Yucatán (Powerpoint presentation provided by CONABIO, n.d.).

58. CBMMx Project, *Mexico Mesoamerican Biological Corridor Indigenous Peoples Development Plan*, 9.

59. CBMMx Project, *Donacion TF-024371*.

60. María Luisa Villarreal Sonora, ed., *Memorias de 1er Seminario de Unidades de Manejo para la Conservación de la Vida Silvestre en el Sureste de México* (Simbiosis A.C.: Chetumal, Quintana Roo, 2006).

61. Arturo Bayona, author interviews conducted April 2008; *Biodiversitas*, "Proyecto Kantemó" (CONABIO monthly bulletin, 2007).

62. López and Jímenez, *Latin America Assessment Environmental Conflict and Cooperation*, 32; Miller et al., *Defining Common Ground for the Mesoamerican Biological Corridor*, 5; Isabel Camacho, Carlos del Campo, and Gary Martin, *Community Conserved Areas in North America: A Review of Status and Needs* (Coatepec, Veracruz: Global Diversity Foundation, 2008), 17; Kaiser, "Bold Corridor Project Confronts Political Reality," 2197.

63. López and Jímenez, *Latin America Assessment Environmental Conflict and Cooperation*, 31.

64. Dzahuindanda Flores, author interviews conducted May 12, 2008, taken from transcript of digital voice recording, translated from Spanish.

65. Miguel Montalvo, author interviews conducted July 2012, taken from transcript of digital voice recording, translated from Spanish.

66. López and Jímenez, *Latin America Assessment Environmental Conflict and Cooperation*, 31–32.

67. Taken from minutes from the symposium "Conceptualización Y Criterios Para Corredores Biológicos En Mesoamérica" (V Congreso de la Sociedad Mesoamericana para la Biología y la Conservación San Salvador, El Salvador, 2008); López and Jímenez, *Latin America Assessment Environmental Conflict and Cooperation*, 30–32.

68. Taken from minutes from the symposium "Conceptualización Y Criterios Para Corredores Biológicos En Mesoamérica," translated from Spanish.

69. World Bank, *Project Appraisal Document*, 3.

70. López and Jímenez, *Latin America Assessment Environmental Conflict and Cooperation*, 32.

71. Radoslav Barzev, *Developing a Methodology for Implementing and Assessing Economic Instruments for the Conservation of the Environmental Goods and Services in the Mesoamerican Biological Corridor* (Managua: CCAD/GEF, 2003), 4.

72. Radoslav Barzev, *Guía Metodológica de Valoración Económica* (Managua: CCAD/GEF, 2002), 40; author's translation.

73. Ibid., 43.

74. Tamayo, *Primera fase del Sistema de Evaluación*, 13, author's translation; Barzev, *Guía Metodológica de Valoración Económica*, 41, author's translation.

75. Miller et al., *Defining Common Ground for the Mesoamerican Biological Corridor*.

76. See for example, section IV.10.4, "Aprovechamiento Sustentable de los Recursos Naturales" in the Quintana Roo *Plan Estatal de Desarrollo 2005–2011*, produced by the government of the State of Quintana Roo.

77. Government of the State of Quintana Roo, *Plan Estatal de Desarrollo 2005–2011*, 32.

78. Grandia, "Between Bolivar and Bureaucracy." See also Liza Grandia, *Enclosed: Conservation, Cattle, and Commerce among the Q'eqchi' Maya Lowlanders* (Seattle: University of Washington Press, 2012).

79. Saleem H. Ali and Mary A. Ackley, "Foreign Investment and Environmental Justice in an Island Economy: Mining, Bottled Water, and Corporate Social Responsibility in Fiji," in *Environmental Inequalities Beyond Borders: Local Perspectives on Global Injustices*, ed. JoAnn Carmin and Julian Agyeman (Cambridge, MA: MIT Press, 2011).

80. Suzana Sawyer, *Crude Chronicles: Indigenous Politics, Multinational Oil, and Neoliberalism in Ecuador* (Durham, NC: Duke University Press, 2004).

81. David Carruthers, ed., *Environmental Justice in Latin America: Problems, Promise, and Practice* (Cambridge, MA: MIT Press, 2008).

82. María Villareal, author interviews conducted March 2008, taken from transcript of digital voice recording, author's translation.

83. María Magdalena Vásquez, author interviews conducted February 2008; Dzahuindanda Flores, author interviews conducted May 12, 2008; Falcon Paz, author interviews conducted May 12, 2008.

84. Arturo Bayona, author interviews conducted April 2008, taken from transcript of digital voice recording, author's translation.

85. María Magdalena Vázquez, author interviews conducted February 2008, taken from transcript of digital voice recording, author's translation.

86. Luis Alfonso Argüelles Suárez, *Diagnóstico y Programas del Corredor de Sian Ka'an-Calakmul. CBM-M* (National Forestry Commission [CONAFOR], 2005), passim.

87. Consultoría Mesoamericana de Asistencia y Desarrollo Popular Asociación Civil [COMADEP], *Creación De Bases Para El Ordenamiento Ecológico Regional Participativo Y Fortalecimiento De Líneas De Acción Detonantes En El Área Focal De La Montaña, Campeche México* (Final Report for the CBMMx Project, 2005), passim.

88. Enrique Galvez, author interview conducted February 2008.

89. CONABIO, *Comercio Sustentable Por Un Consumo Responsable Y Comprometido Con El Medio Ambiente* (Corredor Biológico Mesoamericano/México: México, 2007).

90. Grupo Xcaret, *Balance Social, Cultural y Ambiental: Sustainability Report* (Tourism Bulletin, 2008); CBMMx Project, *Donacion TF-024371*.

91. COMADEP, *Creación De Bases Para El Ordenamiento Ecológico Regional Participativo* (2005), 13.

92. CCAD-PNUD/GEF, *Proyecto Para La Consolidación del Corredor Biológico Mesoamericano*, 10.

93. World Bank, *Project Appraisal Document*, Annex 2, 1.

94. The Sian Ka'an series produced by Los Amigos included the Tabasco protected areas under the newly developed strategy for biological corridor development, for example in Morales, "La Gran Selva Maya," 158. See also CCAD-PNUD/GEF, *Proyecto Para La Consolidación del Corredor Biológico Mesoamericano*, 10; Miller et al., *Defining Common Ground for the Mesoamerican Biological Corridor*, 8, also lists the Tabasco protected areas as part of the CBMMx Project, as does the map presented in Kaiser, "Bold Corridor Project Confronts Political Reality," 2196.

95. World Bank, *Project Appraisal Document*, Annex 2, 1.

96. María Villareal, author interviews conducted March 2008, taken from transcript of digital voice recording, author's translation.

97. María Magdalena Vásquez, author interviews conducted February 2008.

98. María Villareal, author interviews conducted March 2008, taken from transcript of digital voice recording, author's translation.

99. Jim Barborak, quoted in Kaiser, "Bold Corridor Project Confronts Political Reality."

100. Reed Noss, author correspondence via email, October 2009.

101. Miguel Montalvo, author interviews conducted July 2012, taken from transcript of digital voice recording, translated from Spanish.

102. Martín Balám, author interviews conducted March 2008, taken from transcript of digital voice recording, translated from Spanish by author.

103. Donna J. Haraway, *Simians, Cyborgs, and Women: The Reinvention of Nature* (New York: Routledge, 2013); Haraway, "Situated Knowledges: The Science Question in Feminism and the Privilege of Partial Perspective," *Feminist Studies* 14, no. 3 (1988): 575–599; Philipp Pattberg, "Conquest, Domination and Control: Europe's Mastery of Nature in Historic Perspective," *Journal of Political Ecology* 14, no. 1 (2007): 1-9; Karl Jacoby, *Crimes Against Nature: Squatters, Poachers, Thieves, and the Hidden History of American Conservation* (Berkeley, CA: University of California Press, 2014).

104. PADEP A.C., *Evaluación Técnica del CBMMx*, 14; Pilar Rodríguez, *Promoción de la Red de Monitoreo Ecológico Multiescala en el Corredor Biológico Mesoamericano—México* (Mexico City: CONABIO, 2007), 19–21.

105. Gonzalo Merediz Alonso, author interview conducted February 2008, taken from transcript of digital voice recording, translated from Spanish by author.

106. Tamayo, *Primera fase del Sistema de Evaluación*, 6, author's translation.

107. Ibid., passim.

108. Kate Ervine, "Participation Denied: The Global Environment Facility, Its Universal Blueprint, and the Mexico-Mesoamerican Biological Corridor in Chiapas," *Third World Quarterly* 31, no. 5 (2010): 773–790, 774.

109. Grandia, "Between Bolivar and Bureaucracy." See also Grandia, *Enclosed*.

110. Licenciado Tun, author interviews conducted March 22, 2008, taken from transcript of digital voice recording, translated from Spanish by author.

111. Arturo Bayona, author interviews conducted April 2008, taken from transcript of digital voice recording, translated from Spanish by author.

112. Enrique Gálvez, author interviews conducted February 2008, taken from transcript of digital voice recording, translated from Spanish by author.

113. Alfonso Bey, author interviews conducted 2012, taken from transcript of digital voice recording, translated from Spanish by author.

114. PADEP A.C., *Evaluación Técnica del CBMMx*, 21, translated from Spanish by author.

115. Ibid.

116. Taken from minutes from the symposium "Conceptualización Y Criterios Para Corredores Biológicos En Mesoamérica."

117. Camacho, del Campo, and Martin, *Community Conserved Areas in North America*, 14. See also earlier discussion regarding the range of projects developed by civil society ENGOs in corridor zones throughout the 1990s and 2000s.

118. Ibid., 52.

119. See G. Ramos-Fernández, Bárbara Ayala Orozco, Martha Bonilla Moheno, and Eduardo García Frapolli "Conservación Comunitaria en Punta Laguna: Fortalecimiento de Instituciones Locales para el Desarrollo Sostenible" (proceedings from the First International Congress of Successful Cases of Sustainable Development in the Tropics, Boca del Río, Veracruz, México, 2005), which discusses the role of Pronatura in aiding in the implementation of CONANP decrees in Chiapas.

120. State Consultative Council member from one of the Yucatán peninsula states, author interviews conducted March 2008, taken from transcript of digital voice recording, author's translation.

121. Licenciado Tun, author interviews conducted March 22, 2008, taken from transcript of digital voice recording, translated from Spanish by author.

122. Alfonso Bey, author interviews conducted 2012, taken from transcript of digital voice recording, translated from Spanish by author.

123. PADEP A.C., *Evaluación Técnica del CBMMx*, 10–11; Rodríguez, *Promoción de la Red de Monitoreo Ecológico Multiescala*.

124. Budgetary plans for the CBMMx Project from 2005 to 2009 available at CBMMx Project, *Donacion TF-02437I*. See also PADEP A.C., *Evaluación Técnica del CBMMx*, 10–11; Rodríguez, *Promoción de la Red de Monitoreo Ecológico Multiescala*; Enrique Gálvez, author interview conducted February 2008.

125. Enrique Gálvez, author interviews conducted February 2008, taken from transcript of digital voice recording, translated from Spanish by author.

126. María Villarreal, author interviews conducted March 2008, taken from transcript of digital voice recording, translated from Spanish by author.

127. PADEP A.C., *Evaluación Técnica del CBMMx*, 18.

128. Grandia, "Between Bolivar and Bureaucracy"; Grandia, *Enclosed*.

129. Paulette L. Stenzel, "Plan Puebla Panama: An Economic Tool that Thwarts Sustainable Development and Facilitates Terrorism," *William and Mary Environmental Law and Policy Review* 30, no. 3 (2006): 555–623, 567; Claudia Boyd-Barrett, "Environmentalists Protest Dam Project for Ancient River: Sustainable Chiapas" (2002),

https://www.organicconsumers.org/old_articles/chiapas/120902_chiapas.php, accessed June 2015.

130. The upper figure was taken from S. Jeffrey K. Wilkerson, "Damming the Usumacinta: The Archaeological Impact," in *Mesa Redonda de Palenque, Chiapas*, ed. Virginia M. Fields, (Norman: University of Oklahoma Press, 1986), 118–134.

131. Ibid.; Boyd-Barrett, "Environmentalists Protest Dam Project for Ancient River; Stenzel, "Plan Puebla Panama." See also "Action Letter, February 1993," *Global Response*, http://web.mit.edu/hemisphere/events/usumacinta.shtml, accessed June 2015.

132. Sanjeev Khagram, *Dams and Development: Transnational Struggles for Water and Power* (Ithaca: Cornell University Press, 2004), 4.

133. Grandia, "Between Bolivar and Bureaucracy," 491.

134. Kristin Norget, "Caught in the Crossfire: Militarization, Paramilitarization, and State Violence in Oaxaca, Mexico," in *When States Kill: Latin America, the US, and Technologies of Terror*, ed. Cecilia Menjível and Néstor Rodríguez (Austin: University of Texas Press, 2009), 115–142, endnote 16, 139.

135. PADEP A.C., *Evaluación Técnica del CBMMx*, 18.

136. Rodríguez, *Promoción de la Red de Monitoreo Ecológico Multiescala*, 2, author's translation.

137. Grandia, "Between Bolivar and Bureaucracy," 487.

4   Egypt and the Migratory Soaring Birds Project

1. Jeannie Sowers, *Environmental Politics in Egypt: Activists, Experts, and the State* (New York: Routledge, 2013).

2. "Principles of Environmental Justice," *Yes! Magazine*, March 21, 2003, http://www.yesmagazine.org/issues/our-planet-our-selves/principles-of-environmental-justice, accessed July 2015.

3. Richard P. Hiskes, *The Human Right to a Green Future: Environmental Rights and Intergenerational Justice* (New York: Cambridge University Press, 2009), 132.

4. See inter alia, Paul F. Steinberg, *Comparative Environmental Politics: Theory, Practice, and Prospects* (Cambridge, MA: MIT Press, 2012); and Regina S. Axelrod, David L. Downie, and Norman Vig, *The Global Environment: Institutions, Laws, and Policy* (New York: CQ Press, 2010).

5. Fareed Zakaria, "Culture Is Destiny: A Conversation with Lee Kuan Yew," *Foreign Affairs* 73, no. 2 (1994): 109–126.

6. Jeannie Sowers, "Nature Reserves and Authoritarian Rule in Egypt: Embedded Autonomy Revisited," *The Journal of Environment & Development* 16, no. 4 (2007): 375–397; Sowers, *Environmental Politics in Egypt*; Jessica C. Teets, *Civil Society under Authoritarianism: The China Model* (New York: Cambridge University Press, 2014).

7. These flyways begin in Europe and Eurasia, near the Turkey-Syria border, one of which splits off, crosses the Gulf of Suez, and heads south along the Nile Valley through Egypt, Sudan, Eritrea, and Ethiopia. See UNDP/Birdlife, *Mainstreaming Conservation of Migratory Soaring Birds*, UNDP Project Document (UNDP, 2006), http://www.lb.undp.org/content/dam/lebanon/docs/Energy%20and%20Environment/Projects/1472.pdf, accessed August 27, 2015, 2; Yossi Leshem and Yoram Yom-Tov, "Routes of Migratory Soaring Birds," *Ibis* 140 (1998): 41–52; MSEA/EEAA, *Biodiversity Conservation Capacity Building in Egypt* (Cairo: MSEA/EEAA, 2006), 162.

8. Some of the species identified in the project and in interviews include UNDP/Birdlife, *Mainstreaming Conservation of Migratory Soaring Birds*, 2.

9. Graham Tucker, *Migratory Soaring Birds: Review of Status, Threats and Priority Conservation Actions* (Report to Birdlife International, 2005), 188.

10. UNDP/Birdlife, *Mainstreaming Conservation of Migratory Soaring Birds*, 1.

11. Convention on Migratory Species [CMS] Secretariat, "Birds of Prey (Raptors), *Memoranda of Understanding on the Conservation of Migratory Birds of Prey in Africa and Eurasia*, 2015, http://www.cms.int/raptors/en/legalinstrument/birds-prey-raptors, accessed August 27, 2015. See also Mohammed A. Ayyad, Amal M. Fahkry, and Abdel Raouf A. Moustafa, "Plant Biodiversity in the Saint Catherine Area of the Sinai Peninsula," *Biodiversity and Conservation* 9 (1999): 265–281, for a study of biodiversity in the Sinai peninsula; and Esam Ahmed Egypt Elbadry, *Protected Areas of the Mediterranean MedWetCoast Egypt*, project document for the Mediterranean Wetlands Coast Project (c. 2002); and Magdy T. Khalil and Kamal H. Shaltout, *Lake Bardawil and Zaranik Protected Areas*, Publication of Biodiversity Unit, no. 15 (Cairo: State Ministry of Environment, 2006), 531. Zaranik, for example, is a registered Ramsar site with over nine hundred species of flora and fauna, five of which are endemic.

12. Leshem and Yom-Tov, "Routes of Migratory Soaring Birds," 50; GEF/Birdlife, "Bottlenecks for Soaring Migratory Birds—Project Concept Paper," GEF Concept Paper for project titled *Protection of Key Bottleneck Bird Areas for Soaring Migratory Birds in the Eastern Sector of the Africa-Eurasia Flyway (Rift Valley and Red Sea Flyways)* (Washington, DC: GEF, 2003), 3; Gudrun Hilgerloh, "The Desert at Zeit Bay, Egypt: A Bird Migration Bottleneck of Global Importance," *Bird Conservation International* 19 (2009): 332–352; Khalil and Shaltout, *Lake Bardawil and Zaranik Protected Areas*, 534.

13. GEF/Birdlife, "Bottlenecks for Migratory Soaring Birds," 23.

14. István Moldován, author interviews conducted October 11–18, 2008.

15. Wetlands International, *International Update Report on Lead Poisoning in Water-birds* (2000), http://www.nienkebeintema.nl/files/Varia_rapport_loodvergiftiging.pdf, accessed August 27, 2015. See also the African-Eurasian Waterbird Agreement (AEWA), "Special Edition: Lead Poisoning in Waterbirds through the Ingestion of Spent Lead Shot," AEWA Newsletter, Special Issue #1 (2002), http://www.unep-aewa.org/sites/default/files/document/inf2_2special1-engl_0.pdf, accessed August 27, 2015.

16. István Moldován, author interviews conducted October 11–18, 2008, taken from transcript of digital voice recording.

17. EgyBirdGroup, personal communication, September–November 2008; UNDP/Birdlife, *Mainstreaming Conservation of Migratory Soaring Birds*, 8, 137–138.

18. José Luis Tellería, "Potential Impact of Wind Farms on Migratory Soaring Birds Crossing Spain," *Bird Conservation International* 19 (2009): 131–136; UNDP/Birdlife, *Mainstreaming Conservation of Migratory Soaring Birds*, 6–7; Luis Barrios and Alejandro Rodríguez, "Behavioral and Environmental Correlates of Soaring-Bird Mortality at On-Shore Wind Turbines," *Journal of Applied Ecology* 41, no. 1 (2004): 72–81; Frank Bergen, *Ornithological Expert Opinion as a Part of the Feasibility Study for a Large Wind Farm at Gulf of el Zayt, Egypt* (Germany: Report for Deutsche Energie-Consult Ingenieurgesellschaft mbH Norsk-Data-Straße 1 [DECON], 2007).

19. Birdlife International, *Religious, Cultural, and Socioeconomic Importance of Migratory Birds Hunting: In Mediterranean Third Countries of North Africa and the Middle East*, Synthesis Report IV, Birdlife, 2006), http://www.birdlife.org/datazone/userfiles/file/sustainable_hunting/PDFs/SHP_SR4_Religious_Cultural_Socioeconomic_importance.pdf, accessed August 27, 2015.

20. J. Grainger, "'People Are Living in the Park.' Linking Biodiversity Conservation to Community Development in the Middle East Region: A Case Study from the Saint Katherine Protectorate, Southern Sinai," *Journal of Arid Environments* 54 (2003): 29–38.

21. Ann Gardener, "At Home in South Sinai," *Nomadic Peoples* 44, no. 2 (2000): 48–67; Sowers, "Nature Reserves and Authoritarian Rule in Egypt," 388.

22. See EEAA, *EEAA Organization Structure Approved by Central Agency for Organization and Administration* (2006), http://www.eeaa.gov.eg/English/reports/OrgStructure/OrgStructureEnglish.pdf, accessed August 27, 2015; MSEA/EEAA, *Egypt: National Strategy and Action Plan for Biodiversity* (Cairo: MSEA, 1998), 3.

23. UNEP/EEAA, *Biodiversity Conservation Capacity Building in Egypt*, 5.

24. BioMAP Project, Institutional Strengthening of the Nature Conservation Sector and National Biodiversity Department for Monitoring and Assessing of Biodiversity and Natural Heritage (BioMAP) (produced by government of the Arab Republic of Egypt, government of Italy, UNDP, 2004); Egyptian Environmental Affairs Agency

[EEAA], About MSEA—EEAA (2015), http://www.eeaa.gov.eg/english/main/about _detail.asp, accessed August 27, 2015.

25. MSEA/EEAA, *Egypt: National Strategy and Action Plan for Biodiversity*. As indicated throughout the book, the drafting of an NBSAP is part of a party's obligations to the CBD under Article 6.

26. Mohammed Kassas, author interview conducted September 5, 2008; Samir Ghabbour, author interviews conducted October 2008; Tahr Issa, author interview conducted September 20, 2008; Nature Conservation Sector (NCS), *Protected Areas of Egypt: Toward the Future* (Cairo: MSEA/EEAA, 2006), 18; Alaa El Din, author interview, September 2008.

27. MSEA/EEAA, *Egypt: National Strategy and Action Plan for Biodiversity*, passim.

28. EEAA/UNDP, *Self-Assessment of National Capacity in Egypt to Manage the Global Environment*, proposal for GEF-funded project on capacity building (Cairo: EEAA/UNDP, c. 2002), 4; Sowers, "Nature Reserves and Authoritarian Rule in Egypt," 381–382; Saad Eddin Ibrahim, "Reform and Frustration in Egypt," *Journal of Democracy* 7, no. 4 (1996): 125–135, 387.

29. Jennifer Gandhi, *Political Institutions under Dictatorship* (Cambridge, UK: Cambridge University Press, 2008).

30. See the vast literature on Latin American comparative politics, including Larry Jay Diamond, "Thinking about Hybrid Regimes," *Journal of Democracy* 13, no. 2 (2002): 21–35; Guillermo O'Donnell, "Reflections on the Patterns of Change in the Bureaucratic-Authoritarian State," *Latin American Research Review* 12, no. 1 (1978): 3–38; Guillermo O'Donnell, "Latin America," *Political Science & Politics* 34, no. 4 (2001): 809–811.

31. Michael Bratton and Nicholas Van de Walle, *Democratic Experiments in Africa: Regime Transitions in Comparative Perspective* (New York: Cambridge University Press, 1997); Richard L. Sklar, Ebere Onwudiwe, and Darren Kew, "Nigeria: Completing Obasanjo's Legacy," *Journal of Democracy* 17, no. 3 (2006): 100–115.

32. Kevin Koehler, "Authoritarian Elections in Egypt: Formal Institutions and Informal Mechanisms of Rule," *Democratization* 15, no. 5 (2008): 974–990.

33. Lisa Anderson, "Demystifying the Arab Spring," *Foreign Affairs* 90, no. 3 (2011): 2–7, 5. For a discussion on ways in which single-party systems retain power, see Benjamin Smith, "Life of the Party: The Origins of Regime Breakdown and Persistence under Single-Party Rule," *World Politics* 57, no. 3 (2005): 421–451.

34. Sowers, "Nature Reserves and Authoritarian Rule in Egypt," 386–387.

35. Angela Joya, "The Egyptian Revolution: Crisis of Neoliberalism and the Potential for Democratic Politics," *Review of African Political Economy* 38, no. 129 (2011): 367–386.

36. Sowers, *Environmental Politics in Egypt*, 109.

37. Monitoring, Verification and Evaluation (MVE) Unit, *Economic Valuation of the Egyptian Red Sea Coral Reef*, policy brief for the Egyptian Environmental Policy Program (c. 2003), 2.

38. Adel Rady, *Tourism and Sustainable Development in Egypt*, prepared for Plan Blue, Tourism Development Authority (2002).

39. Sowers, *Environmental Politics in Egypt*, 107–108.

40. Joya, "The Egyptian Revolution," 372.

41. Sowers, "Nature Reserves and Authoritarian Rule in Egypt," 381. See also Amr Ismail Adly, "Politically Embedded Cronyism: The Case of Post-Liberalization Egypt," *Business and Politics* 11, no. 4 (2009): 1–26, 10.

42. These areas are visible in Land Utilization Maps available in Egypt's National Biodiversity Strategy and Action Plan (NBSAP). See MSEA/EEAA, *Egypt: National Strategy and Action Plan for Biodiversity*, map 1.

43. Samy Zalat, author interviews conducted September 24, 2008; UNDP/NCS, *Strengthening Protected Area Financing and Management Systems*, GEF Project Identification Form (2008), 3. This was later supported by research conducted at the Nature Conservation Sector of the MSEA/EEAA, where staffers provided me with a copy of the Land Utilization Map for review.

44. Adly, "Politically Embedded Cronyism."

45. GEF/Birdlife, "Bottlenecks for Soaring Migratory Birds—Project Concept Paper," 4, footnote 5.

46. Ibid.

47. One study in particular emphasized the dangers of the bioaccumulation of lead from discarded shot. See Wetlands International, *International Update Report on Lead Poisoning in Waterbirds*.

48. UNEP/AEWA, "Resolution 2.4: International Implementation Priorities for 2003–2007" (c. 2002), www.unep-aewa.org/sites/default/files/document/resolution2_4_0 .pdf, accessed August 27, 2015, 2. Some of the species covered in the Birdlife/ Wetlands 2000 European initiatives and the later MSB project in Egypt include the Dalmatian Pelican (*Pelecanus crispus*) and the Eurasian Bittern (*Botaurus stellaris*). See UNEP/EEAA, *Biodiversity Conservation Capacity Building in Egypt*, 84; and UNDP/ Birdlife, *Mainstreaming Conservation of Migratory Soaring Birds*, 4.

49. Mary Megalli, author interview conducted October 4, 2008. At this time, Sherif had published two books on Egyptian avifauna in 1985 and 1989, *Common Birds of Egypt* and *Birds of Egypt* respectively. See PBS, *Mindy and Sherif Baha el Din* (2010), http://www.pbs.org/saf/1106/hotline/hbahaeldin.htm, accessed June 2010.

50. Personal communication, Mindy Baha el Din; CV of Sherif Baha el Din; PBS, *Mindy and Sherif Baha el Din.*

51. D. E. Pritchard, Statement on Behalf of Non-Governmental Organizations, made at 6th Meeting of the Conference of the Contracting Parties to the Convention on Migratory Species/1st Meeting of the Parties to the African-Eurasian Waterbird Agreement (1999), http://www.unep-aewa.org/sites/default/files/document/proceedings_0.pdf, accessed August 27, 2015.

52. MSEA/EEAA, *First National Report to the Convention on Biological Diversity* (Cairo: MSEA/EEAA, 1997), 30.

53. UNEP/AEWA Secretariat, Action Plan adopted by MOP 2 (2002); See compilation study: UNEP/AEWA Secretariat, *Non-toxic Shot: A Path toward Sustainable Use of the Waterbird Resource*, Technical Series No. 3 (Bonn, Germany: UNEP/AEWA, n.d.).

54. Pritchard, Statement on Behalf of Non-governmental Organizations.

55. L. A. Bennum and L. D. C. Fishpool, "The Important Bird Areas Program in Africa: An Outline," *Ostrich* 71, nos. 1–2 (2000): 150–153; Birdlife, *Middle East IBA Criteria* (2010), http://www.birdlife.org/datazone/sites/middle_east_criteria.html, accessed June 2010; UNDP/Birdlife, *Mainstreaming Conservation of Migratory Soaring Birds*, 22.

56. Sherif Baha el Din, *Important Bird Areas in Africa and Associated Islands—Egypt* (Cambridge, UK: Birdlife International, n.d.), 245.

57. Ibid., 243.

58. Mindy Baha el Din, personal communication and author interview, July 2006; Hala Barakat, personal communication, September 2008.

59. GEF/Birdlife, "Bottlenecks for Soaring Migratory Birds."

60. Ibid., 2, 14. The benefit of taking a site-specific approach to IBA protection is that IBAs are considered small enough to be protected in entirety. See Rachael Adam, "Waterbirds, the 2010 Biodiversity Target, and Beyond: Aewa's Contribution to Global Biodiversity Governance," *Environmental Law* 38 (2008): 88–137, footnote 245.

61. Birdlife International, *Protection of Key Bottleneck Bird Areas*, 5.

62. Graham Tucker, *Migratory Soaring Birds*, passim. This report noted that, of globally important IBAs in Egypt, only Ras Mohammed was protected. The others, including Ain Sukhna, Gebel el Zeit, and Suez, were not covered by any legislation.

63. UNDP/Birdlife, *Mainstreaming Conservation of Migratory Soaring Birds*, 9, footnote 1.

64. Mindy Baha el Din, author interview conducted July 2006; Hala Barakat, personal communication, September 2008; UNDP/Birdlife, *Mainstreaming Conservation*

of Migratory Soaring Birds, 15; István Moldován, author interview conducted October 11–18, 2008.

65. EgyBirdGroup, personal communication, September–November 2008; István Moldován, author interviews conducted October 11–18, 2008.

66. EEAA staffer, author interview conducted September 24, 2008, taken from transcript of digital voice recording.

67. Hala Barakat, personal communication, September 2008, taken from handwritten notes.

68. One study in 1997 puts the number of ENGOs in Egypt at sixty-two. This figure taken from Salwa Sharawi Gomaa, *Environmental Policy-Making in Egypt* (Gainesville, FL: University Press of Florida, 1997), 20 and Appendix 2. In 2003, the Egyptian government counted a few hundred, giving no specific number, in a GEF-funded project assessing the government's capacity for environmental management in EEAA/UNDP, *Self-Assessment of National Capacity in Egypt to Manage the Global Environment*, 3.

69. Sowers, "Nature Reserves and Authoritarian Rule in Egypt," 385; Mohammed Kassas, author interview conducted September 5, 2008; Nature Conservation Sector, *Protected Areas of Egypt*, 4.

70. Mohammed Kassas, author interview conducted September 5, 2008, taken from transcript of digital voice recording.

71. Peter Haas, "Do Regimes Matter? Epistemic Communities and Mediterranean Pollution Control," *International Organization* 43, no. 3 (1989): 377–403; Peter Haas, *Saving the Mediterranean* (New York: Columbia University Press, 1990).

72. Jessica C. Teets, "Let Many Civil Societies Bloom: The Rise of Consultative Authoritarianism in China," *The China Quarterly* (January 2013): 1–20.

73. Sowers, "Nature Reserves and Authoritarian Rule in Egypt."

74. "US Embassy Cables: Egyptian Military's Influence in Decline, US Told," *The Guardian*, Thursday February 3, 2011.

75. Aziza Hussein, "NGOs and Development Challenges," in *Egypt in the Twenty-First Century: Challenges for Development*, ed. M. Riad El-Ghonemy (New York: Routledge, 2002), 203; UNDP/Institute of National Planning, Egypt, *Egypt Human Development Report 2008: Egypt's Social Contract* (Cairo: UNDP, 2008), 92–94.

76. Mohammed Kassas, author interview conducted September 5, 2008, taken from transcript of digital voice recording.

77. Sowers, "Nature Reserves and Authoritarian Rule in Egypt," passim; UNEP/EEAA, *Biodiversity Conservation Capacity Building in Egypt*, 17.

78. UNDP/NCS, *Strengthening Protected Area Financing*, 4.

79. UNDP/MSEA/EEAA, *Strengthening Protected Area Financing*, 14.

80. In 2006 for example, Ras Mohammed generated US$1.9 million in revenue, of which only US$353,000 was reinvested in park upkeep. See MSEA/UNDP/GEF, *Strengthening the National System of Protected Areas* (UNDP/GEF, 2006), 4.

81. R. F. Porter, *Soaring Bird Migration in the Middle East* (Cambridge, UK: Birdlife International, 2005), 141.

82. UNDP/Birdlife, *Mainstreaming Conservation of Migratory Soaring Birds*, 9.

83. Ibid., 27.

84. Bergen, *Ornithological Expert Opinion*, passim. The study concluded with a recommendation that, in light of the lack of certainty about the impact of wind farms on species, and considering the endangered status of several of migratory birds passing through the area, "in terms of strict bird conservation aspects it is highly recommended to avoid construction of a wind power plant within the whole concessionary area [of Gebel el Zeit]" (55).

85. EgyBirdGroup, personal communication, September–November, 2008; István Moldován, personal communication, November 2008. It should also be noted that bird flu was an unlikely cause of this mortality, as at the time of the observation, there were no clear reports that White Stork populations were exhibiting signs of bird flu.

86. Birdlife International, *Protection of Key Bottleneck Bird Areas*.

87. Hala Barakat, author interview conducted September 29, 2008, taken from handwritten notes.

88. Tahr Issa, author interview conducted September 20, 2008, taken from transcript of digital voice recording, emphasis in original recording.

89. UNDP/Birdlife, *Mainstreaming Conservation of Migratory Soaring Birds*, 4.

90. Ibid., 203.

91. Sherif Baha el Din, *Important Bird Areas*, 245.

92. Ibid.

93. István Moldován, author interviews conducted October 11–18, 2008.

94. Sherif Baha el Din, *Important Bird Areas*, 245.

95. Porter, *Soaring Bird Migration in the Middle East*.

96. UNDP/Birdlife, *Mainstreaming Conservation of Migratory Soaring Birds*, 13; USAID, *Biodiversity Conservation: USAIDs Biodiversity Conservation Programs, Fiscal Year 2003*

(USAID, 2004), 37–38; Sherif Baha el Din, *Where to Watch Birds in Wadi el-Gamal National Park and Neighboring Areas* (USAID/Egypt, c. 2008). As indicated in Sowers's article on nature conservation in Egypt, the management of protected areas in Egypt is carried out by identified, quasi-official patrons who have staked out claims in distinct areas. The Red Sea governorate has historically been the province of U.S. action through USAID (Sowers, *Embedded Autonomy Revisited*).

97. Baha el Din, *Where to Watch Birds*.

98. UNEP/EEAA, *Biodiversity Conservation Capacity Building in Egypt*, 48; Porter, *Soaring Bird Migration in the Middle East*; Joseph J. Hobbs, "Speaking with People in Egypt's St. Katherine National Park," *Geographical Review* 86 (1996): 1–21.

99. Ministry of Electricity and Energy, *Feasibility Study for a Large Wind Farm at Gulf of Zayt: Ornithological Field Monitoring Report* (NREA/Decon, 2007), 4; Hilgerloh, "The Desert at Zeit Bay, Egypt," 2.

100. Bergen, *Ornithological Expert Opinion*; Ministry of Electricity and Energy, *Feasibility Study for a Large Wind Farm at Gulf of Zayt*.

101. Ministry of Electricity and Energy, *Feasibility Study for a Large Wind Farm at Gulf of Zayt*; Hilgerloh, "The Desert at Zeit Bay, Egypt."

102. Former Red Sea protectorates manager, author interviews conducted September 2008, taken from transcript of digital voice recording.

103. UNDP/NCS, *Strengthening Protected Area Financing*, 3; UNDP/MSEA/EEAA, *Strengthening Protected Area Financing*, 29.

104. UNDP/MSEA/EEAA, *Strengthening Protected Area Financing*, 29.

105. This is a UNESCO-funded effort to improve knowledge about biodiversity management.

106. Samir Ghabbour, author interview conducted October 2008, taken from transcript of digital voice recording.

107. Former director of Red Sea protectorates, author interviews conducted September 2008, taken from transcript of digital voice recording.

108. UNDP/Birdlife, *Mainstreaming Conservation of Migratory Soaring Birds*, 9.

109. See Sowers, "Nature Reserves and Authoritarian Rule in Egypt," 394.

110. Ahmed, author interview conducted September 15, 2008, taken from transcript of digital voice recording.

111. UNDP/Birdlife, *Mainstreaming Conservation of Migratory Soaring Birds*, 11.

112. Mary Megalli, author interview conducted October 4, 2008, taken from transcript of digital voice recording.

113. Former manager of South Sinai protectorate, author interviews conducted September 20, 2008, taken from transcript of digital voice recording.

114. UNEP/EEAA, *Biodiversity Conservation Capacity Building in Egypt*, 155.

115. EgyBirdGroup, personal communication, September–November 2008; see also http://www.wind-watch.org/documents/huge-wind-farm-in-the-migration-bottleneck-of-zait-bay-egypt/, accessed August 27, 2015.

116. Mary Megalli, author interview conducted October 4, 2008, taken from transcript of digital voice recording.

5 Institutions and Regime Design

1. See Edward L. Miles, Steinar Andresen, Elaine M. Carlin, Jon Birger Skjærseth, Arild Underdal, and Jørgen Wettestad, ed., *Environmental Regime Effectiveness: Confronting Theory with Evidence* (Cambridge, MA: MIT Press, 2002).

2. See in particular, Kal Raustiala, "States, NGOs, and International Environmental Institutions," *International Studies Quarterly* 41 (1997): 719–740.

3. John Duffield, "What Are International Institutions?" *International Studies Review* 9 (2007): 1–22, 7–8.

4. Oran Young, "Institutional Linkages in International Society: Polar Perspectives," *Global Governance* 22, no. 1 (1996): 1–23; Amandine Orsini, Jean-Frédéric Morin, and Oran Young, "Regime Complexes: A Buzz, a Boom, or a Boost for Global Governance?" *Global Governance* 19 (2013): 27–39; Kal Raustiala and David G. Victor, "The Regime Complex for Plant Genetic Resources," *International Organization* 58, no. 2 (2004): 277–309; Karen J. Alter and Sophie Meunier, "The Politics of International Regime Complexity," *Perspectives on Politics* 7, no. 1 (2009): 13–24; Oran Young, Leslie A. King, and Heike Schroeder, eds., *Institutions and Environmental Change: Principal Findings, Applications, and Research Frontiers* (Cambridge, MA: MIT Press, 2008); Sebastian Oberthür and Olav Schram Stokke, *Managing Institutional Complexity: Regime Interplay and Global Environmental Change* (Cambridge, MA: MIT Press, 2011).

5. Young, "Institutional Linkages in International Society." Other scholars who have used Young's typology recently include Alter and Meunier, "The Politics of International Regime Complexity"; G. Kristin Rosendal, "Impacts of Overlapping International Regimes: The Case of Biodiversity," *Global Governance* 7, no. 1 (2001): 95–117, and Oberthür and Stokke, *Managing Institutional Complexity*.

6. John Gerard Ruggie, "International Regimes, Transactions, and Change: Embedded Liberalism in the Postwar Economic Order," *International Organization* 36, no. 2 (1982): 379–415.

7. Young, "Institutional Linkages in International Society," 6.

8. Alexander Betts, "The Refugee Regime Complex," *Refugee Survey Quarterly* 29, no. 1 (2010): 12–37, 13. On parallel regimes see also Alter and Meunier, "The Politics of International Regime Complexity"; and Vinod K. Aggarwal, ed., *Institutional Designs for a Complex World: Bargaining, Linkages, and Nesting* (Ithaca, NY: Cornell University Press, 1998).

9. Raustiala and Victor, "The Regime Complex for Plant Genetic Resources," 279.

10. Stefan Jungcurt, "The Role of Expert Networks in Reducing Regime Conflict: Contrasting Cases in the Management of Plant Genetic Resources," in *Managing Institutional Complexity*, ed. Oberthür and Stokke, 171–198.

11. Rosendal, "Impacts of Overlapping International Regimes.

12. Orsini, Morin, and Young, "Regime Complexes."

13. Robert O. Keohane and David G. Victor, "The Regime Complex for Climate Change," *Perspectives on Politics* 9, no. 1 (2011): 7–23.

14. See the March 2009 special issue of the journal *Perspectives on Politics*, which deals with regime complexity across various issue areas.

15. Lydia Swart and Estelle Perry, eds., *Global Environmental Governance: Perspectives on the Current Debate* (New York: Center for UN Reform Education, 2007).

16. Raustiala and Victor, "The Regime Complex for Plant Genetic Resources."

17. Miles et al., *Environmental Regime Effectiveness*; Helmut Breitmeier, Oran R. Young, and Michael Zürn, *Analyzing International Environmental Regimes from Case Study to Database* (Cambridge, MA: MIT Press, 2006); Oran Young, ed., *The Effectiveness of International Environmental Regimes* (Cambridge, MA: MIT Press, 1999).

18. Ronald Mitchell, "Institutional Aspects of Implementation, Compliance, and Effectiveness," in *International Relations and Global Climate Change*, ed. Urs Luterbacher and Detlef F. Sprinz (Cambridge, MA: MIT Press, 2001), 221–244; Arild Underdal, "One Question, Two Answers," in *Environmental Regime Effectiveness*, ed. Miles, 1–45.

19. Breitmeier, Young, and Zürn, *Analyzing International Environmental Regimes*, 229.

20. Young, "Institutional Linkages in International Society"; Young, King, and Schroeder, eds., *Institutions and Environmental Change*; Oberthür and Stokke, *Managing Institutional Complexity*.

21. Orsini, Morin, and Young, "Regime Complexes," 31.

22. Ibid.

23. Ibid., 32; Keohane and Victor, "The Regime Complex for Climate Change."

24. Keohane and Victor, "The Regime Complex for Climate Change." It is worth noting as well that these issue areas themselves overlap in various fora.

25. Alter and Meunier, "The Politics of International Regime Complexity," 14.

26. Ibid., 16.

27. Sanjeev Khagram, *Dams and Development: Transnational Struggles for Water and Power* (New York: Cornell University Press, 2004).

28. Orsini, Morin, and Young, "Regime Complexes," 36. To be fair, the authors do state that nonstate actors "can also perceive and manage problematic relationships among the different elemental regimes." However, their emphasis is on interstate discussions.

29. Marian A. Miller, *The Third World in Global Environmental Politics* (Boulder, CO: Lynne Rienner, 1995); Marc Williams, "The Third World and Global Environmental Negotiations: Interests, Institutions and Ideas," *Global Environmental Politics* 5, no. 3 (2005): 48–69. This was most aptly summed up in the Founex Report of 1970, produced in light of growing international attention to global environmental problems. See Miguel Ozorio de Almeida, *Environment and Development: The Founex Report on Development and Environment*, no. 586 (New York: Carnegie Endowment for International Peace, 1972).

30. Kathryn Hochstetler and Margaret E. Keck, *Greening Brazil: Environmental Activism in State and Society* (Durham, NC: Duke University Press, 2007).

31. Suzana Sawyer, *Crude Chronicles: Indigenous Politics, Multinational Oil, and Neoliberalism in Ecuador* (Durham, NC: Duke University Press, 2004).

32. Khagram, *Dams and Development*.

33. See, among others, Paul F. Steinberg and Stacy VanDeveer, eds., *Comparative Environmental Politics: Theory, Practice, and Prospects* (Cambridge, MA: MIT Press, 2012); and Regina S. Axelrod and Stacy VanDeveer, *The Global Environment: Institutions, Law and Policy* (Washington, DC: CQ Press, 2014); and Andres Duit, *State and Environment* (Cambridge, MA: MIT Press, 2014).

34. Alter and Meunier, "The Politics of International Regime Complexity," 21.

35. Keohane and Victor, "The Regime Complex for Climate Change," 9.

36. "UNEP Global Biodiversity Assessment," cited in G. Kristin Rosendal, "Interacting International Institutions: The Convention on Biological Diversity and TRIPs—Regulating Access to Genetic Resources," paper presented at the 44th Annual Convention of the International Studies Association, Portland, OR (2003), 3; see also Lyle Glowka, Françoise Burhenne-Guilmin, Hugh Synge, Jeffrey A. McNeely, and Lothar Gündling, *A Guide to the Convention on Biological Diversity* (Gland, Switzerland: IUCN, 1994), 1. This conclusion has also been reiterated in meetings of the administrative bodies of the Convention, including the first Conference of the Parties (COP-1): "The genetic resources are, to a large extent, found in the developing countries" (UN Document, UNEP/CBD/COP/1/Inf.9, December 9, 1994). The Global

Environment Facility was chosen to act as an interim mechanism in the first COP meeting, and was finalized through a Memorandum of Understanding as the permanent financial mechanism in the third COP meeting. See UN Document, UNEP/CBD/COP/3/10, November 15, 1996, which contains a reproduction of the Memorandum.

37. United Nations Environment Programme (UNEP) and Global Environment Facility (GEF), *Sustainable Conservation of Globally Important Caribbean Bird Habitats: Strengthening a Regional Network for a Shared Resource*, project number GF/2713-03 (Washington, DC: Global Environment Facility, 2003), 1.

38. World Bank, *Mexico: Mesoamerican Biological Corridor* (World Bank project document, 2000), 1.

39. UNDP/Birdlife International, *Mainstreaming Conservation of Migratory Soaring Birds into Key Productive Sectors along the Rift Valley/Red Sea Flyway*, UNDP Project Document (2006), 102.

40. Andrea K. Gerlak, "One Basin at a Time: The Global Environment Facility and the Governance of Transboundary Waters," *Global Environmental Politics* 4, no. 4 (2004): 108–141.

41. Defined in Article 2 of the Cartagena Convention as "the marine environment of the Gulf of Mexico, the Caribbean Sea and the areas of the Atlantic Ocean adjacent thereto, south of 30 deg north latitude and within 200 nautical miles of the Atlantic coasts of the States referred to in article 25 of the Convention" (Carribean Environmental Programme [UNEP], Cartagena Convention, Article 2.

42. Kayenne Taylor, "Report on the Legal Imperatives and Implications of the Cockpit Country Conservation Project," report produced for the World Bank (Kingston: n.p., 1999), 10, 76; UNEP, *Sustainable Conservation of Globally Important Caribbean Bird Habitats*, 88.

43. UNEP, *Sustainable Conservation of Globally Important Caribbean Bird Habitats*, 88.

44. Cartagena Convention, Articles 3 and 4.

45. Cartagena Convention, Article 7.

46. UN Document, UNEP(DEC)/CAR IG.19/6, July 13, 2011.

47. Taylor, *Report on the Legal Imperatives*.

48. Patrick Yugorsky and Ann Sutton, *Categorization of Protected Areas in Jamaica* (Kingston: The Nature Conservancy, 2004), 7–8.

49. World Heritage Center, *Operational Guidelines for the Implementation of the World Heritage Convention*, report produced for the United Nations Educational, Scientific, and Cultural Organization (Paris: UNESCO, 2013), http://whc.unesco.org/archive/opguide13-en.pdf, accessed February 2015.

50. Dale Webber and Claudel Noel, *Public Consultations on Defining the Boundaries of the Cockpit Country*, technical report prepared for the Centre for Environmental Management of the University of the West Indies (Kingston: Centre for Environmental Management, 2013), 79.

51. World Heritage Center, *Operational Guidelines*, 87.

52. Interview with unnamed Maroon taken from Webber and Noel, *Public Consultations on Defining the Boundaries of the Cockpit Country*, 104.

53. Kenneth Bilby, *Cockpit Country Conservation Project: Social Assessment Report— Maroon Component*, draft report for 1999 World Bank Cockpit Country Conservation Project (n.d.), 4.

54. Webber and Noel, *Public Consultations on Defining the Boundaries of the Cockpit Country*, 154.

55. Esteve Corbera et al., "Rights to Land, Forests and Carbon in REDD+: Insights from Mexico, Brazil and Costa Rica," *Forests* 2, no. 1 (2011): 301–342; Betsy A. Beymer-Farris and Thomas J. Bassett, "The REDD Menace: Resurgent Protectionism in Tanzania's Mangrove Forests," *Global Environmental Change* 22, no. 2 (2012): 332–341.

56. Beymer-Farris and Bassett, "The REDD Menace; Karin Bäckstrand and Eva Lövbrand, "Planting Trees to Mitigate Climate Change: Contested Discourses of Ecological Modernization, Green Governmentality and Civic Environmentalism," *Global Environmental Politics* 6, no. 1 (2006): 50–75.

57. LBS Protocol, Article V and IX, August 13, 2010.

58. LBS Protocol, Article XV.

59. LBS Protocol, Article XIII.

60. Unidad Coordinadora del Proyecto (UCP), *Plan Operativo Anual Período: Julio 2001–Junio 2002* (Belize City: MBRS, 2001), 1.

61. *Declaración de Tulúm*, Reproduced in UCP, *Políticas de Desarrollo Sustentable de los Recursos Pesqueros, Turismo y Áreas Marinas Protegidas Transfronterizas en el Sistema Arrecifal Mesoamericano* (Belize City: MBRS, 2004), 3–4.

62. CEP-UNEP, *Regional Overview of Land-Based Sources of Pollution in the Wider Caribbean Region*, CEP Technical Report No. 33 (Kingston: UNEP Caribbean Environment Programme, 1994).

63. Ibid., 14.

64. SPAW Protocol, Annexes.

65. Ramsar Convention, "Convention on Wetlands text, as amended in 1982 and 1987," Article 2.

66. Ramsar Convention, Articles 3 and 4.

67. *Declaración Conjunta y Plan de Acción de la Cumbre Tuxtla Gutiérrez II*, "Preamble," February 16, 1996, 26.

68. UCP, *Políticas del Desarrollo Sustentable*, 6.

69. Tilman Jaeger, Natural World Heritage in Latin America and the Caribbean: Options to Promote an Underutilized Conservation Instrument. Report prepared for the IUCN (2013), 6.

70. Memorandum of Understanding on Environmental Cooperation between the State of Acre of the Federative Republic of Brazil, the State of Chiapas of the United Mexican States, and the State of California of the United States of America, (2010) http://www.socioambiental.org/banco_imagens/pdfs/Memorando_Acre_Chiapas_California_REDD_Nov_2010.pdf, accessed March 2015; REDD Offset Working Group [ROW], California, *Acre and Chiapas: Partnering to Reduce Emissions from Tropical Deforestation*. Draft report (c. 2012).

71. Secretaría de Medio Ambiente e Historia Natural [SEMAHN], Comunicada de la Secretaría de Medio Ambiente e Historia Natural del Gobierno del Estado de Chiapas en relación al proceso de "Reducción de Emisiones de Deforestación y Degradación" (REDD+) en Chiapas (Tuxtla Gutiérrez, Chiapas: SEMAHN, 2013).

72. See, among others, Niels Barmeyer, *Developing Zapatista Autonomy: Conflict and NGO Involvement in Rebel Chiapas* (Albuquerque: University of New Mexico Press, 2009); Neil Harvey, *The Chiapas Rebellion: The Struggle for Land and Democracy* (Durham, NC: Duke University Press, 1998); G. Van Der Haar, "Land Reform, the State, and the Zapatista Uprising in Chiapas," *The Journal of Peasant Studies* 32, nos. 3–4 (2005): 484–507.

73. "La Madre Tierra no se vende, se ama y se defiende," letter sent to the Governor of California and the California REDD Working Group (2013), http://libcloud.s3.amazonaws.com/93/a5/b/2890/carta_REDD_version_EG_ChiapasF.pdf, accessed March 2015.

74. Matthew Leggett and Heather Lovell, "Community Perceptions of REDD+: A Case Study from Papua New Guinea," *Climate Policy* 12, no. 1 (2012): 115–134. For a comparative study of cases involving forest conservation and REDD+, see Emma Doherty and Heike Schroeder, "Forest Tenure and Multi-level Governance in Avoiding Deforestation under REDD+," *Global Environmental Politics* 11(4) (2011): 66–88.

75. ROW, *Acre and Chiapas*.

76. D. E. Pritchard, "Statement on Behalf of Non-Governmental Organizations" (6th COP Meeting to the CMS/1st MOP to the AEWA, 1999).

77. Mindy Baha el Din, personal communication and author interview July 2006; Hala Barakat, personal communication, September 2008.

78. GEF/Birdlife, "Bottlenecks for Soaring Migratory Birds—Project Concept Paper," GEF Concept Paper for project titled *Protection of Key Bottleneck Bird Areas for Soaring Migratory Birds in the Eastern Sector of the Africa-Eurasia Flyway (Rift Valley and Red Sea Flyways)* (Washington, DC: GEF, 2003).

79. World Conservation Monitoring Centre (WCMC), *Feasibility Study for a Harmonised Information Management Infrastructure for Biodiversity-Related Treaties* (UNEP-WCMC, 1998); UNEP Division of Environmental Law and Conventions (UNEP-DELC) and UNEP-WCMC, "Joint Core Reporting Elements of Biodiversity-Related Conventions and Agreements," A report from the UNEP Knowledge Management Project (2008), http://old.unep-wcmc.org/medialibrary/2010/11/03/0c3d71c0/1.Report%20on%20joint%20core%20report%20elements_3_Mar_08.pdf, accessed August 27, 2015.

80. UNEP-WCMC, *Toward the Harmonization of National Reporting*, report of a workshop convened by UNEP (2000).

81. UNEP-WCMC, *Toward the Harmonization of National Reporting to Biodiversity-Related Treaties*, report of a separate workshop convened by UNEP (2004).

82. Protocol Concerning the Conservation of Biological Diversity and the Establishment of Network of Protected Areas in the Red Sea and Gulf of Aden, Article 7 (PERSGA [Programme for the Environment of the Red Sea and Gulf of Aden], 2005).

83. See multiple references to the CMS in the *Global Environment Facility Project Document*: UNDP/Birdlife International, *Mainstreaming Conservation of Migratory Soaring Birds*, passim.

84. CMS, Article III and IV, distinguish between Appendix I (endangered) and Appendix II (species that have an unfavorable conservation status) species, yet note that species may be cross-listed between the two.

85. CMS, COP-5, "Recommendation 5.1," April 16, 1997.

86. CMS, Appendix I and II; Tucker, *Migratory Soaring Birds*.

87. CMS, "UNEP/CMS/AERAP-IGM1/8 Agreed Text," September 9, 2008. Additionally, the sites were identified in Sherif Baha el Din, *Important Bird Areas in Africa and Associated Islands—Egypt* (Cambridge, UK: Birdlife International, n.d.).

88. CMS, COP-7, "Resolution 7.5," September 24, 2002.

89. CMS, "UNEP/CMS/AERAP-IGM1/8 Agreed Text.

90. Magdy T. Khalil and Kamal H. Shaltout, *Lake Bardawil and Zaranik Protected Areas*. Publication of Biodiversity Unit. No. 15. (Cairo: State Ministry of Environment, 2006); Ramsar Convention, "The List of Wetlands of International Importance," January 29, 2014.

91. African Convention on the Conservation of Nature, "List of Protected Species under Class A," 15–17.

92. Protocol Concerning Specially Protected Areas and Biological Diversity in the Mediterranean, Annex II, June 10, 1995.

93. Jeannie Sowers, "Nature Reserves and Authoritarian Rule in Egypt: Embedded Autonomy Revisited," *The Journal of Environment and Development* 16, no. 4 (2007): 375–397; Jeannie Sowers, *Environmental Politics in Egypt: Activists, Experts, and the State* (New York: Routledge, 2012).

94. Raúl Gomez, interviewed by author, August 2012, transcribed and translated from digital voice recording by author.

95. Nigel Varty, *Terminal Evaluation of the UNEP/GEF Project "Sustainable Conservation of Globally Important Caribbean Bird Habitats: Strengthening a Regional Network for a Shared Resource"* (Washington, DC: GEF, 2007), 28.

96. This observation invokes one of the core questions about assessing "effectiveness" in environmental regimes and institutions. While using "effectiveness" to describe regimes that lead to positive changes in state behavior is parsimonious and (insofar as advocates of environmental management want states to adopt new regulations) logical, it is difficult to justify using this term to refer to institutions that do not lead to positive changes in environmental outcomes. For discussions on contemplating regime effectiveness, see David Victor, "Toward Effective International Cooperation on Climate Change: Numbers, Interests and Institutions," *Global Environmental Politics* 6, no. 3 (2006): 90–103; Mitchell, "Institutional Aspects of Implementation, Compliance and Effectiveness," 221–224; Carsten Helm and Detlef Sprinz, "Measuring the Effectiveness of International Environmental Regimes," *Journal of Conflict Resolution* 44, no. 5 (2000): 630–652.

97. Orsini, Morin, and Young, "Regime Complexes," 36; Michael J. Struett, Mark Nance, and Diane Armstrong, "Navigating the Maritime Piracy Regime Complex," *Global Governance: A Review of Multilateralism and International Organizations* 19, no. 1 (2013): 93–104.

98. Orsini, Morin, and Young, "Regime Complexes," 36.

99. See Jacob Park, Ken Conca, and Matthias Finger, eds., *The Crisis of Global Environmental Governance: Toward a New Political Economy of Sustainability* (New York: Routledge Press, 2008); Gabriela Kütting and Ronnie Lipschutz, *Environmental Governance: Power and Knowledge in a Local-Global World* (New York: Routledge Press, 2009).

Conclusion

1. For work on Ecuador, see Suzana Sawyer, *Crude Chronicles: Indigenous Politics, Multinational Oil, and Neoliberalism in Ecuador* (Durham, NC: Duke University Press, 2004).

2. Sabrina McCormick, *Mobilizing Science: Movements, Participation, and the Remaking of Knowledge* (Philadelphia: Temple University Press, 2009).

3. LDCs are particularly important to global biodiversity governance, as most of the world's biodiversity is found in the developing world. See inter alia, Marc Williams, "The Third World and Global Environmental Negotiations: Interests, Institutions and Ideas," *Global Environmental Politics* 5 (2005): 48–69; Adil Najam, "Dynamics of the Southern Collective: Developing Countries in Desertification Negotiations," *Global Environmental Politics* 4 (2004): 128–154; Susan Sell, "North–South Environmental Bargaining: Ozone, Climate Change and Biodiversity," *Global Governance* 2 (1996): 97–118, 110. See, in particular, Marian Miller, *The Third World in Global Environmental Politics* (Boulder, CO: Lynne Reinner Publishers, 1995), for a discussion of the Third World as a negotiating bloc in global biodiversity governance.

4. Peter Haas, "Do Regimes Matter?: Epistemic Communities and Mediterranean Pollution Control," *International Organization* 43 (1989): 377–403; Peter Haas, "Introduction: Epistemic Communities and International Policy Coordination," *International Organization* 46 (1992): 1–35; Steven Bernstein, *The Compromise of Liberal Environmentalism* (Chichester, NY: Columbia University Press, 2001); Radoslav Dimitrov , "Knowledge, Power and Interests in Environmental Regime Formation," *International Studies Quarterly* 47 (2003): 123–150; Margaret Keck and Kathryn Sikkink, *Activists Beyond Borders* (Ithaca, NY: Cornell University Press, 1998).

5. See María Guadalupe Moog Rodrigues, *Global Environmentalism and Local Politics: Transnational Advocacy Networks in Brazil, Ecuador, and India* (Ithaca: State University of New York, 2004); Ronald B. Mitchell, "Information and Influence," in *Global Environmental Assessments: Information and Influence*, ed. Ronald B. Mitchell, William C. Clark, David W. Cash, and Nancy M. Dickson (Cambridge, MA: MIT Press, 2006), 307–338.

6. Miller, *The Third World in Global Environmental Politics*; Lawrence Susskind, *Environmental Diplomacy: Negotiating More Effective Global Agreements* (New York: Oxford University Press, 1994); J. Timmons Roberts and Bradley Parks, *A Climate of Injustice: Global Inequality, North–South Politics, and Climate Policy* (Cambridge, MA: MIT Press, 2007).

7. Mac Chapin, "A Challenge to Conservationists," *World Watch Magazine* (Nov./ Dec. 2004), http://tinyurl.com/challenge-conservation, accessed May 2015.

8. Mark Dowie, "Conservation Refugees: When Protecting Nature Means Kicking People Out," *Orion Magazine* (2005), http://www.orionmagazine.org/index.php/ articles/article/161, accessed May 2015.

9. Michele Zebich-Knos, "Ecotourism, Park Systems, and Environmental Justice in Latin America," in *Environmental Justice in Latin America: Problems, Promise, and Practice*, ed. David Carruthers (Cambridge, MA: MIT Press, 2008), 185–212.

10. David Naguib Pellow, *Resisting Global Toxics: Transnational Movements for Environmental Justice* (Cambridge, MA: MIT Press, 2007).

11. McCormick, *Mobilizing Science*.

12. Paul Mohai, David Pellow, and J. Timmons Roberts, "Environmental Justice," *Annual Review of Environment and Resources* 34 (2009): 405–430.

13. See references to the literature throughout this manuscript, including JoAnn Carmin and Julian Agyeman, eds., *Environmental Inequalities Beyond Borders: Local Perspectives on Global Injustices* (Cambridge, MA: MIT Press, 2011); David Carruthers, ed., *Environmental Justice in Latin America: Problems, Promise, and Practice* (Cambridge, MA: MIT Press, 2008); McCormick, *Mobilizing Science*; Mohai, Pellow, and Timmons Roberts, "Environmental Justice."

14. Sanjeev Khagram, *Dams and Development: Transnational Struggles for Water and Power* (Ithaca, NY: Cornell University Press, 2004).

15. McCormick, *Mobilizing Science*.

16. R. F. Porter, *Soaring Bird Migration in the Middle East* (Cambridge, UK: Birdlife International, 2005), 140.

17. Haas, "Introduction."

18. Susanne C. Moser, "Climate Change and Sea-Level Rise in Maine and Hawai'i: The Changing Tides of an Issue Domain," in Mitchell, Clark, Cash, and Dickson, eds., *Global Environmental Assessments*, 201–240.

19. Mohammed Kassas, author interview conducted September 5, 2008, taken from transcript of digital voice recording.

20. Jeannie Sowers, "Nature Reserves and Authoritarian Rule in Egypt: Embedded Autonomy Revisited," *The Journal of Environment & Development* 16, no. 4 (2007): 375–397. See also Sowers, *Environmental Politics in Egypt: Activists, Experts and the State* (New York: Routledge, 2013). Compare these with Haas, "Do Regimes Matter?"

21. Jessica C. Teets, *Civil Society under Authoritarianism: The China Model* (New York: Cambridge University Press, 2014).

22. Karen Litfin, *Ozone Discourses: Science and Politics in Global Environmental Cooperation* (New York: Columbia University Press, 1994).

23. Haas, "Do Regimes Matter?"; Haas, "Introduction"; The Social Learning Group, *Learning to Manage Global Environmental Risks: Volume 1* (Cambridge, MA: MIT Press); Litfin, *Ozone Discourses*.

24. Joanna Burger, Michael Gochfeld, David Kosson, Charles W. Powers, Barry Friedlander, John Eichelberger, David Barnes, Lawrence K. Duffy, Stephen C. Jewett, and Conrad D. Volz, "Science, Policy, and Stakeholders: Developing a Consensus

Science Plan for Amchitka Island, Aleutians, Alaska," *Environmental Management* 35, no. 5 (2005): 557–568.

25. William C. Clark, Ronald B. Mitchell, and David Cash, "Evaluating the Influence of Global Environmental Assessments," in Mitchell, Clark, Cash, and Dickson, eds., *Global Environmental Assessments*, 14. See also Karen Litfin, "Environment, Wealth and Authority: Global Climate Change and Emerging Modes of Legitimation," *International Studies Review* 2 no. 2 (2000): 119–148, 130, where Litfin argues that knowledge generation/internalization is a fundamentally social process.

26. Richard Hiskes, *The Human Right to a Green Future: Environmental Rights and Intergenerational Justice* (New York: Cambridge University Press, 2009).

27. Liliana Botcheva, "Focus and Effectiveness of Environmental Activism in Eastern Europe: A Comparative Study of Environmental Movements in Bulgaria, Hungary, Slovakia, and Romania," *Journal of Environment and Development* 5, no. 3 (1996): 292–308.

28. Kathryn Hochstetler, "Democracy and the Environment in Latin America and Eastern Europe," in *Comparative Environmental Politics: Theory, Practice, and Prospects*, ed. Paul Steinberg and Stacy VanDeveer (Cambridge, MA: MIT Press, 2012), 199–229.

29. Michele M. Betsill and Elisabeth Corell, "NGO Influence in International Environmental Negotiations: A Framework for Analysis," *Global Environmental Politics* 1, no. 4 (2001): 65–85. Similarly, the discussion of epistemic community influence on global ozone management focused on international negotiations on the language and regulatory requirements of the Montreal Protocol. See Peter M. Haas, "Banning Chlorofluorocarbons: Epistemic Community Efforts to Protect Stratospheric Ozone," in *Knowledge, Power and International Policy Coordination*, ed. P. Haas (Columbia: University of South Carolina Press, 1992), 187–224, as well as Radoslav Dimitrov, "Knowledge, Power, and Interests"; and Radoslav Dimitrov, "Hostage to Norms: States, Institutions and Global Forest Politics," *Global Environmental Politics* 5 (2005): 1–24, both of which focus on epistemic community impact on international treaty formation.

30. See for example the contribution of multilevel networks to global governance apart from treaty negotiation in Sanjeev Khagram and Saleem H. Ali, "Transnational Transformations: From Government-centric Interstate Regimes to Cross-sectoral Multi-level Networks of Global Governance," in *The Crisis of Global Environmental Governance: Toward a New Political Economy of Sustainability*, ed. Jacob Park, Ken Conca and Matthias Finger (New York: Routledge, 2008), 132–162.

31. Excerpted from a speech given in the following volume: Audre Lorde, "The Master's Tools Will Never Dismantle the Master's House," *Feminist Postcolonial Theory: A Reader*, ed. Reina Lewis and Sara Mills (New York: Routledge, 2003), 25–28.

32. Alfredo Arrellano Guillermo, author interviews conducted March 2008, taken from transcript of digital voice recording, translated from Spanish.

33. Ildefonso Palermo, author interviews conducted March 2008, taken from transcript of digital voice recording, translated from Spanish.

34. Daniel R. Faber and Deborah McCarthy, "Neoliberalism, Globalization, and the Struggle for Ecological Democracy: Linking Sustainability and Environmental Justice," in *Just Sustainabilities: Development in an Unequal World*, ed. Julian Agyeman and Robert Bullard (Cambridge, MA: MIT Press, 2003), 38–63.

35. Global Environment Facility, *Mainstreaming Biodiversity in Production Landscapes* (GEF Working Paper, 2005), 2.

36. Amitav Acharya, "How Ideas Spread: Whose Norms Matter? Norm Localization and Institutional Change in Asian Regionalism," *International Organization* 58 (2004): 239–275.

37. McCormick, *Mobilizing Science*, 36.

38. McCormick, *Mobilizing Science*.

39. Khagram, *Dams and Development*.

40. Pellow, *Resisting Global Toxics*. See also Anthony Patt, "Trust, Respect, Patience, and Sea-Surface Temperatures: Useful Climate Forecasting in Zimbabwe," in Mitchell, Cash, Clark, and Dickson, eds., *Global Environmental Assessments*, 241–270.

41. See Gabriela Kütting and Ronnie Lipschultz, eds., *Environmental Governance: Power and Knowledge in a Local-Global World* (New York: Routledge Press, 2009); and Jacob Park, Ken Conca, and Matthias Finger, eds., *The Crisis of Global Environmental Governance* (New York: Routledge, 2008) for discussions on this topic.

42. Khagram, *Dams and Development*.

43. Moog Rodrigues, *Global Environmentalism and Local Politics*.

44. Mohai, Pellow, and Timmons Roberts, "Environmental Justice," 407.

Index

Politics, Science, and the Environment
Peter M. Haas and Sheila Jasanoff, editors

Andrew S. Mathews, *Instituting Nature: Authority, Expertise, and Power in Mexican Forests*

Eric Brousseau, Tom Dedeurwaerdere, and Bernd Siebenhüner, eds., *Reflexive Governance and Global Public Goods*

D. G. Webster, *Beyond the Tragedy in Global Fisheries*

Guy Edwards and J. Timmons Roberts, *Continental Divide: Latin America and the Global Politics of Climate Change*

Kemi Fuentes-George, *Between Preservation and Exploitation: Transnational Advocacy Networks and Conservation in Developing Countries*